SO-FAJ-719

FLORIDA STATE
UNIVERSITY LIBRARIES

JUN 2 2 2001

TALLAHASSEE, FLORIDA

THE MITTERRAND ERA

Also by Anthony Daley

STEEL, STATE, AND LABOR: Mobilization and
Adjustment in France

The Mitterrand Era

Policy Alternatives and Political Mobilization in France

Edited by

Anthony Daley
Visiting Scholar
Center for German and European Studies
Georgetown University, Washington, DC

NEW YORK UNIVERSITY PRESS
Washington Square, New York

DC
423
.M575
1996

Selection and arrangement, and Chapter 1 © Anthony Daley 1996
Chapters 2–8 and 10–14 © Macmillan Press 1996
Chapter 9 © Presses de la Fondation Nationale des Sciences Politiques 1994

All rights reserved

First published in the U.S.A. in 1996 by
NEW YORK UNIVERSITY PRESS
Washington Square
New York, N.Y. 10003

Library of Congress Cataloging-in-Publication Data
The Mitterrand era : policy alternatives and political mobilization in France /
edited by Anthony Daley.
p.   cm.
Includes index.
ISBN 0–8147–1872–8 (alk. paper)
1. Mitterrand, François. 1916–   —Influence.   2. France—Politics
and government—1981–   3. Socialism—France—History—20th century.
4. Social change.   5. Political stability.   I. Daley, Anthony.
DC423.M575   1996
944.083'8—dc20   95–6343
                                                              CIP

Printed in Great Britain

Contents

Preface   vii
Notes on the Contributors   x
Abbreviations   xiii

1   **François Mitterrand, the Left and Political Mobilization
    in France**   1
    Anthony Daley

PART I   THE DILEMMAS OF GOVERNANCE

2   **The Limits of Political Economy: Mitterrand and the Crisis
    of the French Left**   33
    George Ross

3   **Exchange Rate Politics in France, 1981–1983: The
    Regime-Defining Choices of the Mitterrand Presidency**   56
    David R. Cameron

4   **Less Exceptionalism than Meets the Eye**   83
    Serge Halimi

5   **The Left's Response to Industrial Crisis: Restructuring in
    the Steel and Automobile Industries**   97
    W. Rand Smith

PART II   POLICY CHANGE AND ECONOMIC ACTORS

6   **An End to French Economic Exceptionalism? The
    Transformation of Business under Mitterrand**   117
    Vivien A. Schmidt

7   **French Socialism and the Transformation of Industrial
    Relations since 1981**   141
    Chris Howell

8   **French Labour Confronts Technological Change: Reform
    that Never was?**   161
    Mark Kesselman

9   **The Dilemma of Unions without Members**   172
    Guy Groux and René Mouriaux

PART III POLITICAL MOBILIZATION AND LEFT POLITICS

10   The Shifting Advantages of Organizational Formats:
     Factionalism and the French Socialist Party   189
     Serenella Sferza

11   French Communism: Party Construction and Party Decline   206
     Martin A. Schain

12   Green Politics and Political Mobilization: Contradictions of
     Direct Democracy   225
     Tad Shull

13   The Politics of *Égalité Professionnelle* Policy: As Symbolic
     Reform becomes More Symbolic   241
     Amy G. Mazur

14   Race, Immigration and the Politics of Hate   258
     Patrick R. Ireland

Index   279

Preface

This volume contains 14 essays on French politics during what I call the Mitterrand era. Along with Charles de Gaulle, François Mitterrand has dominated French political life since 1945. A wily manipulator of Fourth Republic intrigue and in-fighting, he became a determined opponent of de Gaulle's constitution of 1958. Yet, Mitterrand reconciled himself to the institutions of the Fifth Republic, running for president in 1965, 1974, and finally winning election in 1981 and re-election in 1988. His passage from the political landscape marks the end of 50 years of turbulent, and at times controversial, political service.

Mitterrand assumed the presidency in 1981 with a radical programme that promised to remake French capitalism. Like May '68, the Mitterrand experiment captured the imagination of the Left throughout the advanced industrial countries. More importantly, it vowed to complete the empowerment of the French working classes that many felt had been stunted by the domestic repercussions of the Cold War.

The abrupt shift from reform politics to economic orthodoxy in 1983 dashed those hopes. Unemployment crept up to double-digit rates. Even those people with jobs became increasingly insecure about their own economic security. This U-turn altered not just the policies of the Socialist President. It marked a dramatic shift in the thinking of political élites: the notions of 'constraint' and 'limited expectations' entered the political lexicon.

Many would argue that the market-oriented policies of French Socialism were a necessary response to the increasingly open international economy. The inter-nationalization of capital, so the argument goes, puts inexorable pressures on domestic institutions: reformism in one country can only take place with increasing restrictions which not only impinge on economic efficiency but on individual freedoms. Yet, economic orthodoxy also has a *political* price. Old forms of struc-turing social life – especially those centred around trade unions – are weakened by the unwillingness or inability of political élites to intervene in domestic mar-kets. While all the advanced industrial countries have witnessed discord between Left parties and organized labour, France has seen a divorce – for reasons I explain in Chapter 1. Thus, the Mitterrand era has brought policy reversals and political turbulence.

The theme of policy and politics in the Mitterrand years has its genesis in a collective project centred at the Center for European Studies at Harvard University. Under the leadership of George Ross and Andrew Martin, eight North American scholars have been investigating the changing place of labour in European society, and I have been working on the French case. These case studies explore the changes in industrial relations since 1980. In the course of our work,

Chris Howell and I decided to investigate the relations between party and unions, and we co-edited a volume of *The International Journal of Political Economy* (Winter 1992–3).

I wanted to examine in greater depth the political consequences of policy change for France by assembling a group of scholars at Wesleyan University in April 1992. Generously funded by the Pew Charitable Trusts, the workshop 'Labor and the Left: A Decade of Mitterrand' consisted of two days of extraordinarily fruitful interchange. The goal of the workshop was not simply to rehash or bemoan the U-turn. Rather, it was to investigate changes in traditional party and union strategies, the demise of 'workerism' within the Left, attempts to develop new forms of universalism, the development of social movements and the potential loss of French distinctiveness in both policy and politics. In summary, the workshop sought to position the Mitterrand experience within changes taking place in economy and society. What cried out to be explained was the divorce between the French Left and organized labour that was much more basic than those that took place in other rich countries when social democrats held power.

Those papers have been re-worked to fit into the present volume, and the essays by Groux and Mouriaux, Shull, Mazur and Ireland were subsequently solicited. The 14 essays which follow examine the effects of economic orthodoxy on the French Left. They explore the difficulties of governing, the new relationships between the Left and various social actors and political mobilization around issues of gender, environment and immigration. They offer a timely examination of issues affecting the French Left as it attempts to re-invent itself after more than a decade of power.

I owe many thanks to Peter Kilby who, as Director of the Public Affairs Center at Wesleyan University, arranged the funding from the Pew Charitable Trusts. His enthusiasm for a subject well outside his own professional expertise speaks volumes of the intellectual potential of liberal arts schools.

The workshop would not have been possible without the help of several individuals. Gisèle Grayson co-ordinated the workshop – from travel arrangements to accommodations to culinary delicacies – with efficiency and grace. She was a wonderful student at the time and is now a promising scholar. Kimberly Snow ensured that those culinary delicacies evoked constant reminders of the country we were investigating. Eva Smith Ogden arranged for the disbursement of Pew funds. Sue Ferris arranged for and Pam McPheters typed a tapescript of the workshop, which turned out to be an extraordinarily valuable record of our proceedings.

This anthology has also incurred a number of debts. I would like to thank Jane Jenson, who presented material at the workshop but whose commitments prevented further participation. Her typically penetrating comments on individual papers made the essays much stronger. Herb Arnold, Mark Harmon, Cynthia Horan, Cecilia Miller and Brigitte Young also commented on presentations. Many thanks to my students who have heard me hash out these arguments in far more lectures than I can count.

Janet DeMicco used her extraordinary computer talents (and plenty of humour) to prepare a single manuscript out of 14 chapters. Linda Perlstein, another former student and now an editor at *The Washington Post*, did a brilliant job of copy-editing. Thanks to her, these essays are very readable. Many thanks to Joseph Rouse for arranging Linda's temporary employment. Aaron Sedley performed the difficult task of indexing. Keith Povey did an excellent job of finalizing the drafts. I would also like to thank the editors of the manuscript at Macmillan and New York University Press, T. M. Farmiloe, Gráinne Twomey and Niko Pfund.

Most of all I would like to thank Nancy W. Gallagher. She participated in the workshop, commented on papers and helped in the editorial process. She also put up with crazy schedules and an occasionally irritable editor. I dedicate this anthology to Nancy – my spouse, partner and colleague.

ANTHONY DALEY

Notes on the Contributors

David R. Cameron is Professor of Political Science at Yale University. He received his undergraduate degree from Williams College, an M.B.A. from Dartmouth College, an M.Sc. from the University of London, and the Ph.D. from the University of Michigan. He serves as the Chair of the Council on West European Studies at Yale. His comparative research has explored the integration of labour, the role of the public sector, and the conditions for macroeconomic policy-making in the OECD countries. His essays on politics and policy in the European Union have appeared in numerous collections. He has written extensively on French politics.

Anthony Daley is Assistant Professor of Government at Wesleyan University. He is the author of *Steel, State, and Labor: Mobilization and Adjustment in France* (University of Pittsburgh Press, 1995). He has written several book chapters and articles on French unions and politics. He was guest editor (with Chris Howell) of the *International Journal of Political Economy* (Winter 1992–3) for an issue on parties and unions in Europe. His current book project examines organizational and ideological cleavages within the French working-class movement.

Guy Groux is a research associate at the Centre pour l'Etude de la Vie Politique Française (CEVIPOF) at the Fondation Nationale des Sciences Politiques. He is the author of numerous books and articles on the French labour movement, including *Les Cadres* (La Découverte, 1983). Most recently he has co-authored with René Mouriaux *La C.F.D.T.* (Economica, 1989) and *La C.G.T. Crises et alternatives* (Economica, 1992). He has also co-edited with Mark Kesselman *The French Workers' Movement: Economic Crisis and Political Change* (George Allen & Unwin, 1984).

Serge Halimi is Professor at the Institut d'Etudes Européenes at the Université de Paris-8. He is the author of *Sisyphe est fatiqué: Les échecs de la gauche au pouvoir (1924–1936–1944–1981)* (Robert Laffont, 1993). He has also written extensively on American politics. As a journalist for *Le Monde Diplomatique*, he writes regularly on French and American politics and on international economic problems.

Chris Howell is Associate Professor of Politics at Oberlin College. He is the author of *Regulating Labor: The State and Industrial Relations Reform in Post-war France* (Princeton University Press, 1992). He has written articles on French and British industrial relations and political economy. He is currently working on a book, provisionally entitled *Between the State and the Market: British Trade Unionism in Decline*, under the auspices of a German Marshall Fund of the United States Research Fellowship.

Patrick Ireland is Assistant Professor at the University of Denver Graduate School of International Studies. He is the author of *The Policy Challenge of Ethnic Diversity* (Harvard University Press, 1994). He has written several book chapters and articles on immigration. His current research focuses on the interplay between social and immigrant policies in Germany and the European Union.

Mark Kesselman is Professor of Political Science at Columbia University. He has written on public policy, local politics, political parties, and organized labour in France. He is editor of *The French Workers' Movement, 1968–1982* (Allen & Unwin, 1984) and *European Politics in Transition* (Heath, 1992). He has published several journal articles and has contributed to numerous anthologies, including most recently *Policymaking in France: From de Gaulle to Mitterrand* (Pinter, 1989) and *The State, Socialism and Public Policy in France* (Methuen, 1985).

Amy Mazur is Assistant Professor of Political Science at Washington State University. She is the author of *Gender Bias and the State: Symbolic Reform at Work in Fifth Republic France* (University of Pittsburgh Press, 1995). She has also co-edited *Comparative State Feminism* (Sage Press, 1995). She has published journal articles and chapter contributions on women's empirical policy issues in comparative perspective.

René Mouriaux is *Directeur de Recherches* at the Centre pour l'Etude de la Vie Politique Française (CEVIPOF) at the Fondation Nationale des Sciences Politiques, and he teaches at the Institut d'Etudes Politiques. He is the author of numerous books on the French and European labour movements. He has recently co-authored (with Guy Groux) *La C.F.D.T.* (Economica, 1989); *Petits boulots et grand marché européen* (Presses de la Fondation nationale des Sciences Politiques, 1990); (with Guy Groux) *La C.G.T. Crises et alternatives* (Economica, 1992). He has written *Le syndicalisme en France* (Presses Universitaires de France, 1992); and *Le syndicalisme dans le monde* (Presses Universitaires de France, 1993).

George Ross is Morris Hillquit Professor of Labor and Social Thought at Brandeis University and Senior Associate at the Minda de Gunzburg Center for European Studies at Harvard University. He has written *Workers and Communists in France* (University of California Press, 1982) and *Jacques Delors and European Integration* (Polity / Oxford University Press, 1994). He has co-authored *Unions, Change and Crisis*, vol. 1 (George Allen & Unwin, 1982) and vol. 2 (George Allen & Unwin, 1984); and *The View from Inside: A French Communist Cell in Crisis*

(University of California Press, 1984). He has co-edited *The Mitterrand Experiment* (Oxford University Press, 1987) and *Searching for the New France* (1991). He has also co-edited three volumes of *Contemporary France* (Pinter, 1987, 1988, 1989). His recent articles have appeared in numerous journals and edited volumes. Ross is Chair of the Council for European Studies and co-editor of *French Politics and Society*.

Martin A. Schain is Professor of Politics and Chair of the Center for European Studies at New York University. He is the author of *French Communism and Local Power* (St. Martin's, 1985) as well as co-author of *The Politics of Immigration in Western Europe* (Frank Cass, 1994) and *Politics in France* (Harper Collins, 1992). He has co-edited *Socialism, The State and Public Policy in France* (Pinter/Methuen, 1985) and *French Politics and Public Policy* (St. Martin's, 1980). He has also published numerous scholarly articles and book chapters on politics and immigration in France, Europe and the United States, the extreme right in France, political parties in France, and labour unions in Britain and France.

Vivien A. Schmidt is Professor of Public Policy and Management at the University of Massachusetts at Boston where she is Director of the European Studies Program, Director of the Center for Emerging Democracies, and Senior Fellow in the McCormack Institute. She is the author of *Democratizing France: The Political and Administrative History of Decentralization* (Cambridge University Press, 1990) and *Modernizing France: Business and Government in the Mitterrand Years* (Cambridge University Press, 1995). She has published extensively on French politics and French business in scholarly journals and edited volumes.

Serenella Sferza is Assistant Professor of Political Science at Washington University in St. Louis. She is completing a book manuscript on the French Socialist Party, entitled *The Building and Rebuilding of the French Socialist Party*. She has written on French party politics with contributions in *Contemporary France* (1989) and *The Mitterrand Experiment* (1987).

Tad Shull is a Ph.D. candidate in Political Science at Columbia University. His thesis explores the relationships between ecology and socialist parties in France and Germany. He has published several articles on ecological politics.

W. Rand Smith is Professor of Politics at Lake Forest College. He is the author of *Crisis in the French Labour Movement: A Grassroots Perspective* (Macmillan, 1987). He has published numerous journal articles and book chapters on French and Spanish political economy. He is currently completing a book, tentatively entitled *Wrenching Adjustments: Industrial Crisis and Economic Strategy in Social France and Spain, 1981–1993*.

Abbreviations

ANACT	*Agence Nationale pour l'Amélioration des Conditions de Travail* (National Agency for the Improvement of Working Conditions)
CAIF	*Conseil des Associations Immigrées en France* (Council of Immigrant Associations in France)
CERES	*Centre d'Études, de Recherches et d'Éducation Socialiste* (Center for Socialist Study, Research and Education), left wing of the PS
CFDT	*Confédération Française Démocratique du Travail* (French Democratic Confederation of Labour)
CFTC	*Confédération Française des Travailleurs Chrétiens* (French Confederation of Catholic Workers)
CGC	*Confédération Générale des Cadres* (General Confederation of Technical and Supervisory Employees)
CGCT	*Compagnie Générale de Constructions Téléphoniques*
CGE	*Compagnie Générale d'Électricité*
CGT	*Confédération Générale du Travail* (General Confederation of Labour)
CGTU	*Confédération Générale du Travail Unitaire* (Unified General Confederation of Labour)
CNPF	*Conseil Nationale du Patronat Français* (National Council of French Employers), peak employers' association
CREDOC	*Centre de Recherche pour l'Étude et l'Observation des Conditions de Vie* (Research Centre for the Study and Observation of Living Conditions)
CSEP	*Conseil Supérieur de l'Égalité Professionnelle* (High Council for Equal Employment)
CTF	*Comité du Travail Féminin* (Women's Work Committee)
DCF	*Délégation de la Condition Féminine* (Women's Status Delegation)
DRT	*Direction des Relations de Travail* (Employment Relations Office)
EC	European Community
EEP	Equal Employment Policy
EMS	European Monetary System
EMU	Economic and Monetary Union
ENA	*École Nationale d'Administration*
ERM	Exchange Rate Mechanism
EU	European Union
FASTI	*Fédération des Associations de Soutien aux Travailleurs Immigrés* (Federation of Support Associations for Immigrant Workers)

FEN   *Fédération de l'Éducation Nationale*
FN   *Front National* (National Front)
FO   *Force Ouvrière* (Workers' Force), Full title: *Confédération
           Générale du Travail – Force Ouvrière*
GE   *Génération Écologie* (Ecology Generation)
GRAF   *Groupe de Recherche sur l'Activité des Femmes* (Research Group
           on the Activity of Women)
HCI   *Haut Conseil à l'Intégration* (High Council for Integration)
INSEE   *Institut National de la Statistique et des Études Économiques*
           (National Institute of Statistics and Economic Studies)
JALB   *Jeunes Arabes de Lyon et sa Banlieue* (Arab Youth of Lyons and
           Its Suburbs)
MDF   *Ministère des Droits de la Femme* (Ministry of the Rights of Women)
MEP   *Mission pour l'Égalité Professionnelle* (Equal Employment Mission)
MRAP   *Mouvement contre le Racisme et l'Anti-Sémetisme et pour l'Amitié
           entres les Peuples* (Movement against Racism and Anti-Semitism
           and for Friendship between Peoples)
MRP   *Mouvement Républicain Populaire* (Popular Republican
           Movement), Christian Democratic in inspiration
NATO   North Atlantic Treaty Organization
ONI   *Office National d'Immigration* (National Office of Immigration)
PCF   *Parti Communiste Français* (French Communist Party)
PS   *Parti Socialiste* (French Socialist Party), post-1969
PSA   *Peugeot Société Anonyme* (Peugeot Inc.)
PSU   *Parti Socialiste Unifié* (Unified Socialist Party)
RPR   *Rassemblement pour la République* (Rally for the Republic),
           Gaullist political formation after 1976
SEDF   *Secrétaire d'État des Droits des Femmes* (Deputy Minister of
           Women's Rights)
SEDFVQ   *Secrétaire d'État des Droits des Femmes et de la Vie Quotidienne*
           (Deputy Minister of Women's Rights and Daily Life)
SEEF   *Secrétaire d'État de l'Emploi Féminin* (Deputy Minister of
           Women's Employment)
SEF   *Services des Droits des Femmes* (Department of Women's Rights)
SFIO   *Section Française de l'Internationale Ouvrière* (French Socialist
           Party), pre-1969
TU   *train universel*
UAP   *Union des Assurances de Paris*
UDF   *Union pour la Démocratie Française* (Union for French
           Democracy), centrists
ZEP   *Zones d'Education Prioritaires* (Priority Educational Zones)

1 François Mitterrand, the Left and Political Mobilization in France[1]

Anthony Daley

A tremendous popular euphoria accompanied François Mitterrand's election as French president in 1981. After 23 years on the sidelines of national politics, the Left assumed power with a promise to break with capitalism, increase democratic control of the economy, deliver new rights to working people and create a more equitable society. Such a programme promised to alter more than public policy; it sought to forge a realignment of the French party system by sustaining a broad Centre-Left political force. Through new forms of political participation, it attempted to construct deeper relationships between citizen and state.

If the Mitterrand election (and re-election in 1988) represented the flowering of French socialism, then the plant bore strange fruit. By 1983, French economic policy underwent a dramatic U-turn as the government moved from its reform agenda to an economic orthodoxy that won the accolades of the business press throughout Europe. President Mitterrand forged a broad consensus over a strong currency, participation in the construction of Europe and economic 'modernization'. This consensus sustained Mitterrand in power for the longest tenure in the French executive since Napoleon III. Yet it has had disastrous consequences for the French Left.

By the mid-1990s, the political Left had disintegrated in France. The policy framework of the Socialist Party (PS) differs little from those of its rivals on the right. While in power, it clung steadfastly to orthodox economic policies in the early 1990s, as bankruptcies increased, unemployment remained in double digits, and jobs became less stable. The PS's increasingly weaker vote totals in 1992 regional elections, 1993 legislative elections and 1994 elections to the European Parliament suggested that voters had lost patience with a political party that promised a stronger and more equitable economy while delivering higher unemployment and championed a morality of governing while its officials were under indictment. When it lost power in March 1993 and secured fewer seats in the National Assembly than it had received since 1958, the party withdrew into an internal debate that focused more on mobilizing support for individual leaders than on either substantive issues or party renewal.

The French Communist Party (PCF), once the largest party in the country, dwindled to electoral insignificance in the 1980s. It had trouble electing enough

1

deputies for a parliamentary group and lost key municipal bastions. Party leaders were at war with each other over internal political practices, political programmes, and relations with the discredited former regimes of East Europe. The PCF leadership revived a knee-jerk oppositionalism that alienated members and impeded alliance building.

The implosion of the traditional parties of the Left has not led to an immediate resurgence of alternative voices in French politics. Green parties have made inroads into local politics, but they remain divided into two parties with different identities, agendas and alliance strategies. Other social movements – especially those devoted to gender, sexual preference and race – have fractured over political strategies, organizational identities and support for the established Left parties. In the month before the March 1993 elections, former Prime Minister Michel Rocard's call for a 'big bang' – the creation of a new party of the Left out of the remnants of the PS – found little enthusiasm in the PS or in allied groups.

The stagnation of Left parties has been accompanied by disorganization in the labour market. The country of May 1968, the Popular Front and the Commune has become quiescent in the last decade. In the early 1990s, French workers were using work stoppages infrequently, and annual strike volume was among the lowest of the advanced industrial countries. 'Contentious' French workers became de-unionized in the 1980s: the organized work force was cut in half between 1981 and 1993.[2] Trade unions have become increasingly marginalized from decision-making at firm, sectoral and national levels. Employers even began to complain in the 1980s about an absence of legitimate interlocutors and they attempted various remedies to strengthen union organizations.

In short, '[t]he Left no longer has hope, the Right no longer has fear', as two commentators wrote after the French presidential and legislative election campaigns of 1988.[3] In itself, this new political equilibrium constitutes a momentous change in French political history. Three key questions guide the essays in this volume. First, why did the Left fail to sustain its mobilization? Second, how did the *policy* U-turn affect *political* actors? Third, what do the changes of the 1980s portend for the future of French politics?

The French experience has broader implications for comparative politics. Similar changes in the 'respectable Lefts' have occurred throughout Europe. Before losing power in 1990, the Swedish Social Democrats petitioned to join the European Community, ushering in a set of policy changes that undermined the so-called 'third way' (between capitalism and Leninism). When they returned to power after the October 1994 legislative elections, they did not alter their embrace of economic orthodoxy. In Italy, the Communist Party changed its name to the Democratic Party of the Left, emerged as a 'cleaner' party amid the scandals that rocked the political system in the early 1990s, and felt comfortable with economic liberalization. In Spain, the Socialist Party became both the supporter of constitutional continuity and the bulwark of pro-market public policy. The Left has changed everywhere, but the particular way parties and movements change speaks to a broader and more compelling analytical question: what are the opportunities and constraints for elected political officials?

Policy turnarounds and programmatic moderation within the Left are not surprising to those studying European politics. Do not Left parties forge compromises once they attain power? Do not those compromises destabilize the original electorates? Critics continually lament party betrayals. Explanations have run the gamut from 'the Socialists saw the light and recognized reality' to 'the PS used a collectivist rhetoric only for electoral purposes and knew it would betray those ideals'. These resemble the heated debates in Germany and Britain during the 1950s and 1960s: the shift to the Right reflects either reality or deception.

Such finger-pointing leads to sterile analyses. Arguments about reality or deception suggest an inevitability to the U-turn. It is more helpful and more accurate to understand the political, economic, sociological and even cultural frameworks within which political actors formulated policy and forged coalitions – to understand the constraints that faced Left governments after 1981 and the possibilities given those constraints. How have organizations adapted to changing environments after the U-turn?

The French experience differs from U-turns in other countries in at least three ways. First, contrary to its initial optimism in 1981, the French Left had less room in the 1980s for policy manoeuvre than had social democratic governing parties in Austria, Germany, Sweden or even the Labour Party in Britain during an earlier period. The simultaneous internationalization and decentralization of the economy after the mid-1970s critically constrained Socialist economic policy.[4] Therefore, the French Left paid a heavy price for achieving power in the 1980s. Second, the French political executive had the institutional capacity to act decisively. The Left came to power with the most impressive arsenal of policy tools available to change society. The strong French state had developed during the post-war period and had been refined by the successive presidencies of Charles de Gaulle, Georges Pompidou and Valéry Giscard d'Estaing. The Socialists used the power of the French state to adapt economy and society to new domestic and international constraints. The exercise of state power by the Left, however, exacerbated a third feature of the French case – weak party organization and low political mobilization. In the initial period, 'techno-socialists' believed that the central state could engineer social change and were reluctant to entrust non-governmental actors with responsibility.[5] Orthodox economic policies contributed to the demobilization of organized labour. Social and political movements have fractured into a number of antagonistic parts, French interest representation has splintered, and the momentum of 1981 has been lost. Left governance undercut traditional forms of support and failed to nurture new constituencies.

This essay first explores the political constraints that the Socialists encountered when they gained the presidency. The party system limited political mobilization by encouraging fragmented and personalistic parties. In the process, political rejuvenation was discouraged. Second, it argues that the reform project of 1981 was designed for a world gone by. The programme's failure to address adequately the problems that afflicted the contemporary French economy further undercut left mobilization. Socialist policy-making eventually collided with left ideals. Third, it explores the effects of the U-turn on the increasingly remote relationships between Left parties on one hand and organized labour and social movements on the other. Fourth, it places the following 13 essays within the context of new economic forces and an altered political realm. Fifth, it probes the arenas in which political mobilization is taking place in the early 1990s.

PARTIES AND PARTY SYSTEMS IN FRANCE

The Socialists have been operating within a set of constraints created by the particular nature of French political competition. The French party system encouraged all political parties in general and the Left in particular to focus energies on electoral competition at the expense of party organization. This was certainly not unique to France. Combined with the strong state, however, the system of weak political parties encouraged a profound stagnation in programmatic ideas and organizational activity. Such political inertia prevented creative responses to new and turbulent environments.

Party vitality – the capacity to forge linkages to and translate aspirations from the citizenry – depends on factors external and internal to the party organization. France was long considered a case of weakly institutionalized parties. In the Third Republic (1871–1940), political parties consisted of informally linked networks of locally based notables. Politicians assembled political committees at the local level and affiliated with parties at the parliamentary level. To the extent that they were visible, national cleavages were determined by clericalism, support for republican government, regionalism and political opportunism. The Socialist Party (SFIO) was a partial exception, as it mobilized new working-class voters. Yet after the scission of 1920, when those loyal to the Third International broke away from the SFIO, the remaining organization was not a sufficient electoral threat to force the smaller parties of the Centre and Centre-Right to relinquish their cadre-based political organization. Only the PCF developed a mass character before World War II, yet its options were limited by its anti-system programme and its outcast status.

The Fourth Republic (1946–58) revived hopes for a more modern party system. The three forces that emerged from the Resistance – Communism, Socialism and Christian Democracy – all had the potential to develop into mass parties that would channel wide groups of members into the political arena. The SFIO and the *Mouvement Républicain Populaire* (MRP) both failed to forge linkages to increasingly large numbers of members, and they lapsed into rival leadership units that tore apart the MRP, weakened the SFIO and undermined the mass party in France. The explanations for the splintering of the party system ranged from uneven economic development and the absence of a strong working class to the centralized state administration to an incomplete republicanism.[6] At the very least, the atmosphere of crisis that surrounded de-colonization prevented French parties from coalescing around a set of political issues with widespread appeal. The electoral system of the Fifth Republic ushered in a new phase of party competition. The double ballot majority system forced political parties to choose electoral alliances before the second round of voting in legislative and, after the 1962 constitutional reform, presidential elections. While such alliances could be purely tactical, they had the potential to constitute long-term relationships. Between 1958 and 1978, for instance, the share of seats in the National Assembly received by the top four parties increased from 78.6 per cent to 96.9 per cent, and the number of parliamentary groups decreased from ten to four.[7] More important, with the signature of the Common Programme of Government by the PCF, PS, and Left Radicals in 1972, the French party system seemed to have developed into governing and opposition blocs that were relatively coherent and offered the electorate clear choices.

The newfound electoral stability after 1958 cannot be attributed solely to new voting rules, however. De Gaulle's constitution dramatically increased the powers of the presidency, which encouraged co-operation among political forces to capture the prize. The development of the Gaullist party out of a disparate group of Centre-Right political élites suggested that the office of the presidency transcended previously contentious issues. Mitterrand's 1981 victory and the subsequent legislative landslide indicated the important boost that the presidency had given to the electoral fortunes of French parties. Other changes within the French polity reduced representational fractionalization. Secularization of society after 1945 removed religion as a polarizing issue. Decolonization reduced the salience of France's global position. The Cold War limited the appeal of anti-republicanism on the right. Economic expansion privileged social class as a determinant of voting. Thus, societal homogenization combined with the 'presidentialization' of politics encouraged bipolar electoral mobilization either to sustain the president or dislodge him.

The division of the electorate into two rival camps, however, never increased the vitality of French party organizations, for the linkages to societal groups were never strong. The Gaullist movement was created from the top down as a support mechanism for the General. Only with the 1965 election was it imbued with a mass backing, but it remained divided into factions supporting the *barons*, former prime ministers who might be presidential material. Even under the pressure of the electoral law and the allure of the presidency, the SFIO remained so riven by factions that its vote shrank, its membership stagnated and its enthusiasm for campaigning waned until it dissolved itself into the PS in 1969. While the PCF remained a mass mobilization party, its declining electoral reach and lack of internal debate hardly made it a model for other political forces. French parties never developed the mass characteristics of their counterparts in other advanced industrial countries.

Consequently, French parties have had trouble mobilizing the electorate. Because French parties remained cadre- rather than mass-driven, they could not pursue the catch-all strategy adopted by mass parties elsewhere in Europe by the 1960s. According to Otto Kirchheimer, after the war parties sought increasingly to transcend established cleavages (class and religion) to appeal to nationwide constituencies.[8] For Left parties, this broad-based strategy derived partially from the realization, as Adam Przeworski claims, that the blue-collar work force would never constitute a numerical majority and that parties needed to attract different categories of voters.[9] It was also a recognition that political issues were more salient at the national, rather than sectional, level. In Europe, broad appeals became possible because the continuous growth of the postwar period allowed policy élites to contemplate both growth and redistribution. Catch-all parties could simultaneously attract the working classes and the new middle classes with positive sum trade-offs. Their programmes brought a decrease in the ideological content of party platforms and a strengthening of party leaders (giving them the freedom to cut deals with a variety of interest groups). Because French parties were weakly organized, leadership circles were in no position either to impel such changes or to forge linkages to widely different groups of societal interests. The vote-aggregating and system-stabilizing functions of catch-all parties remained illusive in France.

Ironically, the 'backwardness' of the French political system sheltered its parties from the organizational decay that affected their European counterparts in the 1970s.[10] Such decay derived from new issues and new electorates that established parties could not capture. The sources of electoral de-alignment are complex and contentious.[11] For Ronald Inglehart, the passing of generations has impelled wide-ranging shifts in political values and the citizen-party nexus. The sustained economic affluence after 1945 created a generation of voters less concerned with distributional (and confessional) issues. The rise of 'post-materialist' values challenged traditional forms of political representation that depended on distributional issues.[12] Value change has been linked to the development of new political agendas which stress the environment, individual identity, life styles and personal rights. It has also affected the nature of citizen politics: post-materialists prefer direct participation over indirect representation.[13] Changes in the value orientation of electorates therefore put pressure on party organizations to appeal to new groups and advance new issues without undermining their existing bases. Few catch-all parties could simultaneously appeal to new societal groups and reform their internal decision-making practices to weather such changes. Since French parties never adopted the catch-all strategy, they suffered little from the secular trends affecting other political systems.[14] Consequently, they had little incentive to address new issues and constituencies, and thus they remained stuck in a 1940s political discourse.

By 1981, the French political sphere had developed into two blocs, while partisan divisions elsewhere were fracturing. Yet French parties remained loose organizations structured around charismatic individuals. Deceptively coherent blocs within the French party system complicated the Left's attempt to govern during the Mitterrand years.

The two blocs were profoundly unstable. The previous decade of Left unity had been turbulent. The Socialists and Communists coalesced in 1972 with the Common Programme of Government – an electoral pact and joint political statement of the policies of a potential Left government. But the electoral strategy of the PS was based on the eventual weakening of the PCF, and the PCF played into this strategy with a number of ill-timed and poorly formulated political positions on Eastern Europe, internal party democracy and political pluralism in France. Those tensions became more acute as the PS succeeded in poaching votes from the PCF, and the latter forwarded a set of programmatic demands that broke the alliance. The Common Programme coalition fell apart in 1977, although by the 1978 legislative elections, which the Right won, the Socialists had already gained supremacy on the Left. Between 1978 and 1981, the PCF attacked the PS with the same vehemence it usually reserved for the Right. Thus, when Mitterrand won the presidency and the Left captured the National Assembly in 1981, the PCF became a distrustful junior partner in the Left government.

Likewise, the persistence of personality-based party organizations made the linkages to key groups on the Left difficult to sustain. Consequently, French Left parties and their electorates were particularly susceptible to being demoralized if party platforms were not fully implemented. The failure to develop alternative platforms or reform decision-making procedures cast a shadow on attempts to attract constituencies with non-materialist value orientations. This inability eventually undermined the governing capacity of the French Left.

POLICIES FOR A NEW INTERNATIONAL ENVIRONMENT

The Socialists came to power in 1981 with a mandate to increase the democratic control of the economy. Mitterrand defeated Giscard by more than a million votes in the second round. The Socialists alone claimed a majority, and the Left received two-thirds of the seats in the National Assembly. This electoral steamroller gave the government of Pierre Mauroy the political space to implement three structural reforms – nationalizations of industrial groups and major banks, a set of worker rights and decentralization of public administration. Demand stimulation through public-sector spending and wage increases promised to inject purchasing power into the pocketbooks of *le citoyen*, kick-starting the process. These reforms floundered, though, because they did not account for a very different international economic environment.[15] In their place, the Socialists substituted investment for redistribution, private initiative for nationalization, and

Europe for domestic markets. 'Modernization' replaced socialism as the rhetorical model.

The French Left built its policy framework around ideas developed in response to both the Depression and World War II.[16] These ideas centred around the role of the central state in securing a more equitable distribution of resources. The Left in other European countries held similar views in the early post-war period but modified their programmes to adapt to the exigencies of government (Britain), the pressures of party coalitions (Sweden) or the development of middle-class constituencies (Germany). In France, the Left envisioned the state as ensuring income redistribution and modernizing the economy because French capitalists had forever hidden behind protective barriers, familial clans, sweetheart deals and cartels. Despite economic growth in the post-war period, the Left clung to the notion that French capitalists would not modernize on their own. Therefore, it had to capture the 'commanding heights' to push French capitalists into modernity. By the 1970s, however, heavy-handed state direction of the economy was at risk of creating more problems than it could solve.[17]

Centralized political control of the economy through the nationalization of 11 major industrial groups and the remainder of the banking sector not brought under public control after the Liberation failed to tackle new economic conditions that favoured regional and transnational economic organization. The nationalizations were to be used to create large vertically integrated firms for major product categories, a new version of the national champion strategy of the 1970s. These fortified firms would 'reconquer the domestic market'.[18] This had been the reasoning of policymakers in the golden era of economic growth between 1950 and 1975.[19] The policy encouraged economies of scale within mass production industries and prioritized the domestic over the international market – both premises problematic by the 1980s. Innovation, productivity and employment generation have been higher in small firms. Both large and small firms competed increasingly in global markets. The strategy of producing for national consumers was inconsistent with open borders in Europe and became counterproductive with the initiatives on the Single European Market.

Labour reforms also spoke to a different era – one in which employment was stable, trade unions enjoyed wider representation, and collective bargaining was more centralized. Under the Auroux Laws (named after the Socialist Minister of Labour Jean Auroux), employees received the 'right to expression'. Works councils had to be consulted in the event of major changes in personnel, and they received independent powers to assess management plans. Firms had to bargain with their unions annually. Health and safety committees received expanded powers to stop production. Workers for public-sector companies could elect one-third of the board members. These reforms imitated similar attempts in Germany, Italy and the United States (via the Wagner Act of 1935) to regularize the position of labour in shops and offices and carve out an 'economic citizenship'. The new demands of knowledge-based production in the 1980s rendered obsolete such formal modes of employee participation, and the industrial relations reforms fell far short of the Left's intentions. Despite initial resistance, employers found they could use expression groups (and quality circles) to circumvent union organizations and gain important feedback directly from their workforces. Consultation of works councils never implied acceptance of their recommendations. The annual obligation to bargain became an onerous task to a union movement rapidly losing members. After 1981, management became considerably more participative in its search for social harmony, but organized labour has not been a major player.

In contrast to the other two structural reforms, decentralization was a partial success, but increasing administrative flexibility during a period of shrinking resources failed to strengthen political participation. Real powers devolved from Paris. While municipalities and regions previously had looked to the central state for guidance and resources, they received new capacities to tax and spend. The Socialist reforms also created a new political élite at the local level – political bosses who mediated the relationship between centre and periphery. The 1985 law to limit the accumulation of political offices further empowered local élites.[20] But political participation decreased after the reforms. While political and administrative pluralism increased in the next decade, these changes may have weakened national party organizations by reinforcing local interests.[21]

Demand stimulation took place through proactive employment policies, wage increases (stimulated by minimum-wage gains) and increases in transfer payments to the poor. Yet the Left pursued this policy in the midst of what was then the most severe international recession since the 1930s. The Socialists had bet on an American recovery to serve as a locomotive for growth of the European economy. The US recovery did not take place until 1982. Demand stimulation initially flooded the domestic market with imports, and a small trade imbalance turned into a massive one. Reflation in a world of recession increased the differential in price levels between France and its largest trading partners, further weakening the competitive position of French exports.[22] France had a high inflation rate and products that sold poorly at home and abroad.

This macroeconomic instability showed the limits of national economic strategies. The struggles over exchange-rate policy, as David Cameron suggests in Chapter 3, came to symbolize the trade-offs facing the Socialists. The three currency devaluations between 1981 and 1983 were too little, too late, for they neither gave breathing room to French exports nor did they scare off currency speculators. Moreover, the second devaluation of June 1982 was accompanied by a policy that froze wages, prices and some budgetary items. The third devaluation in March 1983 was accompanied by further budget cuts, foreign currency restrictions, a forced loan on taxpayers, higher payroll contributions and the de-indexation of wages. Increasingly conservative approaches had substituted for the initial economic voluntarism.

The Socialists had made a U-turn less than two years into power. As dramatic as the U-turn was, however, it was not sudden. Rather, the about-face resulted from a series of policy choices that whittled away at earlier goals. As the Left government compromised its initial programme, it gave itself increasingly less room for manoeuvre. The alternative of withdrawal from the European Monetary System (EMS), currency restrictions, steady economic stimulus and export-oriented industrial policy became synonymous with autarkic policy. For the politically responsible president, Serge Halimi argues in Chapter 4, autarky became unthinkable. Whether or not the programme was economically feasible, it was marginalized from the very beginning. Each stage of this process was characterized by an absence of intermediate alternatives because of a lack of creative thinking, which, in turn, seemed to have resulted from the Socialists' lack of connection with societal organizations.

After the U-turn, French economic policy revolved around the strong franc, price stability, firm-level profitability and renewed investment. Governments of the Left and then the Right (1986–8 and 1993–5) have trumpeted a strong currency to dampen inflationary expectations while imposing discipline on French producers to maintain production efficiencies, thereby stimulating investment and creating new employment. The firm became the centre of economic creativity. The modernization campaign under Prime Ministers Laurent Fabius (1984–6) and Michel Rocard (1988–91) placed a premium on firm-level adjustment, encouraging managers to allocate resources more efficiently. This did not mean less state intervention in either industrial or labour-market policy.[23] Rather, as Rand Smith suggests in Chapter 5, it showed the extent to which the state could be mobilized to new ends.

In particular, governments sought to dampen collective consumption through economic rigour. National budgetary stringency kept growth in expenditures below increases in national product. France even began reducing national debt for a brief period, facilitated at least partially by the proceeds from privatization in 1986–7 and after 1993. When collective expenses became unavoidable, as with the social security system, households increased their contributions. Rigor increased business confidence and produced an environment favourable to investment (as Vivien Schmidt suggests in Chapter 6).

Restrictive economic policy had a mixed record. After four years of painfully slow growth in the wake of the U-turn, economic activity picked up between 1988 and 1990, during which 750 000 jobs were created. Unemployment dipped into single digits only between 1989 and 1991. The inflation differential with West Germany, France's largest trading partner, was reduced to near zero. After German unification, the advantage turned to the French. Economic growth slowed in the wake of the Gulf War, however. In spite of considerable state-assisted employment, joblessness remained stubbornly high. By late 1994, the unemployment rate had climbed to 12.5 per cent.

Economic policy depended increasingly on more open borders and further integration into Europe, the reasoning being that France could not compete on a national footing.[24] The decision to remain in the EMS marginalized those on the

Left promoting autarkic policies (the so-called 'Albanian solution') and rein-forced Mitterrand's long-standing pro-Europeanism.[25] Afterwards, the acceptance of the Davignon Plan to sort out the troubled steel industry in 1984, the negotia-tion of the Single European Market in 1986, and the promotion of Economic and Monetary Union in the 1991 Maastricht Treaty cemented France's role in Europe. Job creation in the United States after 1983 stunned those bemoaning net losses in France, while the continued success of the Japanese sent shivers up the spines of policy makers who envisioned Europe as the next launching pad after the American market for Japanese firms. Finally, as in the Treaties of Paris and Rome, the Maastricht Treaty was envisioned as a way to constrain Germany – this time with a common currency and European-wide central bank co-ordination.

In their economic orthodoxy and search for European-wide markets for French firms, Socialist policymakers admitted that the policies of nationalization and employment maintenance could not be sustained in an increasingly competitive international environment. This has been most evident in the public sector, which eroded in the decade after the U-turn. In spite of a generation of public consensus for the strong state, French conservatives in the late 1970s had discovered the rhetorical virtues of privatization. After the 1982 nationalizations, the public sec-tor became a politically contentious issue. Already in the early 1980s, municipal governments began contracting out some services. After the Left lost the legis-lative elections in 1986, the government of Jacques Chirac in 1986–8 privatized some firms although the 1987 stock market crash prevented the Right from fully implementing its plans. The Mitterrand re-election campaign of 1988 promised stability in the public sector, while the Edouard Balladur government elected in 1993 pledged a wholesale sell-off. Competition policy in the European Union has pressured French governments into withholding subsidies from public sector firms. The development of Euro-champions in both the public and private sectors came at the expense of massive job losses. Public sector companies needed to be competitive, and employment was no longer guaranteed. At the end of President Mitterrand's second term, the public sector had been transformed from laborato-ries for social experiments into spearheads of French competitiveness.[26]

Likewise, the state has been in the forefront of increasing labour-market flexibilities, in the belief that microeconomic reorganization was critical to firm-level adjustment. Governments after the mid-1980s introduced flexibility into the hiring, firing and use of labour (see Chapter 7 by Chris Howell). For instance, in 1986 Chirac abolished the administrative authorization of layoffs – the procedure by which layoffs needed approval from the Ministry of Labour – and his Socialist successors refused to restore it. Subsequent legislation on layoffs provided for more consultations with works councils. The removal of power from departmen-tal labour inspectors gave employers more prerogatives, some of which had to be shared with union organizations at the firm level. Yet the Socialists did not retreat completely from the labour market. Left governments forced employers to formu-late social plans in the case of job losses and began a new emphasis on worker 'conversion' in workplace restructuring.[27] They encouraged firms to modernize by adopting new technologies and new organizational forms, and streamlining human resources. They gave firms greater discretion in hiring temporary employees. They created an array of programmes to subsidize short-term youth employment, effectively lowering the employment costs to firms. By 1993, France had one of the lowest unit labour costs in Europe.

The irony of the Mitterrand years is that the French economy has never been as market-oriented or as open to the world as after 1983. The policy tools of the strong state forged this market opening strategy. Economic openness, however, has had political repercussions. Both Left parties and the union movement have lost members and vitality. Both have failed to find a replacement for the collectivist discourse that impelled social mobilization before the 1980s. These challenges affected all countries in the 1980s. What distinguished France was the suddenness of the Left's collapse and the decade-long political disorganization that ensued.

THE LEFT, ORGANIZED LABOUR AND SOCIAL MOVEMENTS AFTER THE U-TURN

The Socialists' policy turnabout became synonymous with a collapse in political mobilization. Yet such mobilization always had been hard to sustain in France. Societal organizations have had neither the coherence nor the resources to continuously channel political activity into the political sphere.[28] The choice to respond to trade imbalances and inflation through economic orthodoxy rather than through more redistributive means exacerbated the weak linkages between Left parties and labour unions after the mid-1980s.[29] Furthermore, Left political parties failed to find new ways to mobilize other social movements.

Throughout Western Europe after 1945, Left parties and trade unions developed a set of interconnected understandings, whose details varied among countries. The unions contributed funding, staffing and support to help elect Left parties. In return, they received legislation for goals they could not achieve in collective bargaining. During the long post-war boom, economic exchange supplemented this mobilization function. The unions sought full employment policies and a more developed welfare state, making the workforce less vulnerable to market pressures. In return, they would moderate wage demands when pay increases threatened to surpass productivity levels.[30]

That Left-labour nexus has been historically weak in France. With Socialists and Communists competing for the same pool of working-class voters, party-union deals were difficult to negotiate. Moreover, the inability of unions to respond effectively to a menacing international economic environment further weakened party-union ties.

The character of the labour movement itself also constituted an important political constraint. Political exchange has always been difficult with union organizations that spoke for only a fraction of the workforce. French union membership peaked in the mid-1940s in the excitement of the Liberation and then reached a relatively static plateau of 20 per cent to 25 per cent in the 1960s and 1970s; this low organizational strength was divided among at least five union confederations.

Like their political counterparts, unions developed into charismatic organizations. The method of dues collection – the sale of monthly stamps to members – nurtured a personal relationship between militant and member, but it also contributed to organizational poverty, since members tended to buy fewer than 12 stamps. The tradition of anarcho-syndicalism made unions prone to developing a core of cadres at the expense of wider membership. Internal ideological cleavages put a premium on political conformity, which alienated existing and potential members. The union movement has thus been divided along political, confessional and strategic lines. Constant electioneering for plant delegates and works council members ensured the constancy of division. Unions used their positions as delegates and works councillors to politicize national and work-related issues. The legal framework also facilitated individuals free riding on union organizations. Until the Auroux Laws, any union could negotiate for an entire bargaining unit, and contracts applied to all employees. The state's ability to extend agreements unilaterally to larger categories of workers discouraged membership.

Therefore, even before the 1980s, labour and the Left were internally divided, and the possibilities for a society-wide political exchange were remote. The PCF had been out of power since 1947, and the Socialists had last participated in government under de Gaulle in 1958, so opportunities for economic understandings between a governing party and a union movement did not exist. Party-union linkages contained only political understandings, and they were segmented. The PCF and the *Confédération Générale du Travail* (CGT) had the closest relations of French parties and unions. A faction of the PS found itself close to the *Confédération Française Démocratique du Travail* (CFDT), the so-called 'second Left' that defined itself as less statist than other parts of the party.[31] Before it metamorphosed into the PS, the SFIO had maintained cordial relations with the *Force Ouvrière* (FO). The PS strained those relations by signing the Common Programme.[32]

After the mid-1970s, the understandings that had tied together the Left and labour came under increasing pressure in all the advanced countries. The economic restructuring associated with the exhaustion of mass production fragmented the social bases of unions and Left parties, shrinking the overlap and the commonality of interest between them. Both Left parties and labour unions are much more heterogeneous now than they were 30 years ago. Moreover, the simultaneous decentralization of production and collective bargaining as well as the proliferation of cross-national mergers and strategic alliances have weakened the links in the Keynesian growth dynamic – a cycle in which wage increases stimulate overall demand, thereby inducing greater production, encouraging investment, improving productivity and permitting further wage increases. The de-linkage of wage increases from investment and productivity after the early 1970s meant that the interests of workers were no longer universal. As a result, political élites had less need to work with labour unions, which had become more 'dysfunctional' for the economy. As nation-states lost the capacity to influence important aspects of economic policy, the ability of Left parties to maintain distinct policy packages and to deliver certain goods to unions declined as well. When Left parties were in power, they could no longer maintain full employment. Unemployment, in turn, obviated the need for a political solution to wage inflation.

In France, these general international pressures weakened an already tenuous linkage between the Left and labour. Depressed labour markets, along with the political conflict between the PCF and the PS, impeded the mobilizational capacity of French unions in the 1970s. The state's attempt – in the first years of the Giscard presidency and then between 1981 and 1983 – to insulate France from international forces delayed but did not remove these market pressures.[33] Just as important, it reinforced unions' tendency to seek political solutions to market problems. Until the 1980s, unions had substituted mobilization for organization. When the former declined – membership was halved in the 1980s – the latter could not compensate.

Neither party nor union has succeeded in reversing this organizational decay. Indeed, the splits became even more serious in the early 1990s. Even as its vote waned after 1978, the PCF could still claim to be a coherent organization. It has now lost that leadership homogeneity, and serious divisions separate elected officials from party cadres, union supporters from party activists and proponents of a more open leadership style from the current leadership. The PS has fared better only in electoral results. The bitter struggle over the succession to Mitterrand suggested that important cleavages deepened after 1981. The ousting of First Secretary Fabius by Michel Rocard in April 1993 after the Socialists' defeat in the legislative elections publicly uncovered a set of tensions which had been simmering for years. The dismal performance of the PS in the European elections in June 1994 combined with constant sniping from the president's residence, the Elysée Palace, encouraged Rocard to resign.[34]

Fissures widened even further within the unions. The struggle over relations with the PCF seriously divided the CGT by the end of the 1980s. Fights over relations with other unions rocked the CFDT and partially accounted for the unceremonious resignation of Jean Kaspar in October 1992. The numbers of expulsions – in the CFDT involving postal workers and nurses – and politically induced resignations is alarming for a union movement with so few members. The independent education union (*Fédération de l'Education Nationale*) also split in two in 1992.

Given the tradition of organizational pluralism within the Left and the workers' movement, it is hard to imagine more division. Yet divisiveness increased after the U-turn for five reasons. First, the institution of the presidency and its tremendous powers encouraged the Left to prioritize the needs of individual candidates over those of the party or movement. The joint candidate of the Left in 1965 and 1974 was the winner in 1981 and 1988 – despite only halfhearted support from the Communist Party. Mitterrand was the only Left candidate (at least on the second round of presidential voting) for more than a quarter of a century. This fact alone encouraged the PS to place his electoral needs over doctrinal consistency (see Chapter 2 by George Ross). As the largest force on the Left, the PS came to see after 1981 that securing the presidency trumped any other political goal.[35] This strategy explains why the Socialists introduced proportional representation in 1985 to make cohabitation with the Right easier, although it gave the National Front (FN) representation in the National Assembly.

Second, the dominant Socialists responded to political difficulties in ways that discouraged the political mobilization of new categories of electors. The Socialists were in the key position to include such new voters in their ranks, yet the use of highly developed factions (*courants*) to organize the party prevented the infusion of new members and new issues, which could upset a delicate balance of power (see Chapter 10 by Serenella Sferza). When the party reached out to social movements – supporters of civil rights for immigrants, women and environmentalists – it attempted to co-opt them for its own electoral advantage (see Chapters 12, 13 and 14 by Tad Shull, Amy Mazur, and Patrick Ireland). Presidentialism encouraged *courant* system leaders to act instrumentally. The struggles within the party among these 'elephants' have been efforts to position candidates for the inevitable succession to Mitterrand.

Third, the decline of the Communist Party has drained the Left of a core of dedicated militants. Perhaps the key political change of the Mitterrand presidency has been the unambiguous decline of the PCF. Martin Schain in Chapter 11 suggests that the PCF after the 1960s was unable to avail itself of the growth formula it had used in previous periods. For 50 years, it had grown and prospered by integrating different generations of immigrants into French political life. But immigrants since the 1970s have been largely non-white, and the party could not attract them into their ranks. The reasons behind such failure – particularly stark when compared to the success of the Italian Communist Party – can be found in the group formed around former Secretary General Georges Marchais. This clique prevented the debates over ideology, strategy and party composition, which might have led to rejuvenation.

Fourth, the governing Left came increasingly to resemble the Right in both policy and rhetoric, a move that did not facilitate political mobilization. Having adopted the market, the Socialists could not find a creative way to convince voters that a Socialist state would improve their lives. Both labour and the Left continued after 1981 to view the state as the primary vehicle of social change. Yet state leadership was being used increasingly to carve out market niches. Therefore, the Socialists could argue that their policies of facilitating entrepreneurial activity in the economy was socially progressive, but it was unlikely

Table 1.1   Strike Activity 1981–1990

Working Days Lost in Work Stoppages per 1000 in Total Labour Force (annual average)	
Italy	1624
Greece	454
Spain	340
UK	226
Portugal	92
US	86
France	55
Germany	23

Note: Data for Spain excludes Catalonia (1981–6) and the Basque country (1986–90).

Source: ILO, *Yearbook of Labour Statistics*.

to lead to lasting bonds either to the institutions of labour or other social movements.

Fifth, the logic of inter-union competition prevented unions from coalescing to protect workers from the effects of market-oriented policies. The world of work changed dramatically for union organizations (see Chapter 8 by Mark Kesselman and Chapter 9 by Guy Groux and René Mouriaux), yet union leaders seemed more intent on scoring points against their rival organizations than on developing new strategies. Militancy has been particularly difficult to generate, as indicated by annually declining strike rates: By the early 1990s France would be among those countries with the *lowest* rates (see Table 1). In an earlier period, French unions compensated for their organizational inadequacies through local mobilization to trigger state responses.[36] That has become increasingly difficult since 1983. Union leaders knew that memberships were shrinking, but the institutionalization of union activity in a host of different elected and appointed positions gave the illusion of activity.[37] More responsibility fell on fewer shoulders. The *movement* aspects of union activity were neglected in favour of the more overtly *political* facets.

Political parties and labour unions failed to come up with a sustainable discourse after the U-turn.[38] European integration could hardly be a rallying cry when it became synonymous with restrictive economic policy, slow growth and unemployment. Likewise, 'modernity' rang hollow when it came to signify economic restructuring, stagnant wages and less employment security. The only rhetorical device that the ruling PS developed was 'solidarity'. This was used only in a compensatory manner – for deficits in the social security system or to spread out work – and not as an essential ingredient of social change. The Socialists promoted 'civil society', but the concept had little real substance to counter suspicions of justifications of rising social inequality. The governing Left found itself caught within the logic of market metaphors, and the oppositional Left, the PCF, was not sufficiently credible to challenge it. The Left has had trouble forging innovative political strategies to create and sustain linkages to a society itself undergoing radical social change.

According to Henri Mendras and Alistair Cole, France is experiencing a 'Second Revolution', in which social mores, cultural frameworks, economic rules and political instincts have been thrown into doubt.[39] Even if they overdramatize the consequences of social change, the divisions that separated town from city, worker from employer, and popular from 'bourgeois' culture have become increasingly blurred in the 1980s and 1990s. Consequently, political parties and social movements have needed to adapt their practices to a changing environment.

The 1993 legislative elections seemed to indicate the incapacity of the governing Socialists to adapt to these societal changes. Vote for the PS shrank from 34.8 per cent in 1988 to 17.6 per cent in 1993.[40] Most commentators interpreted the results as an overwhelming rejection of Socialist stewardship.[41] The PS had relinquished its linkages to important social groups and in the process had lost the capacity to mobilize constituencies.

The Right has not been much more successful at strengthening political organization and sustaining increasing voting shares. In the March 1993 legislative elections, the coalition of the *Rassemblement pour la République* (RPR) and *Union pour la Démocratie Française* (UDF) captured the largest percentage of seats of any coalition in the 20th century, but its percentage of votes on the first round (39.6 per cent) actually decreased relative to 1986 and only increased by 1.9 per cent over its performance in 1988. The electorate has not shifted massively from the Centre–Left to the Centre–Right.

As conventional platforms and mobilization strategies fall on deaf ears, alternative parties on the Right and Left gain ground. The FN (12.7 per cent) continued its pitch for French nativism and its assault on the political class. It captured a larger number of working-class votes than did the PCF, and the latter's 9.1 per cent masked its absence from wide areas of the country. The success of the environmental parties in the 1992 regional elections (*les Verts* and *Génération Écologie* totalled 14 per cent) and their subsequent rise in public opinion polls (peaking at 19 per cent) indicated a public malaise with established leaderships and the issues they championed. Their mediocre score in the 1993 elections – together the two parties received only 7.6 per cent – may have reflected the infighting within their electoral coalition, which dissipated their anti-establishment appeal. Nonetheless, allied environmental groups gained ground, and the total vote for environmental candidates reached 10.9 per cent.

The materialist Left in France has shrivelled from internal turbulence and external pressures, although no political force has taken its place. The PCF is a shell of its former self. The PS has been badly bruised by its experience in government. The trade unions are struggling for existence. The suicide of former Prime Minister Pierre Bérégovoy on 1 May 1993 symbolized the Left's anguish. Rather than using state tools to re-orient policy in ways that could institutionalize a new set of strong linkages between left parties and French citizens, the Left undermined traditional support and failed to develop new constituencies.

THE MITTERRAND ERA

Along with Charles de Gaulle, François Mitterrand has been one of the two key actors in post-war French politics. His influence extends beyond political longevity (51 years of governmental service beginning with a post as junior minister in the post-Liberation cabinet). He defined the terms of political competition in the Fifth Republic. He served as president during a time period of profound economic change. He presided over dramatic changes in domestic political organization and European construction. The essays in this volume evaluate the Mitterrand presidency in terms of its effects on political mobilization and on the Left. They explore the quandaries facing Socialist governments, the interaction between the Left and economic actors, and the effects of governmental participation on political mobilization.

The Dilemmas of Governance

The erosion of national economic policy autonomy – via the Single European Market, the internationalization of business and distinctive localized production strategies – has circumscribed public policy in individual European countries. Mildly redistributive Keynesianism, the backbone of social democracy in Europe, has become increasingly difficult to implement in an international system that can foster competition based on wages and labour standards. French Socialists, like their counterparts elsewhere, had to govern within these new international constraints, and they have struggled with unemployment rates that stubbornly resist traditional remedies.

George Ross suggests that the combination of Mitterrand's personal style and the institution of the presidency undermined the capacity of the French governing Left to mend and strengthen its political organization. The presidency permits its occupant to wield enormous policy levers *and* to stamp an imprint on those policy orientations. Mitterrand is a political leader nurtured on the intrigues of the Fourth Republic who became an astute tactician, and who learned to play off forces within the Socialist Party in the 1970s and within his governments in the 1980s. These strengths served the Socialist president in terms of his ability to manage the U-turn, to jockey with the Right and to secure his re-election in 1988. They led him, however, to obscure the advantages of a possible programmatic and organizational renewal in the PS and to overestimate the benefits of European policy. As a result, the Socialists have been left with a weak organization, without a clear identity and with very uncertain electoral support.

David Cameron argues that the policy U-turn was not as inevitable as a number of observers have claimed. He eschews both the 'reality' and the 'betrayal' arguments that have dominated discussion of exchange rate policy, participation in the European Monetary System and the austerity policies of 1983. Instead, he provides a chronicle of the exchange rate policies that narrowed the room for manoeuvre between 1981 and 1983 and that eventually led to large domestic policy shifts. He finds that Left policy élites knew they had an alternative path (*l'autre politique*) in the form of monetary and fiscal expansion, industrial modernization and devaluation of the franc. They rejected *l'autre politique* not because of its demerits, but because of presidential preferences, the capacity of the Treasury to set the terms of debate and the 'tyranny of small decisions'. The consequences of this U-turn were still being felt more than a decade later through slow growth, high unemployment and the unravelling of the Left coalition.

For Serge Halimi, the about-face provides more continuity than change for the French Left. While the U-turn was dramatic, it was consistent with the experiences of other Left governments in the 20th century – the *Cartel des Gauches* in 1924 and the Popular Front of 1936. In all three instances, the Left retreated behind the arguments of 'external constraint' and 'political responsibility'. He finds that the Left consistently refuses to devalue the currency, while the Right feels comparatively unencumbered. This economic dogmatism undercuts attempts to cement long-lasting political coalitions. This recurrence of political suicide, Halimi explains, has resulted from the Left's hopes that the problem will solve itself, its desires to appear responsible and its attention to diplomatic imperatives.

The weakness of organized labour, argues Rand Smith, made pro-market policies politically easier for the Socialists. Industrial policy, so the Left thought in 1981, would be one arena in which the Left could simultaneously redistribute resources to its constituencies and create the conditions for long-term national prosperity. Those dreams of modernization were quickly dashed within the economic context of the early 1980s: reform became difficult in a sea of red ink. The steel and automobile industries became the focus of Socialist modernization strategies after the U-turn. Smith finds that the Left government used policy levers to direct investment choices, select top management, and manage massive job losses. Industrial policy in steel and automobiles enabled companies to return to profitability. The Socialists, therefore, brought new meaning to state action. Orthodox restructuring resulted from an absence of sufficiently powerful countervailing forces within the political economy.

Policy Change and Economic Actors

After the U-turn, the French Left trumpeted the virtues of entrepreneurial activity. For the business community, this was the first period of sustained celebration in the post-war period. For labour, it weakened the basis for organization precisely when individual unions found themselves incapable of attracting new members.

An important irony of the Mitterrand era, writes Vivien Schmidt, is that the Left promised to break with capitalism but instead rehabilitated and revived French capitalists. During the 1980s, the business community became considerably more internationalized. While recruitment channels for the business élite remained largely the same, managers were younger, more aggressive and more open to participative management. The public came to see the firm as a positive force in society, while employees developed greater trust in management. This ideological turnaround, along with public policy, improved conditions for business. Nationalization injected much-needed capital into cash-starved firms and permitted the massive restructuring to achieve profitability. Privatization gave managers more room for manoeuvre. Policies to bring together the banking and business communities transformed old-style French *dirigisme* into more subtle forms of intervention. The governing Socialists changed the state into a tool of competitiveness.

Chris Howell finds that attempts to improve competitive capacity conflicted with policies to strengthen societal organization. The Left in power tried to rewrite the rules of industrial relations to make work more 'human' and to create a new form of economic citizenship. The five Auroux Laws sought both to induce collective bargaining and to place the firm at the centre of labour relations. But the laws had the unintended consequence of encouraging firms to avoid dealing with organized labour. Therefore, while the Socialists thought they were strengthening a potential constituency, they were weakening labour at the workplace. Instead of reinforcing union organizations, the laws focused on institutions and procedures that could be wielded by either managers and workers. In the crisis atmosphere of the 1980s, with considerable employer mobilization and increased union weakness, French business turned flexibility to its advantage. Ironically, managers grew fond of *autogestion* as a way to merge the interests of workers with those of the firm.

According to Mark Kesselman, labour-market flexibility need not be inherently detrimental to organized labour. Its effect will depend on the capacity of institutions to represent employee interests and manage technological change. The Auroux Laws promised to give traditionally weak French unions opportunities to participate in management. The provisions mandating consultation of works councils during the introduction of new technologies might have enabled unions to play a key role in workforce management. In his micro-level study of the banking and chemical sectors, Kesselman found that works council members did not have time to evaluate managerial proposals and that managers frequently vetoed the hiring of an independent expert. The increase in bargaining also stretched already slim union resources. In a period of anxiety over job loss, the unions could not find a way to show how the subtleties of technological change would affect worker interests. Finally, the unions remain uncertain about participation in a process that involved outcomes counter to traditional union goals. The Socialists facilitated a form of participation that contributed to a marginalization of the labour movement.

The Mitterrand era may forever be known as the period in which traditional unionism was fatally wounded. Guy Groux and René Mouriaux examine the organizational fragmentation of French unions. They find that unions have too many responsibilities in the workplace and the political arena, over-taxing their resources. New levels of responsibility have not encouraged either mobilization or membership, as both dropped precipitously during the 1980s. The combination of administrative responsibilities and diminished support has rendered French unions even less influential over the terms of economic change. Moreover, the new forms of state intervention have increased labour market flexibility and weakened the collectivism that trade unionism historically provided. The authors examine labour's efforts to address de-unionization and find that the persistence of organizational rivalries undermines co-operative strategies.

Political Mobilization and Left Politics

The policy U-turn and the implosion of organized labour confronted left political actors with a number of problems, not the least of which was the identity of the Left itself. The third set of essays examines how political forces have responded to the constraints the Left has faced. The traditional core of the materialist Left was shrivelling and the understandings tying party to union, which were never very strong, were collapsing. The non-materialist Left was making itself presence felt in the streets, in political networks and potentially at the ballot box. In the context of social demobilization, political parties and social movements have sought new strategies and coalitions.

Serenella Sferza explores the relationship between party organization and political environment. The Socialist Party used a factional (as opposed to territorial) mode of party organization to renew itself in the 1970s. Factionalism facilitated debate when previous programmatic statements seemed mired in opportunism. It helped expand membership as different *courants* fought to control agendas. It forged a linkage between party programme and leadership that had ossified after Liberation, and provided an outlet for dissent without undermining the organization. Yet this mode of organization failed the PS after 1981. Debate was shunned in the interest of governmental harmony. The U-turn rendered factional identities obsolete. Leaders became entrenched in their factions, incapable of addressing new issues or sustaining mobilization. Factional organization was based more on materialist concerns than on the 'new' issues of Europe, the environment and race. The disharmony between factions and issues discouraged potential members. Morcover, the necessity to moderate rivalry among *courants* led to a pause in recruitment. Finally, deprived of programmatic identity, the *courants* became identified with pure political ambition. Thus, the environment of the 1970s encouraged a self-contained turmoil while the demands of government favoured unity. Sferza suggests that party renewal in the 1990s may take place through a more careful orchestration of internal debates that factions provide.

For Martin Schain, the rise and decline of the Communist Party offers lessons on how to conceptualize party development and how to re-mobilize constituencies. The PCF electorate and its organization were constructed between 1920 and 1960 on different bases, and he identifies three sequential layers of constituencies – the peasantry in southwestern France, industrial workers in the suburbs around major cities and immigrant workers in manufacturing. Managing these three constituencies required ingenuity, although the message of oppositionalism spoke to their experiences. The core constituencies declined after the mid-1970s, at least partially because of socio-economic change: the peasantry is ageing and the industrial working class is declining. Ideological rigidity and organizational conformism, however, sapped a capacity either to find new or strengthen old constituencies. Confronted with competition from the PS, the party chose to strengthen its own identity by sabotaging the Common Programme in 1977. The workerist and pro-Soviet rhetoric after the late 1970s did not correspond to the aspirations of new segments of French society. The outmoded identity cost the party electors and members. The leadership accelerated the shrinkage of its core without finding adequate replacements. In particular, the PCF failed to attract new immigrants from North Africa, who have been mobilized around an Islamic identity – which the party finds a threat rather than an opportunity. This analysis suggests that political organizations need to respond flexibly to changes in class structures and social identities.

The environmental movement, writes Tad Shull, offers an example of political renewal. The two green parties, *les Verts* and *Génération Écologie*, have challenged the PS and PCF not simply on environmental issues but on work-sharing, the underclass, lifestyle concerns and participatory democracy. While they gained no seats in the National Assembly in the 1993 legislative elections, they have developed a permanency in the French political spectrum. Given their performance in the 1989 European and 1992 regional elections, this force of 'neither Left nor Right' expected to receive vote totals comparable to those of the PCF or the FN. Broad agreement exists among green members and voters on a critique of industrial society, but political strategy has perpetually divided them. Debate and practice pits strategies for political autonomy (the 'pure-green' strategy) versus alliances with other Left parties (in practice the PS). This choice strikes at the heart of Left politics in France: old-style politics has become increasingly unpopular with electors, yet parties need to influence political outcomes to attract voters. The successful resolution of this debate depends upon both internal struggles for power and internal pressures. The poor performance of the two green parties in the 1994 European elections – a combined vote total of less than 5 per cent – indicated that alternatives to French Socialism have not yet coalesced.

Amy Mazur suggests that the labour-market policies that followed from the U-turn overwhelmed the Socialists' attempt to forge alliances among women.

Between 1965 and 1981 Mitterrand had succeeded in reversing the Left's historic tendency of attracting more men than women. He had long worked with a group of women in the PS and social movements to develop an agenda favouring equal treatment, access to education and more day care. Later he proposed the legalization of contraception. This strategy established political channels for women to make claims on the party's leadership before and after 1981. The Mauroy government created a Ministry of the Rights of Women, which forwarded proposals to reduce gender-based disparities in pay, increase the number of women political candidates, reduce sexist advertising and expand access to contraception. It envisioned its law on professional equality as a centerpiece of a strategy to appeal to women. The 1983 law on *égalité professionnelle*, Mazur argues, was a compromise between feminists who sought a strong version protecting individual women's rights and policy makers who feared adding administrative burdens to the state or employers. Because formulation had been confined to a sub-community of the ministry and women's groups, policy had been weakened even *before* the U-turn. State actors, parties, unions and employers only supported the policy as long as it was not enforced. A weak reform became symbolic over the subsequent decade, as employers evaded rules and state actors declined to enforce them. As a result, the law did little to change the position of women in the labour market. The Socialists stalled on gender rights because they refused to upset traditional social relationships.

The identity of the Left was challenged the most by the social conflicts involving race and ethnicity. This cluster of issues – housing, welfare services, criminality, religious tolerance and cultural difference – confounded all political forces in France (and elsewhere in Europe) in the 1980s. Yet the Left had to struggle the most with the tensions pitting integration against ethnic difference and universalism against cultural pluralism. France has long been a country of immigrants, writes Patrick Ireland, but the non-European immigration after the 1960s differed from earlier patterns in that it was less white, less Christian, and less First World. The assimilation of European populations was never easy, but the labour movement, the Catholic Church and political machines succeeded in channelling social interests while the army and the school system inculcated republican virtue. The assimilation of North and Central African as well as Asian populations, however, became increasingly difficult in the 1970s. With higher levels of unemployment, the non-French became scapegoats. Moreover, a second generation asserted a non-French identity, challenging the Left values of republicanism, universalism and equality. Left policy after 1981 sought to balance integration with cultural pluralism. The U-turn, Ireland argues, complicated this balancing act by increasing the potential for scapegoating and by whittling away at the Left coalition, giving the governing Socialists less electoral margin for manoeuvre. By manipulating the electoral law to stem party losses for the 1986 legislative election, the Socialists facilitated the entry of the National Front into the National Assembly. By tilting toward assimilation and away from pluralism, they encouraged the mobilization of second-generation *beurs*. The PS tried to redirect the energies of various associations, but the *beurs* generation rejected both the republicanism of Left parties and class-based analyses of labour unions, and chafed under assimilationist policies. Cultural identity had become politically explosive and difficult to merge into the established Left.

By the 1990s the Left was fractured. The organizations of the PS and PCF seemed incapable of speaking to new constituencies. The old partnership of Left parties and labour unions no longer provided the ideas or the mobilizational impetus to sustain a united movement. Linkages between the PS and other social groups seemed more cynical and opportunistic rather than principled and mutually beneficial. Mitterrand presided over a sustained period of political degeneration.

POLITICAL RENEWAL?

The capacity for political renewal seems meagre in the short term, as the constraints are enormous. The institution of the presidency continues to offer incentives to prioritize the individual over broader social and political forces. Standard operating procedures, as the PCF has shown, are remarkably resistant to change. Party organizations are difficult to create from the ground up, as the greens have discovered. Not much unites the critics of the PS except for a distaste for the lame-duck president. Political mobilization seems difficult to initiate, even harder to sustain and almost impossible to aggregate.

Yet politics does not stop when established political actors falter. Some have recognized that past choices have been counter-productive and are searching for creative alternatives. The increase in political apathy, the dispersion of votes and the weakening of trade union organizations are signals to the political class that traditional rhetoric and practice have not met constituency demands. Deciphering those expectations, of course, employs innumerable consultants and spin doctors. The inability of established political actors to address new issues offers political opportunities for emerging forces. The amount of agitation and activism in the early 1990s is reminiscent of the political clubs of the 1960s that sought explicitly to revitalize institutions. At the grass-roots level, numerous political groups mobilize along parallel, if not similar, progressive lines.

Dissidents within and outside the Communist Party are speaking openly against the party leadership.[42] By focusing exclusively on the Socialists' U-turn, these critics argue, the Marchais group provided a profoundly demobilizing message. Instead, the party needs to examine its strategy of deliberate isolation and its practices of stifling dissent. The party needs more internal democracy. These were not new critiques, but they tap into an organizational malaise compounded by electoral failure and the changes taking place in Eastern Europe. Consequently, they have elicited tactical confusion in party headquarters that range from expulsions to attempts to institutionalize dialogue. While some dissidents ran on alternative tickets in the 1988 presidential, 1989 municipal and 1993 legislative elections, their results were mixed at best. Their importance rested more with the party's inability to contain them. Thus, the Mitterrand era has witnessed not only the decline of the party but also the decay of democratic centralism. Rigid and hierarchical organization faces strong resistance, and the dead weight of that form of political mobilization had been largely removed from the French political landscape by the time of Marchais' announced resignation in September 1993. Dissatisfaction also developed within the Socialist Party after the mid-1980s. In the immediate aftermath of the U-turn, party leaders and deputies preferred to lobby the government to protect their regions from plant closures rather than question the soundness of the policy reversal. Opposition voices developed later within the party. Several scandals involving party financing (and personal gain) diminished the moral authority of party leaders. Presidential interference in party affairs – in the promotion of Fabius as heir apparent, in the covert financing of social groups (such as *SOS-Racisme*) and in the support of key centrist leaders, such as Bernard Tapie – rankled party members.[43] The Maastricht referendum in September 1992 drove a wider wedge between the government and critics of disinflation within the party. By the 1990s, the gleam was off presidentialism. Not only was the historic leader unpopular in the party he helped forge, but the state-centred approach to solving social problems was receiving a heavy dose of scepticism.[44] The *courant* system of organizing the PS also came under close examination in the aftermath of the 1993 legislative defeat: leadership selection took place by a direct delegate vote at the October congress at Le Bourget, although the residual power of the *courants* undermined Rocard's brief leadership of the party. Finally, disinflationary economic policy was rejected by the PS after it lost power.

Released from the totalizing discourse of Leninism and the reliance on centralizing institutions of Jacobins, French political actors will need to find ways to forge linkages to citizens. It is interesting that *autogestion* experienced a rhetorical comeback in the 1990s as political clubs – more malleable than established parties – have promoted new forms of citizen participation. Within this context, the decentralization reforms may provide the mechanism that will allow political experimentation. The relaxation of political centralization has encouraged the development of self-sustaining industrial districts.[45] It has also allowed important policy experiments in labour policy at the regional and local levels. Such change in the political economy requires new forms of trust and co-operation among social actors. There are some indications that the labour movement has begun rethinking such fundamental questions as social alliances, welfare provision, local co-operation and firm-level activity.[46] The self-examination within the parties of the Left and among the unions does not in itself guarantee political rejuvenation. Rather, it provides a precondition for facilitating political mobilization. Any sustained mobilization requires a revitalization of organizational capacity.

No French political party has a lock on voter loyalties. The 1994 European elections showed the RPR-UDF coalition vulnerable to breakaway lists. Despite Rocard's defeat, the combined total of the Left actually exceeded that of 1989. The problem is bridging political fissures. Populism, via such political figures as Bernard Tapie (who has promised to outlaw youth unemployment), offers one solution. A longer-term solution will require careful organization. Political parties of the Left will need to develop grass-root organizing potential around their traditional values – social and economic equity and greater acceptance of the public sphere – while addressing social difference, religious tolerance and civil rights. They will need to open up their organizations to greater participation while eschewing the temptations of political power that ensnared so many Socialist officials in corruption scandals. Finally, they will need to promote a new spirit of collective action. These are not easy tasks.

Some commentators have celebrated a long-awaited 'normalization' of French politics.[47] The Revolution of 1789 had introduced an irreconcilable ideological chasm of the two sides of the political spectrum, which had only been exacerbated by the electoral system of the Fifth Republic in 1958. The 'revolutionary ethic' declined after 1981, as the Left accepted the market and the right accepted 'modernity'. This diminished the ideological variance among the parties, thereby reducing political anxieties and increasing the number of possible political coalitions. This is the victory of society over state, de Tocqueville over Rousseau, and the Girondins over the Jacobins.

The following essays confirm the proposition that French politics followed a fundamentally different trajectory after 1981. Without the normative slant, however, they examine the seachange that affected both political parties and organized interests. The Left experienced a dramatic policy turnaround after Mitterrand was elected president. Mitterrand and his Left governments confronted many difficult constraints in the economy and within the French political system. Yet, these political actors had choices about policy alternatives and political mobilization. Understanding these constraints and choices can help locate opportunities for future renewal.

Notes

1.   The author would like to thank the following individuals for helpful comments and criticisms: Nancy W. Gallagher, Serge Halimi, Chris Howell, George Ross and Serenella Sferza.
2.   See Charles Tilly, *The Contentious French* (Cambridge: Harvard University Press, 1986).
3.   Olivier Duhamel and Jérôme Jaffré, 'Dix leçons de 1988', *L'État de l'opinion. Clefs pour 1989* (Paris: Seuil, 1989) p. 238.
4.   In many respects, the Socialists' predicament resembles that facing the British Labour

Party with the run on the pound between 1964 and 1967. In contrast to the British case, however, production has taken on an even greater European dimension. Moreover, as discussed below, the decentralization of production has pulled policy-making in another direction.

5. See George Ross, 'Turning Technocratic: Euro-Socialists and 1992', *Socialist Review* 21, no. 2 (April–June 1991) pp. 133–57.

6. Philip M. Williams, *Crisis and Compromise: Politics in the Fourth Republic* (Hamden, CT: Archon, 1964).

7. Frank L. Wilson, *French Political Parties under the Fifth Republic* (New York: Praeger, 1982) pp. 17–8.

8. Otto Kirchheimer, 'The Transformation of the Western European Party Systems', in Joseph LaPalombara and Myron Weiner, eds., *Political Parties and Political Development* (Princeton, N.J.: Princeton University Press, 1966).

9. Adam Przeworski, *Capitalism and Social Democracy* (Cambridge: Cambridge University Press; Paris: Editions de la Maison des Sciences de l'Homme, 1985).

10. See Frank L. Wilson, 'When Parties Refuse to Fail: The Case of France', in Kay Lawson and Peter H. Merkl, eds., *When Parties Fail: Emerging Alternative Organizations* (Princeton, N.J.: Princeton University Press, 1988).

11. See Ivor Crewe and David Denver, eds., *Electoral Change in Western Democracies: Patterns and Sources of Electoral Volatility* (London: Croom Helm, 1985); Russell Dalton, Scott Flanagan and Paul Allen Beck, eds., *Electoral Change in Advanced Industrial Democracies: Realignment or Dealignment?* (Princeton, N.J.: Princeton University Press, 1984).

12. Ronald Inglehart, *The Silent Revolution: Changing Values and Political Styles Among Western Publics* (Princeton, N.J.: Princeton University Press, 1977).

13. Russell J. Dalton, *Citizen Politics in Western Democracies: Public Opinion and Political Parties in the United States, Great Britain, West Germany, and France* (Chatham, N.J.: Chatham House, 1988) pp. 77–95.

14. France has also scored consistently low on post-materialist rankings, thereby putting less pressure on established political practices. See Inglehart.

15. A number of excellent studies have investigated this period of government. See Michel Beaud, *La politique économique de la gauche: Le mirage de la croissance*, vol. 1 (Paris: Syros, 1983); and *La politique économique de la gauche: Le grand écart*, vol. 2 (Paris: Syros, 1985). See also David Cameron, 'The Colors of a Rose: On the Ambiguous Record of French Socialism', *Center for European Studies Working Paper*, no. 12 (1988).

16. George Ross, 'Adieu vieilles idées: The Middle Strata and Decline of Resistance-Liberation Left Discourse in France', in Jolyon Howorth and Ross, eds., *Contemporary France* (London: Pinter, 1987); and Jane Jenson and George Ross, 'The Tragedy of the French Left', *New Left Review*, 171 (September/October 1988) pp. 5–46.

17. See Élie Cohen, *L'État brancardier: Politiques du déclin industriel (1974–1984)* (Paris: Calmann-Lévy, 1989).

18. Bertrand Bellon and Jean-Marie Chevalier, eds., *L'Industrie en France* (Paris: Flammarion, 1983); and Ministry of Research and Industry, ed., *Une politique industrielle pour la France: Actes des journées de travail des 15 et 16 novembre 1982* (Paris: Documentation Française, 1983).

19. André Gauron, *Histoire économique et sociale de la Cinquième République: Le temps des modernistes*, vol. 1 (Paris: La Découverte, 1983); and *Histoire économique et sociale de la Cinquième République: Années de rêves, années de crises (1970–1981)*, vol. 2 (Paris: La Découverte/Maspero, 1988).

20. Before the 1985 law, political élites could engage in a *cumul des mandats*. They

could simultaneously serve as deputy or senator, deputy in the European parliament, regional councillor, departmental councillor, and mayor or local councillor. The new law limited service to only two positions.

21.   Vivien A. Schmidt, *Democratizing France: The Political and Administrative History of Decentralization* (Cambridge: Cambridge University Press, 1991) p. 291.
22.   Alain Fonteneau and Pierre-Alain Muet, *La gauche face à la crise* (Paris: Presses de la Fondation Nationale des Sciences Politiques, 1985).
23.   On Socialist industrial policy, see Schmidt, 'Through "More State" and "Less State"', The French State Goes On: Patterns of Industrial Policy-Making in France 1981–1991', paper presented to the annual meeting of the APSA, Washington, D.C., August 1991. On labour policy, see Anthony Daley, 'Socialist Employment Policy in France: 1981–1993', *Studies in Political Economy* 42 (Autumn 1993) pp. 7–43.
24.   Wayne Sandholtz and John Zysman, '1992: Recasting the European Bargain', *World Politics* 42, 1 (October 1989) pp. 95–128.
25.   See the account in Pierre Favier and Michel Martin-Roland, *La décennie Mitterrand: Les ruptures (1981–1984)*, vol. 1 (Paris: Seuil, 1990).
26.   See Anthony Daley, 'The Travail of Sisyphus: French Unions After 1981', in George Ross and Andrew Martin, eds., *The Changing Place of Labour in European Society*, forthcoming.
27.   See Daley, 'Socialist Employment Policy'.
28.   See Tilly.
29.   See Kay Lawson, 'Political Parties and Linkage', in Lawson, ed., *Political Parties and Linkage: A Comparative Perspective* (New Haven, CT: Yale University Press, 1980).
30.   For greater elaboration, see Chris Howell and Anthony Daley, 'Introduction: The Transformation of Political Exchange', *International Journal of Political Economy* 23, no. 4 (Winter 1992–3).
31.   See Hervé Hamon and Patrick Rotman, *La deuxième gauche: Histoire Intellectuelle et politique de la CFDT* (Paris: Éditions Ramsay, 1982).
32.   Relations between Catholic unionism and the remnants of French Christian Democracy were also close after the war.
33.   Alain Lipietz points out correctly that the national-centred approach to economic policy changed to a more open borders policy when Raymond Barre replaced Jacques Chirac as prime minister in August 1976. After the defeat of the Left in the 1978 legislative elections, Barre was able to implement more fully his version of economic liberalism. See 'Quelle base sociale pour le "changement?"' *Les temps modernes*, no. 430 (May 1982) pp. 1898–1930.
34.   The relationship between Mitterrand and Rocard had been rocky for 15 years. Rocard challenged Mitterrand for the leadership of the PS after the 1978 legislative defeat and lost. He used his high standing in the polls to attempt a presidential campaign, only to defer to Mitterrand in early 1981. Mitterrand rewarded Rocard with the Ministry of the Plan, a relatively insignificant post. Later he was 'promoted' to Minister of Agriculture, a difficult post for any political élite in France. In 1985, Rocard resigned from the government over the decision to alter the electoral law for the 1986 legislative election from the double-ballot majority system to proportional representation, a change that promised to limit the losses of the PS but also to give legislative representation to the National Front. Mitterrand appointed Rocard prime minister after the 1988 presidential and legislative elections, largely on the basis of his high standing in public opinion polls. Rocard lasted three years in the job and was dismissed in favour of Edith Cresson, as the president prepared for the 1993 legislative elections by attempting to depict his government as left of centre. Meanwhile, Rocard had defeated Fabius, the president's choice, to head the PS in 1988 but acquiesced to Fabius' leadership in 1992 under the condition that he be promoted

as the 'virtual candidate' for the 1995 presidential elections. The 1993 coup against Fabius represented an attempt by Rocard to reassemble the party for the 1995 presidential elections. His 1994 resignation was seen as an admission that he was unable to mobilize the Left.

35. Eric Dupin, *L'Après Mitterrand: Le parti socialiste à la dérive* (Paris: Calmann-Lévy, 1991).
36. This form of industrial relations was not new to the postwar period. See Edward Shorter and Charles Tilly, *Strikes in France 1830–1968* (Cambridge: Cambridge University Press, 1974); and Val Lorwin, *The French Labour Movement* (Cambridge, MA: Harvard University Press, 1954).
37. This included participation in workplace institutions (works councils, plant delegates and health and safety committees), boards of nationalized companies, broader labour market responsibilities (administration social security fund, and the arbitration of grievances) other labour market initiatives (local and regional employment committees), national labour market oversight (within the Ministry of Labour for training and job creation) and policy advising (national and European economic and social councils).
38. George Ross, 'French Intellectuals from Sartre to Soft Ideology', in Charles C. Lemert, ed., *Intellectuals and Politics: Social Theory in a Changing World* (Newbury Park, CA: Sage, 1991).
39. Henri Mendras with Alistair Cole, *Social Change in Modern France: Towards a Cultural Anthropology of the Fifth Republic* (Cambridge: Cambridge University Press, 1991).
40. For an analysis of the distorting effects of the double-ballot majority system in which less than 39.7 per cent of the vote can translate into 77.8 per cent of the seats, see Howard Machin, 'Representation and Distortion in the 1993 French Election', *Parliamentary Affairs* 46, no. 4 (October 1993).
41. See 'Législatives 1993: La fin d'un cycle politique?' *Revue politique et parlementaire*, no. 964 (March–April 1993) special issue.
42. See George Ross, 'Party Decline and Changing Party Systems: France and the French Communist Party', *Comparative Politics* 25, no. 1 (October 1992) pp. 43–61; and Michel Dreyfus, *PCF: Crises et dissidences* (Paris: Editions Complexes, 1990).
43. Tapie's list for the 1994 European elections received 12 per cent of the vote. Mitterrand offered considerable media support for his former Minister of Urban Affairs – a successful businessman, owner of the Marseilles football club and controversial political leader who was being investigated for a number of shadowy financial dealings. Most of Tapie's vote total came at the expense of the Socialists.
44. The reports of Mitterrand's close personal connection to political figures of the far right further undermined his moral authority within the party. See Pierre Péan, *Une jeunesse française: François Mitterrand, 1934–1947* (Paris: Fayard, 1994); and Emmanuel Faux, Thomas Legrand and Gilles Perez, *La Main droite de Dieu: Enquête sur François Mitterrand et l'extrême droite* (Paris: Seuil, 1994).
45. José Arocena, *Le développement par l'initiative locale: Le cas français* (Paris: l'Harmattan, 1986); and Georges Benko and Alain Lipietz, eds., *Les régions qui gagnent. Districts et réseaux: Les nouveaux paradigmes de la géographie économique* (Paris: PUF, 1992).
46. There are even indications in the early 1990s that the unions have stopped the haemorrhage of members. While density reached a nadir of roughly 9 per cent, all unions reported membership increases in 1993 and 1994. See Daley, 'The Travail of Sisyphus'.
47. François Furet, 'La France unie . . .', in Furet, Jacques Julliard and Pierre Rosanvallon, *La République du centre: La fin de l'exception française* (Paris: Calmann-Levy, 1988).

Part I

The Dilemmas of Governance

2 The Limits of Political Economy: Mitterrand and the Crisis of the French Left

George Ross

Left parties in power have been constrained since the late 1970s by new and difficult trends. The end of high post-war economic growth meant an end to the magic moment when a reformist Left could promise jobs, economic security, social protection and optimism. The globalization of economic life has obliged the Left to reconfigure its policies to seek international competitiveness, a very different task from redistributing the fruits of growth. Finally, these fundamental changes have occurred simultaneously with the post-industrialization of class structures. The combination of these three tendencies – to which one might add the collapse of Communism after 1989 – has produced crisis and confusion. Widespread incapacity to produce rewards for supporters has been compounded by a need to promote economic flexibility and rapid structural change. Both processes, plus changes from industrial toward service employment, have weakened workers and their unions, traditionally the Left's key constituencies. Simultaneously, Left-leaning middle strata have lost tolerance for 'old Left' workerist perspectives and moved toward 'post-materialist' and 'identity' concerns. Earlier social alliances around programmes for full employment, protection against harsh market outcomes and the democratization of capitalist institutions have been disrupted. As a consequence of such changes, most Lefts, including the French, have not been able to find ways to avoid austerity, rising unemployment and labour market deregulation or to find policies to encourage capital growth.

Social democratic élites, who never had an easy time conciliating markets and reformism, as Serge Halimi reminds us in this volume, face new challenges.[1] There are many conceivable paths, however. It is difficult to predict specific political and ideological changes from underlying economic trends. Choices in particular cases, like France since 1981, are often explainable only by reference to mediating factors, political institutions in the first instance. This essay will claim that the role of *one* institution, the French presidency, has been central to the policies and political fate of the French Left since 1981.

The Fifth Republic's 1958 constitution gave the French presidency great control over policy options. The president appoints and dismisses the prime minister and governments, calls elections, can completely disregard Parliament in certain circumstances and has a vast reserve of power over foreign and defence affairs.

The direct election of the French president, which began in 1965, reinforced this by making presidential elections the political event around which everything else revolves. *Becoming* president is now the most important activity, by far, in French politics. Charles de Gaulle, who invented the institution, was clearly trying to conciliate democracy and monarchy.[2] He did a good job, since the Fifth Republic's presidential regime has no peer for concentrated executive power in the democratic world.

The great powers of the presidency as an institution inevitably, and powerfully, mediate the course of any French government, including Left ones. Moreover, given the the vast scope and centrality of this institution, the strategic approaches and political styles of any incumbent become a major dimension for analysing the course of French politics. This essay will review, in broad strokes, the primordial role of the French presidency and the particular approaches of François Mitterrand as they have impinged upon the French Left during the 'Epinay cycle', from the late 1960s until now.[3] During this time, the political centrality of the presidency as an institution combined with the definition of the uses of this institution by Mitterrand have strongly hurt the French Left. The partisan Left in France has always seen itself, and claimed to be, an emanation of social forces and a mobilized instrument for change in their interests, both in opposition and in power. This vision has been a major casualty of the Mitterrand era.

FROM PRESIDENTIALIZING THE SOCIALISTS TO SUBORDINATING SOCIALISTS TO THE PRESIDENT

The history of the Socialists prior to 1981 had already demonstrated the changes brought by the Fifth Republic presidency as an institution and François Mitterrand's own understanding of it. Mitterrand started out in 1981 as a Comrade-President – simultaneously party leader responsible for his troops and president responsible for all the French – carrying out a programme that was as much the Left's as his own, even though his own political work had created it. The role of Comrade-President imposed constraints on the exercise of presidential power. The president was supreme arbitrator to implement the programme of the presidential majority. Once the lifetime of this programme ended in 1983, however, Mitterrand's role had to change.

Despite his opposition to the change of constitutions in 1958, Mitterrand gained his initial, and perhaps most important, advantages from success in the first direct elections to the presidency in 1965.[4] Subsequent recognition by most of the non-Communist Left of the useful political capital that a plausible *présidentiable* (potential presidential candidate) bore then gave Mitterrand the resources to begin pursuing the strategic and organizational regrouping of the Left. One important dimension of this involved bringing Socialists and Communists to accept the institutions of the Fifth Republic, including the presidency.[5] Mitterrand's projects, after complicated detours around May–June 1968, led to the creation of the new Socialist Party (PS) in 1971. The evolution of this party in the 1970s established the role of Comrade-President that Mitterrand would initially play.

The PS was primarily a vehicle for François Mitterrand to sustain his position as the most plausible Left *présidentiable*. To achieve these goals Mitterrand gambled both politically and organizationally.[6] *Union de la Gauche*, the political gamble, was meant to allow the PS, the more respectable of the two partners, to gain electoral strength at the expense of the French Communist Party (PCF). The PS presidential candidate would simultaneously profit from this, as Mitterrand did in 1974, and promote it. Presidential elections could only be won at the centre, which only a PS candidate could plausibly approach. The electoral 'halo effect' of serious presidential efforts would redound to the benefit of the party more generally. If all went well, the Communists, co-opted into such a dangerous gamble by their need to overcome Cold War isolation, would lose strength relative to the PS. This in its turn would further increase the credibility of a PS presidential candidate and allow the PS to fish for new support among the middle strata, who had traditionally been wary of PCF power.

The organizational gamble was to create a new PS that allowed free play to organized factions and tied the political balance of the party's direction to their relative weight.[7] This particular form – which resembled a gang of alley cats spitting at one another – had a number of advantages. It encouraged militantism and active outreach. It put the new PS in contact with the range of ideological options offered on the Left. And it allowed the party to be like a Hydra in its appeals, gathering support from all sides. Most important, the party's general interest lay in being led by a plausible *présidentiable*. As long as Mitterrand could sustain his claim to this role, which gave him a certain external authority over the party, which suited his particular approach to politics, he would be able to manipulate the PS's kaleidoscope of internal factions in his own interests.[8]

Mitterrand's gambles bound any future presidency, at least initially, to a programme derived from the culture and concerns of the party itself rather than from Mitterrand's own preferences. In the circumstances of the 1970s this involved commitment to a set of outlooks closer to those desired by the Communists than many Socialists would have preferred, and strongly out of step with conventional social democratic wisdom. The Common Programme of 1972 proposed a rhetoricized rerun of 1944 more than a creative response to the 1970s and 1980s. The new strategy was also foreign to certain important Left constituencies, in particular Left Catholics, the 'post-materialist' new middle strata and the intelligentsia. The relative alienation of such groups, despite their participation in the mobilization that sapped the strength of de Gaulle and his successors in the 1960s and 1970s, and their considerable political and cultural strength (central positions in the media, publishing and intelligentsia, among others) would be important in subsequent events.[9] All of this meant that any Mitterrand presidency would initially be mortgaged by its policy commitments and political problems.

Until 1981, Mitterrand's fate depended upon the success of these gambles. His position in the PS was secure only insofar as he remained the leading *présidentiable*. The party itself had to be able to perceive that it was moving steadily toward power. The PCF presented the first major obstacle. When the electoral success of the Mitterrand strategy became clear in the mid-1970s, the Communists rebelled and tried, ineptly, to reverse the situation, ending in the failed attempt to 'actualize' the Left Common Programme in 1977. The divisions of the Left that followed cost it the 1978 legislative elections. This made Mitterrand vulnerable. The attack by Michel Rocard on Mitterrand's leadership that followed was designed to establish Rocard's own claim to be a more plausible *présidentiable* than Mitterrand. It was based on a contention that Mitterrand's general strategy was 'archaic' and that Mitterrand was a loser who would drag the PS down with him. Mitterrand beat back this challenge, not without difficulty, by manipulating the internal balance of PS factions and seducing the PS's Left (CERES) back into the majority, at the cost of further alienating the Catholic and new middle strata 'second Left'. At the same time Mitterrand ably parried the PCF's erratic aggressiveness by pursuing a position designed to assign blame for the Left's problems entirely on the PCF.[10] The price for this, however, was to bind Mitterrand's presidential candidacy even further to the policy outlooks of the Left Common Programme and the left-most factions of the PS. The 1980 *Projet Socialiste*, a controversial policy statement whose outlines turned up in slightly diluted forms in Mitterrand's 1981 campaign, demonstrated this. To Mitterrand, however, *l'Elysée valait bien une messe*.

Comrade President – Party and President during the Reform Period

The political circumstances of Mitterrand's relationship to the Left were bound to change with accession to the presidency. While Mitterrand's position in the party prior to 1981 had been open to challenge, his position as President guaranteed him huge independent institutional power, longevity and relative autonomy from his original political base. But the logic of the pre-1981 period meant that President Mitterrand at least initially would be bound by programmatic commitments made earlier by Candidate Mitterrand. General de Gaulle, the pioneer of Fifth Republic presidents, had been the bearer of programmes around which his supporters were obliged to gather (although sometimes grudgingly and, after 1968, rebelliously). Those who came after him, although much less successful (Valéry Giscard d'Estaing in particular), attempted to follow the same model. Mitterrand, in contrast, would initially be a Comrade-President, bound by commitments whose origins were in the culture and organization of the Left.

Thus the new Left Unity government followed blueprints set out in the President's campaign platform, themselves built upon the PS's public commitments of

the 1970s. Industry nationalizations, industrial policy, decentralization, the Auroux
Laws, legal reforms and other measures were the products of a Left regime whose
directions were shared by the President and ministers (except, of course, second
Left personalities such as Rocard and Jacques Delors, never a part of this consensus and who expressed their reservations periodically). To be sure, Mitterrand
arbitrated governmental conflict. He also developed his own approaches in foreign and defence policy, the traditional *domaine reservé* of Fifth Republic Presidents, quickly backing away from early Third-Worldism toward more conventional
postures.[11] Still, this first period of the Left in power was largely one of collaboration between the President, his party and the Left rather than more traditional
Fifth Republic Gaullist presidential domination. This relationship, in which the
President acted as the dedicated instrument of a programme that was as much his
party's as his, was new for the Fifth Republic.

Arbitrating Fundamental Choices

Change began when the programme that Mitterrand had used to create and bind
to him the PS collapsed in failure. The period from mid-1982 to mid-1983 was
the turning point. France's differential inflation level, accentuated by the first
months of Left rule, interacted with the consequences of the Left's very mild
1981 *relance* to create a severe balance of payments and monetary crisis. Vigorous short-term measures, pushed mainly by Delors, the Minister of Finance,
imposed *rigueur* but failed to stop the bleeding. During the famous few days in
March 1983 when everything turned around, key figures in the government and
among the President's close advisers were divided on whether to leave the European Exchange Rate Mechanism.

The President decided the course finally taken, while dealing with political
differences, the March 1983 municipal elections and the Germans. Commitments
were made to rapid reduction of inflation and solidifying the franc vis-à-vis the
deutsche mark. Budget deficits were to be reduced in ways that seriously limited
future social spending, even though the turn toward deflation was certain to bring
more unemployment. The change brought fundamental decisions to regenerate
France's international competitiveness as well. Profits had to be encouraged at the
expense of wages to stimulate investment. France's capital markets had to be
energized. Public firms had to be pushed toward profitability and cease being
buffers for containing unemployment. In general, France's focus had to shift from
Leftist reform to a new crusade for economic 'modernization', the term used by
Mitterrand when in November he presented his first elaborate picture of the new
strategy. *Libération* then covered its front page with the headline, in Beaujolais
season, '*le Mitterrand Nouveau est Arrivé*'.

What is interesting about this moment – beyond the sheer political accomplishment of completely turning around a querulous set of political groups to endorse

policies they had unanimously rejected a few months earlier – is the degree to which Mitterrand made virtually all fundamental decisions, concealed their implications for a considerable period and protected himself from their consequences. Here there was an important dose of *Mitterrandiste* style and method: others took 'point positions' and assumed the risks for him. Rather than decreeing and ordering policy from first principles, as de Gaulle would have done, or micromanaging, as Giscard d'Estaing would have, Mitterrand encouraged his ministers and minions to fight with one another and then induced his choices from the outcomes. Behind his decisions lay the logic of the presidency, however. Mitterrand had to think through the medium-term consequences for his own political resource base and his chances for re-election.

Because of this presidentialist logic, the change promised major political difficulties for the PS and the Left more broadly. Decreeing long-term austerity, promising greater employment insecurity and taking a series of measures overtly designed to seduce capital – policies the Right would never have dared to promote – could only be seen by parts of the Left electorate as a betrayal. There were some – Centrist and Rocardian parts, mostly – who believed that the new politics could be a *stratégie de rechange* on its own, that the 'people of the Left' could be mobilized for a grim pursuit of international economic success for the benefit of capital, perhaps in the name of nationalist virtue. Everyone else had difficulty accounting for what was happening. From an electoral point of view the Socialists were certain to pay heavily. From a coalitional point of view the Communists were certain to leave the Left government (they did in July 1984) and re-establish the state of war that had been suspended in 1981. Even though the Communists had been severely wounded, they could still cause problems.

The direct consequences for the Socialists were very difficult. They had to live through massive change without any plausible alternative strategy, live in contradiction and take their lumps with the only recompense – a large one – of staying in power. A certain amount of new cynicism was the product for some, a slow conversion experience to neo-liberalism with a human face was the result for others. The French Left, however, had to go without firm convictions of its own. The policy shift was initially masked by contradictory claims and rhetorical fog. Mitterrand himself was elliptical, as usual. Others, including Prime Minister Pierre Mauroy, persisted in denying that any fundamental shift had occurred and that instead, hard times had interrupted reforms, which would be back on the agenda as soon as possible.

TOWARD A TRADITIONAL PRESIDENTIAL STRATEGY

Initially, Mitterrand had assumed the role of maximum leader of a programmatically committed presidential majority. This made him the final arbitrator among different proposals from that majority in working the most fundamental domestic policy shift of his presidency in 1982–3. From then on, however, Mitterrand moved toward a much more independent definition of his role. Henceforth he, and not his political family of origin, would make fundamental choices and carefully sculpt the shorter-run choices of his governments for his own, rather than their, political interests.

Mitterrand was well aware that a new strategic outlook was needed to pull his presidency from the depths of 1982–3. Not embedded in a broader stategy, the policy changes of those years were political losers, since they hurt Left supporters and rewarded the Left's opponents. A new strategy would have to make sense of the new policies in both specific and general terms and uncover good reasons why a winning coalition of different social groups should continue to support Mitterrand. The 'Europe Option' was the President's answer.

Replacing the 1981 programme of domestic reforms with another proposing renewed European integration was not an obvious choice. Mitterrand himself had been part of the French élite that had done much of the founding of the New Europe, but the broader French Left had been persistently divided about European integration. Important Left elements persisted in nationalist-*dirigiste* and anti-European sentiments all along. Such positions had, moreover, been strongly reinforced in the Gaullist years and by much in the Left's programmes of the 1970s.[12]

By the early 1980s, the European Community had fallen into a collective action trap. Since each EC member state had confronted economic crisis with its own national strategy, EC-level co-ordination was less and less possible. The British, bitter about the financial terms of their entry in the 1970s, were determined to hold up anything European until the problem of their excessively large net contribution to the EC budget could be settled. In addition, once Margaret Thatcher's government came to power in 1979, the British consistently blocked any EC regulatory policy initiatives, especially in the area of social policy. The Germans, logical candidates for taking up EC budgetary slack, refused to give in to British budgetary demands. Greece, who entered the Community in 1982, refused to allow Spain and Portugal to join unless it received sufficient payoffs, creating new disagreements about regional policies.

The French quest for social democracy in one country after 1981 had been another of the EC's problems, but the 1983 policy shift made new convergence with the Germans possible. And because this was largely on liberal ground, it created new openings for discussion with the British. Mitterrand seized the opportunity, particularly during the French presidency of the EC in the first half of 1984. Energetically mobilizing to resolve outstanding EC problems and clear the decks for new initiatives, Mitterrand brokered a solution to Britain's budget problem, removed the roadblocks to Spanish and Portuguese membership and nominated Jacques Delors to be the next President of the European Commission.[13]

Mitterrand's deeper logics were borne more from classical *realpolitik* than Left thinking. The 1982–3 turnabout had ended the quest for French distinctiveness through radical and nationalist reformism. Using the EC as a new vehicle for affirming French national interests conformed both to Mitterrand's deeper European commitments and to the diplomatic configurations of the moment. US monetary policy under Ronald Reagan had been so damaging for Europe that it almost by itself made a new European initiative conceivable.[14] Export-oriented Germany had a strong interest in promoting new European economic activity. The British might go along as long as the measures were liberal. But despite their economic strength, the Germans, because of their history, could not take the lead. Britain's timid commitment to the EC meant that it also could not be the leader. Diplomatic opportunities thus fell to the French, provided they could regenerate and sustain the Franco–German couple, a task at which Mitterrand had been working carefully for some time. Moreover, in the EC context French administrative élites had a comparative advantage, and the EC was already well-colonized by French personnel and techniques. French defence positions could also confer strength. Delors, as President of the European Commission, was an asset as well.

The 1985 White Paper, *Completing the Single Market*, and the 1987 Single European Act were the launching pads for the Europe option. Largely the product of reinvigorated ideas that had long languished in the closet, the '1992' programme was strongly supported by the French and Germans while simultaneously appealing to British neoliberalism. The programme made Mitterrand's Europe option a political reality, more or less in the terms Mitterrand had envisaged. '1992' then proved a quick public success, particularly with business interests.

The idea of renewed European integration as a *stratégie de rechange* after 1982–3 did not lack nobility. EC member states no longer had sufficient leverage or autonomy to promote full-blown national development models. This made it preferable to work toward an EC-level model, over whose evolution the French could have more control than anyone else if they played it correctly. This model could preserve, perhaps even enhance, what Delors came to call the 'European model of society', a mixed economy in which market harshness was mitigated by welfare states and civilized industrial relations systems, with an important regulatory role reserved for the state. Such an outcome was clearly preferable to one in which each country separately faced the huge tides of US and Japanese economic power, the even higher waves the global market could create and the assaults of neoliberalism. Europe could become a powerful zone in this global market, limiting damage from outside. At the same time, invoking the economic self-restraint needed to pursue such a noble cause could prove a very useful tool to many EC governments, including the French.

The vision was thus not simply geostrategic. Mitterrand also saw it as a replacement programme and appeal for a Left whose programmatic stock in trade was exhausted. This was true not only in the traditional 'big think, big project' terms that the French Left had traditionally used, but also in more practical terms of electoral and ideological support. The new vision was meant to be one of social democracy on a European scale led by the French. The liberal basis of

'1992' would bring capital on board, initiating a new wave of investment and growth. France's leadership role in Europe might also be appealing, particularly if it were able to advocate Euro-level social and economic policy regulation. While awaiting such payoffs, the Europe option would provide both leverage and arguments to governments to justify shorter-run problems. Austerity would no longer be simply a necessity for bad times, but a commitment to make the broader European programme go forward to bring larger payoffs down the line.

The Europe option was a big gamble, however. Much was at stake, and the odds against success were great. Europe had to pay off economically to make the political side plausible. The French had to be able to maintain leadership over Europe's direction – German priorities had to be recognized but integrated into larger French visions and British hyper-liberalism marginalized. The Left, or at least enough of it, had to be persuaded that this path made political sense, while its constituencies had to believe payoffs to come in order for them to accept structural adjustments in the economy and limitations on economic sovereignty. Nothing could be guaranteed.

That the substance of the Europe option as strategy was problematic was one thing. The fact that it was almost completely the creation of the presidency was yet another. The new strategy was a turning point in relationships between Mitterrand as President and the Left. The Socialist Party and the broader Left had very little role in its development even though it implied a basic change in political discourse for both. Europe had been built diplomatically, by political executives working quietly, often secretly, under the cover of their 'foreign relations' prerogatives.[15] The Fifth Republic was characterized by the particularly large space it granted to its presidents to shape and implement diplomatic strategies. François Mitterrand used this space to the fullest in developing the Europe option in the mid-1980s.

Diverging Interests between President and Party

The substitution of the president for parties as strategist for the Left was the ultimate result of the 1982–3 policy shift. The Socialists no longer could design their political future. After 1983 the identity of political interest between the President, his party and the Left would become less clear. If the President dominated strategically, his political purposes would dominate those of the PS, and quite likely this would be at the party's expense.

Presidential-party relationships changed not only because Mitterrand decided to reassert a more traditional Fifth Republic presidential approach. The Socialists' standing in public opinion had collapsed along with its austerity and 'modernization' programme in 1983, the party-induced fiasco of school reform in 1984 and the consequent ending of *Union de la Gauche* that summer.[16] With little hope for the 1986 legislative elections, the Socialists became dependent on prospects for the Left's candidate in the 1988 presidential elections. As a result, partisan tactics, both in government and in outreach to different constituencies, had to be subordinated to those of Mitterrand himself. There would inevitably be a period of *cohabitation* after 1986, and for Mitterrand to stand a chance in 1988 he had to maximize available political resources for his personal use during this period. Moreover, he also had to position himself for what promised to be a difficult election campaign in 1988. In some of these matters the interests of party and President coincided, in others less so.

At best *cohabitation* would be a complicated game, with opponents whose objective would be Mitterrand's political destruction. For the President, then, gathering resources for *cohabitation* meant doing everything reasonable to prevent the Centre-Right from winning a landslide in the 1986 legislative polls. A Right landslide would weaken Mitterrand and make it impossible to win this game. This implied exploiting the Right's divisions. Limiting Right success in 1986 was an objective the PS and Mitterrand could share, to a point. But it was the President, and not the PS, who designed the steps necessary to accomplish this objective. The first, and perhaps most important, step was the appointment of Laurent Fabius as Prime Minister in 1984 – here Mitterrand was returning to tried and true Gaullist techniques for, when appointing prime ministers, thinking of who would best ensure presidential electoral success.

Having bit the economic modernization bullet after 1983, Mitterrand needed clear results. Inflation and the deficit had to decline, and, more generally, signals had to be sent to the private sector that the government was serious. It was essential for the new prime minister to look as different as possible from his predecessor. Fabius fit this bill rather well, both because of his youth – he was the youngest prime minister in modern French history – and his allure, the brilliant young technocrat in a hurry. If a Socialist, Fabius was clearly of a different kind than Pierre Mauroy. And if he might also seduce some centrist voters with the rhetoric of 'democratic modernization', so much the better.

By nominating Fabius, the President thus informed the Socialists in which policy directions to move to prepare for 1986. Fabius' daily actions were somewhat more independent of the President than those of his predecessor: Mitterrand let his dauphin run the government in some detail. This was paradoxical, however. For the President, positioning for 1988 meant distancing himself in 1984 from a government under presidential injunction to pursue painful economic policies and condemned to lose the next legislative elections. No matter how well Fabius succeeded, the government would remain tainted by the Socialists' earlier failures. Mitterrand, who intended to run at the centre in 1988, had to clear his name.

Dividing the Right – or rather helping the Right further divide itself – was the next manoeuvre. Here Mitterrand chose a simple, time-honoured ploy: changing the electoral law. The existing single-member constituency, two-round system had always polarized runoffs into Left–Right duels, obliging each side to paper over differences to form winning coalitions. Installing proportional representation, as Mitterrand insisted upon doing in April 1985 (at the expense of Michel Rocard's resignation) could change this. Each component of Left and Right would have to campaign on its distinctiveness. Divisions between neo-Gaullists and Giscardians had allowed Mitterrand's 1981 success, and they were severe enough. But since 1982, the rise of the National Front (FN) made the Right's situation even more complicated. The different segments of the 'moderate' Right then had to decide whether to pander to the National Front's xenophobic positions to limit its success, to ignore the National Front or to combat it.

Whatever the choice, Mitterrand was likely to win. If any part of the moderate Right moved to co-opt National Front xenophobia, then Mitterrand's position in *cohabitation* and in occupying the Centre in 1988 would be eased. If there was no such pandering, the National Front would win a number of seats in the National Assembly and cut down on the 'moderate' Right's majority, making the Left–Right balance more equal. The designated loser was the PS. By faithfully voting electoral reform and carrying out Mitterrand's tactics, the PS promoted the National Front's electoral and ideological success for short-run electoral gain. Mitterrand had no scruples about giving the xenophobic extremist FN the institutional space to consolidate its positions.[17] The PS, obliged to follow, lost credibility as a defender of core Left and Republican values.

Despite its costs to the PS, Mitterrand's pre-electoral strategy made him, in 1988, the first president of the Fifth Republic ever to be re-elected. Fabius as Prime Minister, plus the reformed electoral law, limited the relative victory of the 'moderate' Right in 1986 and cut PS losses. The balance of forces that resulted granted Mitterrand the space to 'game' the Right government during *cohabitation*. He began to do this immediately by appointing Jacques Chirac Prime Minister, thereby consecrating his most easily defeatable 1988 opponent as the Right's 'virtual' candidate. Mitterrand's strategy of positioning himself in the Centre was pursued by very careful efforts to use presidential authority only when he could clearly communicate that he was acting to prevent the Chirac government from taking overly partisan right-wing action. Chirac, wearing his Reaganite costume, played into this hand. Inept handling of privatizations allowed Mitterrand to denounce RPR colonization of the state, while the botched response to student demonstrations in late 1986 allowed him to depict Chirac's team as repressive. Good luck, as in the stock-market crash of October 1987, which put an end to many of the Right's liberal dreams, played its role. Ultimately Mitterrand was skilful enough to ensure that Right candidacies other than Chirac's (Raymond Barre's, for example) were set aside while Chirac himself was labelled politically fickle. Simultaneously, Mitterrand turned to the studious manipulation of 'new' political techniques, using image professionals to remanufacture his identity into 'Tonton', avuncular font of France's wisdom, ideal of the 'Mitterrand Generation' of young people. This operation, crowned by the publication of the President's 'letter to all the French' in Spring 1988, was masterfully successful.[18]

TWILIGHT OF THE GOD

From the mid-1980s on, presidential interventions played a determinant role in the evolution of the French Left. The constitutionally created interactions between presidential and legislative elections in the Fifth Republic made this inevitable. In an elective monarchy, presidential campaigns are as important a source of resources for parties as are their own platforms, organizations and campaigns. Thus they cannot avoid subordinating their interests, different in important ways from those of presidents, to presidential electoral purposes. For the PS, the consequences of policy failure and unpopularity after 1982–3 made Socialist electoral politics and political discourse almost completely dependent upon Mitterrand's strategy for reelection for 1988. Presidential constraints on the PS did not cease after 1988 either. Mitterrand used his prerogative of prime ministerial appointment to shape the general course of political events, largely with an eye on the next presidential election in 1995. Moreover, the PS governments from 1988 to 1993 were corseted by obligations to play out Mitterrand's Europe option.

'God', as the press referred to the President, won an extraordinary victory in 1988. By re-centreing his image, Mitterrand dissociated himself from his own political family, with the complicity of a PS that knew its only possible salvation was a Mitterrand victory. Re-centreing was undoubtedly a shrewd move for Mitterrand, but it was certain to leave the Socialists confused and politically vulnerable. Government policies after 1983 and Mitterrand's strategies had both neglected the needs of the PS's own base, while winning them no new support beyond it. Still, these issues would turn out to matter less for the Left than the President's miscalculations after 1988. These, combined with the effects of presidentialization, led the Left into uncharted new territory.

The most immediate difficulties for the PS followed from the ambiguities of Mitterrand's strategy. It was evident in 1988 that Mitterrand, beyond re-centreing his presentation, was toying with a major change in coalitional outlooks. If circumstances were propitious, he was prepared to abandon Left unity for a Left–Centre alliance. This would have involved further exploiting divisions on the Right and depended upon the willingness of Centrists to risk crossing the aisle. Changing coalitional outlooks made some sense because the Left would be unable to generate a plausible parliamentary majority soon, given its relative electoral decline since 1981.[19] It also would have had immense implications for the PS, which would have had to remake its identity yet again. In any event, Mitterrand found no takers (aisle crossing might have been very costly, since the Chirac government restored the old electoral law), quickly backed away from '*ouverture*' and dissolved parliament – another way his re-centreing hurt the PS.

Mitterrand was no longer a man of the Left in identifiable political terms, and he quite specifically tailored his 1988 campaign to demonstrate this. This meant that the coat-tail effect of his success no longer worked as effectively as it had in 1981 (or indeed, as it almost always had in the Fifth Republic). French voters made the distinction Mitterrand had wanted them to make. The President was the wise and shrewd uncle. The Socialists were those who had made such a mess of things and betrayed their promises after 1981. One result was that the Socialists were unable to win a majority in the 1988 parliamentary elections, thenceforth depending for majorities upon the erratic goodwill of the Communists, the fragmentation of the Right, and the Constitution.

If the coalitional and electoral consequences of Mitterrand's re-centreing were largely negative for the Socialists, so, it can be argued, was Mitterrand's clever, highly professional, image remanufacturing. It was inevitable, given the way in which France's presidents were elected and the centrality of television, that hyper-personalization of candidates and the professional reconstruction of personae by image makers and advertising agents would occur. The stuff of Left politics in France, on the other hand, had almost always been programmatic, usually in terms of promises of change and hope to constituencies that were in need of such things. As of 1988, the PS was dangerously out of steam in terms of programmatic self-presentation. The success of Mitterrand's image plastic surgery would tempt many potential new PS leaders to explore personalization and self-marketing as a substitute rather than a supplement for finding a new programme. In that way, Mitterrand could lead the PS toward political cynicism rather than reconstruction.

'God' Loses Touch

One of the more important powers of any Fifth Republic president is the appointment of prime ministers. In 1988 some found it surprising that the President would appoint Michel Rocard, whom he despised. In fact, the choice was quite logical, at least in Mitterrandist terms. Mitterrand was in his second, and certainly last, term. Rocard was in a good position to be the PS's leading *présidentiable*. Sequencing prime ministers had become a routine. The first prime minister in any presidential term had always been a foot soldier to do the dirty work. Successors, usually appointed after three years, were assigned to tidy things up before the legislative elections leading to the next presidential poll. In appointing Rocard, Mitterrand was thus aware how much dirty work there was to do after 1988. Following through on the Europe option meant continuing austerity, a programme unlikely to do the prime minister charged with implementing it much good in career terms. Rocard was appointed, in other words, to be used up. If all went according to plan, he would be removed, *présidentiable* glow totally dissipated, in time for Mitterrand to promote a successor more to his taste.

Things did not go according to plan, however, as Rocard did rather well. The combination of his truthful technocratic style, fastidious avoidance of risk and, most important, the economic boomlet of the late 1980s meant that he was not ground up by the job and his *présidentiable* aura stayed intact. In retrospect, it is clear Rocard was trying to beat Mitterrand at his own game by carefully dissociating his own presidential image from governmental policies. Rocard's success thus went into his account and did little for the PS. A frustrated Mitterrand finally had to dismiss him summarily in May 1991, without any particularly good explanation. The Rocard episode was the first major sign that the President was losing his touch.

There were other indications that the presidentialization of Fifth Republic politics, intensified by Mitterrand's presidency, was undermining the capacities of the PS to find its own way. Socialist debate about new ideas and programmatic identities had been desultory after the 1982–3 collapse, but what little of it there had been was predictably tied to PS factions. The Mitterrandists talked about democratic versus authoritarian economic modernization. The Rocardians talked about reconfiguring patterns of representation in less statist ways. The ex-CERES group, *Socialisme et République*, talked about renewed Jacobinism and Republicanism. But there were more important matters at issue, however, in particular succession to Mitterrand. Pretenders thus began to copy what they thought to be Mitterrand's 1960s model, trying to establish position as plausible *présidentiables* and accumulate power inside the PS by playing the internal faction game. There turned out to be a Hobbesian dilemma in this, however. Except for Rocard, a relative outsider, there were no obvious successors, while there were too many contenders.[20] Ideas, instead of being contributions to a real discussion, became weapons to advance presidential ambitions.

Mitterrand's efforts to control this game complicated matters. After Lionel Jospin's 1988 resignation, the President, assuming that Rocard would be destroyed by the premiership, intervened to procure a favourable starting point for Laurent Fabius as new First Secretary of the party. Fabius was not a popular figure, however, particularly with Jospin. Moreover, other PS pretenders, who understood Mitterrand's action as a clear attempt to block their campaigns, banded in opposition. Pierre Mauroy was thus elected, 63–54, in a head-to-head *bureau executif* confrontation with Fabius, and Mitterrand was publicly disavowed. Fabius' failure led him to multiply his patented clientelism (partly through use of his position as President of the National Assembly) to strengthen his clan for the next confrontation.

The result of all this was the ignominious PS Rennes Congress in 1990, where the various PS 'elephants' fought it out, in the process defying Mitterrand's desire to make Fabius party leader once again. Exposed for all to see was a gaggle of power-hungry middle-aged men invoking vague ideas and deploying rhetorical gunmen to block one another's chances. Missing was any sense that the PS was interested in new ideas that could bring back public support. Only Rocard, shielded by his position as Prime Minister, emerged unscathed, his status as *présidentiable* enhanced. This compounded the irony of the situation. Mitterrand, trying to use and destroy Rocard, had instead handed him a position that he could use as a launching pad. The PS elephants, many of whom also disliked Rocard, acted 'objectively' to enhance Rocard's chances by blocking those of Fabius.

There was no mistaking the logic behind this undignified and politically costly display (which, moreover, would continue into the 1990s). The presidency as an institution had deeply changed, and perhaps corrupted, the PS. Becoming a *présidentiable* had become more important than developing viable Left politics, which would have to wait until after electoral success. Power, rather than programme and principle, had gained the upper hand. Mitterrand at least had a strategy. The pretenders to his succession simply wanted to be first in line.

Contradictions in the Europe Option

Mitterrand's gamble on the Europe option was what structured governmental action for the Left (and, to a certain degree, the Right between 1986 and 1988). The line, more fully elaborated by the later 1980s, had acquired an unmovable anchor in the *franc fort* policy, whose objective was to bring French inflation down to German levels and turn the franc into a rock-solid currency. The premise of this new monetarism was that France needed financial credibility comparable to the Germans' to influence the construction of Economic and Monetary Union. EMU was seen as the critical step in the Europe option, the way to lock the Germans into the kind of Europe France wanted. There was an entry fee for EMU, however. France had to accept Bundesbank monetary predominance and become a plausible monetary partner for the Germans. When monetary union came it would involve a massive new pooling of sovereignty. In the long run, EMU would imply the development of something like real economic policy union. At that point, the French would get leverage over German economic policy, rather than the Germans controlling Europe through their monetary power.

The medium-term implications of this scenario were harsh, however. Governments had to promote price stability, compress the budget deficit, control the trade balance and keep interest rates at or below German levels – leaving few resources for reform. Moreover, these restrictive policies had to be pursued in a setting in which firms were encouraged to be more flexible (a task made easier by the growing weakness of the union movement, discussed in Chapter 1). This also implied further transfers of national income to profits at the expense of wages. Avoiding *dirigisme* and Keynesian reflationary techniques was gospel. It was Rocard's good fortune that he could avoid the worst effects of this line because economic activity grew. Unemployment levels nonetheless continued to rise, and evidence of growing inequality abounded. Social exclusion, particularly of immigrants, increased in urban areas, as did crime and urban insecurity. Unemployment hit hard on young people, who had an ever more difficult time making the transition from school to work, underlining the contradiction between Socialist commitments to increasing numbers receiving the *baccalaureate* and the difficulty of employing such graduates. Young people became cynical and impervious to Left appeals.

Mitterrand and other advocates of the Europe option believed its payoffs would come only after a difficult period. Then the Single Market, economic and monetary policy convergence, austerity and restructuring would bring an era of strong growth. When this began, economic success would provide the cushion needed to renew reformism, including at the European level, and give Social Democrats a second wind. But this scenario began to come apart in the early 1990s. The EC overloaded its agenda after 1989, partly in response to the end of the Cold War, making decision-making more difficult and prompting some member states to drag their heels. The 1991 Maastricht Treaty, meant to consecrate Europe's qualitative leap forward, reflected this and was a mediocre and confusing document. EMU, its one solid accomplishment, consecrated policy covergence criteria that dictated restrictive monetarism in France at least until full EMU would be established, probably in 1999. Ratifying Maastricht in 1992 brought more unfavorable news.[21] Political malaise had spread across the EC. Leaders such as Mitterrand, Kohl, Gonzalez, British Tories and the Italian Christian Democrats had been in power for too long. Voters demonstrated growing mistrust of élites, prompting commentators to talk of a 'crisis of politics'. Finally, the years 1991 and 1992 brought the worst recession since the 1930s. The Danish 'no' to Maastricht in June 1992, the first great shock, turned out to be the tip of a public opinion iceberg. A strong minority of Europeans, including the French, disapproved of the new Europe.

Renewed European integration had been advertised as an economic magic bullet. Instead, it had brought few remedies to Europe's relative economic decline. Official French unemployment rose to 3 million, 12 per cent of the workforce, during Maastricht ratification. (Real levels were much higher if those who had given up looking for work were factored in.) In the baleful tones of the European Commission's 1993 White Paper, *Growth, Competitiveness, and Employment*, 'Was the single market process merely a flash in the pan? The truth is that although we have changed, the rest of the world has changed even faster.'[22] In the absence of new growth, what became most salient about the new Europe was its liberal bias. The social dimension had not produced enough to assuage the less economically secure. There was also renewed sensitivity, particularly after Maastricht, to the EC's chronic democratic deficit. Other EC member states, including the Germans, who faced huge unification costs, had begun to retreat from earlier strong commitments to 'more Europe'. Second-order effects, such as the currency disorders of 1992 and 1993, which nearly destroyed the EMS and cast grave doubts about the future of EMU, were devastating. The headlong rush toward renewed European integration thus slowed to a stop.

The devastating consequences of this for Mitterrand's domestic strategy were illustrated most clearly in the 1992 referendum on Maastricht.[23] On the day after the Danish 'no' result, Mitterrand announced there would be a French referendum in September. No doubt Mitterrand felt the renaissance of European integration after 1985 to be very much his work, and a successful referendum could restore its momentum after the Danish shock. Since Maastricht could have been ratified by parliamentary vote alone (the two houses of Parliament voted overwhelmingly for the pre-ratification constitutional amendments proposed by the *Conseil*

Constitutionnel), the referendum decision made sense only if there were other agendas. Mitterrand was also trying to play on the Right's new divisions on Europe.[24] It was too tempting for Mitterrand, with parliamentary elections only six months away, to resist using a referendum to whip up civil war on the Right. Mitterrand had miscalculated yet again. The Maastricht referendum offered various national populist forces, both Right and Left, a golden opportunity to coalesce against the EC, Maastricht and anything else that came to mind. The complex Maastricht text was its own worst enemy. The independent Left and many others cursed the neoliberal conspiracy. Communists talked about a capitalist plot, and Left Socialists, behind Jean-Pierre Chevènement, marched against Maastricht for 'Republican patriotism'. The Right of the Centrists and Gaullists articulated soft national populism. The extreme-Right National Front lumped Maastricht with the coming of immigrant hordes. The Greens divided and waffled, as was their wont, but overall opposed the treaty. Reasons for the 'no' votes included the conflict in Yugoslavia, the failure of social Europe, foreigners voting in French local elections, Brussels bureaucrats, the menace to Camembert cheese, threats to French agriculture from Common Agricultural Policy reform, the General Agreement on Tariffs and Trade, Eastern Europe, unemployment, the need for trade protection, fears about the loss of the *franc* and foreign policy and defense autonomy. Finally, there was regicide in the air. Polls showed that a majority of the French believed that *le vieux* had been around too long!

A month before the referendum, polls were 50–50 with 'no' forces leading in momentum and energy. The government, the pro-Maastricht opposition around Giscard and economic élites then pulled out all stops. Socialists and conservatives spoke on the same 'yes' platforms around France. Great writers, actors and intellectuals placed full-page 'yes' petitions in the daily papers.[25] The *'petit oui'* – 51 per cent yes, 49 per cent no – was by and large rich, urban and well-educated.[26] The 'no' voters were farmers; blue-collar workers, particularly those in social crisis-ridden suburbs and delining industrial areas; lower-level white-collar workers; and the less-educated. François Mitterrand had – barely – won one part of his bet. A French rejection of Maastricht would have finished the treaty and put the Community in an enormous crisis. But he had clearly lost another. Maastricht had been saved by the leaders and voters of the Centre–Right, and Mitterrand's enemies, Chirac and Giscard, ended ahead of the game. Worse, the referendum's effects encouraged an emerging cleavage in French politics, which bode ill both for Europe and the Left. Protectionist national populists would henceforth confront élite internationalists advocating freer trade, austerity and European integration.

Leaving the PS as it was Found

The collapse of the Europe option was background for a very long list of presidential tactical failures that further debilitated the PS. Mitterrand's choice of

Edith Cresson to replace Rocard in spring 1991 came from the same tactical concerns that had brought Laurent Fabius in 1984. The feisty Cresson would become France's first female prime minister, and the President hoped that this would bring some of the same benefits that the appointment of the thirtysomething Fabius had had, for the time had come to prepare the 1995 presidential election. Cresson was a tough-talking rhetorical Leftist with old-fashioned *dirigiste* instincts, qualities that the President judged useful to revitalize the PS Left against Rocard and in preparation for a new cohabitation after 1993. The appointment was a major miscalculation, however. The new Prime Minister was somewhat incompetent and prone to frightful political gaffes. Even without such deficiencies, however, Cresson would have had difficulties with the elephants of the PS's factions, many in her government, who resented her presence. Some felt that the position ought to have gone to someone more deserving (Pierre Bérégovoy carried on a guerrilla war against her), others resented the high-handed way that Mitterrand had imposed her, and, last, many resented her for her sex.[27] After less than a year, Mitterrand replaced her with Bérégovoy to minimize the inevitable disaster in the 1983 legislative elections.

Bérégovoy was left with an impossible job. The European recession had a dramatic effect on French unemployment. On top of this, the franc fell under serious speculative pressure after Britain's exit from the ERM in September 1992. Containing this pressure intensified Bérégovoy's personal obsession with the *franc fort*, leaving even fewer resources to help French victims of the recession and unemployment. In this context the emergence of anti-European policy options – which in some cases involved proposing new *dirigisme*, the end of the *franc fort* and reflation – gave the opposition a near-monopoly on serious proposals for reform. The PS looked bereft of ideas. Worse still, the party and a number of its leaders lurched from scandal to scandal. The President's own entourage came under suspicion for using its privileged contacts for personal purposes, particularly in an insider-trading episode involving Mitterrand's longtime friend Roger-Patrice Pélat. Bérégovoy, who accepted an interest-free loan from Pélat, was so troubled that he would commit suicide after the 1993 elections. Laurent Fabius had to face lingering questions about the horrible scandal in 1985 in which HIV-contaminated blood was distributed in hospitals. Finally, the PS was rocked by accusations about illegal fund-raising (in which consulting agencies billed municipal governments for fake services and kicked back the payments to campaign chests). A campaign finance reform in 1990, which included full amnesty for past PS practices, added insult to injury.[28]

In the March 1993 parliamentary elections, the PS, with 17 per cent of the vote in the first round, managed to lose 4 million of the votes it had won in 1988. After the second round, it held only 67 seats (with its allies) in the new Assembly, down from 282 in 1988. Mitterrand could not have been in a more difficult situation to confront a second *cohabitation*. The Left had evidently failed to find any credible answers to the underlying tendencies of a post-boom economy, globalization and changing stratification, and the French electorate knew it. A substantial minority of the PS's and PCF's former voters either retreated into apathy or began searching for non-Left alternatives, including the dangerous national populist ones being proposed by the FN and others.

The story was not over, however. Whatever the state of the PS and the Left electorally, the designation of the Left's presidential proto-candidate remained a live issue. This in turn perpetuated warfare among PS elephants.[29] As of 1993 the PS seemed determined to demonstrate that the only important thing was cynical struggle for political positions and precedence. In this convoluted setting, Michel Rocard, still the 'virtual' candidate of the PS for 1995, decided to remove Laurent Fabius, who had finally become PS first secretary in 1992 (after forming an alliance with Rocard, despite their deep personal antipathy) and assume party leadership himself. The step was a fundamental strategic error, however.[30] It simultaneously placed him in the elephants' line of fire, for Rocard was still regarded as an interloper, and obliged him to accept leadership of the Socialist list for the 1994 European elections. These elections, run on a strict proportional representation basis, had never been favourable to the PS, since given their relative lack of consequences, they tended to elicit protest voting and disaggregate large political families into their smaller factions. Worse still, in 1994 the Socialists remained tainted by the failure of their period in government and, more important, by the difficulties of Mitterrand's Europe option.[31]

In these impossible circumstances, Rocard ran a bad campaign, Mitterrand quietly encouraged Bernard Tapie's own demagogic effort (Tapie led a list that won 12 per cent), and the PS ended up with 14.6 per cent, the worst Socialist showing in decades. Rocard's credibility as *présidentiable* was destroyed, and he was obliged to resign as first secretary. François Mitterrand had succeeded in destroying Michel Rocard. Rocard would not be the 1995 PS presidential candidate. The dark side to this success, however, was that the PS had *no* plausible presidential candidate to succeed Mitterrand. François Mitterrand had indeed left the PS in the state he had found it. French Socialism, and the broader French Left, was divided, electorally weak and without ideas.

CONCLUSIONS

The great powers of the Fifth Republic presidency and its electoral centrality for everything else creates huge space for *présidentiables* and incumbents to shape French politics. For the Left, the Presidency as an institution and the specific purposes of any Left President would fundamentally structure any experience in power. After 1981, therefore, Mitterrand's choices would be switchpoints for a French Left compelled to seek new answers for a new and difficult era. The end of the post-war boom years, economic globalization and post-industrializing class relationships meant that the French Left would have to change no matter what.

Because of the presidency, whatever Mitterrand did and however he decided to configure relationships between himself and his family of political origin, the Left would never have complete control over these changes.

After a brief moment as Comrade-President, Mitterrand turned to a more classic Fifth Republic presidential role in the face of the collapse of the Left's initial programmes. Thereafter, he subordinated Left governments to a plan designed to win his own re-election in 1988. In doing so, he put into place a grand strategy, the Europe option, designed to replace the one that had failed in 1982–3. His re-election plan by necessity drew the PS toward the centre. The Europe option, itself premised upon liberal economic hopes and a long period of austerity, did likewise. The Left and the PS were simultaneously drawn away from their natural bases and from profitable confrontation with longer-term strategic issues. By Mitterrand's second *septennat*, these choices had brought the PS to a dead end. Instead of devising new ideas, it settled into a Florentine battle for succession to the President, replete with all of the public relations techniques of personalized politics that Mitterrand himself had adopted to ensure re-election. In the absence of new approaches, the Socialists could only discredit themselves.

It could have been otherwise. The presidency in the Fifth Republic creates remarkable space for a president to define and conduct a personally chosen strategy. With a president other than François Mitterrand, the specific choices might have been different. To be sure, few options that were not centrist – pro-capitalist and anti-Left – were on offer anywhere during the two Mitterrand terms. This should not obscure what is really the central lesson, however. The presidency in the Fifth Republic, with its huge powers, is an institution that drags French political groups toward the centre of the spectrum and the strategic options of *présidentiables* and presidents. If the Left wanted power, it had to submit to being dragged. Choosing centrist options was thus quite as much a function of the ways French institutions worked as of any needs of capital, however great these needs may have been. The Left, obliged to embrace the institutions of the Fifth Republic in order to be taken seriously, very nearly succumbed in the process. Now it is on the cusp of an irreparable choice between reconstructing itself *as a Left* or committing permanently to a presidentialized agenda in which personality and skilful manipulation of polls wins power. The latter is the overwhelmingly likely outcome. Such will be François Mitterrand's immediate legacy. It will also be Charles de Gaulle's triumph.

Notes

1.   See also Halimi's longer essay in *Sisyphe est fatigué: Les échecs de la gauche au pouvoir* (Paris: Robert Laffont, 1993).

2. De Gaulle had numerous predecessors in these efforts, as Marx reminds us in his very pertinent *Eighteenth Brumaire of Louis Bonaparte.* Current glorification of de Gaulle, although exaggerated, is correct in underlining the degree to which the General actually did conciliate the democratic side with the monarchical, even though the glorifiers tend too often to overlook both the dark sides of the monarchical and the historical antecedents of de Gaulle's creation.

3. The best analysis of the PS and its relationships with Presidents and the phenomena of power is Alain Bergounioux and Gérard Grunberg's *Le Long Remords du pouvoir* (Paris: Fayard, 1992). For the Epinay cycle, see Part IV. On the period reviewed in this section their analysis is quite close to mine (see Chapter XVI). Their one flaw is to place inordinate weight on the need for the PS to accept the realities of power and governance, in contrast to outreach.

4. Mitterrand then obliged the incumbent General de Gaulle, theretofore regarded as untouchable, to campaign seriously in the runoff of the election. Mitterrand lost honourably, winning 45.5 per cent of the vote. This was a key moment in the desanctification of de Gaulle.

5. The classic study of this process, in general terms, is Olivier Duhamel's *La Gauche et la Ve République* (Paris: PUF, 1980).

6. See Bergounioux and Grunberg, Chapter XVII.

7. The most vivid account of Mitterrand's takeover of the PS via manipulation of different fractions is Albert Du Roy and Robert Schneider, *Le Roman de la rose* (Paris: Seuil, 1982).

8. Mitterrand was thus able to organize the party and his relationships to it in his preferred, two-tiered and nested way. He continued to cultivate his own inner circle of trusted operators. Connected to this, but at much greater distance from Mitterrand himself, were PS faction leaders. Many of these had strong political bases of their own. By the later 1970s, however, Mitterrand had sought out a number of promising younger leaders and brought them to top PS leadership. Although these people were all talented, the fact that they owed their careers to Mitterrand made them dependent upon him. The complexity of this two-tiered structure combining a political Praetorian Guard and semi-dependent official party leadership allowed Mitterrand to organize PS life in the sinuous ways that he liked – setting competing groups identical problem-solving tasks and waiting for things to 'decant' before him, choosing the solution he preferred, manipulating existing conflicts among fractions to his advantage, and so on, all the while protecting his privacy and freedom to manoeuvre. There are many portraits of this side of Mitterrand, most hostile. See Franz-Olivier Giesbert, *François Mitterrand ou la tentation de l'histoire* (Paris: Seuil, 1978) and *Le Président* (Paris: Seuil, 1990); William Shonfeld, *Ethnographie du PS et du RPR: les éléphants et l'aveugle* (Paris: Economica, 1985); and Danielle Lochak, *La CIR. François Mitterrand et le socialisme* (Paris: PUF, 1977).

9. On this question see the Georges Lavau, Gérard Grunberg and Nonna Mayer, eds., *L'Univers politique des classes moyennes* (Paris: Presses de la Fondation Nationale des Sciences Politiques, 1983).

10. The PCF's erratic behaviours undoubtedly played a significant role in saving Mitterrand's career. Beyond the implausibility of the various posturings of PCF leaders, sabotaging success in the 1978 elections was a fundamentally erroneous strategic move. Had the Left won in 1978 Mitterrand would have had to become Prime Minister in difficult political and economic circumstances. Politically, he would have had to cohabit with Valéry Giscard d'Estaing. Economically, he would have had to face stagflation. Moreover, in such circumstances the PCF, if somewhat weakened, would still have had a great deal of leverage and considerable governmental power. It is difficult to imagine that Mitterrand's presidential credibility

would have survived such circumstances, and the PS would undoubtedly have suffered along with him.

11. See Pierre Favier and Michel Martin-Roland, *La Décennie Mitterrand: Les Ruptures*, Vol. 1 (Paris: Seuil, 1990).

12. Giesbert recounts a 1973 PS bureau meeting where a proposal from Mitterrand to strengthen the PS's EC contacts won by only 12 to 8, leading Mitterrand to threaten to resign unless the PS leadership took a more enthusiastic position on the EC. See *La fin d'une Epoque* (Paris: Seuil, 1993) pp. 281–2. Beyond the PS, the PCF's anti-Europeanism was notorious. Moreover, these outlooks reflected considerable nationalism in the Left's base.

13. Simon Bulmer and Wolfgang Wessels document the unusual efforts of Mitterrand at this point in *The European Council* (Basingstoke: Macmillan, 1987).

14. Mitterrand had firsthand experience with this at the Versailles G-7 meeting in 1982, where Reagan's indifference to the French plight was patent.

15. There is much evidence that the EC's founders believed that this was the only way to make European integration happen and that European leaders consistently saw the pursuit of European integration in diplomatic camera as advantageous.

16. Polls had turned against the Left as early as 1982. The PCF continued its collapse towards 10 per cent while the Socialists declined somewhat less dramatically. The 1983 municipal elections were a defeat – the Left won 44.2 per cent in the first round, even if they benefited from a rallying effect in the second round. Thirty-one cities changed majorities to the Right. At the 1984 European election, more difficult because of proportional representations, the PS won only 20.86 per cent and the PCF 11.79 per cent.

17. Mitterrand had begun to play on the FN even before this, pressuring to allow it television time in the 1984 European elections, also run on a proportional representation basis. The Front then won 11 per cent, dropping to 9.8 per cent in the 1986 legislative elections, enough to win 35 seats.

18. The facts of the remanufacturing of Mitterrand's image by public relations professionals such as Jacques Séguela, Jacques Pilhan and Gérard Colé have not been seriously analysed, to my knowledge. However in Erik Orsenna's historical novel, *Un Grand amour* (Paris: Seuil, 1993), they are a central theme.

19. This was the perspicacious contention of Georges Lavau in his prophetic contribution to George Ross, Stanley Hoffmann and Sylvia Malzacher, eds., *The Mitterrand Experiment* (Oxford: Polity/Oxford University Press, 1987). Barring very unlikely changes, Lavau argued, the Left would be unable to gather enough votes to win a parliamentary majority. The PCF's electoral hold was ever-diminishing, while the PS would be quite unable to reproduce the near-40 per cent totals of 1981, created by the divine surprise of Mitterrand's presidential election.

20. Giesbert cites a rank-ordered list of his preferred successors that Mitterrand allegedly gave to a friend in 1991. It went as follows – Jacques Delors, François Léotard, Raymond Barre, Valéry Giscard d'Estaing, Jacques Chirac, Mitterrand's dog, then Michel Rocard. See *La Fin d'une époque*, p. 33.

21. The treaty created negative effects at precisely the moment when actual '1992' policies had begun to bite, particularly for employment. This was as the European Commission's Cecchini Report, *The Costs of Non-Europe*, had predicted. The payoffs of completing the single market would come in the medium term. In the short run, as firms restructured, states deregulated and nationalized activities privatized to confront new market geography, there would be considerable dislocation and unemployment costs.

22. See EC Commission, *Growth, Competitiveness and Employment: The Challenges and Ways Forward into the 21st Century* (Brussels-Luxembourg: EC, 1993).

23. Mitterrand also mishandled German unification, advocating prudence (largely out of concern for Mikhail Gorbachev) against Helmut Kohl's desire to move fast. Mitterrand even undertook a state visit to the GDR at a point where the crisis was very advanced. The strange saga of Mitterrand's idea for a European confederation, a new and different transnational organization to incorporate ex-socialist countries, was another abject failure.

24. The neo-Gaullists and the Centrists were deeply split, with half the Gaullist deputies voting against changing the constitution.

25. It was an interesting sidelight that both sides invoked the German menace, the 'no' voters asserting that Maastricht meant surrender to German power and the 'yes' voters that Maastricht was the best way to contain this power.

26. Results and analysis can be found in *Le Monde*, 22 September 1992.

27. Elisabeth Schemla's *Cresson* (Paris: Flammarion, 1993) tries to make a case that Cresson was a victim of sexism, particularly by PS leaders. She does not succeed in proving anything more than that elements of sexism were present.

28. For a brief summary of the events see Pascale Robert-Diard, 'L'argent obsédant', in *Le Monde, Dossiers et Documents, 21 mars–28 mars 1993, Elections législatives* (Paris: Ed. Le Monde, 1993) pp. 12–4.

29. A rough list of the players would include Fabiusians (with Fabius having become First Secretary); Mitterrandists (co-ordinated by Lionel Jospin, whose relationship with Fabius was poisonous); Rocardians, in their eternal situation of marginality to the Epinay party; *quadras*, a grouping of younger ministers whose main bond was distaste for the elephants; and various Left factions, including Jean-Pierre Chevènement's increasingly nationalist group, which would eventually leave the PS altogether.

30. Undoubtedly Rocard's logic was that without doing so his presidential campaign would be tainted by the public spectacle of Socialist infighting and subject to all sorts of sabotage from his enemies.

31. On this see Elisabeth Dupoirier, 'L'Enjeu européen dans l'opinion publique française', in *French Politics and Society* (Summer 1994). See also *Le Monde*, 14 June 1994, pp. 10–1, for revealing exit poll results.

3 Exchange Rate Politics in France, 1981–1983: The Regime-Defining Choices of the Mitterrand Presidency

David R. Cameron

In the evening of 10 May 1981, as the supporters of François Mitterrand celebrated his election as President of France, everything seemed possible for the *Parti Socialiste* and its allies.[1] For at least seven years, they would control an office whose potential powers exceeded those of any political executive in the democratic world. They could reasonably expect the President's coat-tails would help them win a majority of seats in the *Assemblée Nationale* in the legislative elections that would soon be called. And then, with executive and legislative power secured, they could deploy the highly developed administrative apparatus of French government and its extensive role in the economy to implement the plethora of changes articulated in Mitterrand's *Cent dix propositions*.[2]

Perhaps in no other country and at no other time in recent history was there a more promising moment to anticipate the transformation of an advanced capitalist economy into one that was more humane, more egalitarian and more fully imbued with the progressive principles of socialism and social democracy. But now, those ambitions and dreams seem as if from another era, cruel reminders of what might have been, visions of a possible future that for some reason eluded the Left. Instead of presiding over a transformation of French capitalism, the Socialist Party appears only to have achieved such conservative policy objectives as a reduction in inflation, a resurgence of corporate profitability and investment and a strong currency, at the expense of economic growth and employment. Not surprisingly, it suffered an accelerating erosion in its electoral fortunes – first in the 1983 municipal elections, then in the 1986, 1988 and 1993 legislative elections, and, most recently, in the 1994 elections for the European Parliament.[3] Bereft of much of its early electorate, dispirited and divided, the PS grimly awaited the 1995 presidential election and its likely eviction from the *Elysée*.

The erosion in electoral support was perhaps the inevitable consequence of having been in power for so many years. But it was also, at least in part, self-inflicted, the result of growing disaffection as the government abandoned its early commitments to reflation, employment and redistributive spending in favour of such eminently conservative goals as price stability, external balance, fiscal and monetary restraint and a strong currency. The pursuit of those objectives could only cause its supporters to ask whether the Socialist Party and its allies stood for anything other than their own retention of power. Given the high electoral costs, why did economic policy evolve as it did during the Mitterrand presidency?[4] Why did a Socialist-dominated government in control of a large number of policy instruments through which it could intervene in the economy gravitate toward a policy that increasingly diverged from its initial programmatic commitments? And why, above all, did the shift from a reflationary and redistributive economic policy to a more contractionary one begin so *early* in the presidency – not in the second *septennat*, when the Party's political and institutional resources had been depleted, but, rather, in the early years of the *first* septennat, when it still held a secure majority in the *Assemblée*?[5]

In part because the turning point occurred early in the Mitterrand presidency, when it still had considerable political resources at its disposal, a conventional wisdom has developed that the shift to a contractionary economic policy could not have been avoided. Typically, this view emphasizes the *external* constraints faced by the government – the fact that currency reserves were sparse relative to the large trade deficit; that the government therefore needed to continue financing the deficit with international loans; that the scarcity of reserves, coupled with the high level of international debt, made it impossible to float the franc or devalue by a large amount; that in any event, given its place at the heart of the European Community, France could not withdraw the franc from the Exchange Rate Mechanism of the European Monetary System, and, therefore, in order to restore French competitiveness in export markets and reduce the trade deficit, it was necessary to reduce the rate of inflation through fiscal and monetary contraction. Thus, Hall concludes:

> while some variation in the timing and intensity of devaluation and the macroeconomic stance might have improved the overall level of France's economic performance in 1981–85, the room for maneuver was probably not great. French levels of growth, unemployment and inflation were close to the European averages, and there are few grounds for thinking that macroeconomic policy could have been substantially different given prevailing international economic and domestic constraints.[6]

Similarly, Bell and Criddle conclude that:

> It is difficult to see what else the Government could have done, given the international constraints on the French economy and the need for European co-operation. . . .[7]

Likewise, in speaking of the 'force of external constraint on French policy', Loriaux concludes that:

The claim that the Socialists had options they chose to ignore loses much of its power when the costs of those options are assessed. The external constraint operating on the monetary policies of France and its European neighbors was a compelling one.[8]

As plausible as this conventional view is, a careful examination of the early years of the Mitterrand presidency suggests that, despite the obvious international constraints, the government *did* in fact have a choice in policy and that, indeed, every important figure in the government understood very well that such a choice existed. The international constraints were obvious and real. But the best and most appropriate response in the face of those constraints was by no means as obvious, and radically different responses could be imagined. When the Socialist government moved, in its first two years in office, from its initial reflationary and redistributive fiscal and monetary policy to a more contractionary one, it did so not because it was *forced* to shift by external constraints but, rather, because it *chose* to do so. And it made that choice not because of unavoidable external constraints but, rather, because the supporters of a contractionary policy triumphed over the adherents of an alternative policy in a protracted, *political* struggle that preoccupied the government throughout its first two years – and that, more than any other issue, defined the subsequent course of the Mitterrand presidency. This chapter describes that struggle.

EXCHANGE RATE POLICY: OPTIONS AND CHOICES

Although commentators often described the '*tournant*' simply in terms of the shift to a more contractionary fiscal and monetary policy, the regime-defining choices of the Mitterrand presidency actually involved exchange rate policy. In particular, they involved exchange rate policy vis-à-vis the European Monetary System – whether the franc would remain in the ERM or be withdrawn, and, if remaining, whether, when, and by how much it would be devalued vis-à-vis other member currencies.[9] In the first years of the Mitterrand presidency, the Socialist government confronted a fundamental choice. It could opt for a large devaluation of the franc, whether through negotiation within the EMS or by a withdrawal from it, that would allow it to continue its expansionary macroeconomic policy, thereby boosting growth and employment, and, through the relative price effect, alleviating the trade deficit. Such a devaluation would, however, fuel inflation – already in double digits – and would therefore have to be accompanied by fiscal and monetary restraint and an effective incomes policy. On the other hand, it could opt for a more modest devaluation – the most likely result of one negotiated within the ERM, since the country's trading partners with strong currencies would have to agree to *re*value their own currencies – or no devaluation at all. A modest, negotiated devaluation would enable the government to repair the trade deficit, to some extent, while moderating the rate of inflation and keeping the country's European commitments intact. It would, however, require that interest rates be kept high, in order to support the franc and reduce demand, and it would also require fiscal and wage restraint in order to reduce inflation and demand for imports and increase the price competitiveness of exports.

During the first two years of the Mitterrand presidency, the Socialist-dominated government was embroiled in an ongoing debate about various permutations of these two alternatives. Ultimately, it chose the second alternative, eschewing any devaluation when it took office, keeping the franc in the ERM, and negotiating three modest devaluations – in October 1981, June 1982 and March 1983 – each of which was accompanied by a shift to a progressively more contractionary fiscal and monetary policy. Those exchange rate decisions constituted a plausible response to the complex array of economic problems faced by the government – continued recession, double-digit inflation, a large trade deficit, an overvalued currency, etc. But they were by no means the *only* decisions that could have been made – as Mitterrand himself was to observe later (and as the sustained ERM crisis in 1992–3 demonstrated).[10] In light of that fact – and the subsequent adverse economic and electoral developments that can be attributed to those decisions – understanding how and why Mitterrand and the Socialist government made them is central to an appraisal of the Mitterrand presidency.

The Decision Not to Devalue: May 1981

When Mitterrand and the new Socialist government came to power in 1981, they inherited an economy mired in stagflation. The economy had been in recession for a year; after barely growing during the first six months of 1980, the real gross domestic product had decreased by about 0.5 per cent from mid-1980 to mid-1981, and the number of unemployed had increased from about 1.4 million to 1.7 million by the time of the 1981 elections. Despite the year-long recession, inflation continued to accelerate, to slightly more than 13 per cent,[11] and the trade deficit continued to grow to well in excess of 50 billion francs, having tripled in 1980. Despite the large and increasing trade deficit, and the large and increasing difference between the French and German inflation rates, the government of Raymond Barre had rejected any devaluation of the franc after the formation of the EMS. As a result, the franc had become increasingly overvalued relative to the German mark, thereby further accelerating the deterioration of the balance of trade and requiring the *Banque de France* to impose high interest rates to prop up the franc.

One of the great ironies of 1981 is that while Mitterrand and the Socialist Party came to power with a comprehensive and detailed programme, their views about exchange rate policy – the domain of policy that more than any other would shape the evolution of the presidency – were at best sketchy and inconsistent. For all the detail regarding their ambitions in the areas of nationalization, social policy and labour relations, Mitterrand and the Socialist Party came to power without a well-developed view about exchange rate policy, the franc and the EMS. Thus, while one of the '110 Propositions' (#20) committed the party to defending the franc against speculation, the programme from which it was drawn rejected the EMS on the grounds that it committed weak-currency countries to shadowing German monetary policy and instituting austerity.[12] Both Jean-Pierre Chevènement, who was primarily responsible for drafting the *Projet Socialiste* after the 1979 Congress, and Pierre Bérégovoy, who headed the group that turned the *Projet* into a more concise campaign document in 1981, not only wanted to devalue the franc but to leave the EMS altogether, thereby letting the franc float and presumably effecting a larger depreciation in its value than could be negotiated within the EMS.[13] Notwithstanding their views, however, Mitterrand, Jacques Delors, Pierre Mauroy and others had decided before the second round of the presidential election not to devalue.[14]

Exchange rate policy was on the agenda of the Socialist government well before Mitterrand and the *Parti Socialiste*, with its left-wing allies, formally took office. For one thing, capital had been fleeing the country as the prospects of a Socialist victory increased, and Mitterrand's victory in the second round only accentuated the flight. Driven down by investors' efforts to convert out of franc-denominated assets, the French currency fell toward its floor in the EMS. Indeed, the day after Mitterrand's victory, the franc dropped to its floor against the mark for the first time in the two-year existence of the EMS, and the *Banque* was forced to spend 3 billion francs worth of reserves in defence of the currency (and, as part of that defence, raise its seven-day intervention rate from 13.5 to 16 per cent).[15] In the first four days of business after Mitterrand's victory, 3 billion dollars in foreign exchange reserves flowed out in defence of the franc against speculators who, anticipating a devaluation, were moving out of the franc. In each of the next three days the losses were in the 700 million to 1 billion dollar range. And on the day of Mitterrand's inauguration, 21 May, well over 1 billion dollars was lost in defence of the franc against the attacks of speculators. In all, some 15 billion francs left the country in the four days between May 18 and May 21,[16] and over the ten days between Mitterrand's election and inauguration, the *Banque* lost roughly one-third of its total reserves.[17]

Underlying these movements in the currency markets was the fact that the country's external account was deeply in the red and deteriorating and its rate of inflation relatively high and rising, despite the year-long recession. To those holding franc-denominated assets, the rising deficit and accelerating rate of inflation were sure signs that the franc was overvalued and likely to be devalued. True, the Socialists had vowed not to devalue. But could one reasonably expect them to adhere to that commitment – especially when Gaullist presidents had not hesitated to devalue upon entering office in less pressing circumstances?[18] To many, devaluation seemed imminent. Indeed, as he left office, Raymond Barre told Valéry Giscard d'Estaing that the new government would have to devalue and do so quickly. (To which Giscard responded – correctly as it turned out – 'No, they won't dare.'[19]) Likewise, Jean-Yves Haberer, the director of the *Trésor*, believed a devaluation was inevitable, as did Daniel Lebègue, a high civil servant in the *Trésor*.[20] The Governor of the *Banque de France*, Renaud de la Genière, was so certain the new government would devalue and blame the *Banque* for the weakness of the franc that he tendered his resignation at a meeting with Pierre Mauroy, the new Prime Minister, on 21 May and had to be reassured otherwise in order to remain on the job.[21]

The exchange rate was literally the first issue confronted by Mitterrand and the new government. At the *Elysée* in the morning of 21 May, Michel Rocard pulled Mauroy aside and told him it was necessary to devalue immediately, within 48 hours, while the blame could still be placed on the previous government. The devaluation should be a large one, he said, about 15 per cent, so that it would not only offset the 7 to 8 per cent inflation differential with Germany but also give French firms a competitive advantage. If its EMS partners refused a realignment on that scale, Rocard said France should leave the Exchange Rate Mechanism.[22]

Shortly after the conversation with Rocard, Mauroy rode with Mitterrand to the memorial to the Unknown Soldier at the *Arc de Triomphe*. On the return to the *Elysée*, he mentioned that the franc was doing badly that morning and reserves continued to drain away – perhaps as much as 1.5 billion francs that day – and that some, such as Rocard, favoured floating the franc while others, such as Delors, the Minister of Finance, favoured remaining in the ERM and defending the existing value of the franc. He mentioned the measures his staff had already prepared and asked whether the President still thought the franc should not be devalued. Mitterrand replied that they had always thought the franc should not be devalued and, in Mauroy's words, that 'political common sense dictates the solution: one does not salute the victory of the Left with a devaluation.'[23] Besides, Mitterrand told Mauroy, alluding to his inauguration, 'one does not devalue on a day like today . . . one does not devalue the money of a country that has just placed its confidence in you . . . one can not go up the *Champs-Elysées* and lower the franc.'[24]

With that, the decision not to devalue had been made. Mauroy returned to the *Matignon* and, after assuring Renaud de la Genière that there would be no devaluation, set to work with Delors, Haberer of the *Trésor*, as well as two advisers, Jean Peyrelevade, an economist with Crédit Lyonnais who was to become his chief economic adviser, and Jean Deflassieux, another banker, to draft a set of measures that could be decreed that evening to support a franc that was obviously overvalued and yet would not be devalued. Drawing largely on proposals Haberer had prepared for Barre, the group decided upon such measures as an increase in interest rates, a strengthening of exchange controls and a limitation on import credits.[25]

Why did Mitterrand resist devaluation? For one thing, as noted earlier, the campaign platform had committed itself to not rewarding financial speculators and a devaluation would have done exactly that. There were pragmatic, political calculations as well: a devaluation before the upcoming legislative elections could have exposed the new government to charges of incompetence in economic policy. Also, there were historic parallels to be avoided – in particular, the experiences of the Centre-Left governments of 1924 and 1936, both of which began their short-lived stays in office with devaluations.[26] Finally, devaluation might have called into question the patriotic credentials of the government; certainly a government that would likely include Communist ministers after the legislative elections could not appear willing to cheapen the value of such an important symbol as the nation's money.[27]

The new government's decision not to devalue when it came to power may have reflected the constraining effects of international pressures. The anxieties of western allies over a new Socialist government that would probably include Communists, the fear of unleashing an even greater flight of capital and a run on the franc, the perception that EMS partners (most notably, Germany) would oppose a large devaluation, and that France, as a founding member of the EC and the EMS, could not leave the latter, undoubtedly influenced the government's decision not to devalue or float the franc. As one of Mauroy's advisers put it:

> to be efficacious, the devaluation would have to be large, something our partners judged unacceptable. In retrospect, it was necessary to let the franc float in leaving the European Monetary System. There again, the first signal that the new government would have given on the international scene would have been a setback in respect to European solidarity. Furthermore, the success of the Left in France had already aroused astonishment and distrust in most of the western capitals. And the Socialist leaders knew that this nervousness was going to increase, a month later, when the Communists entered, inevitably, the new government. How, then, could the government take the risk of floating the franc? It risked being sharply attacked, which would rapidly drain away the reserves. Where might the slide stop and did this not run the risk of inaugurating Mitterrand's term with a catastrophic monetary skid?[28]

However real these anxieties and concerns were, though, they were only that, anxieties and concerns based on perceptions – and, possibly, *mis*perceptions as well – of foreign reactions.[29] It is by no means obvious they reflected actual constraints that *forced* the government to maintain the existing exchange rate. Certainly international financial markets had been expecting a devaluation for some time – in part, because one was fully warranted in light of the overvaluation of the franc and continued deterioration of the trade deficit. Indeed, with the benefit of hindsight, it may well be that, notwithstanding the anxieties that some in the government had about the reactions of EMS partners and international markets, the proverbial window of opportunity for a significant devaluation was wide open in May and June 1981 – in fact, much more open than it would be at any later moment in the Mitterrand presidency.

Some time later, after the Socialist government had gone through its third devaluation and completed its shift to a contractionary macroeconomic policy, Mitterrand looked back on the decision not to devalue in May or June 1981 and acknowledged that he had let an opportunity slip by. To one interviewer, he admitted, 'I committed an error in not devaluing in 1981.'[30] To another, he identified the major reasons for the decision not to devalue:

> We had the legislative elections ahead of us – that delayed it a few weeks. It would have been impossible to devalue before the elections. We would have broken the electoral dynamic. No, that was unthinkable at the time. But the question could have been raised after the elections, after the appointment of the second Mauroy government. If it was not – it was, however, the right time, whether it was a question of a devaluation or floating the franc, or both – it was because Delors insisted that he was in charge of money.[31]

The presidential decision not to devalue, coupled with the effectiveness of the defensive measures to stem the outflow of reserves and the government's desire to project an image of tranquillity, competence and responsible financial management in the legislative election campaign, postponed any correction in the exchange rate. Immediately after the legislative elections, Chevènement, a *Ministre d'Etat* and the Minister of Research and Technology, spoke with Mitterrand and insisted that France leave the EMS.[32] But while some important figures – for example, Bérégovoy, the new Secretary-General of the *Elysée*, and Jean Riboud, Mitterrand's close friend and the head of Schlumberger – agreed that France should leave the EMS, a larger number of equally important figures in the government, such as Mauroy, Delors, Haberer and Jacques Attali, the President's closest counselor in the *Elysée*, opposed the move. Thus, for the time being, both methods of adjusting the value of the franc – the moderate one of negotiating a devaluation of the franc within the EMS and the more radical one of leaving the EMS and floating the franc – were ruled out, and the summer passed without any correction in the exchange rate.

The First Devaluation: October 1981

The government's wish to deprive the money speculators of their anticipated profits by maintaining the existing exchange rate only guaranteed a further deterioration in the balance of trade and postponed the inevitable correction in the value of the franc. The time for that correction came in the early autumn of 1981, when the franc again came under speculative attack. By that time, the franc was probably overvalued relative to the mark by almost 20 per cent, given the cumulative difference in French and German inflation rates since the founding of the EMS in 1979.[33] As painful as it may have been to admit, it was increasingly apparent that the speculators (and those such as Barre, Haberer, Lebègue, Rocard, and Chevènement, among others) were correct in thinking that some type of adjustment in the value of the franc was necessary and inevitable. The balance of trade had continued to deteriorate through the summer, as the pre-election *relance* produced by the Barre government and the growing cumulative difference between the inflation rates of France and its trading partners increased the demand for imported goods and reduced the competitiveness of exports. In addition, the revised budget deficit for 1981 announced in August and the even larger deficit projected for 1982 had raised the spectre of high and accelerating inflation and continued deterioration of the trade account. Businesses, especially international firms, became increasingly reluctant to hold francs and began moving into other currencies at an accelerating rate, and the *Banque de France* was forced to spend its already-dwindling foreign exchange reserves to buy francs. By the end of September, it was losing about 1 billion dollars a day in reserves, and it had lost about 4.5 billion dollars in reserves since July. De la Genière warned the government that could not go on much longer.[34]

Delors, the Minister of Finance, and Haberer, the Director of the *Trésor* in the ministry, had never believed that leaving the EMS was an option for France. But by the end of September, both decided the time had come to negotiate a devaluation of the franc within the EMS. Although initially reluctant, by early October Mitterrand agreed, and he authorized Delors to open negotiations in Brussels through the Monetary Committee.[35] Those negotiations prepared the ground for a meeting of the Ministers of Finance of the EC on 4 October 1981 that agreed upon a devaluation of the franc and revaluation of the mark and guilder.

In late September, Delors had estimated that a realignment of the franc against the mark of 12 to 15 per cent, while not fully neutralizing the accumulated difference in inflation rates, would at least have repaired a good deal of the loss in competitive position over the past two years. However, German and Dutch opposition to large revaluations of their currencies (which would hurt their export competitiveness in other European markets as well as in France) and Delors' desire to maintain solidarity within the EMS led him to accept a more modest devaluation. The mark and the Dutch guilder were revalued by 5.5 per cent, while the franc (and Italian lira) were devalued by 3 per cent. Thus, the franc was in effect devalued by 8.5 per cent vis-à-vis the mark – well under the cumulative inflation differential since the founding of the EMS and well below the range sought by Delors.[36]

Upon returning to Paris, Delors immediately proposed a number of measures to accompany the devaluation – measures one observer called 'a sort of hors d'oeuvre of the programme of *rigueur* that would be refined later on.'[37] But the measures – a proposal to freeze or otherwise moderate price increases, reduce expenditures by 10 billion francs and freeze another 15 billion francs – were challenged by virtually every other member of the Council of Ministers. In particular, Laurent Fabius, the *ministre délégué* for the budget who, by Mitterrand's decision, was alone responsible for the budget, challenged Delors' right to propose alterations in spending. Both Mitterrand and Mauroy supported Fabius, but, in order to placate Delors, who threatened to resign, they accepted the latter's idea of a freeze of 15 billion francs of expenditures.[38]

The Second Devaluation: June 1982

The October devaluation improved France's competitive position vis-à-vis its trading partners, but only to a degree. German resistance to revaluation of the mark, coupled with French reluctance to press the Germans, had produced a modest adjustment that erased less than one-half of the cumulative difference since 1979 in the two countries' inflation rates. The trade deficit, driven by the surge of imports during the second-half recovery in 1981 and a growing inflation differential with some partners, increased at an accelerating rate in the months following the devaluation. With those deficits, and inflation continuing in excess of 13 per cent, speculative pressures on the franc forced the *Banque* into currency markets and foreign exchange reserves flowed out in large amounts once more. Thus, for example, in the week before the cantonal elections in March 1982, reserves worth some 10 billion francs were spent in defence of the currency. The day after the second round, the franc fell to its floor against the mark, and both within and outside the government, devaluation or perhaps even departure from the EMS became the topic of conversation and rumor.[39]

As the balance of trade continued to deteriorate through the winter of 1981-2, advisers attached to the President, Prime Minister and Minister of Economy and Finance began to construct a new package of economic measures. By April 1982, Peyrelevade and Henri Guillaume, another adviser to the Prime Minister, were warning Mauroy that a second devaluation was inevitable – by September or October at the latest – because of the negligible corrective effect of the previous devaluation.[40] Mauroy asked them to prepare a *note* he could submit to the President, so they, together with Philippe Lagayette of Delors' *cabinet*, prepared a plan that would encompass the main elements of *rigueur* – a negotiated realignment of the franc vis-à-vis the mark in the range of 12–14 per cent, price and wage controls, cuts in expenditures, and higher interest rates. After seven drafts, they produced a 40-page plan that Mauroy and Delors could both accept. The Prime Minister signed it and on 28 May 1982 delivered it to the *Elysée*.

While the Mauroy–Delors package commanded considerable support, a number of individuals in the government and outside began to recommend an alternative policy. Instead of opting for a second modest, negotiated devaluation accompanied by *rigueur*, they proposed a larger devaluation or exit from the EMS altogether. The special virtue of the latter, they felt, was that by freeing the franc from the narrow range of fluctuation vis-à-vis such strong currencies as the guilder and the mark it would be possible to lower interest rates significantly, thereby reducing the cost of capital and inducing firms to invest and modernize and, in so doing, create jobs. In addition, of course, the lower relative prices of exports would presumably increase sales abroad and jobs at home.

Among the leading proponents of this alternative policy were Chevènement, who had been urging the President to leave the EMS since the 1981 elections; Bérégovoy, who had become convinced at the time of the first devaluation in the early autumn of 1981 that the franc should be withdrawn from the ERM; and Fabius. In addition, a variety of friends and informal advisers of the President – in particular, Jean Riboud of Schlumberger, Georges Plescoff of the Suez financial company, and Jean-Jacques Servan-Schreiber – argued in favour of leaving the EMS and pursuing an industrial strategy that would enable firms to invest, modernize, and improve their competitive position in both foreign and domestic markets.[41] In contrast to the emerging Mauroy–Delors programme, the alternative programme would, its proponents claimed, allow the government to continue the policy of economic expansion and job creation advocated by the *Projet socialiste* while also enhancing the competitive position of French firms.

Mitterrand and his close advisers were caught up in the preparations for the summit of the Group of Seven that would take place at Versailles in early June. Thus, when Mauroy pressed the President for a response to his note of 28 May, Mitterrand said, 'Let me have my summit. After that, we'll see.'[42] Just after the last luncheon of the summit, Mauroy pulled the President aside to one of the small rooms off the Hall of Mirrors and pleaded for a decision, saying that the country could not keep going on with its high rate of inflation in a deflationary world. Mitterrand finally agreed and, several days later, held a press conference to prepare the way for the *tournant*.

In his press conference on 9 June 1982, Mitterrand spoke of moving to a new and more difficult stage in reform, likening it to ascending a steep mountain after crossing a plain. Although he avoided any mention of devaluation (or the word *rigueur*), speculation in currency markets drove the franc to its floor in the EMS, where it remained despite an intervention of some 3 billion francs by the *Banque de France*. Devaluation became inevitable, and on 11 June, Mitterrand approved the initiation of new EMS negotiations. The next day the Monetary Committee agreed to, and the Ministers of Finance ratified, a 5.75 per cent devaluation of the franc (and a 2.75 per cent devaluation of the lira) and a 4.25 per cent revaluation of the mark and the guilder. Thus, the franc was devalued by 10 per cent versus the currency of its largest trading partner. Again, as in October 1981, the devaluation was less than Delors and other French ministers had hoped for, and it was not enough to eliminate the cumulative difference in French and German inflation rates. Nevertheless, it did represent a large change in the relative values of the mark and the franc – larger than in October 1981, even though it occurred only nine months after the earlier realignment while the 1981 realignment was the first in more than two years.

If the devaluation of the franc vis-à-vis the mark was, from Germany's view, generous, that may have reflected the fact that Delors' German counterpart, Manfred Lahnstein, recognized that Germany had profited greatly from the French recovery of 1981–2 and, for that reason, was willing to accept a larger revaluation of the mark than had been recommended by the Bundesbank.[43] In return, however, Delors committed France to remain within the EMS and to practise an austerity strong enough to bring it within the logic of deflation currently being practised throughout the West. Reflecting that commitment, the final accord of the Monetary Committee noted that it had 'taken into consideration the important programme that the French government planned to put into effect. The ministers noted their appreciation of this programme.'[44] The programme, of course, was the Mauroy–Delors package of price and incomes restraints and budget cuts – the programme of *rigueur* which, although not yet officially approved by the French government, had been the subject of secret discussions and commitments between Delors and the German officials for two weeks! The day after the devaluation, the government formally adopted the various provisions of the Mauroy–Delors package, freezing prices for four months, freezing salaries for the same period, lowering the target for the growth in the money supply and cutting some expenditures.

The decision to negotiate a second devaluation and pursue the programme of *rigueur* terminated the debate over exchange rate policy for the time being. There were, of course, some within the government – chiefly Bérégovoy, Chevènement and Fabius – who continued to protest the turn toward economic orthodoxy. But Bérégovoy and Chevènement were pre-occupied with new duties – the former having been named Minister of Social Affairs and the latter having added the Ministry of Industry to his other portfolios. Thus, one year after having come to power in the elections of May and June 1981, economic policy had fallen firmly under the control of a loose coalition of pro-EMS partisans of *rigueur*: Delors and his advisers in the Ministry of Economy and Finance; Mauroy and his team of economic advisers in the *Matignon*; and the President's advisers in the *Elysée* – in particular, Jacques Attali, Jean-Louis Bianco, the new Secretary-General, Christian Sautter, a councillor for international finance and the new Assistant Secretary-General; and François-Xavier Stasse, a councillor for economic affairs. Leaving the EMS no longer seemed to be an option – except to the one person whose views counted most; in concluding the Council of Ministers meeting of 16 June 1982 that formally approved the Mauroy–Delors package, Mitterrand said:

> We find ourselves in a typical case of class struggle, one that is both national and international at the same time. We are not able to count on any of the great capitalist powers because, for them, the goal is to demonstrate that we are not able to isolate ourselves. That situation would have led us to quit the EMS . . . If we fail in this second phase, a third one could lead us to leave the EMS.[45]

The Third Devaluation: March 1983

In late 1982, the debate about exchange rate policy resurfaced again. In spite of the June devaluation, the balance of trade continued to deteriorate, the franc remained under speculative pressure, and foreign exchange reserves continued to drain away. According to Delors, reserves had dropped by about 65 billion francs over the past year to a total of about 260 billion francs in foreign exchange reserves and gold.[46] In September, the government negotiated a line of credit with 14 American, Arab, Japanese and other international banks for 28 billion francs (approximately 4 billion dollars) – the largest line of credit ever taken by a government.[47] But the franc remained weak and continued to face downward pressure in the financial markets, and Mitterrand began to express misgivings about the policy of restraint.

Despite the fall of Helmut Schmidt's government in Germany in October, the franc remained under attack throughout the autumn, not only from the stronger European currencies but also from the rising American dollar, and reserves continued to drain away. By year's end, the trade deficit was approaching 100 billion francs. The depletion of reserves and rising trade deficit forced the government once again to arrange a large international loan, and in December it negotiated a loan of 14 billion francs, in the form of dollar deposits for pre-export credits in the *Banque de France*, from the Saudi Arabian Monetary Authority. As a result, over the course of 1982 the country's international debt had doubled to 40 billion dollars.[48]

Many of Mitterrand's advisers shared his concerns about *rigueur* and about the apparent failure of the two devaluations to alleviate the trade deficit and the weakness of the franc. They painted an increasingly pessimistic view of the future: 'given the direction of the external deficit and our inflation differential with our trade partners,' one adviser said, 'in two months France will be a colony of the German mark, and by January, 1984, it will be the International Monetary Fund which rules in Paris.'[49] Within the government, some ministers – most notably Fabius, Bérégovoy, and Chevènement – pressed again for *l'autre politique*, for a withdrawal of the franc from the ERM and a return to a policy of expansion that required, above all, a sharp reduction in interest rates which had reached 18 per cent. And the various *visiteurs du soir* who consulted with Mitterrand at the *Elysée* did likewise, presenting once again the case for leaving the EMS and floating the franc, at least temporarily, as the only way to bring rates down and spark an expansion.[50] The advantages of *l'autre politique*, some of its partisans noted, were political as well as economic; for example, according to Bérégovoy, the sacrifices required could be made more palatable by wrapping the policy in nationalism:

> I supported a departure from the EMS coupled with an extremely firm policy of *rigueur*. Politically, we had the possibility of designating our adversaries outside the country. We would have had the Communists with us, saying it's the fault of the Germans and the Americans.[51]

Mitterrand had decided not to make a decision about exchange rate policy and, more generally, macroeconomic policy until after the municipal elections in March

1983.[52] To some, it appeared that the supporters of the 'other policy' were close to convincing the President to leave the EMS and float the franc. But those who were committed to the existing policy were not about to concede defeat, and over the several months preceding the elections, a deluge of official *notes* on economic and monetary issues flowed from the partisans of *rigueur*. In particular, the '*club des Cinq*', a group of young presidential advisers in the *Elysée* – Attali, Bianco, Sautter, Stasse and Elisabeth Guigou, a civil servant detached from the *Trésor* – who had been meeting nearly every day for several months, prepared notes and memoranda outlining the possible adverse consequences of a withdrawal of the franc from the EMS. In late February, for example, Guigou drafted a *note* for the President that predicted that leaving the EMS would cause the franc to drop immediately by 10–15 per cent. The external deficit would increase by 2 billion francs a month. France had exhausted all possibilities for international loans, she wrote, and if it left the EMS it would find itself having to borrow from the EC or the IMF and having to satisfy conditions specified by those lenders. In the margin of the note, Bianco wrote, 'Mr. President, leaving the EMS will put us in the hands of the IMF.'[53]

In the first ballot of the 1983 municipal elections, on 6 March, the Left parties suffered a setback that exceeded the predictions of the polls. Evidently viewing the results as an electoral indictment of *rigueur*, Mitterrand decided at some point during the next week, prior to the second ballot of the elections, to endorse the arguments of Chevènement, Bérégovoy, Fabius, Riboud and the others who advocated *l'autre politique*.[54] He would withdraw the franc from the EMS and let it float, impose controls on imports, lower interest rates to stimulate investment, maintain price controls to prevent an acceleration of inflation, and institute a system of bargaining between employers and unions to restrain wages.[55]

Mitterrand informed Mauroy of his decision to leave the EMS on 14 March, the day after the second round of the municipal elections. The Prime Minister opposed the decision and said he would have to resign. Fortified by the arguments of his councillors about the risk of an unlimited drop in the value of the franc and an exhaustion of reserves, and fearing such a policy would also lead to a relaxation of budgetary policy and a resurgence of inflation, Mauroy told the President he could not lead a government committed to such a policy – that he 'didn't know how to drive on an icy road.'[56] He suggested that, rather than withdrawing from the ERM, France should initiate negotiations with the Germans about a third devaluation. Without reversing his decision, the President agreed to explore that possibility and, toward that end, sent Bianco on a secret mission that evening to discuss the matter with Helmut Kohl, the German chancellor.[57] Meanwhile, the President gathered those who supported a float of the franc – Fabius, Bérégovoy and others – and asked them to prepare a concrete plan of action.

The next day, the backers of *rigueur* mobilized in support of the existing policy. Attali, for example, visited Delors and told him that it was important to convince someone in the other camp to defect and join the partisans of *rigueur*.

He persuaded Delors to let Fabius speak with Michel Camdessus, the director of the *Trésor*, about the state of reserves, calculating that the weak link in the solidarity among the supporters of a float was the Minister of the Budget.[58] The following morning, 16 March, Mauroy met with Mitterrand at the *Elysée*. Guessing the Germans might agree to a sizeable revaluation of the mark – they had not as yet formally responded to the Bianco overture – he told the President he would be willing to continue as Prime Minister despite his disagreement with the new policy.[59] Meanwhile, before the meeting of the Council of Ministers that day, Attali asked Fabius to verify 'for the President' the state of offical reserves from Camdessus. (After the meeting, the President, encouraged by Attali, took Fabius aside and asked him what he would do if he were finance minister.) Upon his return to the ministry, Fabius contacted Camdessus, who told him almost verbatim what Guigou had said in her *note* in late February and what Delors had been saying as well – that there were only 30 billion francs of official reserves on hand; that a departure from the EMS would lead to a drop of at least 20 per cent in the franc; that such a depreciation would raise the country's international debt – already at 330 billion francs – by a comparable amount; that the country had used up its sources of international borrowing; that leaving the EMS would deprive the country of European support for the franc; and that the only means of defending the franc would be to increase interest rates significantly, perhaps as high as 20 per cent.[60]

Whether events would have transpired as Camdessus predicted – whether his forecast was a reasonable assessment of what would happen, a prudent civil servant's 'worst case' scenario, or simply a bluff by a partisan of *rigueur* – is uncertain.[61] It does appear, however, that he used a very narrow definition of reserves rather than the more conventional one used by the IMF which he would later head; as noted earlier, according to the IMF, France had considerably larger foreign exchange reserves – more than 100 billion francs – as of the end of 1982.[62] In any event, whether accurate assessment or misleading bluff, Camdessus' argument convinced Fabius; as he later said, 'I drew from this conversation the certitude that if we left the EMS, the expected advantages of the decision would lead us to an even greater *rigueur*, because the franc would collapse.'[63] 'I understood that leaving the monetary system was impossible.'[64]

Fabius immediately passed the information to Mitterrand, who asked Gaston Defferre, the Minister of the Interior and another partisan of the exit option, to check the figures. In meetings that day, the President pressed those who supported the decision to leave the EMS for guarantees about the size of the depreciation of the franc and the reputed adverse consequences of the policy. A few, such as Bérégovoy and Jean-Jacques Servan-Schreiber, held to the exit option. But others, when confronted with the Camdessus scenario, joined Fabius in agreeing with the opponents of the decision to leave the EMS.[65] Mitterrand accepted the advice – although with some reluctance, for by now he had convinced himself that the EMS posed enormous constraints on French policy:

We do not control our policy. In remaining in the EMS, we are in fact condemned to the policy of the dog that kills itself swimming in the current. Only for the profit of Germany.[66]

Despite his misgivings, Mitterrand agreed to keep the franc in the EMS and endorsed the plan of Delors and Mauroy to seek, for the third time, a negotiated devaluation of the franc – although he retained the exit option as a bargaining chip in those negotiations. That evening, he asked Delors to investigate the possibility of another negotiated realignment of exchange rates within the EMS. Delors immediately contacted the German Minister of Finance, Gerhard Stoltenberg and invited him to Paris to discuss a realignment in the values of the two currencies.

Travelling incognito, Stoltenberg arrived in Paris the next day. He offered a 5 per cent revaluation of the mark without a franc devaluation. But Mitterrand had told Delors to negotiate a realignment of the two currencies in the range of 10 per cent, with most of that coming from a revaluation of the mark, since, the President said, the source of the problem was the mark's undervaluation.[67] The negotiations continued into the evening, over dinner in Saint-Cloud. But they failed to produce an agreement and Stoltenberg returned to Bonn.[68]

The conversation between Delors and Stoltenberg resumed in Brussels two days later, when the ministers of finance of the EC met, at France's request, to negotiate a multi-currency realignment in the EMS. Delors approached the negotiation with a target adjustment in the value of the mark and franc of 10 per cent or thereabouts, most of which – 8 or 9 per cent – would result from a revaluation of the mark.[69] The Germans offered to revalue by 6 per cent, provided France devalue by 2 per cent and provided, also, that the fluctuation bands of the ERM be increased from 2.25 per cent in either direction to 4 per cent – all of which would result in an effective adjustment between the two of 8 per cent and possibly as much as 12 per cent.[70] After two days of negotiation, the ministers decided to keep the ERM's bands of 2.25 per cent and agreed on a total adjustment between the mark and the franc of 8 per cent. The mark was revalued by 5.5 per cent and the franc was devalued by 2.5 per cent.[71]

To an even greater degree in the previous June, the decision to opt for a negotiated devaluation within the EMS also represented a decision to opt for fiscal and monetary restraint. And as was the case in 1982, the restraint was, to a considerable degree, imposed on France by its negotiating partners – chiefly Germany – as the price for revaluing their own currencies. Thus, in the realignment negotiations, Germany demanded 'supplementary guarantees' of fiscal restraint by France in exchange for revaluation of the mark.[72] In particular, the German negotiators insisted that France increase the social insurance contribution of wage earners, impose a compulsory loan on taxpayers and reduce expenditures by 20 billion francs. As Lagayette, the head of the Delors *cabinet* – and hardly a proponent of *l'autre politique* – said, "This is the soft version of the IMF, the mark zone.' To Bérégovoy, and undoubtedly to the others who advocated the exit option, the German conditions represented an 'unacceptable diktat'.[73] But at its next meeting after the devaluation, the Council of Ministers dutifully endorsed the programme of fiscal restraint demanded by the Germans, and the government turned from *rigueur* to full-fledged austerity.[74]

EXPLAINING FRENCH EXCHANGE RATE POLICY

Exchange rate policy in 1981–3, and the domestic macroeconomic consequences of that policy, set the course for the remainder of the Mitterrand presidency. The decisions in that domain of policy resulted in a shift during the first two years of the Mitterrand presidency to a tighter, contractionary fiscal and monetary policy that, in turn, contributed to a deceleration in inflation, a sustained period of low growth and an increase in unemployment (see Table 3.1). Yet because the rate of inflation in France, although dropping sharply, continued to exceed that in Germany, where it also dropped sharply, the still-overvalued franc became even *more* overvalued, relative to the mark. As it did, the trade deficit with Germany began to soar once more and that, in turn, forced the subsequent governments to adhere even more vigorously to the tight monetary and fiscal policy that had been adopted in the early 1980s. As a result, the rate of economic growth continued to stagnate, the level of unemployment remained in double digits for most of the next decade, and electoral support for the Socialists and their allies dropped precipitously.

Table 3.1   Inflation, Unemployment and Growth in France, 1979–86

	1979	1980	1981	1982	1983	1984	1985	1986
Rate of Inflation *(Annual % Change in Consumer Prices)*	10.8	13.3	13.4	11.8	9.6	7.4	5.8	2.5
Rate of Unemployment *(% of Total Labour Force)*	5.9	6.3	7.4	8.1	8.3	9.7	10.3	10.4
Rate of Economic Growth *(% Change in Constant-Price GDP)*	3.2	1.6	1.2	2.5	0.7	1.3	1.9	2.5

Source: Organization for Economic Co-operation and Development, *Economic Outlook 532, June 1993* (Paris: OECD, 1993), Tables R 1–15; and earlier volumes.

How are we to account for the 'regime-defining' decisions made in exchange rate policy in the early years of the Mitterrand presidency? Despite the *post hoc* conventional wisdom, those decisions were not inevitable and preordained, the inexorable consequence of 'international constraints'. The government *chose* to take the path it did. Therefore, to understand why it moved from a reflationary policy to one of *rigueur* and eventually outright austerity, one must understand why it made the choices it did in exchange rate policy – why, upon assuming office, it forsook devaluation altogether, and why, subsequently, it decided on three occasions to negotiate modest devaluations within the ERM that, because they did not fully redress the deterioration in France's external competitiveness, had to be accompanied by *rigueur* and austerity.

To a large extent, of course, these choices reflected the preferences, concerns, and anxieties of one man – François Mitterrand – since exchange rate policy was, in the final analysis, a presidential decision. That being the case, a complete understanding of them must await Mitterrand's memoirs – and perhaps more extensive analyses of the presidential psyche than are now available. But however important such personalistic factors were in shaping those decisions, other factors appear to have contributed to the policy by shaping the context within which presidential decision-making occurred. Four, in particular, seem to have been important in shaping that context: the weakness of French labour and its marginality – despite the partisan composition of the government – in the debate over exchange rate policy; the weakness and lack of political influence of the French export sector and its absence from that debate; the public ownership and control of the financial sector and the representation of its interests in the debate; and the powerful, authoritative role within the dense network of policy advisers to the President, Prime Minister, and Minister of Finance of officials of the *Trésor*.

Perhaps the most striking feature of the two-year debate over exchange rate policy is the extent to which, in a government dominated by the Socialist Party that, moreover, included several Communist ministers, the voice of organised labour – a voice that might have argued for the alternative policy of continued reflation, high growth, full employment and an early and large devaluation or exit from the EMS – was virtually silent. One reason for that silence was the legendary weakness of the French labour movement. French labour was then (and is now even more so) largely unorganized and the organized minority was divided among several federations that were affiliated, in varying degrees, with different parties or were non-aligned.[75] Moreover, while organized (and unorganized) labour represented an important component of the Socialist electorate, it was only one of several components and, indeed, as the party enjoyed electoral success in the 1970s and became increasingly heterogeneous in its social composition, the importance of labour within the party diminished. Thus, the Socialist Party, and the government it formed in 1981, was not the exclusive agent of organized labour, the interests it espoused were not exclusively those of organized labour, and organized labour itself was fragmented and representative of only a small portion of the labour force.

The marginality of labour in the Socialist-dominated government was accentuated by the position of the Communist Party. Because the PS unexpectedly won a secure majority of the seats in the *Assemblée*, the bargaining power in the government of the Communist Party and its allied labour confederation (the CGT) was greatly diminished relative to expectations before the election. While they were not needed for the parliamentary majority, the Communists received four ministries – undoubtedly to assure the party's co-operation with the government. But they were relegated to minor ministries and played no significant role in the debate over economic policy.[76]

The organizational weakness of French labour, coupled with its subordinate role in the Socialist Party and the marginality of the Communist Party in the Socialist-dominated government, allowed the government a greater degree of autonomy from organized labour than has typically been the case for Social Democratic or Labour-dominated governments in Europe. The government did, of course, institute progressive reforms in such domains as social assistance, industrial relations and employment that, to a greater or lesser degree, served the interests of organized labour. But transcending as it did the particularistic interests of organized labour, the government was not confined to the satisfaction of those interests and was free to pursue a course that was at once more radical and more conservative than the one typically pursued by European Social Democratic governments. Thus, while it enacted some policies long since abandoned by most if not all European Social Democratic and Labour governments – for example, expansion of public ownership and the imposition of a wealth tax – it simultaneously pursued other policies – most notably, in the domains of exchange rate and macroeconomic policy – that were more orthodox and conservative and less 'labourist' than those typically implemented by other leftist governments.[77]

No less striking than the lack of influence of organized labour in exchange rate policy in France in the early 1980s was the absence – with one notable exception – of any significant advocacy by industry of a large devaluation or a float of the franc as a means of promoting exports. One might anticipate that the export-oriented portion of the business community, recognizing the adverse consequences of *over*valuation, would have been a vocal advocate of devaluation or even withdrawal of the franc from the ERM. Yet throughout the long-running debate over exchange policy, few voices were heard from the export sector in favour of either a large devaluation or a float as a means of increasing exports. Jean Riboud, the head of Schlumberger – a company that produces oil-drilling equipment and sells most of its production outside France – *was* one of the more frequent *visiteurs du soir* and was a strong proponent throughout the debate over exchange rate policy of *l'autre politique*. But he was the exception rather than the rule, and his prominence seems to have derived from his long and close friendship with the President rather than as a spokesman for the export sector. Whether because it was poorly organized, subsumed within a business peak association (the *Patronat*) that was outspoken in its hostility to the Socialist government, or more concerned with controlling inflation and moderating wages than promoting exports (and thus sympathetic to the contractionary policy advocated by Mauroy and Delors), the export sector appears to have had little influence in the debate over exchange rate policy.

In marked contrast to the near-invisibility of export-oriented industry, the interests of the financial sector were kept at the fore throughout the debate over exchange rate policy. Indeed, if one were to judge by the results of policy, the financial sector would appear to have been its primary beneficiary. Thus, while the currency was devalued, the devaluations were modest. Interest rates were kept at high levels. Inflation was driven down by a contractionary macroeconomic policy. And membership in the ERM and the close tie of the franc to the mark were retained. That the financial sector's interests were reflected in policy was not simply the product of its size relative to the export sector. Rather, it was a reflection of the sector's organizational and institutional attributes – most notably, the fact that most of it was owned (even before the 1982 nationalizations) by the state and controlled by the Ministry of Finance. Control over the state-owned portion of the sector by the ministry not only further enhanced its extraordinary power relative to the other ministries but also assured that the sector's interests were incorporated into policy making – indeed, that they were presented as the interests of the ministry itself.

It is, of course, conceivable that if the Minister of Finance had not been as fervent a defender of the value of the franc as Delors was, and as committed to the policy of modest devaluations negotiated within the ERM and accompanied by *rigueur*, the apparent influence of the financial sector on exchange rate policy might have been muted. On the other hand, the exchange rate policy pursued later when Bérégovoy was minister suggests the limits of ministerial voluntarism and, conversely, the power of the ministry in assuring that its institutional interests are manifest in policy. Although Bérégovoy was one of the leading proponents of leaving the EMS, and although he continued to believe, after March 1983, that the exit option might have been viable at various times in the first two years of the Mitterrand presidency, when he served as Minister of Finance in 1984–6 and 1988–92, France pursued a policy of a strong franc, the *franc fort*, that maintained the existing franc–mark parity, despite the difference in French and German inflation rates and overvaluation of the franc during much of that time.[78]

Another facet of the institutional context within which decisions about exchange rate policy were made involved the role of the finance ministry's *Direction du Trésor*.[79] As the Socialist government debated and defined its exchange rate policy in its first years in office, a dense network of officials in the *cabinets* of the President, the Prime Minister and the Minister of Finance played an important advisory role. Within this network, officials of the *Trésor* were especially influential – even authoritative – regarding the definition of feasible, and unfeasible, policy. Thus, such individuals as Lebègue, a *trésorien* attached to Mauroy's office, Guigou, another official of the *Trésor* assigned to the *Elysée* as an advisor on international monetary affairs, and, of course, Haberer and Camdessus, the directors, figure prominently in the exchange rate decisions of 1981–3. Not only were officials of the *Trésor* located throughout the dense network that provided data and advice to the Prime Minister, Minister of Finance, and President. They appear to have brought a common perspective to the debate over exchange rate policy – most notably, a commitment to the value of the franc, an opposition to devaluation, and a visceral hostility to currency speculators. Thus, in his study of the *Trésor* – which he calls a 'power machine' – Mamou quotes two heads of the office in charge of balance of payments and currency markets (office G1): 'We are all very attached to the defence of the franc. That is the true spirit of the place,' says one. And according to another, 'From the moment one arrives at the *Trésor* until one leaves, we are certain that our most important instruction, whoever the minister, is to defend the franc.'[80] Given the role of *Trésor* officials in the debate over exchange rate policy and the views they brought to it, and the finance ministry's power and its internalization of the interests of the finance sector, juxtaposed against the political weakness of organized labour and the export sector, it is perhaps not surprising that in the end, and against his better instincts, Mitterrand was persuaded to keep the franc in the EMS, negotiate a series of modest devaluations, and impose an increasingly contractionary macroeconomic policy.

CONCLUSION

Less than one year after Mitterrand's triumph in the 1981 presidential election, the Socialist-dominated government shifted from an expansionary macroeconomic policy to one that was more contractionary and marked by fiscal and monetary restraint. Within two years, in the wake of the third negotiated devaluation of the franc, *rigueur* had given way to full-fledged austerity that set the parameters for subsequent policy during the remainder of the Mitterrand presidency. This chapter has examined the process by which the Socialist government in France adopted an increasingly conservative macroeconomic policy and why, in particular, it shifted to such a policy so early in its life, at a time when its political, electoral and institutional resources were still intact.

We have argued that, contrary to the conventional wisdom, the Socialist-dominated government *did* have a choice regarding economic policy and that it exercised that choice on several occasions in the early years of the Mitterrand presidency. The essential choices about domestic macroeconomic policy were made, we argued, in the domain of exchange rate policy. They involved a series of decisions about whether the franc should remain in the EMS, or be withdrawn, and, if remaining, whether, when, and by how much it should be devalued. The choice boiled down to one between an orthodox response espoused by Delors, Mauroy and their economic advisers, on one hand, and *l' autre politique* espoused by Bérégovoy, Chevènement, Fabius and others, on the other hand. The former involved keeping the franc in the EMS, negotiating modest devaluations of the franc and instituting *rigueur* and austerity. The latter involved withdrawing the franc from the EMS and letting it float, or at least enacting a large devaluation, and instituting an import-competing and export-oriented industrial policy.

The story told here is about how the proponents of the orthodox policy alternative defeated the advocates of *l'autre politique*. It revolves around the decision not to adjust the value of the franc when the Socialist government first took office and the subsequent decisions, taken on three occasions in the government's first two years in office, to negotiate modest devaluations of the franc within the EMS. In failing to negotiate a devaluation immediately upon entering office (as its Gaullist predecessors had done on two occasions, and as Mitterrand later recognized he should have insisted upon), in failing later to negotiate devaluations large enough to eliminate the cumulative inflation differential with Germany, and, ultimately, in failing to leave the EMS (at least temporarily) the government consigned itself to remaining in the EMS with an overvalued currency. In so doing, it consigned itself to the pursuit of an orthodox deflationary policy marked by fiscal restraint and tight money that inevitably resulted, over time, in low growth and high and rising unemployment. As the government abandoned its initial commitments and objectives in favor of such eminently conservative goals as price stability, external balance and a strong currency, French voters on the left could be excused for their growing disenchantment with the Socialists and their allies.

Especially in the early phase of the Mitterrand presidency – in particular, in mid-1981, before the accumulation of a large amount of external debt and the draining of reserves that occurred in 1982 and 1983 and at a time when the economic problems could reasonably be attributed to its predecessor – the government could have addressed the problem of an overvalued franc either by a substantial devaluation of the franc within the EMS or by an exit from the EMS and float of the franc. In retrospect, the decision not to follow either of those strategies at a time when many 'responsible' individuals – Giscard, Barre, Haberer, Renaud and Rocard among others – thought devaluation appropriate and, indeed, inevitable was perhaps *the* lost opportunity of the Mitterrand presidency.

To say that the window of opportunity for an aggressive exchange rate policy was wide open in May and June 1981, and that it remained open for some time thereafter, is not to deny that it slowly closed as time went by, as the external debt increased and reserves flowed out. Nor is that to say that 'the other policy' would have worked as its proponents claimed, and that it would not have produced the dire consequences forecast by its opponents. Nevertheless, as with the issue of devaluation, the plausibility of *l'autre politique* as a 'feasible' alternative depended to a considerable extent on timing. Notwithstanding the possibility that the famous Fabius–Camdessus interchange of 16 March 1983 may have underestimated the country's foreign exchange reserves and exaggerated the danger associated with floating the franc, the probability that the 'other policy' could be implemented successfully in fact may have been lower in March 1983 than it was

78   *Exchange Rate Politics in France*

in the autumn of 1982, just as it may have been lower in the autumn of 1982 than it was in mid-1981. On the other hand, in light of the possible exaggerations that may have found their way into the various worst-case scenarios of Attali, Delors, Camdessus, Guigou, and others in the *Elysée*, *Rivoli*, and the *Matignon* as they mobilized against *l'autre politique* in early 1983, that alternative may have been more feasible than was assumed at the time. Certainly, several of its better-informed proponents thought so; for example, looking back on the period, Bérégovoy (who by then had considerable experience as Minister of Economy and Finance) said:

> The franc would have floated, it would have dropped, then it would have straightened itself out . . . Once that had happened, it would have been able to rejoin the EMS. I remain persuaded that rather than having to accept a discipline imposed from the outside, we would have been able to find within ourselves the strength needed to discipline ourselves.[81]

And in the same vein, he told another interviewer:

> I am not European; . . . I believe in my country, because geography does not change . . . To leave the EMS in 1983 was like 1940 – a time to bind our energies together . . . the easy solution in March, 1983 was to remain in the EMS.[82]

We will, of course, never know. Mitterrand – faced with the dire predictions of Delors, Attali, Guigou, Bianco, Camdessus and others, the firm opposition of Mauroy, the vacillation of Fabius and the vague and imprecise nature of the proposals put forward by the adherents of *l'autre politique* – pulled back at the last moment from what appeared to be, increasingly, *une aventure* and opted for orthodoxy – for keeping the franc in the EMS, negotiating yet another modest devaluation and implementing the progressively more contractionary economic policy that accompanied such devaluations. And in so doing, he set the course for the remainder of his presidency.

Notes

1. For helpful comments and suggestions, I wish to thank Suzanne Berger, Anthony Daley, Serge Halimi, Peter Hall, Mark Harmon, Chris Howell, Cynthia Horan, Denis Lacorne, George Ross and Martin Schain.
2. The One Hundred and Ten Propositions were drawn up after Mitterrand was officially declared the candidate of the *Parti Socialiste* at its Congress of January 1981. For the most part, they restate positions developed by the PS after its 1979 Congress at Metz. See *Projet socialiste pour la France des années 80* (Paris: Club Socialiste du Livre, 1980).

3. In the 1981 elections for the *Assemblée*, the PS won 37.5 per cent of the vote and a large majority of seats. In 1986, it won 31.6 per cent of the vote and lost its majority to a conservative coalition of the neo-Gaullist *Rassemblement pour la République* and the *Union pour la Démocratie Française*. In the 1988 legislative election, immediately after Mitterrand won re-election, the PS won 35.9 per cent of the vote but failed to win a majority of seats in the *Assemblée*. In March 1993, it won only 18 per cent of the vote, and in the 1994 European election, it won 14.5 per cent of the vote.

4. For discussions of the Mitterrand presidency, and the economic policies pursued by it, see, among many, Philippe Bauchard, *La Guerre des deux roses: Du Rêve à la réalité 1981–1985* (Paris: Bernard Grasset, 1986); D. S. Bell and Byron Criddle, *The French Socialist Party: The Emergence of a Party of Government* 2nd ed. (Oxford: Clarendon, 1988); David R. Cameron, 'The Colors of a Rose: On the Ambiguous Record of French Socialism', *Center for European Studies Working Paper Series*, Harvard University, 1988; Philip G. Cerny and Martin A. Schain, eds., *Socialism, the State and Public Policy in France* (New York: Methuen, 1985); Stéphane Denis, *La Leçon d'automne: Jeux et enjeux de François Mitterrand* (Paris: Albin Michel, 1983); Pierre Favier and Michel Martin-Roland, *La Décennie Mitterrand: 1. Les ruptures (1981–1984)* (Paris: Seuil, 1990); Alain Fonteneau and Pierre-Alain Muet, *La Gauche face à la crise* (Paris: Fondation Nationale des Sciences Politiques, 1985); Peter A. Hall, *Governing the Economy: The Politics of State Intervention in Britain and France* (New York: Oxford, 1986), ch. 8; Hall, 'The Evolution of Economic Policy under Mitterrand', in George Ross, Stanley Hoffmann, and Sylvia Malzacher, eds., *The Mitterrand Experiment* (New York: Oxford, 1987); Serge July, *Les années Mitterrand: Histoire baroque d'une normalisation inachevée* (Paris: Grasset, 1986); Michael Loriaux, *France After Hegemony: International Change and Financial Reform* (Ithaca: Cornell, 1991), Ch. 8; and Marie-Paule Virard, *Comment Mitterrand a découvert l'économie* (Paris: Albin Michel, 1993).

5. Favier and Martin-Roland, pp. 401 and 424, identify the '*tournant décisif*' or '*tournant majeur*' as having occurred in June 1982. Virard, p. 51, identifies the same moment as the '*grand tournant*' of the presidency. For a useful comparative analysis of major turning points in the policies of governments, see Organisation for Economic Co-operation and Development, *Why Economic Policies Change: Eleven Case Studies* (Paris: OECD, 1988).

6. Hall, 'The Evolution of Economic Policy', pp. 63–4.

7. Bell and Criddle, p. 162.

8. Loriaux, pp. 229, 231.

9. The European Monetary System (henceforth EMS) had come into being in March 1979 as the successor to the ill-fated 'snake' that had been created in April 1972. All currencies in it (except the Italian lira) were to fluctuate within a range of 2.25 per cent in either direction from their predetermined central rate with each other currency. Currencies that could not be maintained within that range were to be realigned in negotiations conducted by the Monetary Committee of the EC and/or the Ministers of Finance. For the definitive account of the creation of the EMS, see Peter Ludlow, *The Making of the European Monetary System: A Case Study of the Politics of the European Community* (London: Butterworth, 1982).

10. No currency had ever been withdrawn from the ERM prior to September 1992. In that month, both the British pound and Italian lira were withdrawn. See David R. Cameron, 'British Exit, German Voice, French Loyalty: Cooperation, Defection, and Domination in the 1992–93 ERM Crisis', presented at the Annual Meeting of the American Political Science Association, Washington, D.C., September 1993.

11. Data are reported in *International Financial Statistics Yearbook 1991* (Washington, D.C.: International Monetary Fund, 1991), pp. 117, 154, 138–44; and in *OECD Economic Outlook 58* (Paris: OECD, 1991), Table R18, p. 208.
12. See Serge Halimi, *Sisyphus is Tired: The French Left and the Exercise of Power, 1924–1986*, Ph.D. dissertation (University of California, Berkeley, 1990) p. 626.
13. See Bauchard, pp. 13–5.
14. Favier and Martin-Roland, p. 60.
15. See Virard, pp. 25–8.
16. *Ibid.* p. 28.
17. Bauchard, pp. 9, 27; Favier and Martin-Roland, p. 50.
18. In discussing his government's exchange rate policy, Mauroy notes that the franc was devalued by 17.5 per cent in December 1958 and by 11 per cent in August 1969. See Pierre Mauroy, *A Gauche* (Paris: Albin Michel, 1985) p. 99.
19. Denis, p. 13.
20. *Ibid.* p. 14. Lebègue soon became an adviser to Mauroy. In mid-1984, he replaced Michel Camdessus (who had succeeded Haberer in February, 1982) as director of the *Trésor* when Camdessus was appointed Governor of the *Banque de France*.
21. See Thierry Pfister, *La Vie quotidienne à Matignon au temps de l'union de la gauche* (Paris: Hachette, 1985) p. 246. Pfister served as a counsellor to Pierre Mauroy in the office of the Prime Minister. See, also, Favier and Martin-Roland, p. 60.
22. Favier and Martin-Roland, p. 57.
23. Pierre Mauroy, *C'est Ici le Chemin* (Paris: Flammarion, 1982) p. 19.
24. The first phrase is reported in Pfister, p. 246, the second in Bauchard, p. 10, and the third in Virard, p. 30.
25. See Favier and Martin-Roland, p. 60; and Pfister, p. 247.
26. On the *Cartel des Gauches* (1924–26) and the *Front Populaire* (1936–38), see Halimi.
27. See Denis, pp. 14–6.
28. Pfister, p. 242.
29. Note, for example, Pfister's confusion over what a float entailed. Obviously, a float – as opposed to a devaluation to a new exchange rate vis-à-vis other currencies – would not require the *Banque* to intervene and spend reserves, since, by definition, a floor for the currency would not exist.
30. Quoted in July, p. 110.
31. Quoted in Denis, p. 15.
32. Bauchard, p. 33.
33. In 1979, the French rate of inflation was 10.8 and the German rate was 4.1, of which 2.0 was offset by the revaluation of the mark in September. In 1980, the rates were, respectively, 13.3 per cent and 5.4 per cent, and in 1981, they were 13.4 per cent and 6.3 per cent.
34. See Denis, p. 41; and Bauchard, p. 55.
35. The Committee consisted of the deputy governors of the central banks and deputy ministers of finance of the member countries of the European Community.
36. On Delors' position and attitudes toward the negotiations, see Bauchard, p. 56.
37. Bauchard, p. 57.
38. See Favier and Martin-Roland, pp. 406–7.
39. *Ibid.* p. 414.
40. See Favier and Martin-Roland, pp. 412–6; and Bauchard, pp. 88–90.
41. See Bauchard, pp. 91, 100.
42. *Ibid.* p. 416.
43. *Ibid.* p. 426.

44. Bauchard, p. 102.
45. Favier and Martin-Roland, pp. 428–9.
46. *Ibid.* p. 444, 451. The IMF's data reveal considerably larger reserves in 1982 – a year-ending balance of slightly more than 100 billion francs, of which 96 billion was in foreign exchange, as well as another 240 billion francs (by national valuation) in gold. See International Monetary Fund, *International Financial Statistics Yearbook, 1991* (Washington, D.C.: IMF, 1991), pp. 371–3.
47. Bauchard, p. 124; Favier and Martin-Roland, p. 444.
48. *Ibid.* p. 450–51.
49. July, p. 85. On Mitterrand's views, expressed to Mauroy, see *Ibid.* p. 120, and Pfister, pp. 255–6.
50. Bauchard, p. 120. The term *visiteurs du soir*, taken from the title of a 1940s film by René Clair, was coined by Mauroy in reference to those he saw waiting to see Mitterrand in the late afternoon as he was leaving the President's office. To Mauroy, it appeared that 'during the day, Mitterrand worked with a government which followed the policy decided in June, 1982. But during the evening, he received a concubine which proposed to him a completely different policy.' Quoted in Favier and Martin-Roland, p. 441.
51. *Ibid.* p. 442.
52. *Ibid.* p. 451.
53. *Ibid.* p. 461.
54. On the timing of Mitterrand's decision, see July, pp. 88, 90, 94–5. In his diary for 13 March, Attali noted that Mitterrand told him that day that it was necessary to leave the EMS. See Favier and Martin-Roland, p. 466.
55. See *Ibid.* pp. 86–7, and Bauchard, pp. 140–1, 143.
56. Favier and Martin-Roland, p. 468.
57. Favier and Martin-Roland, p. 468. According to these authors, after the Bianco visit, Kohl pressured the German Minister of Finance and the Bundesbank to accept a large revaluation of the mark for the sake of solidarity with the French.
58. *Ibid.* p. 469.
59. See Pfister, pp. 257–65. Also, July, pp. 90–5; Bauchard, pp. 141–2; and Favier and Martin-Roland, pp. 467–9.
60. On the Fabius-Camdessus conversation, see Favier and Martin-Roland, pp. 471.
61. One adviser to an anti-EMS minister said of the 16 March exchange, 'Camdessus a bluffé Fabius. C'est ça. Il l'a bluffé.' Personal interview, Paris, June, 1988. Favier and Martin-Roland, p. 469, use the same term (le bluff) as the subtitle of their account of the events of that day.
62. See IMF. We might note, also, the surprising suggestion in Camdessus' conversation – especially surprising given his later role as Managing Director of the IMF – that reserves would have been required in order to defend a floating franc. In fact, of course, floating the currency meant precisely that the government would *not* have to defend the franc, unless it wished for some reason to defend a particular rate.
63. Favier and Martin-Roland, p. 471.
64. Bauchard, pp. 144–5.
65. See July, pp. 95–6. Another proponent of the exit option, Chevènement, had secretly resigned his portfolio as Minister of Industry in February, after several heads of state-owned enterprises took their complaints about his intrusions to Mitterrand, who ordered him to desist. The resignation was held by Mitterrand until after the municipal elections and the announcement of a new government, but undoubtedly diminished his influence on the issue.
66. *Ibid.* p. 96.
67. Bauchard, pp. 145–6.

82   *Exchange Rate Politics in France*

. On the Stoltenberg visit, see Favier and Martin-Roland, p. 472.
69. *Ibid.* p. 474.
70. July, pp. 96–7.
71. In addition, the Dutch, Danish and Belgian currencies were revalued – the guilder by 3.5 per cent, the krone by 2.5 per cent, and the franc by 1.5 per cent – and the Italian lira and Irish punt were devalued – by 2.5 per cent and 3.5 per cent, respectively.
72. Bauchard, pp. 145–7.
73. July, p. 97.
74. The only significant change from the terms stipulated by the German negotiators was the substitution of a proportional 1 per cent surtax on incomes in place of the increase in the social insurance contribution by wage earners after Bérégovoy, the Minister for Social Affairs, vigorously opposed the latter.
75. On the French labour movement, see, among many, Anthony Daley, *State, Steel, and Labor: Mobilization and Adjustment in France* (Pittsburgh: University of Pittsburgh Press, 1995) and Chris Howell, *Regulating Labor* (Princeton: Princeton University Press, 1992).
76. The PCF's participation in the government in these circumstances undoubtedly contributed to the subsequent electoral decline it experienced. Perhaps recognizing as much, the PCF quit the government in 1984, when Fabius replaced Mauroy in the *Matignon.*
77. Compare, for example, the Mauroy government's exchange rate policy with those pursued by the British Labour government in 1979 and the Swedish Social Democratic government in 1982. In Britain, James Callaghan, the Prime Minister, decided not to join the Exchange Rate Mechanism of the EMS (despite the fact that he had participated in its design) because he feared its likely consequences for interest rates, employment and electoral support for the Labour Party in the next election. In Sweden, the first measure enacted by Olaf Palme's government, upon its return to power, was a 15 per cent devaluation of the krona – despite the fact that the non-socialist government had devalued the currency by 10 per cent the previous year. The two devaluations fuelled an export boom that contributed to a marked reduction of unemployment in the mid-1980s.
78. See David R. Cameron, 'From Barre to Balladur: Economic Policy in the Era of the EMS', in Gregory Flynn, ed., *Remaking the Hexagon: The New France in the New Europe* (Boulder: Westview, 1995), ch. 7.
79. On the role of the *Trésor*, see, among others, Philippe Jurgensen and Daniel Lebègue, *Le Trésor et la politique financière* (Paris: Montchrestien, 1988); Yves Mamou, *Une Machine de pouvoir: La Direction du Trésor* (Paris: La Découverte, 1988); and Alain Prate, *La France et sa monnaie: Essais sur les relations entre la Banque de France et les gouvernements* (Paris: Juillard, 1987).
80. *Ibid.* pp. 33–4.
81. Favier and Martin-Roland, p. 489.
82. Quoted in Denis, pp. 137–9.

4 Less Exceptionalism than Meets the Eye
Serge Halimi

In 1988, a few weeks after the re-election of President François Mitterrand, three prominent French authors heralded the 'Republic of the Centre' and announced 'The End of the French Exception'.[1] A year later, Paris celebrated the bicentennial of the fall of the Bastille amid a gathering of world aristocrats – the heads of delegations of the Group of Seven industrial nations (G-7). Mitterrand, the triumphant leader of the French Left, a movement whose symbolic birth coincided with the victory of the *sans-culottes*, had invited George Bush, Helmut Kohl and Margaret Thatcher to join him in burying the 200-year-old corpse called the Revolution.

The symbolism of such a paradox has encouraged many observers to decree that after 1981 the French Left achieved its most remarkable turnaround, its most final break with an old discourse made only of sound and fury that signifies nothing. The break is indeed remarkable. But is it unique, and will it be permanent? Before we freeze history into an 'end' called 'modernity', before we decree that the French Left has 'finally' understood that it can do little more but manage a capitalist economy without altering its course and challenging its principles, we may need to turn to history and see whether or not the *Mitterrand Experiment* was as exceptional as we have been led to believe.[2] In other words, did Mitterrand modernize the French Left by 'normalizing' it along Anglo-American lines once and for all?[3] Or did he instead repeat its very old mistakes?

The clash between progressive discourse in the opposition and conservative practice in government is such a recurrent phenomenon for the French Left and has affected so many issues that it is difficult to isolate one area of analysis. This chapter will focus on the unglamorous subject of monetary policies, for one reason: the French Left usually blames its lack of leftist priorities in government on economic constraints it could neither surmount nor ignore. But how serious were these constraints?

Every time the Left came to power, it faced a mediocre economic legacy at best. For a change in a coalition advocating change, the difficulty is almost inevitable: it is unlikely to be called to office when the incumbent administration presides over peace and prosperity; when it takes over in a relatively unfavourable context, its ability to fulfill its progressive mandate is drastically compromised. In 1924 Edouard Herriot, the head of the *Cartel des Gauches* (the electoral alliances forged between Socialists and Radicals), had to liquidate the financial legacy of

World War I. In 1936 the leader of the Popular Front, Léon Blum, had to reverse the deflationary policies enacted by Pierre Laval in the wake of the Great Depression and prepare the country for war. In 1944, the Left faced a 'legacy of ruins', a country that was 'decimated, torn apart and surrounded by malicious neighbours.'[4] Lastly, in 1981 Mitterrand came to the Elysée bemoaning his 'disastrous legacy' – a high inflation rate and a quadrupling of unemployment over the previous seven years. This brings to mind La Fontaine's fable of a left-cicada and a rightant. Financial disaster, economic depression, collaboration with the enemy, massive unemployment – with ants like these, what could a cicada squander?

As far as the monetary policies are concerned, three cases are striking by their similarity: 1924, 1936 and 1981. Each time, the Left in power had to address the same constraint: an overvalued currency. Each time, it failed to do so. Each time, the failure (or the choice) has been explained in very similar terms. Here, incidentally, one can be reminded of Karl Marx, and not only because of his comment (spurred by the French case) on history repeating itself from tragedy to farce. In his introduction to Marx's book on the Paris Commune, *The Civil War in France*, Friedrich Engels wrote of 'the holy respect with which [the Communards] stopped before the gates of the Banque de France.'[5] Little would change until (tragedy? farce?) the 'holy respect' before the gates became the widespread corruption with the contents these gates protected.[6]

In 1924, the problem was debt. A huge fraction of it had been subscribed during World War I (to pay the cost of 'victory') and the amount, far from being whittled down after the war, had kept increasing to cover the cost of reconstruction. When Herriot was appointed to Matignon, the national debt, much of it short-term, amounted to 335 billion francs. With annual fiscal receipts of 30 billion francs, France had to pay war pensions of 4.2 billion francs, interest payments of 12 billion francs and refinance 150 billion francs in short term debt by issuing new bonds. Should a significant fraction of the bondholders have asked to be repaid, the country would have spiralled into financial chaos. Originally, the state tolerated this extraordinary constraint – 'the daily plebiscite of the bondholders', it was called at the time – but expected it would not last: German reparations (initially set by the French at 230 billion francs) would easily have solved any potential crisis of confidence. By 1924, however, the hope that Germany would pay had been shattered by Germany's monetary disintegration and by the meagre returns of Raymond Poincaré's show of force in the Ruhr (occupied by French troops in January 1923).

If he had the will, Herriot would have been in a position to build a new policy on the ashes of the old one. Having just vanquished the Right at the polls in the wake of a particularly acrimonious campaign, he could have reversed its failed strategy and acknowledged the futility of its past expectations. Then, as would be the case later, the 'wall of money' (an expression Herriot coined) had to be broken by a devaluation of the currency, which would automatically have brought down the real amount of the national debt. As Pierre de Mouy, the director of the

Mouvement Général des Fonds (today's Treasury) wrote to Herriot: 'One cannot refuse to take into account the fact that Germany's failure to pay, with the consequences which this entails for the balance of our budget, constitutes a legitimate motive to revise the commitments the Treasury has made [to limit its borrowing from the Banque de France], commitments that were based upon the obligations subscribed by Germany.'[7]

Unless he chose to stay the course taken by the Right, Herriot was faced with three options: higher taxes, more debt leading to more inflation and devaluation. In the wake of an election victory owed in part to a denunciation of Poincaré's 20 per cent regressive tax increases, Herriot could seek the revenue he needed through a tax on capital, which incidentally belonged in the programme of the Radical Party. In his memoirs, Herriot would write: 'In 1920, I had stated that we should not fear the prospect of a tax on capital. . . . In Britain, it had been initiated by the Conservative Party. . . . But I am coming to think that, in matters of money, France might well be the most reactionary country in the world.'[8] This stress on collective psychology should not, however, conceal the fact that Herriot would propose the tax on capital only a few days before his cabinet was overthrown, at a time when his government's fate had already been sealed.

The second option before the *Cartel des Gauches* would have been to raise the amount of money the state could borrow from the *Banque de France*. In 1924, this amount was set by law (to reassure bondholders about monetary stability), and the *Banque de France* operated as a semiprivate financial institution. When Herriot arrived at Matignon, the state's legal ceiling with the bank had been reached and the Radical leader had no financial operating space. To be sure, lifting this ceiling (as Treasury director de Mouy recommended) would have been perceived as inflationary, but a country faced with huge debts has worries beyond a dose of inflation, which anyway could reduce its debt. Herriot chose not to follow de Mouy's advice despite the fact that the latter's non-socialist credentials were impeccable. The Radical leader feared that a round of inflation might threaten the value of the franc.

A currency devaluation was the third option before the *Cartel des Gauches*, one whose necessity appears almost beyond discussion. Officially, the value of the 1924 franc was exactly what it had been in 1914 – which was also its value in 1804. In reality, the value had gone down significantly after the outbreak of World War I, but this decline was deemed temporary: the return to the parity of 1804 was proclaimed to be a paramount national obligation. The currency had therefore become a fetish. A strong franc bespoke as strong a France as existed in the year Napoleon crowned himself emperor. Although a devaluation would have automatically cut down in real terms the debt owed to bondholders, at the time the idea seemed downright unpatriotic and the functional equivalent to a legal theft. Herriot – like Blum in June 1936 and Mitterrand in May 1981 – rejected such a move. It would be implemented by his conservative successor (who also happened to have been his predecessor). When in 1928 Poincaré devalued the franc down to one-fifth of its 1914 value, eliminating 80 per cent of the state's debt, he was called the saviour of the franc.

The lesson was lost on Blum in 1936. But this is surprising, given that the Socialist leader had not only witnessed the unfolding of Herriot's financial débâcle, he had also warned the leader of the *Cartel des Gauches* against the pitfalls of monetary orthodoxy: 'Too often, we have had to seek the forbearance of the banks, which have been free to refuse or make pay. A democratic government cannot accept this kind of servitude. It cannot go on living like this. From month to month, from week to week, the indispensable steps, acknowledged as such by the government, have been postponed.'[9]

When Blum became prime minister, his foremost problem was economic depression, not debt. The crisis of the 1930s had reached France later than the United States or Great Britain and, because of France's uneven industrialization, it had been less severe. Yet the deflationary policies of Pierre Laval and other conservatives had inflicted upon the country a 'great penance' of Malthusian economics meant to wring out what was perceived to be a problem of oversupply. To his credit, Blum understood the crisis in Keynesian terms and sought to stimulate production through deficit spending and higher wages: 'This crisis was caused by a breakdown of the balance between production and the general ability to buy. . . . The deflation worsens the crisis, it slows down production and it decreases the yield of taxes.'[10] But what represented a good analytical start was partly negated by a reckless pledge Blum had made during the campaign: 'Neither deflation, nor devaluation.'

Keeping that pledge meant that the stimulus of rising demand would be contradicted by an overvalued currency, especially in a setting of free trade. But breaking that pledge would diminish the Left's political standing and its economic credibility. Kept between May and October 1936, the pledge would then be broken twice – first in October 1936, then in July 1937. Here, one cannot help being struck by an analogy between the Popular Front and the Mitterrand years. Elected in May 1981, Mitterrand would contradict his reflationary strategy by refusing a devaluation and then consenting only to insufficient ones in October 1981 and June 1982. Moreover, in a parallel to the 1983 debate on '*l'autre politique*' (see Chapter 3), Blum was presented with the following choice a few days before he entered Matignon: either enact exchange controls, strict government supervision of the economy, autarky and authoritarianism, or open borders, the free trading of currencies and a coalition of democratic regimes. Who would have chosen the first option of this dilemma?

In 1981, the central challenge before the governing Left – slow growth and a weak industrial base – was somewhat different from that of 1924 (debt) and 1936 (depression). But since the Socialists had blamed the sharp increase in unemployment between 1974 and 1981 on monetarist policies that had sacrificed the 'industrial imperative', the value of the franc became a critical issue once again. The Socialist programme drafted in 1980 sought a reflation of the economy through public spending and simultaneously a 'reconquest of the domestic market' (without which the reflation might unleash a flow of imports).[11] This reconquest entailed investing in industry to make it competitive while putting an end to the *de facto* subsidy to imports an overvalued currency represented. As in 1936, reflation and devaluation were inseparable, but this time the Socialists knew that short of new monetary and trade policies, their whole economic strategy was doomed to fail. This understanding was explicitly acknowledged in their 1980 programme and had led them to denounce the European Monetary System (EMS).[12] Yet, the Left repeated the crucial mistake of failing to provide a speedy and significant monetary stimulus.

The fact that the monetary decision of 1981 would be essentially identical to the earlier ones is all the more remarkable in that its context was substantially different. In 1924, Herriot controlled neither a stable parliamentary majority nor the pace of monetary creation. In 1936, Blum became almost immediately distracted from a necessary devaluation by the social explosion of the June strikes and outbreak of the Spanish civil war. In 1981, in contrast, save for a predictable run on the franc, Mitterrand held three formidable assets neither Herriot nor Blum could have imagined: a parliamentary majority for the Socialist Party (PS), one of the strongest executives in the Western world and substantial control over the financial sector, through direct ownership of the largest banks and the public administration of credit. Why, then, did he repeat the mistakes of Herriot and Blum? Why was 1981 so unexceptional in this respect?

EXPLAINING THE LEFT'S UNEXCEPTIONALISM

Three reasons stand out to explain the recurrent monetary timidity of the Left: hope that a devaluation might be avoided, the temptation to display firmness by proving even more ruthless than the Right in implementing monetarist policies and the desire to see domestic economic strategy mesh with France's standing in a pro-Western diplomatic alliance.

When the Left came to power, the argument runs, it did not wish to ruin the celebratory mood by being the bearer of bad news. It hoped that the financial problem would work itself out without a devaluation. This mindset was most explicitly acknowledged in 1981, as shown in the memoirs of Pierre Mauroy, Mitterrand's first prime minister:

> 21 May 1981. I look at François Mitterrand saluting the crowd from a convertible car driving us to the Elysée.... Since 10 May [the day of Mitterrand's election], the franc has lost value and our currency reserves have diminished. A rapid decision must be made. Some, like Michel Rocard, favor . . . an immediate devaluation. Jacques Delors . . . on the other hand, wants us to defend our currency and its standing in the EMS. I share their analysis. The President, distrustful of those who seek monetary drama, judges that political common

sense dictates the answer: One does not salute the victory of the Left with a devaluation.[13]

Buoyed by unexpected electoral success, the President refused, therefore, to answer the crowd's salute with an immediate devaluation. He thus committed himself to sustaining the unsustainable – an overvalued parity of the franc within the EMS. Moreover, he gambled on a rapid American-led recovery that would have mitigated the need for a monetary drama he was loth to interpret. Lastly, Mitterrand was preparing to call for new parliamentary elections (to be held in June), and he did not want to shatter his state of grace before his party had won decisively. Yet when those elections were over, the governing Left still postponed the inevitable until October 1981. By then, the Right could claim that the devaluation was the cost – or the first instalment of it – for five months of financial mismanagement. Here, Mitterrand repeated the historic mistake of the Popular Front government.

Blum, however, was significantly more constrained than Mitterrand. Whereas Mitterrand would remain evasive on the subject of a currency adjustment, Blum had made 'Neither deflation, nor devaluation' a campaign pledge. In doing so, he was merely emulating the old Radical device of defining oneself by simultaneously rejecting contradictory choices without stating too precisely what one was standing for. Blum restated this pledge immediately after he assumed office: 'The country should neither expect nor fear from us that we might, some morning, cover the walls with the white [official] posters announcing a devaluation.'[14] How could Blum make this commitment despite the fact that 40 currencies, including sterling, had been devalued since the beginning of the Great Depression? Part of the answer is that he hoped that his economic policy might succeed painlessly: he anticipated that production would be stimulated by the reduction of unit costs triggered by increases in purchasing power and consumption, itself a result of the wage benefits won by the workers in June 1936. As Jean-Marcel Jeanneney summed it up in 1966, 'Léon Blum hoped that the economy would be pliable to his enthusiasm.'[15]

In 1924, Herriot, whose understanding of economic and financial affairs was sketchy at best, was pulled away from a devaluation by two hopes: that the *Banque de France* would co-operate in a short-term patching up and that Germany would contribute to a long-term solution by paying its war reparations imposed by the Treaty of Versailles. The co-operation of the *Banque de France* would have enabled the state to continue to borrow surreptitiously while pretending to abide by the legal ceiling placed on monetary creation. In other words, Herriot was prepared to break the law and thus provide his political foes at the *Banque de France* with the ammunition they could and would use against his government, rather than follow through on the recommendation of the director of the Treasury.[16] The naiveté and optimism of such a course of action are truly unbelievable: Herriot counted on the kindness of his opponents. He would also rely too much on the wealth of strangers. Yet when it came to the chimera of waiting for Germany's gold, the leader of the *Cartel des Gauches* was only one of many French politicians of the time seeking this painless remedy to their own financial mismanagement. By 1924, however, it had become clear that the political context (rise of nationalism across the Rhine) and the financial situation (collapse of the Reichmark) prevented the German government from doing anything more than agreeing to reschedule – and considering scaling down – its debt. It would rapidly become clear for Herriot, as it would for Blum and Mitterrand, that there would be no way around the monetary drama, no foreign economic saviour (be it Germany in 1924 or the United States in 1981), no painless cure (such as economic growth in 1936).

Another possible explanation for the recurrence of mistaken monetary choices is the 'guest-in-power' syndrome.[17] Simply stated, it is the ambition to prove oneself on the very terrain of the opposition. For the Left, this belief is translated into a policy firmness that means being even more ruthless than the Right when it comes to implementing orthodox economic policies. Conceived as merely a fluke in history, the victorious Left should therefore rearrange as modestly as possible an order of things it is managing only transitionally until it relinquishes control to the legitimate owners. It should act as the trustee of the Conservatives, watching over their silver in their short absence. At best, the Left can hope to improve upon what Mauroy called in 1982 its past 'record of longevity'. To succeed is thus to last in power. Regarding monetary matters, the result of that mindset is simple enough: suspected to be careless or ignorant, the Left will manage the currency even more prudently than the Right ever did.

In 1981, as he concurred with François Mitterrand to refuse monetary drama, Mauroy explained:

> The governor of the *Banque de France* appears sceptical about our ability to hold the parity of the franc. . . . I affirm our will to defend the franc. . . . The Left refuses monetary facility. . . . When he entered the Elysée [in 1974] Valéry Giscard d'Estaing had been unable to keep the franc within the European Monetary System. We meet that challenge. . . . My first decision is therefore to defend the currency, although, unlike our predecessors, we are not monetarists.[18]

So, here we have the absolute paradox of a victorious Left whose first decision is to 'meet that challenge' on the very monetarist terrain of the Conservatives and that seeks to be more successful there than they were themselves. Upon becoming president, both Charles de Gaulle in 1958 and Georges Pompidou in 1969 had devalued the franc (by 17 per cent in the first case and 12.5 per cent in the second); Giscard had allowed it to float twice (in 1974 and 1976) until it re-entered, at a lower rate, the European system of the day. The Left, on the other hand, chose to defend the currency although it was 'not monetarist'. It could only fail to defend the indefensible – three devaluations would take place between October 1981 and March 1983 – and this (improvised) priority not only did not belong in its programme but also contradicted the reflation of the economy, which should have been its foremost objective. When it bemoans the constraints of power, the Left is fond of emphasizing the difference between one's will and one's ability: Mauroy's explanation cited above demonstrates that there have been occasions when the Left overrode its ability by stressing its will. It rarely had much to do with fighting for a progressive agenda, however.

For the Left, a slowing down of reform had almost always represented the first step toward a full-fledged retreat. By 1983, a Socialist President committed to promoting better income distribution would come to stress the need to reduce income taxes, which he said 'choke off the economy, limit production and discourage [individual] energy'.[19] By 1986, a Socialist president elected to protect and create jobs (*'D'abord l'emploi!'*) would assert, in the face of rising unemployment, 'Our great priority is inflation.' And, summing up with candour and precision the policies of his Left government, Laurent Fabius acknowledged that he was performing 'the dirty work of the Right' by cutting many unprofitable jobs.

In 1936, the attempt to prove oneself a good guest in power had been less brazen yet still noticeable, especially once the proletarian tide of strikes had ebbed. By the end of the year, Léon Blum diagnosed that 'after the immense changes we have introduced in the social and economic order, the country's health imperatively demands a period of stability and of normality.'[20] And as he prepared to announce a 'pause' in the reform process – which is exactly what Jacques Delors, Mitterrand's first finance minister, would do 45 years later – the leader of the Popular Front went on to acknowledge, much like Mitterrand would: 'There is no doubt that we have gone ahead of the [global] recovery. There is no doubt that we have acted as if tomorrow's prosperity were certain'.[21] Soon enough, the practical meaning of 'pause' would become clear to all. In February 1937, the government decided it would protect bondholders against inflation, a protection wage-earners had just been refused, although for them rising prices had all but dissipated the income gains of June 1936. In March 1937, Léon Blum appointed a committee of experts almost exclusively composed of conservative economists. They advised Blum – no surprise – to enact conservative economic policies. One of them, Jacques Rueff, who would work for de Gaulle after his return to power in 1958, had claimed, based on the British case during the 1930s, that unemployment benefits were the cause of unemployment. Maybe because of what he called 'the fear to frighten' adversaries, Blum acknowledged his own version of performing the dirty work of the Right: 'We pushed economic liberalism as far as any past government, and maybe even further than any other government would have done in the present circumstances.'[22]

In this respect too, if the Popular Front foretold the Mitterrand years, it also repeated the *Cartel des Gauches*. In his memoirs, Herriot stressed 'the analogy between the difficulties faced by Léon Blum and those I had encountered in 1925. Léon Blum, the doctrinaire Socialist, was obliged to propose a 'pause' in January [*sic*] 1937, to reverse the steps taken against capital flight and to reinstitute the free trading of gold.'[23] A bemused observation of the Popular Front's difficulties and of its conservative economic turn hardly suffices, however, to exonerate Herriot for his own capitulation before the 'wall of money'. Moreover, when the Radical leader refused to follow de Mouy's advice in June 1924, he, not Blum, explained his decision to reject a course of action that 'would have completely disentangled us' by the fact that the proposed strategy 'might have appeared inspired by a spirit of partisanship. It would not have been a national solution.'[24] Here we have political capitulation at its finest: in order not to embarrass the Right by disclosing the extent to which it had deceptively broken with monetary orthodoxy, Herriot pretended that the situation he had inherited was sound and sustainable. He thus entangled himself and his government in a policy whose only shred of credibility was that its bankruptcy had not been revealed. He there-fore doomed his Left coalition to a reckless course and, subsequently, reaped the blame for a predictable failure. Compared with this outcome, a 'spirit of partisan-ship' would have been providential for the *Cartel des Gauches* and for the coun-try. It might not have burdened the French Left with a taint of financial incompetence that only increased its sense of insecurity and its predisposition to behave as timidly as a guest in power.

A last explanation for the Left's reluctance to devalue the franc outright – and thus break the monetary stranglehold that risked choking off its Keynesian eco-nomic strategy – has much to do with the Left's diplomatic priorities. In order to confront the 'wall of money' before capital flight made it crumble upon the new coalition, and in order to protect against a flood of imports taking advantage of a domestic stimulus (thus causing it to fail), the Left needed to challenge the liberal economic order and its dogma. This entails confronting its architects and beneficiaries – Britain, the United States and Germany. But the electoral victory of the French Left was quite unwelcome there. The problem then becomes an obvious one. Whether it was Herriot and his diplomatic attempt to resurrect close ties with Britain, Blum and his desire to build a strong democratic alliance against Nazi expansion, or Mitterrand and his passionate support for NATO and its nuclear buildup of the early 1980s, the governing Left did not think it could afford the diplomatic price of a lonely (and potentially contentious) monetary strategy.

One of the first foreign visitors Mitterrand met in June 1981 was George Bush. The US Vice President officially expressed his country's concern about the pres-ence of Communist ministers in non-essential departments. He was immediately assured that this would lead to no departure from the Atlanticism extolled by the victorious Socialist candidate throughout his political life and presidential cam-paign. This desire to reassure foreign capitals about the intentions of the Left logically entailed its monetary consequences. In 1981, these constraints would be known as 'European solidarities': in order to demonstrate its commitment to the

European Community, the Left endorsed a trend towards trade and monetary integration that could not but contradict its primary economic strategy. Asked why Mitterrand had decided to postpone a devaluation of the franc, Delors pointed to 'the necessary correspondence between the economic policy of the President of the Republic and his foreign policy, especially . . . his efforts to accelerate the construction of Europe.'[25] Thierry Pfister, Mauroy's political adviser, would later elaborate on the comment: 'The first signal given on the international scene [by an immediate devaluation in 1981 or by a withdrawal from the EMS] would have been a withdrawal from European solidarities. But the victory of the left in France already arouses surprise and distrust in most Western capitals. . . . And this apprehension is likely to be compounded when the Communists will join the new majority after the parliamentary elections of June 1981.'[26]

In the same way the Left had been inclined to placate its domestic capitalists, it attempted in this instance to reassure foreign partners who would keep on requesting reassurances. The political leanings of Helmut Kohl, Margaret Thatcher and Ronald Reagan all but guaranteed that the search for solidarities with them would oblige the Left to veer far from the 'European social space' for which it had originally intended these solidarities. Beseeching a common ground with conservative European capitals, the Socialists would also accept Germany deciding the size of its devaluations and the level of France's interest rates. It is difficult to see what sort of leftism the Left got out of these solidarities.

Once again, such a Faustian bargain had not been without precedent. In 1936, the Popular Front, seeking to strengthen a democratic alliance with Britain and the United States to stop the territorial expansion of fascism, sacrificed major pillars of a progressive economic strategy (trade protection and sanctions against capital exports). But it neither contained Hitler in Austria, nor did it succeed in defending the republic in Spain. The issue of exchange controls is quite exemplary here. Although they represented an explicit part of the Left's economic programme in 1936, they would be imposed by the Right in 1939, after the demise of the Popular Front.[27] The Left's 'fear to frighten' and its desire to do nothing that might displease London or Washington had led the Popular Front to renounce the project altogether. And, acknowledging the dissonance between his domestic strategy and his international priorities, the Socialist leader explained: 'The normal leaning of our domestic policy would lead us to take coercive measures against capital exports and speculation. . . . But there would be a contradiction with our policy seeking a community of action with the great Anglo-Saxon nations.'[28]

In 1924, gasping for motives to justify his disastrous decision to remain in the trench to defend a grossly overvalued currency, Herriot too had raised the international factor, albeit in a slightly different way. Referring to the French–British summit of June 1924, during which he attempted to re-create a Paris–London axis badly damaged by Poincaré's German policy in the Ruhr, Herriot accounted for his rejection of de Mouy's advice:

We were on the eve of an international conference essential to the future of our country and, more particularly, to the future of our finances. The disclosure to the world of the situation of our Treasury [the fact that the legal ceiling placed on monetary creation had been broken] would have shattered the trust placed in our currency.[29]

Here, the explanation appears doubly unconvincing. First, Herriot's accomplishment in the conference was essentially to give up Poincaré's German policy in its entirety without obtaining anything in exchange (such as a forgiving of France's debt owed to Britain). Although necessary, the French concession hardly required a prior display of financial strength. Moreover, since that strength was totally artificial, shattering its appearance would not have been damnable, nor would it prove avoidable. Finally, calling a deception covered by illegal acts 'trust' seems to stretch the flexibility of our common political vocabulary.

In June 1982, Mitterrand, host to the Versailles summit of the G-7, refused to devalue the franc a second time, in part to not overshadow the splendour of France's welcome in the palace built by Louis XIV. There, too, the illusory strength achieved through temporary deception gained the Left nothing: during the summit, Mitterrand failed his paramount objective, which was to prod Reagan, Thatcher and Kohl to stimulate their economies by lowering interest rates. Six days after the summit, the franc was devalued.

In 1982, seeking to explain why the French Left, 'not monetarist' though it might be, attempted to 'inflate a punctured tyre'[30] by digging in the trench of the franc's defence while trying to promote economic growth, Mauroy wrote with his uncanny sense of paradox: 'We must not repeat the mistakes of the past.'[31] And in 1977, retracing the chronicle of Herriot's debacle, Jean-Noel Jeanneney titled his book: *History Lesson for a Left in Power*. Jeanneney summed up the lesson in this way: 'The Left loses itself when it chooses a policy consisting in the sole play of market mechanisms in order to reassure the moneyed interests. . . . Not only does it compromise its mission, it also performs the task less well than would its adversary. In that case, it would be better to leave the place to him.'[32] In 1988, Jeanneney joined the first government of Mitterrand's second presidential term. Between 1988 and 1993, conservative economic policies were once again enacted. In March of that year, the Left relinquished control to its adversary.

CONCLUSION

In one fundamental way, the 1981 case stands out from the previous ones. For the first instance in its history, the Left had time on its side. Controlling a parliamentary majority and endowed with a strong executive, it could not just engineer a sunbath and then let its successor manage its consequences. It could not attribute its rapid failure to a conspiracy against progressive reforms either – from the 'wall of money' in 1924 or the so-called '200 families' who would choose Hitler rather than the Popular Front in 1936. It could not even explain its economic retreat by a 'pause' after which the serious work of change would resume. In the context of a sustained stay in power, 'to manage the duration' (*gérer la durée*) would oblige the Left, discursively and theoretically, to renounce the radical programme it had once advocated and to extol the moderate policies it would enact shortly. In other words, instead of preserving its self-proclaimed revolutionary identity by grudgingly acquiescing to temporary conservative adjustments to its original platform, the governing Left after 1983–4 presented its endorsement of markets and its inducements to capitalists as the new mantra of its modernity. Giving up its old compass, it risked stumbling upon the landscape of the Right, losing its constituency in the process. In its 1992 programme, 'A New Horizon', the PS acknowledged that 'capitalism circumscribes our theoretical horizon'.[33] In summary, after repeating the mistakes of its distant past, the French Left has attempted to bury its history once and for all. Ironically, the severe electoral sanction for that apostasy may make the idealism of yesterday shine brightly when appraised against the returns of the new realism.

Henri Emmanuelli, leader of the PS after June 1994, reflected this new understanding when he identified his first priority as repositioning the Socialists to the left. Such a shift, however, is hardly uncommon when the Left is in opposition. If history is any guide, it rarely foretells much about what the Left might do when it returns to power.

In December 1992, Socialist parliamentarian Austin Mitchell wrote that his party was

> a grey party looking for colour, . . . a united party with no message, a present-able corpse where dissent has neither base, nor role, an organization tamed as mass parties die. We have diluted socialism, the state, growth, cheap money and intervention. We have abdicated weapons of economic management, and that degree of distance from the European Community which is necessary to rebuild our . . . industrial base. We have done so just in time to see [the Conservatives] move back to the positions we have abandoned. Have the last 13 years been a waste of [our] time? A fundamentalist revolt against the compromise and dilutions necessary for the seventies was followed by a reversal out of that chaos into soft options and vacuous niceness which was completed just as hard times returned. The Conservatives have begun to unlearn the eighties. Socialists will find the reversal more difficult. Yet Mitchell's law of leadership states that leaders can only lead their parties in the opposite direction to that from whence they came.[34]

Mitchell is not French, but British. He wrote of his own party, not of Mitterrand's. It may be then that once we are through with a historical analysis of the French Left in power, we shall also need to look at the rest of the world and find we already know the story. The 'exceptionalism' of the French Left of 1981 seems rather mundane after all.

Notes

1. François Furet, Jacques Julliard and Pierre Rosanvallon, *La République du centre: La fin de l'exception française* (Paris: Calmann-Levy, 1988).
2. George Ross, Stanley Hoffmann and Sylvia Malzacher, eds, *The Mitterrand Experiment: Continuity and Change in Modern France* (New York: Oxford University Press, 1987).
3. Serge July, *Les années Mitterrand: Histoire baroque d'une normalisation inachevée* (Paris: Grasset, 1986).
4. Charles de Gaulle, *Mémoires de Guerre*, vol. 3 (Paris: Plon, 1959) pp. 279, 283.
5. Karl Marx, *La guerre civile en France* (Paris: Editions Sociales, 1968) p. 22.
6. The case of 1944 is different from these other experiences. There too, however, the monetary situation might have called for a bold move, which the Left chose not to make. Still, whereas an overvalued franc doomed any strategy of economic reflation in 1924, 1936 and 1981, the currency had become almost worthless in 1944. A drastic shortage of basic goods, not unemployment, was the paramount issue facing the new authorities even as they kept fighting the war.
   In 1944–5, an economic debate took place over how to avoid the destruction of the currency. As head of the provisional government, Charles de Gaulle refused the drastic steps toward monetary deflation – an immediate exchange (at 25 per cent of nominal value) of existing banknotes. Instead, in March 1945, he decided to count on inflation and an increase in production to lead to adjustment between the value of the currency and the supply of goods. See Serge Halimi, *Sysyphe est fatigué. Les échecs de la gauche au pouvoir: 1924–1936–1944–1981* (Paris: Robert Laffont, 1993) pp. 314–16; de Gaulle, pp. 143–9; and Jean Lacouture, *Pierre Mendès-France* (Paris Seuil, 1981).
   The explanations for the policy choice were also different. The hope that a painful move might be avoided was not nearly as reckless as it had been in 1924 and 1936 and as it would be in 1981. Moreover, the final decision had nothing to do with the desire to beat the Right at its own game: in 1944–5, the Right was so weak it appeared irrelevant. When it comes to the restraint imposed on a Left economic strategy by diplomatic imperatives, this case only remotely resembles those of 1924, 1936 and 1981. De Gaulle refused a more demanding strategy in part so he would not be distracted from his priority of re-establishing France as a leading European and war power. Yet unlike Herriot, Blum and Mitterrand, de Gaulle would have been free to act differently, since the Americans and British were preoccupied with other geopolitical issues.
7. See Halimi. The details of the 1924 case are also laid out superbly in Jean-Noël Jeanneney, *Leçon d'histoire pour une gauche au pouvoir: La faillite du Cartel* (Paris: Le Seuil, 1977); and *François de Wendel en République. L'argent et le pouvoir: 1914–1940* (Paris: Le Seuil, 1977).
8. Edouard Herriot, *Jadis: D'une guerre à l'autre* (Paris: Flammarion, 1952) p. 219.
9. Herriot, p. 216.
10. This comes from the Socialist budget proposal for 1933. See Fondation Nationale

des Sciences Politiques, *Léon Blum chef de gouvernement* (Paris: Presses de la Fondation Nationale des Sciences Politiques, 1981) pp. 305–6.

11. See the programme of the Socialists, *Projet Socialiste: Pour la France des années 80* (Paris: Club Socialiste du Livre, 1980).

12. For details of the Socialist programme on trade and currency, see Halimi, pp. 383–8.

13. Pierre Mauroy, *C'est ici le chemin* (Paris: Flammarion, 1982) pp. 16–9.

14. Assemblée Nationale, 6 June 1936, cited by Alfred Sauvy, *Histoire économique de la France entre les deux guerres* (Paris: Fayard, 1965) p. 261.

15. Fondation Nationale des Sciences Politiques, p. 231.

16. One of Herriot's opponents was François de Wendel, an outspoken conservative and the most influential member of the *Banque de France*'s Council of Regents.

17. This expression was coined by Joseph LaPolombara, *Interest Groups in Italian Politics* (Princeton, NJ: Princeton University Press, 1964) p. 316.

18. Mauroy, pp. 24–8.

19. Television programme, 'L'enjeu', TF 1, 15 September 1983.

20. Cited by Georges Lefranc, *Histoire du Front Populaire* (Paris: Payot, 1974) p. 205.

21. Léon Blum, 31 December 1936, cited by Lefranc, p. 226.

22. See Lefranc.

23. Herriot, p. 643. In this quote, Herriot confuses dates. The 'pause' took place in February 1937.

24. Herriot, p. 204.

25. *Le Nouvel Observateur*, 24 October 1981.

26. Thierry Pfister, *La vie quotidienne à Matignon du temps de Pierre Mauroy* (Paris: Hachette, 1985) p. 242.

27. Halimi, p. 205.

28. Assemblée Nationale, 26 February 1937, cited in Lefranc, p. 230.

29. Herriot, p. 205.

30. Sauvy, p. 245.

31. Mauroy, p. 28.

32. Jeanneney, *Leçon d'histoire*, p. 60.

33. Parti Socialiste, *Un nouvel horizon: Projet socialiste pour la France* (Paris: Gallimard, 1992) p. 82.

34. Austin Mitchell, 'The Yolk of Power', *The Guardian*, 15 December 1992.

5 The Left's Response to Industrial Crisis: Restructuring in the Steel and Automobile Industries

W. Rand Smith

Industrial firms – the locus of both capitalist exploitation and heroic class struggles – were a natural focus for the Left's economic plans in 1981. Through such measures as nationalization of large firms and banks, the Left planned to use industrial policy to boost immediate investment as well as reshape economic structures. For many on the Left, such reforms also implied that new institutions at the firm and corporate-group levels would empower employees and their unions.

Despite their aspirations for reform, the new Socialist leaders were far from embracing a Marxist-style assault on capitalist power. On the contrary, these leaders argued that a wide-ranging industrial policy was needed to combat French capitalism's *weakness*, not its excessive might. The main economic problem, they claimed, was a lack of capital available for industrial investment, a problem that stemmed in large part from the nature of the financial system. French finance capital, derived mainly from bank loans rather than equity markets, made industrial investment depend largely on the price and availability of bank-supplied credit. During the 1970s, banks had turned increasingly toward investments such as real estate that offered high short-term profits rather than longer-term but less profitable investments in industrial firms. The result, Socialists asserted, was a failure of French companies to invest in their productive capacity and a consequent penetration by foreign competition in the domestic market.[1]

To reverse this trend, Socialist leaders argued that the state had to play an important supply-side role, helping companies restructure by furnishing them with new sources of capital. This intervention, spearheaded by the promised nationalization of 12 industrial groups, 36 banks and two finance companies, would help 'reconquer the domestic market'. Industrial policy, François Mitterrand claimed in his first news conference as President, would be 'a weapon for defending French production'.[2] Underlying this approach was a belief that new government policies could reverse the sliding fortunes of French industry.

Such optimism was soon dashed, however. Within a few months, government leaders realized that French industry's ills were far graver than they had thought. Part of the difficulty was a plague common to all industrialized countries in the

97

early 1980s: the global slowdown triggered by the 1979 oil shock and the subsequent recession induced by high US interest rates. But several industries were
also chronically underfinanced, inefficient and technologically backward. Many
firms, especially in older industries such as steel, automobiles and textiles, were
losing money and ceding market share to foreign competitors.[3] After 1979, these
problems were exacerbated by France's membership in the European Monetary
System (see Chapter 3). Given the country's relatively high inflation level (especially vis-à-vis Germany) coupled with the EMS's requirement that currency
exchange rates remain relatively stable within the system, the franc tended to
become increasingly overvalued, which further eroded France's trade position.
Finally, the Socialist Party's stimulative policies in the first year aggravated these
problems by discouraging domestic investment and stimulating imports.

Thus, within two years of coming to power, the Socialist government faced
unforeseen industrial challenges. The Left had vowed to 'break with capitalism
in crisis',[4] but by 1983 it faced the virtual breakdown of French capitalism itself.
Understanding how it responded is crucial to understanding the Mitterrand presidency. Industrial policy posed an acute dilemma for the Left. On one hand, the
goal of transforming French industry was central to its economic programme; a
more productive industrial sector would help fight unemployment and make the
country more competitive internationally. On the other hand, the severity of the
industrial crisis imposed sharp limits on the government's ability to achieve that
transformation. The government would find it difficult to be both architect and
firefighter, to redesign French industry according to its blueprint while seeking to
save the structure from collapse.

In the 1980s, the steel and automobile industries – each of which was dominated by two giant firms – were important for the politics of industrial restructuring because of their combination of economic vulnerability and political
sensitivity. Both industries had experienced foreign penetration into domestic
markets and declining market shares in global markets. By 1983, faltering sales
and operating losses forced a reconsideration of basic strategy; at the least, these
firms had to contain and reverse their losses. From a market perspective, therefore, there were strong arguments to eliminate thousands of surplus jobs. But
many union and management officials asserted that these firms could not simply
be abandoned to market forces, given their importance for regional development
and even national security. Thus both industries combined economic weakness
with mobilized constituencies which resisted market discipline – a pattern that
made the dilemma of Socialist industrial policy especially acute.

Despite a rhetorical turn toward less state intervention, the government's
industrial restructuring efforts shared much in common with traditional *dirigiste*
approaches of previous governments. Far from stepping aside to allow market
forces to operate in these and other crisis industries, the government was most
concerned with modernizing and rationalizing them. Far from permitting these
firms to restructure on their own, the Socialists sought to guide this process

through such measures as replacing recalcitrant and ineffective company heads (in the case of nationalized firms), mandating or negotiating manpower reductions with management and unions, and choosing 'winners' and 'losers' in product lines. The government thus followed the broad operating assumption of all French governments since 1944 – that French capitalism is too important to be left to capitalists; it must be led by the state. In this sense, the Left's fabled turn to the market obscured a deeper continuity in state-industry relations.

Also, the government encouraged a modernization of these industries that produced a decidedly non-Socialist result: massive job losses among production workers. What is striking is not the fact of job cuts *per se* but rather their scale. This result is all the more remarkable in light of the considerable public protest that the cuts provoked, including the spectacle of Left leaders being denounced as traitors by their own erstwhile supporters. This raises the question of why these leaders took actions that so directly and negatively affected a core group of constituents.

Finally, from a profit-loss perspective, these policies generally worked. By the early 1990s, although all of their structural problems had not been eliminated, the targeted industries were stronger financially and more competitive internationally. Indeed, compared with their Gaullist and Giscardist predecessors, as well as with other contemporary European governments, the Socialist government was at least as successful (if not more so) in restoring the conditions of capitalist profitability.

These are indeed surprising outcomes for a government that came to power so fervently aspiring to reform the economy along socialist lines. That the Left's rhetoric did not match its subsequent achievements is a recurring theme in assessments of the Mitterrand presidency.[5] What is less clear is how the gap between rhetoric and achievement can be explained. In seeking to explain this gap, the analysis first examines the Mitterrand government's restructuring policies in the steel and automobile industries. Second, a conceptual framework is proposed for explaining these policies. This framework, derived from the recent literature on the state, distinguishes between state 'autonomy' (or the ability to define a set of policies) and 'capacity' (the ability to execute a given set of policies). The central argument here is that the Mitterrand government exercised relatively little autonomy, especially internationally, but considerable domestic capacity to execute the policy imposed on it. That is, although the government had little choice about the basic direction its policies would take, it executed those policies effectively, even in the face of considerable protest. Third, this chapter suggests several factors that help account for this pattern of low autonomy and high capacity.

RESTRUCTURING IN THE STEEL AND AUTOMOBILE INDUSTRIES

Two broad sets of measures comprised Socialist industrial policy: those aiming to *promote* promising industrial activities and those seeking to *restructure* troubled firms or sectors. In practice, such measures were deployed simultaneously across a wide range of both 'sunrise' and 'sunset' industries. A key instrument in these efforts was the 1982 nationalizations that brought into the public sector several large firms including CGE (electrical equipment, electronics), Péchiney (chemicals, pharmaceuticals, metallurgy), Rhône-Poulenc (synthetic textiles, chemicals, pharmaceuticals), Saint-Gobain (glass, computers) and Thomson (consumer and professional electronics). Once nationalized, these firms were then recapitalized and reorganized under state auspices. On balance, such measures helped restore most of these firms to financial health, with the clearest evidence being the enthusiastic investor response to the re-privatization of several such firms by Jacques Chirac's government in 1986–7.[6] Moreover, the government attempted, through a series of 'sectoral plans' in 1981–2, to restructure such industries as machine tools, leather goods, textiles, furniture and toys – all of which had been affected by imports or shrinking markets.

Restructuring was particularly controversial in the steel industry. It took the form of two modernization plans, in 1982 and 1984, that sought to close obsolete plants, consolidate production in profitable market segments and reduce manpower requirements. By the early 1990s, these and other measures had wrought a veritable transformation in the industry. The two main firms, Usinor and Sacilor, had merged into a single firm, Usinor Sacilor, which by 1988 had become a profitable and active acquirer of American and other foreign companies.[7] Accompanying these changes, predictably, was a drastic reduction in personnel; by 1991, the French steel industry employed about 54 000 workers – less than half as in 1980.[8]

When the Left came to power in 1981, these changes were far from inevitable. At that time, only two elements of its steel policy were well-defined. The first was that the government would nationalize the industry, a pledge first made in the 1972 Common Programme. This action was indeed carried out during the first five months, but it was widely viewed as a financial manoeuvre rather than a power shift, since it merely transformed the firms' state-owned debt into state-owned shares.[9]

The second defining element was the lamentable state of the industry itself, for by the early 1980s steel had become chronically unprofitable and dependent on state aid. The industry's plight stemmed: from both world trends and domestic mismanagement. European firms in general had fared poorly in an industry marked by stagnating demand, geographic shifts in production and consumption (mostly from the United States, Western Europe and Japan to the newly industrializing countries and non-market economies of Eastern Europe, Soviet Union and China) and growing international competition.[10]

French steel, no exception to the European downturn, also fell victim to its own strategic errors. Although output quadrupled between 1946 and 1960, by the mid-1960s the industry was burdened by overcapacity, obsolete technology and low productivity.[11] In response, government and industry officials fashioned successive restructuring plans in 1966, 1977 and 1978, the ultimate impact of which was to foster industry consolidation, job loss and growing state financial responsibility. Despite these efforts, the industry became increasingly unprofitable and indebted.[12] This cycle reached its logical end in the 1978 plan, when the state, by assuming the industry's debt, took a controlling equity interest in Sacilor (77 per cent) and Usinor (64 per cent).[13]

Thus the steel industry initially presented an ambiguous opportunity for the Left. On the one hand, with ownership of the two largest firms, the state had direct authority over investment, production and employment. Control over an industry the Socialists considered 'an indispensable link in the coherence of France's industrial tissue' could provide an important instrument in the Left's drive to transform industrial policy.[14] On the other hand, the industry's dire financial condition hardly made it an ideal instrument. Moreover, the Left's options were limited by European Community policies to stabilize the industry. Beginning with the 1977 Davignon Plan, EC members had sought to maintain price stability by erecting a *de facto* producers' cartel. The EC had attempted to regulate national production by setting mandatory minimum prices and quotas on members' production and capacity, overseeing investment plans, limiting government subsidies and limiting imports.[15] The government thus would have to share authority over steel policy with EC officials in Brussels.

Within nine months of nationalizing the industry, the government presented its first modernization plan in June 1982. The plan declared the 1986 production goal to be 24 million tons, a 15 per cent *increase* over 1981 output and a level only attained in a much more favourable world market (1972–4). From 1982 to 1985, the government would provide 17.5 billion francs of new investment capital, an increase of 50 per cent over the previous government's last four years.[16] The plan, which called for the elimination of 10 000 to 12 000 jobs (about 10 per cent of the workforce), was widely viewed as unrealistic, especially since it also required the main firms to break even by 1 January 1986. (The EC had already declared that all state subsidies had to cease by that date.)

As the government began implementing the 1982 plan, divisions emerged within the industry and labour. Interfirm rivalry grew fierce, as managements for Nord-based Usinor and Lorraine-centred Sacilor lobbied to win state subsidies and avoid plant and personnel reductions. Discord also arose among the two main labour confederations, the Communist-aligned *Confédération Générale du Travail* and the independent but Socialist-leaning *Confédération Française Démocratique du Travail*, both of which opposed the plan, albeit for different reasons. The CGT rejected all job reductions, whereas the CFDT generally accepted the need for job cuts but accused management and the government of withholding information and failing to consult with them.[17] Despite these differences, both confederations were reluctant to break openly with the government and therefore attempted no national-level protests.

Even as the 1982 plan was announced, its inadequacy was apparent. Given declining customer orders, the Industry Minister admitted that production would have to be cut 15 per cent from the 1981 level.[18] Thus the September 1982 plan postponed but did not resolve the industry's basic problems, as losses continued to mount, from 7 billion francs in 1981 to 11 billion francs in 1983.[19] The government could not continue to cover losses of that magnitude and finance the industry's modernization indefinitely, especially given the EC subsidy cutoff date of 1986.

An equally compelling reason was that by early 1983 the government faced a turning point in its macroeconomic policy, for the stimulative policies of the first year had worsened trade and budget deficits, boosted inflation and dampened domestic investment. In response, the March 1983 Delors Plan raised taxes, cut defence and social expenditures and channelled some of the savings into industrial investment.[20] The government also ordered public enterprises in competitive markets to break even within three years. In a further effort to cut the budget deficit, the government in November 1983 froze public-firm subsidies at current levels. Since the steel industry's losses continued to climb, the 1982 plan would have to be revised drastically, making further layoffs inevitable.

Thus the government in January 1984 began new talks with management and unions to revise the plan. As with the 1982 consulting round, the process was marked by conflicts – between firms, regions and even top government officials. The focal point of contention was a Sacilor proposal to build a 2 billion franc universal rolling mill (*train universel*, or TU) in Gandrange in Lorraine. Supporters included all the firms' unions, the CGT and CFDT metalworkers' federations, local political and business leaders and, within the government, Laurent Fabius, a Mitterrand protégé who had become Industry Minister a year earlier. This coalition argued that the investment would help modernize the firm's 'long products' (rods, beams, etc.) and revive a demoralized region. Opposing this plan were Usinor's management and unions, as well as Prime Minister Pierre Mauroy, a Nord native and mayor of Lille, who claimed the TU would jeopardize existing long-product plants in his region.[21] As an alternative, this group proposed its own rationalization plan that would obviate the need for massive new investment by Usinor.

Despite the important regional stakes, both plans would require massive job cuts. Given the marginal position of the Communist Party, the only political force favouring expansion backed by protectionism, the internal debate centreed on how to reapportion a diminishing pie. Given the various divisions, Mitterrand had to make the final decision himself by choosing between his two top officials. In a decisive Council of Ministers meeting on 30 March 1984, Mitterrand backed Mauroy's position, thus defeating the TU proposal. Lorraine would therefore bear the brunt of the cuts, which were estimated to reach at least 25 000 jobs, or more than a quarter of the industry's workforce.[22]

Although most of those affected would be covered by early retirement (for workers over 50) and 'reconversion leaves' (job retraining for up to two years at

70 per cent of the last salary),[23] workers responded angrily. Yet protests remained scattered and disunited. At the national level, union reaction was divided and largely ineffectual. The harshest critic, the CGT, opposed the cuts but could mobilize only limited demonstrations, while all other unions at least tolerated the decision.[24] As for the Communist Party, it criticized the plan – and even announced its own counterplan, which would increase production nearly 25 per cent – but remained in the government for the time being. (It finally withdrew three months later, when Fabius replaced Mauroy as Prime Minister.) Popular mobilization against the decision thus remained localized and fragmented. Although these actions temporarily hurt Mitterrand's popularity, they were insufficient to force the government to rescind its plan.[25]

The March 1984 decision by no means resolved France's steel crisis. The following two years witnessed continued scattered protests, interfirm bickering, postponements of scheduled plant closings and governmental requests to the EC for deadline extensions. Yet the plan did establish the principle that the industry had to become self-sufficient, which meant permanent pressure to cut production and personnel. Moreover, by 1986 there were signs that the plan had improved the industry's health, as worker productivity had increased 22 per cent since 1980 (versus West Germany's 13 per cent).[26] During that same year, the 'cohabitation' government headed by Gaullist Premier Chirac further consolidated the industry by merging the two firms into the world's second largest steel firm.

This push to modernize continued into the 1990s. The government's strategy was to allow management flexibility in redeploying labour, including layoffs, and then to provide income-support and retraining programmes to soften dislocations for the workers affected. The industry still faced recurrent market crises and the prospect of further job cuts; for example, the global recession beginning in 1991 caused European producers to call for a new Davignon Plan to staunch falling prices.[27] After turning profits in 1988–90, Usinor Sacilor lost money in 1991 and 1992.[28] But the Mitterrand government did not waver from the 1984 policy, namely that the industry must be a competitive market player that progressively weans itself from state aid.

Restructuring in the automobile industry contrasted with the steel industry in both timing and form, differences that stemmed from the two industries' structures and relations with government. First, the two main auto firms, Renault and Peugeot Société Anonyme (PSA), have dispersed production since the 1960s, installing most new plants outside of the Paris region, either elsewhere in France or abroad. Since the pain of auto restructuring was spread across many sites, labour and other interests were unable to mount the regional defence protests characteristic of the steel industry.[29]

Second, compared with steel, the auto industry has had less involvement with the state. Until the early 1980s, auto firms were generally profitable and thus less dependent on the government. Whereas Usinor and Sacilor became wards of the state, in the automobile industry ownership was mixed. Renault had been nationalized in 1945 in order to punish its founder and owner, Louis Renault, for Nazi collaboration. Since that time, although it remained a public firm, Renault operated largely autonomously. PSA was a family-held company that guarded its independence.

Thus, restructuring in the auto industry would be considerably less institutionalized than in steel. Because of the lack of tradition of state intervention, government leaders, company officials and unionists had to define not only the content of restructuring – that is, such questions as what plants would close and what workers would be affected – but also the process whereby that content would be decided. New decision-making norms had to be created. Because the government exercised less direct control over the firms, its ability to impose decisions was more limited, especially in the case of PSA. Therefore, restructuring in the auto industry would be less likely to take the form of a grand plan, as it did in steel. The state's role would be more contested, its authority less sweeping, its decisions more *ad hoc*.

PSA restructuring took place in a context of deteriorating finances and growing worker protest. As with steel, PSA's financial problems stemmed from both a global market downturn and management errors. Of the latter, the most serious were the acquisitions of Citroën in 1974 (with the help of ample government incentives)[30] and, in 1978, of Chrysler's European operations, which were renamed Talbot. Many of these firms' plants and dealer networks were inefficient, and PSA had great difficulty absorbing them. By mid-1980, these problems caused the company to begin layoffs, most of which were handled through 'pre-retirement' plans or severance payments to entice immigrant workers – especially North Africans, who comprised more than half of Citroën's and Talbot's production force – to return home.

After the Left's election in 1981, workers' anxiety over job security became increasingly organized. This mobilization owed much to a newly militant CGT seeking to increase its influence, especially within Citroën and Talbot plants, where unionism historically had been repressed. Thus, beginning in the spring of 1982 the CGT sparked a wave of work stoppages, centreed in two plants, a Citroën facility of 6500 workers in Aulnay-sous-Bois and a Talbot plant of 17 000 in Poissy. By mid-1983, the combination of declining markets and work disruptions had generated a three-year loss of 6 billion francs and a debt of 30 billion francs.[31]

From mid-1983 to mid-1984, management attempted to slash jobs, first at Talbot and then Citroën. At Talbot the plan called for the dismissal of nearly 3000 workers, most of them production workers in Poissy, while the Citroën plan cut an equivalent number, mainly in Aulnay. Because labour law required government approval for collective layoffs, even by private firms, both plans became highly politicized, as government officials negotiated with management and top union officials while local unions sought to mobilize workers.

Since the administrative framework brought the ultimate decision on Talbot and Citroën to the government's door, these restructuring efforts bore a similar dynamic.[32] Initially, the government rejected the firm's requests but appointed a neutral expert to study whether the job cuts were economically justifiable. Thus the government sought to buy time while testing the degree of worker resistance. Meanwhile, the government began talks with top union and management officials about a possible compromise. The Talbot case was handled by the Communist Minister of Employment, Jack Ralite, whose apparent task was to contain the CGT. This strategy succeeded in the short run, as CGT officials entered co-operatively into negotiations. On the other hand, the CFDT, which had only a small union section at Poissy, was only occasionally consulted. For Citroën, talks were conducted by the Minister of Social Affairs, Pierre Bérégovoy.

With centralized negotiations thus largely excluding the local unions, workers at Poissy, Aulnay and elsewhere used whatever means they could to defend their jobs – including work stoppages, strikes and factory occupations. Workers only partially supported these actions, however, because the unions themselves were highly divided. Not only did the two main unions, the CGT and CFDT, clash constantly, but both were actively (and sometimes violently) opposed by pro-management unions, which sought to stop the strikes. At Talbot–Poissy, the minuscule CFDT section, taking a maximalist, no-layoffs position, led a plant occupation for several weeks in December 1983, which the local CGT, in order to save face, was forced to follow.[33] Several months later, however, at Citroën–Aulnay, the union roles were reversed. In the spring of 1984, with the Communist Party now openly opposing the government's austerity policies, the CGT hardened its line regarding layoffs. At Aulnay, it led a one-week occupation.[34]

Finally, despite intensive local protests, both conflicts ended with the government and management agreeing to carry out most, but not all, of the proposed dismissals. (Strangely, but perhaps not coincidentally, the numbers in both cases were virtually identical: at Talbot, the initial dismissal request of 2900 was cut to 1905, whereas Citroën's demand was reduced from 2937 to 1909.)[35] Although local unions opposed the accords, they lacked the power to prevent their application.

These settlements established a precedent for the next decade of market adaptation by PSA: the government might press management to increase its layoff benefits, but it would not stop management from restructuring, as the latter saw fit, in order to meet competitive pressures. One indication of the government's increased concern over industrial competitiveness was its slight and reluctant role in a bitter seven-week strike over wages within the Peugeot division in September and October of 1989. Faced with a chief executive, Jacques Calvet, who virtually rejected negotiations, rank-and-file workers and even several prominent Socialist leaders pressured Premier Michel Rocard to intervene, but he refused, claiming that the conflict was one of 'private law' in which the government should not impose a solution. Rocard finally appointed a mediator after five weeks but kept his distance throughout.[36]

In the Renault case, restructuring came later than at PSA, in part because management at the state-owned firm – in particular, chief executive Bernard Hanon – sought to avoid political problems for the government (and himself) by laying off thousands of workers. Restructuring was thus delayed as long as possible.[37] By 1984, however, escalating investment costs and declining markets had made adjustment necessary. During the late 1970s, Renault had embarked on an expansive strategy abroad, including an effort to penetrate the American market by buying American Motors. It had also invested heavily in new production technologies, such as robotics. But after the government abandoned its initial attempt in 1982 to stimulate the economy, the domestic auto market contracted sharply. Renault, in particular, suffered – its market share dropped from 39 per cent in 1982 to 31 per cent in 1984.[38] From modest profits in 1979–80, the firm's performance steadily declined, culminating in a 1984 loss of 12.5 billion francs.[39]

During this period of decline, Hanon sought to demarcate himself from PSA executives by advocating a 'soft' approach to restructuring in which Renault would work closely with the unions to trim unneeded personnel, avoiding outright dismissals.[40] By January 1985, however, with the government firmly committed to reducing subsidies to public firms, top government officials had concluded that Hanon's approach would no longer suffice, and they summarily replaced him with Georges Besse, an engineer who had overseen restructuring at newly nationalized Péchiney. By May, Besse's new approach had become clear. Unlike Hanon, who sought the unions' cooperation, Besse largely ignored them, making decisions in secret. In a further effort to quiet the unions, Besse did not publish a grand plan for Renault, but rather carried out restructuring in incremental, unannounced steps.[41]

Not surprisingly, the CGT, which by 1985 strongly opposed the government's austerity measures, declared virtual war against Besse from the outset. Tensions culminated in an October 1985 strike wave, centred in Renault's Le Mans and Boulogne-Billancourt plants. The CGT mobilized only a quarter of the workers, however, and the confederation finally called off the strike. Such was the union's isolation that three other unions organized a demonstration *against* the strike![42] The CGT's defeat, according to some observers, constituted a turning point for the automobile industry because it ended the system whereby the CGT had long shared power with Renault management.[43]

By late 1985, then, Renault's direction was clear: Whatever the impact on the workforce, management's mandate was to make profits. By November 1986, when Besse was assassinated by terrorists, Renault had reduced its workforce by nearly 20 000 under his management.[44] Besse's successors, Raymond Lévy (1987–92) and Louis Schweitzer (1992–present), continued to restructure with minimal government involvement, including a share-exchange agreement with Volvo that partially privatized the firm. In 1987, for the first time since 1980, the firm became profitable and has remained so. Finally, the emphasis on productivity resulted in further cuts in the workforce, which declined from 86 000 to 58 000 between 1986 and 1992.[45]

POLICY RESPONSE: AN EXPLANATION

This analysis of restructuring in the steel and auto industries permits three general conclusions. First, the Socialist government's approach to crisis industries remained, like that of its predecessors, a *dirigiste* one that saw the state intimately involved with such questions as manpower levels, investment strategies and selection of top management. What changed throughout the 1980s was not the reality of state intervention but rather the goal. From early pretensions to recapitalize French industry in order to combat unemployment, the government shifted by 1983 to promoting international competitiveness. All the while, the state retained a quite visible hand in promoting market-driven behaviour. In this sense, one can plausibly argue that far from representing a withdrawal of the state from the industrial sector, the Socialists' shift was an effort to maintain and even reinforce the state's power to influence industry under conditions of intensifying international competition.[46]

Second, the steel and auto restructuring plans produced a controversial downsizing of the work force. In these and other basic industries – including coal, shipbuilding, machine tools and textiles – hundreds of thousands of jobs disappeared during the 1980s. Affected workers, as we have seen, did not go quietly. What is surprising is that a government that took power incorporating the Socialist and Communist parties and the two main labour confederations would encourage such sweeping changes that angered so much of the government's electoral and activist base.

Finally, the plans generally worked in that they allowed, and even forced, these firms to become more adaptable to market conditions. While the Socialist government did not miraculously transform all ailing industries into successful global competitors, it certainly forced them to become more competitive by relying less on state financial support.

How can these responses to industrial crisis be explained? How can we account for the Socialists' ultimate embrace of a modernizing industrial strategy that placed productivity and profits well ahead of the promotion and protection of employment? In the cases under consideration, we must ask what policy choices the government could have exercised in an international economy marked by technological change, increasing trade competition, and unpredictable shifts of capital and labour,[47] and what factors shaped its decisions.

These questions can be addressed using concepts derived from recent work on the state, specifically from the debate over state 'strength'. Some states, it is argued, possess 'strong' institutions – typically, executives and bureaucracies with concentrated, wide-ranging powers – which can wield powerful economic policy influence, whereas 'weak' states lack such institutions.[48] Thus a state's relative institutional strength helps determine the kinds of economic policy responses that are feasible. This logic suggests that the explanation for the Socialists' restructuring strategies should be sought in an assessment of the strength of the French state. While this is a promising insight, the concept of state strength is limited in at least two ways.

First, the concept lacks parsimony, since it embraces a multitude of potentially distinct attributes or dimensions, including autonomy and capacity.[49] The former refers to a state's ability to formulate its own goals – that is, to select its own course of action or to act on the policy preferences of state officials, even when those preferences diverge from those of external (non-state) actors. An autonomous state, Eric Nordlinger writes, 'invariably acts as it chooses to act, and does not act when it prefers not to do so'.[50] This definition, while essential, goes only so far, for it implies nothing about the state's capacity – that is, the ability to achieve its goals, whether or not that policy has been selected autonomously.

While interrelated – for example, officials will tend to prefer and select policies that can achieve their intended goals – autonomy and capacity are distinct attributes that may vary independently.[51] For one, a state may have the ability to formulate a particular policy (autonomy) but lack the policy instruments to carry it out (capacity). Examples here include Salvador Allende's Chile, Kwame Nkrumah's Ghana and Harold Wilson's Britain during the 1960s sterling crisis. Obviously, such situations are highly unstable, since the lack of capacity to carry out a declared policy will eventually undermine the government's legitimacy and credibility.

Also, a state may lack autonomy but possess significant capacity. That is, a state may not be able to formulate and act on its own preferences, and thus it may be obliged to carry out the preferences of external actors. Yet even though a state may be forced to enact a policy that diverges from the preferences of state officials, it may possess significant authoritative powers to execute that policy effectively.

A second limitation of the state strength concept is that it normally refers to a state's power vis-à-vis its domestic environment, or what Peter Hall labels the 'organization of state-society relations'.[52] While the domestic environment is obviously important, so too, especially in the case of economic and industrial policy, is the international environment. Thus the concept of state strength must be enlarged to take account of a state's relations with principal global actors, including other states, transnational firms (including banks), and multilateral bodies such as the International Monetary Fund and the World Bank.

In the steel and auto industries, the government largely lacked international autonomy but possessed considerable domestic capacity: although it had relatively little choice about the basic direction its policies would take, it executed those policies effectively, even in the face of opposition. On one level, it is clear that the government lacked international autonomy: French industry had declined in competitiveness and profitability during the 1970s, and the Socialist government faced international pressure to improve these conditions.[53] Moreover, the stimulative policies of the first year only worsened the trade and budget deficits. Thus by 1983 the government needed to reduce subsidies to losing firms, curb consumer spending and encourage business investment. In steel, the government had to abide by the additional financial restrictions imposed by the EC's Davignon regime, while auto firms confronted a sharp erosion of their domestic market share at the expense of German and other European producers. In a word, the government needed to enact some version of austerity.

But what kind of austerity? It has become common to think of austerity as mainly a process of lowering labour costs by depressing wages, giving managers more flexibility in deploying labour, discouraging unionism and the like. Yet it is far from obvious that bolstering a nation's international competitiveness has to mean squeezing labour. Just as governments' stimulative policies may vary, so may their austerity regimes, since a key issue is the apportioning of sacrifice. If some workers must lose buying power and others their jobs, compensations can be provided in the form of work-time reductions, expanded vocational training and a stronger voice for labour in economic decisions. Workers do not automatically reject measures to sacrifice immediate economic well-being if they anticipate a *quid pro quo*.[54] In return for labour concessions, governments and employers can offer non-monetary inducements that expand the power of employees and their organizations. There is no guarantee that such a policy could have worked; obviously, it would have faced sharp opposition from many quarters. Yet there is reason to suggest it could have constituted a plausible alternative to the orthodox modernization policies ultimately adopted.

The Socialist government, however, considered but never seriously pursued such an alternative path (see Chapter 3). As the steel and auto cases reveal, the route chosen was largely a 'welfarist' one, which provided some financial cushion for dislocated workers but did nothing to alter the institutional structure to empower labour in both private and public enterprises. This conclusion holds *a fortiori* for the government's efforts at industrial relations reform, the Auroux Laws.[55]

One critical reason the Socialists did not pursue this alternative path was the nature of the governing coalition. In simplest terms, the government was permeable to international capitalist influence because its potential support base – the Socialist and Communist parties as well as the major trade unions – failed to mount an effective challenge. First, the governing coalition's dominant element, the Socialist Party, remained controlled by Mitterrand, who demonstrated little attachment to left-wing ideological goals (see Chapter 2). Moreover, the PS was decidedly élitist in structure, autocratic in internal practices and isolated from the organizations that defended workers' interests.[56] It thus tended to exclude from representation and power the very interests that would likely be hurt by a restructuring programme.

Second, the other elements of the governing coalition were generally weak and divided, thus further ensuring Socialist Party dominance. The Communist Party was rapidly losing voters, having shrunk from more than 20 per cent of the vote during the late 1970s to about 10 per cent by the mid-1980s. Although Mitterrand allowed the French Communist Party (PCF) four cabinet ministries from 1981 to 1984, the party had little impact on economic policy, especially after June 1982. Organized labour, in particular, lacked policy influence. Although most PS members also belonged to a union, the party had no formal attachments to any labour confederation. Moreover, the two main confederations, the CGT and CFDT, carried out constant ideological and organizational warfare. Most seriously, the movement generally was experiencing a sharp drop in membership and militancy (see Chapter 9). All of these traits were in evidence in the cases of steel and automobiles, as the main working-class organizations – the PCF, CGT and CFDT – could not decisively affect the firms' plans or defend against employment cuts.

Despite a lack of autonomy, the Socialist government exhibited considerable domestic capacity to undertake an orthodox restructuring strategy. This capacity was bolstered in particular by the Fifth Republic's centralization of power in the executive's hand (on condition that he be supported by a parliamentary majority). In steel, the final decision on the 1984 plan was taken by Mitterrand himself, while in the automobile case, the key actors were top ministers who negotiated directly with management officials. In three of the four main firms in these industries, the state held direct control, while even in the one case of private ownership (PSA), the restructuring plan had to be approved by government officials, who decisively affected the conditions under which workers were dismissed. These institutional relationships, in turn, reinforced organized labour's exclusion.

While the international economy limits the range of feasible industrial policies, states can exercise some measure of choice. How they choose depends on many factors, including the organizational and institutional resources the government can wield. For Left or social democratic governments in general, ties with the labour movement constitute a critical organizational resource.[57] While a strong labour presence is no guarantee that Left governments will execute restructuring programmes that depart from orthodox prescriptions, such a presence is necessary for any attempt. In the case of industrial restructuring under Mitterrand, labour's relative weakness meant that the government faced few pressures for an alternative policy. Without such pressures – especially in a context of economic and industrial crisis – most Socialist leaders came to view market adjustment as the only realistic approach, and for them any deviation from this approach was economically foolhardy and politically suicidal.

Notes

1.   For an influential statement of this thesis, see Alain Boublil, *Le Socialisme industriel* (Paris: Presses Universitaires de France, 1977). See also the Socialist Party, *Projet*

Socialiste pour la France des années 80 (Paris: Club Socialiste du Livre, 1980) pp. 185–97. Of this analysis the Communist Party agreed only with the conclusion – namely, that vigorous state intervention was needed – and not the premises. The PCF continued to hold that France's main problem was a form of 'state monopoly capitalism' whereby monopolistic firms use their power to capture the state, which in turn aids these firms in counteracting falling profit rates. See Anicet Le Pors, *Les Béquilles du capital* (Paris: Seuil, 1976).

2. *Le Monde*, 26 September 1981.
3. W. Rand Smith, '"We Can Make the Ariane, But We Can't Make Washing Machines": The State and Industrial Performance in Postwar France', in George Ross and J. Howarth, eds, *Contemporary France*, vol. 3 (London: Frances Pinter, 1989) pp. 175–202.
4. *Projet Socialiste*, p. 172.
5. See Chapters 3 and 4 in this volume, as well as Ross *et al*, eds., *The Mitterrand Experiment: Continuity and Change in Modern France* (Oxford: Polity/Oxford University Press, 1987).
6. W. Rand Smith, 'Nationalizations for What? Capitalist Power and Public Enterprise in Mitterand's France', *Politics and Society* 18, no. 1 (March 1990) pp. 75–99.
7. 'France is Quietly Forging a Steel Empire', *Business Week*, 30 April 1990, pp. 90–1.
8. Eurostat, *Iron and Steel – Yearly Statistics 1991* (Brussels: European Community, 1991) p. 12.
9. *Le Monde*, 10 October 1981.
10. For example, between 1972 and 1986, European Community firms experienced a 23 per cent drop in production and a 44 per cent drop in employment. By contrast, total world steel production remained roughly constant during this period. See Organisation for Economic Cooperation and Development, *The Iron and Steel Industry* (Paris: OECD, various years); Thomas R. Howell, *Steel and the State: Government Intervention and Steel's Structural Crisis* (Boulder, CO: Westview Press, 1988) pp. 17, 29; and OECD, *World Steel Trade Developments, 1960–1983* (Paris: OECD, 1985).
11. Stephen Woolcock, 'The International Politics of Trade and Production in the Steel Industry', in John Pinder, ed., *National Industrial Strategies and the World Economy* (Totowa, NJ: Allanheld, Osman, 1982) p. 59; Pierre Judet, *L'Evolution des débouchés de la sidérurgie française: perspectives à moyen terme* (Paris: Ministère de l'Industrie, 1982) p. 73.
12. By 1978, industry debt had reached hopeless proportions: 112 per cent of revenues, compared with about 20 per cent for the United States and West Germany. See Philippe Zarifian, 'La Politique industrielle dans la sidérurgie française de 1977 à 1983: le jeu de l'échec', *Cahiers du CRMSI*, 9 (August–September 1984) pp. 9–10.
13. For useful analyses of industry–government relations in the steel industry since 1945, see Jean G. Padioleau, *Quand la France s'enferre* (Paris: Presses Universitaires de France, 1981); and Anthony Daley, 'Industrial Adjustment in the French Steel Industry', in Richard E. Foglesong and Joel D. Wolfe, eds., *The Politics of Industrial Adjustment: Pluralism, Corporatism, and Privatisation* (Westport, CT: Greenwood Press, 1989) pp. 107–26.
14. *Projet Socialiste*, p. 194.
15. Howell *et al*, *Steel and the State*, p. 78; Loukas Tsoukalis and Robert Strauss, 'Community Policies on Steel, 1974–1982: A Case of Collective Management', in Yves Meny and Vincent Wright, eds., *The Politics of Steel: Western Europe and the Steel Industry in the Crisis Years, 1974–1984* (Berlin: Walter de Gruyter, 1986) pp. 186–221.

16. Judet and *Le Monde*, 10 June 1982.
17. Claude Durand, 'Les Syndicats et la politique industrielle du plan acier', *Cahiers du CRMSI*, 7 (April–May 1984) p. 58; and *Le Matin*, 29 June 1982.
18. *Libération*, 29 September 1982.
19. *Le Secteur public industriel in 1985* (Paris: Observatoire des Entreprises Nationales, Ministère de l'Industrie, des P. et T., et du Tourisme, 1986) pp. 188, 225.
20. Peter A. Hall, *Governing the Economy: The Politics of State Intervention in Britain and France* (New York: Oxford University Press, 1986) p. 203.
21. *Le Nouvel Observateur*, 6 April 1984.
22. The most detailed account of this decision is found in Pierre Favier and Michel Martin-Roland, *La Décennie Mitterrand. Les épreuves*, vol. 2 (Paris: Seuil, 1991) pp. 43–70.
23. *Les Echos*, 30 March 1984; *Financial Times*, 18 April 1984.
24. *Le Matin*, 1 April 1984; *Le Monde*, 14 April 1984.
25. *Le Point*, 9 April 1984.
26. OECD, *The Iron and Steel Industry*.
27. *Financial Times*, 24 November 1992.
28. *Financial Times*, 29 January 1993.
29. Jean-Jacques Tur, 'L'Industrie automobile en France: bilan et perspectives', *L'Information Géographique* 53, no. 4 (1989) pp. 155–71.
30. Carl Cavanagh Hodge, 'The Future of Four Wheels: Government and the Automobile Industry in France and West Germany, 1971–1985', *Governance* 4, no. 1 (January 1991) pp. 42–66.
31. *Le Monde*, 14 July 1983.
32. The following synthesis has been drawn from press reports and interviews with several key government and union officials.
33. See CFDT (section syndicale Talbot), *L'Effet Talbot ou les raisons profondes d'un conflit* (Paris, 1984).
34. For the CGT perspective, see the interview with metallurgy federation leader André Sainjon in *Révolution*, 18 May 1984.
35. *Le Monde*, 25 August 1984.
36. Pierre Mathiot and René Mouriaux, *Conflictualité en France depuis 1986: Le cas de Peugeot-Sochaux* (Paris: CEVIPOF, 1992).
37. Daniel Labbé and Frédéric Périn, *Que reste-t-il de Billancourt? Enquête sur la culture d'entreprise* (Paris: Hachette, 1990).
38. *Le Point*, 21 January 1985.
39. *Financial Times*, 22 January 1985.
40. *Le Monde*, 25 September 1984; *Financial Times*, 3 October 1984.
41. *Le Matin*, 10 May 1985.
42. The three other unions were the *Confédération Générale de Cadres, Force Ouvrière* and the *Confédération Française des Travailleurs Chrétiens*. They were protesting the CGT's occupation of the Boulogne-Billancourt plant (*Les Echos*, 15 October 1985).
43. *Le Monde*, 17 October 1985.
44. *Le Monde*, 9 November 1990.
45. *Libération*, 5 December 1992.
46. A similar argument is made with respect to Socialist government changes in monetary policy by Michael Loriaux, *France After Hegemony: International Change and Financial Reform* (Ithaca, NY: Cornell University Press, 1991) Chapter 8.
47. See W. Rand Smith, 'International Economy and State Strategies: Recent Work in Comparative Political Economy', *Comparative Politics* 25, no. 3 (April 1993) pp. 351–72.

48. See, for example, Peter J. Katzenstein, ed., *Between Power and Plenty: Foreign Economic Policies of Advanced Industrial States* (Madison: University of Wisconsin Press, 1978).
49. Theodore J. Lowi, 'The Return to the State: Critiques', *American Political Science Review* 82, no. 3 (September 1988) p. 891.
50. Eric A. Nordlinger, *On the Autonomy of the Democratic State* (Cambridge, MA: Harvard University Press, 1981) p. 8.
51. Nordlinger, pp. 193–4.
52. Hall, pp. 259–83.
53. *OECD Economic Surveys: France* (Paris: OECD, 1984) p. 48.
54. For an example drawn from Spain, see Robert M. Fishman, *Working-Class Organization and the Return to Democracy in Spain* (Ithaca, NY: Cornell University Press, 1990) p. 222.
55. See Chris Howell, 'The Contradictions of French Industrial Relations Reform', *Comparative Politics*, 24, no. 2 (January 1992) pp. 181–97.
56. Hugues Portelli, *Le Socialisme français tel qu'il est* (Paris: Presses Universitaires de France, 1980).
57. See, for example, John Stephens, *The Transition From Capitalism to Socialism* (London: Macmillan, 1979); David R. Cameron, 'Social Democracy, Corporatism, Labour Quiescence and the Representation of Economic Interest in Advanced Capitalist Society', in John H. Goldthorpe, ed., *Order and Conflict in Contemporary Capitalism* (Oxford: Clarendon Press, 1984) pp. 143–78.

Part II

Policy Change and Economic Actors

6 An End to French Exceptionalism? The Transformation of Business under Mitterrand[1]

Vivien A. Schmidt

At the time of the bicentennial celebration in 1989, commentators spoke of the end of French exceptionalism, and the end of France as a revolutionary country. France had not seen a revolutionary upheaval for more than a century, a radical overhaul of governmental institutions since 1958 or a student uprising since 1968. Economically, however, French exceptionalism was still very much a reality during the 1980s. During the decade, the country's economy went though a series of mini-revolutions: from expansionary neo-Keynesianism in 1981 to economic austerity and increasing financial deregulation as of 1983; from nationalization of banking and industry in 1982 to privatization in 1986 to the '*ni-ni*' period of neither nationalization nor privatization as of 1988. And just as each political revolution served to transform the polity, bringing it one step closer to democracy, so did these economic mini-revolutions serve to bring the economy, step by step, closer to modernity.

Over the past decade, France has modernized and internationalized its industries, deregulated its markets and prepared for the Single European Market of 1993. Ironically, the French Socialist Party (PS), having entered office vowing to establish a socialist economy, ended up creating a more modern, capitalist one. This decade saw the restructuring of industry, both in terms of firm activities and their ownership and control; the improvement of the business environment through the rehabilitation of business; the renewal of the managerial élite, with a younger and more dynamic although no less élite leadership; and the reform of managerial practice, with closer labour-management relations, more management participation, less centralization of top management decision-making and the beginnings of change in management recruitment and promotion systems.

Businesses that had been tightly controlled and facing inward at the beginning of the decade had loosened up and turned outward by the end, combining and acquiring with abandon both inside and outside of France. The economy that had been deindustrializing in the previous decade, leaving its businesses vulnerable to foreign takeover, had been reindustrializing, making it possible for its business to take over foreign concerns. Industries that had been undercapitalized, horizontally diversified and increasingly in the red were recapitalized, vertically integrated and

117

for the most part more profitable. Finally, and perhaps most importantly for the future of industry, firms that had been part of the 'protected capitalism' of the past, having been controlled by 'hard cores' (*noyaux durs*) of private investors, became part of today's 'dynamic capitalism', that mixed ownership and control: public and private companies and banks controlled one another through cross-holdings.

Attitudes toward business, moreover, changed almost as dramatically as the outlook for the economy and the structure of business. Nationalization brought with it a shift in popular views of business: the public – and the Socialists – who had mistrusted business and its top executives, seeing them as exploiters of labour, came to see business as the creator of riches and business heads as heroes and friends of the worker. And privatization, rather than generating a widespread conversion to *laissez-faire* capitalism, elicited a popular rejection of all economic ideology with the realization that, private or public, business is business.

Management practice also underwent a major transformation. Heads of business who had been autocratic and paternalistic, overly eager to centralize, distant from and mistrustful of labour, and often conservative and behind the times in their management, changed. They became more dynamic, introducing modern management techniques; closer to labour; less autocratic and somewhat less centralizing. Their profile, however, remained remarkably similar to that of their predecessors. The new heads tended to be from upper-middle-class families, had received an élite education at one of the *grandes écoles*, became members of an élite civil service corps, had extensive experience in state service, including in a ministerial cabinet, and had a comparatively brief business career begun at the top. Such an élite recruitment and promotion system, although guaranteeing that well-qualified individuals head French firms, nevertheless has had a negative impact on the corporation, since it blocks access to top positions, thus lowering morale and undervaluing achievement. But this, too, has begun to change, as firms diversified their recruitment in response to the modernization and internationalization of business.

In the United States and Great Britain, a decade of ideologically driven policies intended to promote *laissez-faire* capitalism has not stemmed their decline, and their leaders are wondering whether a renewal is possible. In such a context, the French case is extremely useful. It suggests that the remedies of both the declinists, who recommend removing structural impediments to economic revival, and the revivalists, who believe only renewed leadership and values can halt decline, may be necessary. The French case makes clear that changes in business and government structures, cultural values and political and industrial leadership are all important for revival.

THE NEW ENVIRONMENT FOR BUSINESS

By the end of the 1980s, the deindustrialization begun in the 1970s had been reversed.[2] Most economic indicators improved steadily since 1983, when the economic austerity programme was put into place: France's rate of inflation, one of the highest in Europe at the beginning of the decade, was one of the lowest by the end; production, household consumption of industrial goods and gross fixed capital formation in the manufacturing industry, after significant fluctuations in the early 1980s, grew at acceptable annual rates; and the level of savings increased greatly, allowing a higher level of investment and external growth.

French firms reaped the benefits of the improved economy. Investment in research and development was up, capital investment rose considerably, and industrial productivity grew at an unprecedented rate. Moreover, the nationalized firms that were suffering great losses at the beginning of the decade were making such large profits by the end that they were able to finance ambitious international merger and acquisition programmes. Although they incurred some debt, this enabled them to remedy some of their problems of inadequate size and internationalization.

Certain structural weaknesses remain, though, including a high unemployment rate, a comparatively slow rate of increase in industrial production, a negative balance of trade, a decrease in *per capita* gross national product, a decrease in the size of the workforce and a smaller market share worldwide. France's industrial base continues to be too small, its industry lacks specialization, its small and mid-sized businesses and industries are not large enough, and its products are not competitive enough. France has continued to have insufficient investment, an inadequate savings rate and too much public expenditure. The educational system does not produce enough skilled employees at any level and focuses too much on the education of an élite group of managers in the *grandes écoles*.[3]

Still, the economy has been revitalized. When asked to explain this, an overwhelming majority of French business executives responded that the industrial policies of nationalization and privatization had little to do with economic recovery in either a positive or negative way.[4] Bankers and Treasury officials credited governmental macroeconomic policy, deregulation and business internationalization, arguing that where a firm was weak or had a poor business strategy – as in the machine tool, textile and wood industries – no amount of industrial policy made a difference.[5] The industrialists added to this an emphasis on the modernization of business, and their own leadership.[6] Only Ministry of Industry officials, past or present, suggested that industrial policy focused on the microeconomic level was important. They argued that macroeconomic policies were necessary but not sufficient to explain the economic recovery.[7]

Restructuring Industrial Ownership and Control

Industrial policy played an important role in the transformation of the French economy, albeit often in ways not anticipated by the governments themselves. Nationalization dramatically increased state ownership of industry and banking, leaving the state owning 13 of the 20 largest firms in France and all but a few family-owned banks. But it did not alter capitalism in the way the Socialists had predicted.[8] As Dominique Strauss-Kahn, Minister of Industry in the governments of Edith Cresson and Pierre Bérégovoy, explained, assuming that ownership *per se*, whether through nationalization or privatization, could lead to profound changes was wrong. It affected property rights, but not the structure of the economy or the strategies of CEOs.[9] State control, however, did make a difference, in that it both recapitalized the nationalized industries and engineered their change from horizontally diversified firms to vertically integrated ones. By focusing each firm's efforts on one main kind of product, government restructuring enabled the nationalized firms to avoid destructive competition, duplication and the dispersion of investments, sites and research programmes; they could grow to an internationally competitive size while eliminating jobs and closing obsolete plants without the labour unrest they would have encountered as private concerns.[10] Through government nationalization and industrial policy, the Socialists performed quickly and in an organized manner what a decade of takeovers and acquisitions did in the United States, and they did this with less waste, more rationality and fewer problems with employee morale.

Privatization was the next sensible step. In a curious twist, denationalization became necessary because the now-profitable nationalized concerns needed more capital than the government was willing (or able) to provide. But even before the neoliberal, or *pro-laissez-faire* Right, came to power in 1986, *de facto* denationalization was taking place, with many firms having floated non-voting shares and others having sold their subsidiaries illegally, albeit with the full knowledge of the government. Privatization involved selling off close to one-third of the 65 companies the neoliberal government had anticipated selling before the stock market crash of October 1987 halted their efforts, and included such symbols of state authority as the national television station, TF1, the industrial giant Saint-Gobain and the bank Société Générale. The move was welcomed by most CEOs as a way of gaining more capital and greater freedom.[11] The heads of the nationalized concerns saw privatization less as a rejection of social *dirigisme* than simply a sensible next step for firms requiring new infusions of capital. Most nationalized firms, now financially solvent, modernized and streamlined, were interested in conquering the global market, an easier task once privatized.

The process of privatization itself tended to reassure established businesses since it did not unleash the unbridled forces of competition neoliberal campaign rhetoric had promised. On the contrary, privatization in many cases appeared to be an orderly divvying up of the market by the government in favour of the most interested parties. In the case of the privatization of the telecommunications firm CGCT, for example, analyst Henry Ergas found, 'Far from seeing a liberalization of the market, we're seeing a freezing of market share.'[12] This was true of other companies as well, since privatization granted control to a *noyaux dur* made up of large companies holding anywhere from 15 per cent to 30 per cent of the stock.

These cross-holdings re-created something akin to the traditional 'protected capitalism' of the pre-nationalization period, when a majority of publicly quoted

French firms were controlled by a small group of investors with enough shares in the company to capture all seats on the board.[13] There were two significant differences, however. First, the banks acquired a significant share of industrial capital for the first time. Before, the banks held a negligible interest in industry, less than 5 per cent. By comparison, the state as of 1 January 1986 had a controlling interest in more than half of the 50 largest industrial firms in France. Family-owned firms accounted for approximately 25 per cent, and foreign concerns held about 20 per cent.[14] Second, the nationalized banks and industries also held shares in the privatized companies, making the distinction between nationalized and privatized firms a bit confusing. For example, as of 1 April 1988, Saint-Gobain's largest shareholders were the nationalized banks BNP (about 4 per cent) and Suez (about 4 per cent), the private Générale des Eaux (about 3.5 per cent) and the nationalized insurance company UAP (about 2.3 per cent); CGE's were the same, although in this case the private Générale des Eaux held the most shares (between 8 per cent and 9 per cent); while the bank CCF had a mix of nationalized and privatized companies, including the nationalized pharmaceuticals company Rhône-Poulenc (2.5 per cent), the private insurance company Axa (2.5 per cent), and the private cement maker, Lafarge Coppée (3.4 per cent).

The period of the *ni-ni* further confused ownership patterns. Although the official policy of the Michel Rocard government allowed neither privatization nor renationalization, the government allowed for exceptions (in the cases of Pechiney and Renault). And, to generate new capital it could not provide directly, it arranged for the recapitalization of industry through the trading of shares among nationalized industries and banks. The picture was further complicated with the end of the *ni-ni* policy in Spring 1991: private and privatized companies now can gain up to 49 per cent interest in nationalized companies. Privatized companies have taken advantage of this new landscape. The CEOs of some privatized and nationalized firms are now at the centre of networks of private and public enterprises. For example, Jean-Louis Beffa, chief executive of privatized Saint-Gobain, put his group in the centre of a network of public and private enterprises, including the Générale des Eaux, BNP, UAP and Suez. And Jean-Yves Haberer, head of the nationalized Crédit Lyonnais, gained seats on the boards of private as well as public companies such as Bouygues, Club Med, Crédit National, Framatome, Hachette, Matra and Lyonnaise des Eaux-Dumez, when his bank became a principal shareholder in these companies.

This means of providing new capital has a potentially dramatic impact on the structure of control of the nationalized industries. Where the state directly owned and exercised leadership over industry, the Rocard government began the move toward a model in which the state would control the nationalized industries only indirectly and nationalized industries and banks would control one another in such a way that they look increasingly like French private enterprises, with a *noyau dur* of investors, in this case other corporations and banks, to ensure stability and good management. While the Socialists were in office, however, the law governing the composition of the boards of directors – a third employees, a third state representatives and a third *personalités* – ensured that the shift in control from direct to indirect was not automatic, because nothing guarantees firms that have bought into a nationalized company a seat on the board. Only once the law changes will bankers and corporate executives formally exercise the oversight function that in the past the Ministry exercised. Because the boards of directors of public as much as private companies have exercised little of the control they officially have, however, this change will probably not represent more than a guarantee of continued top management autonomy.

The government has not renounced all interventionism. It retains the ability and will to intervene where it deems an industrial action of national strategic importance. But even in many of these cases, industry ultimately gets its way. This was shown in the 1991 alliance between Bull and NEC, which Prime Minister Cresson held up for a year on the grounds that no Japanese company should gain a share in French nationalized industries, then ultimately approved because of Bull's need for Japanese participation. Industry also prevailed in the abortive initiative under Cresson to create a new super-firm linking the state's semiconductor, consumer electronics and nuclear industries.

Changes have also affected the scope of the operations of French companies, as they have internationalized in response to the pressures of European integration. The French have been on a worldwide shopping spree: in the United States alone, for example, Accor acquired Motel 6; Péchiney, National Can; Rhône-Poulenc, Rorer; Saint-Gobain, Norton; and Bull, Zenith's computer division. Unlike the US mergers and acquisitions based solely on financial profit, these were motivated by strategic reasons.[15] Thus, new CEOs are more powerful than previous ones, not only because of the new networks of interlocking directorships and growth of their companies but also because French industry and banks, public and private, are becoming much more independent of the central government at the same time they are themselves interdependent. French CEOs in the 1980s also benefited from a change in political attitude, an indirect result of governmental industrial policy.

Changing Attitudes toward Business

Up until the 1980s, the French were hostile to business. Nationalization and privatization together altered much of this attitude. Nationalization, which made Socialists responsible for business, served to free them from the old ideological apparatus and led to the replacement of the image of the exploitative, greedy capitalist with that of the dynamic entrepreneur, creator of riches for all. Privatization, which enabled the neoliberal Right to put into practice the Thatcherite and Reaganite policies of *laissez-faire* capitalism that they had been preaching ever since the Left came to power, served to demonstrate that the free market, with all its unbridled competition and uncontrolled business, was not the panacea anticipated and that business does not change the way it operates, whether it is nationalized or privatized.

This produced a seachange in French societal attitudes toward business, evident not only in the rehabilitation of business generally but also in an amelioration in labour-management relations. Studies showed a softening of labour militancy and a more positive approach to the firm by workers, and business leaders shifted their attention from personnel problems to questions of profitability. Top managers, the group most likely to intuit any change in attitude, credited the Socialists with rehabilitating business and fostering more co-operative labour-management relations. Instead of a profiteer and an enemy, the business executive came to be seen as an entrepreneur in the service of the public, making money in order to invest it in the future, not to exploit the worker. Although most CEOs were quite pleased with this change in image, for one Socialist banker, it went too far, because the Socialists 'rehabilitated not just the enterprise but the entrepreneur. They liberated profits, but they kept salaries down; they created an inheritance tax that . . . punished widows on fixed incomes . . . and allowed owners of businesses to escape. . . . With this, the Socialists went too far. They abandoned socialism.'

The Socialists, in other words, became good capitalists, certainly the last thing that the capitalists themselves could have imagined on the eve of the Left victory of 1981. Business executives at that time were concerned that the state would, among other things, limit their freedom to fire and set wages. On management issues, they feared that they would themselves be treated as pariahs instead of recognized as 'the ones who make the economic engine run', who are in 'the front lines of the battle of competition'.[16] Little did they know that they were to become the new heroes.

Confronted with a Socialist government and nationalized means of production, labour also had to make an about-face. With its allies in power, it felt less able to strike than before, feeling bound to accept the government's urgings to consider the good of the company and of the nation, despite government indifference to their demands for wage increases.[17] By 1986, labour itself had changed its views of the firm. It was no longer seen as the place of alienation, and work was no longer exploitation. Instead, personnel at all ranks came to characterize their relations with the firm primarily in terms of trust (55 per cent), solidarity (43 per cent) and *sympathie* or likeability (33 per cent), as opposed to antipathy (2 per cent), contempt (2 per cent), hostility (3 per cent), discord (12 per cent) or mistrust (19 per cent). Workers *were* less enthusiastic about the firm than were upper-level managers, having less trust (53 per cent vs. 67 per cent), feeling less solidarity (39 per cent vs. 56 per cent) and finding it less *sympathique* (27 per cent vs. 33 per cent). But this was still a significant change from the past.[18] This is not to suggest that all problems have been resolved: the high rate of unemployment alone ensures a high level of alienation among the jobless, while the recession increased tensions even within the firm as employers try to keep wages down and cut where they could. But even if under the new right-wing government labour unrest increases, it will remain contained, not only because of the changed attitudes of labour but also because of the weakening of organized labour.

This change in attitudes and discourse began relatively early in the Socialists' tenure. By 1983, the climate for business had already changed. This was aided not only by the nationalizations but also by the fact that the Socialist leadership, confronted with the continuing deterioration of the economy, made the decision to reverse its expansionist macroeconomic policies and institute economic austerity while pledging to do everything possible to increase business competitiveness. Business executives had been demanding such 'realism' for some time already, and the public agreed. Ninety per cent of those polled by Cofremca, a major management consulting firm, agreed either completely (61 per cent) or for the most part (29 per cent) that for the economy to get better, it was first necessary for French enterprises to become competitive.[19] By 1986, public confidence in the private sector saw an increase of 11 points over 1982. Public confidence in CEOs also increased, going from 44 per cent in 1981 to 56 per cent in 1985. And finally, 39 per cent of French saw profit as a negative concept in 1980, while 37 per cent thought it was a positive term. In 1982, however, 42 per cent thought it was positive, 33 per cent negative.[20]

With the neoliberal experiment, the pendulum – which in 1983 began slowly moving from the Left toward the centre with the Socialists' restrictive macroeconomic policies, deregulatory policies in financial markets and informal denationalization – took a quick swing to the Right. Just as the Socialists had come to power in 1981 with what seemed to many a rather extreme leftist economic programme of nationalization and state industrial policy, so the neoliberals came to power in 1986 spouting a rather extreme rightist programme of privatization and deregulation. And much like the Left, their programmes and policies turned out to be not nearly as radical as they claimed. Most importantly, however, instead of ushering in a decade of Thatcherite or Reaganite capitalism, they lost power as the populace as a whole turned away from all extremist economic programmes, Right or Left. The lesson, gleaned from eight years of back-and-forth on economic policies and ideology, is that through nationalization and privatization, through state control of business and proclaimed state non-intervention, as well as through government-sponsored industrial co-operation and government promotion of seemingly unbridled competition, business does not change its ways.

The public tended to back away from the programmes of both the Left and the Right once they were implemented. In April 1980, 40 per cent were in favour of nationalization, while 38 per cent opposed it. By October 1983, only 34 per cent remained in favour versus 46 per cent opposed. And by 1986, only 10 per cent of the French claimed to be satisfied with the nationalization of the banks and industry.[21] Similarly, public support for solving economic problems by business and giving business greater freedom jumped immediately after the nationalizations and climbed steadily until the neoliberals' privatization programme was in full swing. At that point it plunged dramatically, as if to conclude that privatization and deregulation had gone far enough. More specifically, whereas in September 1978, 49 per cent of the population agreed that to solve economic problems the state should control business and regulate it more strictly, this number had plunged to 31 per cent in December 1982, in the middle of the Socialist government's nationalization and restructuring programme, and to a low of 26 per cent by October 1986, during the initial phase of the neoliberal government's privatization and deregulation programme. By May 1987, it increased. By contrast, whereas in September 1978 33 per cent of the public agreed that to solve economic problems businesses should be given greater freedom, this number jumped to 58 per cent in December 1982 and reached 65 per cent in October 1986. It then plunged to 55 per cent in May 1987. In the end, the public remained more in favour of greater freedom for business than it had been at the outset.

The public's attitudes towards change, whether to nationalization or privatization, were more moderate than those of its leaders. As Rocard explained, after ten years of considerable modernization, 'The French have acquired an economic culture that they didn't have before and which makes them at the same time clearseeing and severe with regard to demagogues.'[22] And like the public, the executives too were less ideologically inclined than the goverments that appointed them.

RENEWING THE MANAGERIAL ELITE

The overall success of the nationalized industries has much to do with their new leaders, who were younger, more on the Left, more dynamic and more open to new ideas and management techniques. Otherwise, they differed little from the CEOs of the past, conceiving of management as value-neutral – that is, as removed from political values of the Left or Right – and often coming from the same élite background. Such attributes may have ensured that the new leadership retained a certain kind of legitimacy that helped minimize the disruption any abrupt change in ownership and management might have caused – thus ensuring a smooth transition from private to public and, in some cases, back to private-sector enterprise.[23]

The Profile of the New Managerial Elite

Following the traditional pattern of recruitment and promotion meant that the shift in ownership did little to engender change in personnel. Just as Pierre Mauroy found in 1982 that 'we have nationalized the banks but not the bankers', so Jacques Chirac may have discovered that he denationalized the banks but, again, not the bankers.[24] The Socialist and neoliberal governments both appointed as heads of the nationalized enterprises managers who, after attending the National School of Administration (ENA) or the *École Polytechnique* and one of the professional engineering schools, generally joined one of the prestigious civil service corps. As members of one of the élite corps, the future CEOs will have spent a few years working in a ministry. And the majority will have gained a high civil service position or been in a ministerial cabinet before being parachuted into a vice-presidency or even a presidency of a major industrial group.

The Socialists, in their appointments to head nationalized industries and banks, did little to challenge the dominance of the traditional interpenetrating political-financial-industrial élite held together by family and school ties, and by *pantouflage*, or the shuttling of members from top levels of the civil service or politics into the highest reaches of business.[25] After ten years of Socialist rule, of the 30 top managers in industry and banking, one-third came from *Polytechnique*, one-third from the corps of the *Inspection des Finances* (and thus ENA), and nearly half had also passed through a ministerial cabinet. Almost all of them had the same upper-middle-class social background: there were only two farmers' sons and no children of blue-collar workers.

Of the initial PS appointees to the major, newly nationalized industries, all but one had graduated from a *grande école*, and all but two were also members of one of the élite civil service *grand corps*. These last two, along with three others, had been in a ministerial cabinet. Their predecessors, along with those the Socialists reconfirmed, were somewhat less élite or statist in their credentials, with half having spent their entire careers in business. In banking and insurance, by contrast, where politics played a larger role in the appointment process, three out of 12 Socialist appointees did not have impeccable élite credentials, whereas all of their predecessors did. The Socialists, moreover, reconfirmed more than 40 per cent of the chief executives in place before 1981.

In both industry and finance, however, there were a few individuals who did not fit the traditional profile. Neither Loïk Le Floch Prigent of Rhône-Poulenc nor Jean Peyrelevade of Suez had major responsibilities in business prior to their appointments, though Peyrelevade did graduate from *Polytechnique* and the *Institut d'Etudes Politiques*. That almost all top ministry and industry officials were quick to point this out in interviews demonstrates how aware they were of the exceptions to the rule.[26] Notwithstanding these exceptions, throughout their first mandate the Socialists appointed to nationalized firms individuals who, if anything, had greater élite status than the previous business leaders.[27] And the neoliberals who followed them only continued this pattern.

The neoliberal government's appointments seemed to have had more to do with politics than they did either with a commitment to neoliberalism or with some new kind of free-marketeering credential. The profile of the new executives was quite similar to that of the executives under the Socialist government, as well as under previous regimes: no self-made individuals here. All new appointments were men with élite credentials, while reappointments primarily depended upon track record, except a number of politically inspired appointments of CEOs on the Right and dismissals of those on the Left.

The recruitment pattern did not change after the Socialists' return in 1988. They appointed executives – on both the Left and Right – who had been turned out by the neoliberals. The Socialists, however, also left in place a number of neoliberal appointees. They also reconfirmed their own first-round appointees the neoliberals left in place. The privatized companies did not change their leaders either. Throughout the decade, the major nationalized and privatized firms were led for the most part by CEOs with élite educational credentials and *grands corps* membership. The pattern was quite different from that of the major private industries, which had not been touched by either nationalization or privatization. Here, the large majority were businessmen who sometimes had élite schooling, but rarely combined élite schooling with *grand corps* membership.

French top management recruitment and promotion, consequently, remains as it has always been, quite distinct from that found in most other advanced industrialized countries. In Germany, top managers tend to be regular university graduates, with little distinction made among universities. In Great Britain, some are products of public school who went directly into business rather than to university, and some are university graduates. In the United States, no easy pattern can be discerned: while the heads of major firms may be self-made individuals, they are often graduates from élite liberal arts and business schools. The Japanese model, in which the heads of industry tend to be the graduates of Tokyo University, comes closest to the French, although it does not place the same emphasis on technical schooling.[28]

France probably has the most exclusive recruitment system for top managers. In France, of the CEOs of the top 200 firms in January 1986, half were graduates of one of six first-class *grande écoles*. What is more, more than one-third were graduates of two of these schools, *Polytechnique* and ENA. Universities, by comparison, produced a mere 6.6 per cent of CEOs of the top firms – far behind the number of top CEOs with no formal higher education (at 13.7 per cent).[29]

In many ways, this recruitment pattern is more open than in Japan, where there is only one main feeder for future CEOs, Tokyo University. The comparison, however, ends upon graduation. Whereas most Japanese destined to lead their firms enter business immediately upon graduation, few French do. In France, the best and the brightest have traditionally gone to work for the state before entering business. By age 26, 84 per cent of top managers in the United States and 81.2 per cent of those in Japan had begun their careers in business, compared with only 49 per cent of the French. By 35, moreover, while virtually all future CEOs in the United States (99 per cent) and Japan (97.8 per cent) had started their business careers, a sizeable number of France's future top managers (20.2 per cent) had yet to begin theirs.

The figures are equally striking when considering the age at which CEOs had entered the firms they would ultimately lead. By age 29, only 29.8 per cent of future French CEOs had begun their in-house careers, far behind the Americans (at 50 per cent) and the Japanese (at 77.4 per cent). Moreover, after age 48, a time when they would presumably enter only into the top management ranks, 25 per cent of the French began their in-house careers, a number almost double that of the Americans (13.5 per cent), and almost four times the percentage of Japanese (6.5 per cent).

Among the top 200 firms in France, only the CEOs of subsidiaries of foreign multinationals have come close to matching the Japanese pattern of long in-house business careers and élite educational credentials. Of the 16 French heads of the 20 largest foreign subsidiaries in 1986, eight attended *grandes écoles* (but only three went to the most prestigious, *Polytechnique*), only one had any state experience, and all but one entered business and the firm in which they would later become CEO in their twenties (as opposed to the French firm percentage of 66.3 per cent for entry into business and 29.8 per cent for entry in the firm they were later to lead).

Family-owned firms are the greatest exception to the typical French management profile, since they are not only long on in-house business careers, they are also short on élite educational credentials. In all, of the 42 heads of family-owned firms in the top 200, just over 21 per cent had élite educations. Among the 21 family-owned firms run by the founder, there were six times as many *autodidactes*, or self-made men, as there were graduates of the *grandes écoles*. Of the remaining 21, six out of 21 attended élite schools. Even though the CEOs of French family-owned firms lack the typical credentials, they are still far ahead of Great Britain's top 100 owner-managed firms, where only 5 per cent of CEOs have a university degree and 91 per cent have the O-level (not quite equivalent to the *baccalaureate*) or below.[30] Excluding family-owned firms and foreign-owned subsidiaries from consideration, relatively few top managers have had a regular career in business, in particular in the firm they lead. Of the 64 French non-family-owned firms among the top 200 in January 1986, only 30 were led by people whose careers were exclusively based on and in business; of these, only 12 had had full careers in the firm they then led.[31]

For all firms other than those that were family-owned or subsidiaries of foreign multinationals, then, managers' career paths are more likely to depend upon their education and membership in a corps and state experience than on their business accomplishments. This is only partially due to the highly competitive educational system, which, through the process of elimination, funnels the best students (at least those most capable of succeeding in the French examination system) to the ENA and *Polytechnique*. It also has to do with the *corporatisme*, or the tendency of the *grands corps* to stick together, which ensures that *Polytechnique* or ENA graduates at the head of a company surround themselves with their fellows.

Quite typical is the story told of Claude Bébéar, head of AXA, the private insurance group, when he took over another, larger insurer. In his first meeting with the top one or two hundred managers, Bébéar, a product of *Polytechnique*, singled out the seven or so other products of *Polytechnique* by greeting them with the familiar '*tu*' (a peculiarity of graduates of *Polytechnique* that distinguishes them from all others) rather than the formal '*vous*', the usual greeting. In this simple gesture, everyone in the firm immediately understood that a new, exclusive management team was being formed.

The system does not rely solely on this sort of informal cronyism. The technical corps (composed of graduates of *Polytechnique* who subsequently attended technical schools and joined such civil service corps as the *Corps des Mines, Ponts, Télécom,* and *Aéro*) in particular take care of their own, through an efficient system that begins with the head of the corps, in conjunction with the personnel directors of the concerned ministries, deciding on the position a young recruit is to take. The recruit has little choice in the matter and may refuse a position only once or twice. The *Corps des Mines* tends to be the most authoritarian in this regard, but corps members generally do not mind, given the jobs they get, often at a very young age. It also tends to be most active in tracking members throughout their careers, helping them find employment when they lose their jobs and even protesting when a corporation whose CEO had traditionally been a member of the corps appoints a non-member.

The result is that top management teams in public and private French corporations that are not family-owned are rife with graduates of *Polytechnique* and ENA who are also corps members.[32] Of the CEOs of the top 200 firms in France in 1986, one-quarter were members of a *grand corps.*[33] With their appointments to the nationalized firms, the Socialists increased the hold of the graduates of élite schools and members of élite civil service corps on top management.

The neoliberals did nothing to change this pattern of recruitment. After all, they had only recently been reborn as *laissez-faire* capitalists, having been statist and credentialist in the 23 years they had been in power before the Socialist victory of 1981, and therefore responsible for the élite recuitment patterns of the past. And whatever the rhetoric of entrepreneurialism and *laissez-faire* capitalism, the reality was otherwise. The neoliberals did not seek to appoint as heads of the nationalized firms entrepreneurs or self-made individuals who had a demonstrable commitment to *laissez-faire* capitalism or ability in free-market methods. Moreover, the firms that were chosen to constitute the *noyau dur* were picked more on the basis of the shareholders' friendships with the Prime Minister than on their neoliberal or entrepreneurial flair. Only the acquisition of TF1 by Francis Bouygues, the construction magnate (although himself a graduate of the number two engineering *grande école, Centrale*) could be said to fit the neoliberal *laissez-faire* ideology. Moreover, that the privatized industries and banks did not see fit to throw out the CEOs placed there by neoliberals and Socialists alike is probably as much testimony to their good business sense – after all, these were good managers, and too much turnover is never good – as it was to their own comfort with the executives' élite credentials.

Why did the Socialists, who had a long history of opposition to just such patterns of business recruitment and control, and who had vowed to make radical social changes, perpetuate the traditional élite recruitment patterns? The key lies in the Socialists' commitment to social justice and economic efficiency. Social justice was served by the worker democracy laws (the 1982–3 Auroux Laws and the 1983 law on public enterprises). Economic efficiency, however, could only be appropriately ensured by recruiting those with top managerial qualifications – those with élite educational and career histories.

Most Socialists saw the élite status of the new CEOs as a necessary evil, if they saw it as an evil at all. After all, there was little reason for the Socialists to mistrust the graduates of the ENA and *Polytechnique*. Élite education did not preclude left-wing values, especially with the sixties generation. And the new CEOs appointed in 1981 were very much part of that generation. As students at the élite schools during that decade, they were part of a large majority solidly on the Left. Among ENA graduates in the late sixties, those on the Left made up 58.5 per cent, as opposed to 31.2 per cent on the Right. The graduates of the École des Mines, themselves generally graduates of *Polytechnique*, have been only somewhat less on the Left. This was not the case for the less prestigious engineering school, *Centrale*, often students' second choice behind *Polytechnique*. There, the Right, at 46.9 per cent, was only slightly larger than the Left, at 44.2 per cent, or the most prestigious business school, the *École des Hautes Etudes Commerciales* (HEC), where the Right was close to 3 percentage points larger than the Left.[34]

Given this division, it is understandable that the Socialists, upon coming to power, turned to this generation of graduates of the ENA and of *Polytechnique-Mines*, the most prestigious schools, for recruits, and tended to ignore graduates of HEC, let alone *Centrale*. In so doing, they killed a number of birds with one stone: they renewed top managers with a younger generation of appointees who were not only of the appropriate political stripe but also had legitimacy, given their élite educational background.

Regardless of values, these managers were bourgeois. The fathers of this cohort of potential CEOs were in mainly upper-middle-class professions. On average, whereas the children of the Socialists' targeted constituency of blue-collar workers (at 3.1 per cent) and middle managers (at 11.4 per cent) together make up 14.8 per cent of graduates of the élite schools that produce the most CEOs (ENA, *Polytechnique* and *Mines*), the children of upper-middle-class professionals make up 67.1 per cent of these graduates. In brief, only a relatively small percentage of these potential CEOs are from those to whom the Socialists made an appeal in their electoral campaigns.

Elections, the Socialists might retort, are one thing; running nationalized enterprises is another. To run the nationalized enterprises efficiently, they felt they had to appoint those who could do the job, regardless of social origins; otherwise they would lose the support of even their natural constituency. This was certainly the perception among CEOs on the Right, who felt that the Socialists appointed individuals with élite credentials in order to retain credibility. The more cynical view, however, and the most widely cited, especially on the Right, is that this was a phenomenon of caste. For Michel Drancourt, director of the Business Institute, it was simply a matter of the next generation of Young Turks taking over a bit earlier, a question of clans taking power; for Jean-Louis Descours, CEO of the Groupe André, it was the clash of different groups of Young Turks who had opted for the Socialists or the neoliberals not from deep belief but from their calculation of the easiest way to the top. On the Left, somewhat less cynically, it was seen as a way of wresting control of the economy away from the conservative élite.[35]

Whatever the reason, the Socialists did little to challenge the dominance of the traditional political-financial-industrial élite. One could even argue that it only increased during their tenure in power.[36] Moreover, this caste's hold has only been reinforced as a result of the structural changes attendant upon the periods of privatization and of *ni-ni*, in which business heads are now part of networks of interlocking directorships.

The interlocking directorships give these leaders tremendous power, which is only enhanced by relationships based on previous working experience and old school ties. There are now linkages between the heads of UAP, BNP, Suez and Saint Gobain based on interlocking directorships, as well as special relationships between CEOs based on schooling and career histories. Members of the new Socialist establishment are being accepted more and more by members of the old, conservative establishment. Not only have some of these Socialist-appointed CEOs been kept on by the neoliberal government and by companies once they were privatized, a number of them have also become part of the *Conseil Nationale du Patronat Français* (the trade and employers' association representing large businesses). Caste, in short, has been more a determinant than political sympathies in the re-creation of business networks following the nationalizations of industry.

The Values of the New Élite

Although the new Socialist CEOs had much in common with the conservative CEOs they replaced, they differed from their predecessors in their more dynamic approach to management, their openness to new management techniques, such as participative management, and their age. They were members of a younger generation, most – but not all – of whom would probably in the end have acceded to the top position in the firm. As such they were, in the words of the sociologist Elie Cohen, 'true capitalists' who, even if they went to the same schools, were, 'compared to their elders, carriers of a modern capitalism, of movement, conquerors and European.'[37] As capitalists, moreover, whether 'true' or not, they also carried no political ideology, Socialist or otherwise, into internal management practice.

When asked why Socialist CEOs did not seek to imbue the firm with Socialist values (whatever that might mean), almost all the executives queried responded with the same refrain: there is no such thing as management of the Left or the Right, there is only good or bad management. This was as true for top managers no matter their political allegiance. Jean Grenier, director-general of Eutelsat, noted that although politics may have influenced the firing of people at the very top, 'underneath, the rest remained the same, and there was no political pressure to change anything in management.'[38]

Only a handful of Socialist top managers suggested that Socialist values could be involved in some way in management. One Socialist banker insisted that Socialist values determine how to spend the money earned. In most cases, however, it is as if the Socialists felt that ownership by the state of the means of production, together with greater worker democracy through the Auroux Laws was sufficient. But such democracy did not extend to participation in top management decision-making, or to *autogestion*, the rallying cry of the more grass-roots Left in the seventies.

The Socialists' value-neutral approach to management should have come as no surprise. What little discussion there was of Socialist management before nationalization suggested that there would be few 'Socialist' changes to the firm once the party took power. Three years before the Socialists' accession to power, one of the leading 'pink', or left-leaning, managers, Alain Gomez, at the time senior vice-president at Saint-Gobain but soon to become head of the newly nationalized Thomson, tellingly argued that within the context of a government of the Right, 'there was no difference between a *patron*, or boss, of the Right and of the Left: he is required to work within the rules of the game established by the environment and the society.'[39] Gomez' wife, Francine Gomez, at the time chief executive of Waterman, was equally opposed to the possibility of democratizing recruitment and promotion practices because, 'You can't always be liked; you can't have the CEO elected, or you would end up like politicians. And then the best will not necessarily be in charge.' Similarly, François Dalle, then chief executive of L'Oréal and a close friend of President François Mitterrand, contended: 'One has to avoid ideology. Men can't manage themselves; they need to find a leader.'

At a time when the *autogestion* movement was in its heyday, top managers with ties to the PS seemed to intimate that the more democratic forms of management demanded by activists would not arrive. It should come as no surprise, therefore, that left-leaning CEOs, once placed at the head of industries and banks nationalized by their comrades, did not seek to infuse the firm with Socialist values. In fact, that was the furthest thing from most of their minds. Rather, they sought to defend their firms against any encroachments by the Socialist government. This was as true of those without élite training and corps membership as it was of those who were nurtured by it.

It should come as no surprise, therefore, that most Socialist appointees to the nationalized firms were very much in favour of denationalization when it presented itself. In addition to the more than 70 cases of illegal sales of subsidiaries of public enterprises, the heads of such nationalized concerns as Rhône-Poulenc, Thomson, CGE, Paribas and Suez had also been working on denationalization plans ahead of the Right's return to power. This list included even such non-élite CEOs as Loïk Le Floch Prigent, head of Rhône-Poulenc.[40]

For most leaders of the nationalized enterprises, privatization was simply the next step for firms requiring a new infusion of capital, enabling them to be more flexible in their strategies. Moreover, by 'flexibility', the heads of the nationalized concerns generally meant new ways of raising capital rather than, as the neoliberals would have insisted, an end to excessive Socialist *dirigisme*.

Is there any difference between managers of the Left and those of the Right? Peyrelevade, now considered the pivot of the new establishment, stated that 'We are, it is true, very "business-minded".' But he still saw CEOs of the Left as different – they have a longer term view and probably different relations with labour from the owner-capitalists. But this is the extent of it. He certainly felt no overriding obligation to the Socialist Party: 'The interest of the enterprise [comes] first.'[41]

REFORMING MANAGERIAL PRACTICE

The nationalizations provided a climate for change at the same time they became an excuse to clean house, to rationalize operations and to introduce a new management style and culture into the organization. French managerial practice over the past ten years has been transformed through modernization and internationalization. The greatest changes have been in personnel and labour relations and in the introduction of modern management techniques; the smallest have been in the executives' management style, recruitment and promotion.

Although not all CEOs would agree that modernization started with the Socialists, and that they are therefore the only 'true' capitalists, they are all convinced that it accelerated under them, beginning with the new appointments to head the nationalized industries. In particular, they see a better ability to manage human resources and a better management strategy, and they credit the Socialists not only with an increase in the entrepreneurial spirit but also with unblocking labour-management relations.

French managers have come to recognize that the client needs to penetrate the enterprise, and that marketing should start from the needs of the client. Japanese management techniques are the rage. In many cases, firms have decentralized operations, democratized management and modernized personnel evaluation systems.[42] A study by Cofremca found these changes already in evidence in 1984, with a greater concern for productivity and efficiency on the parts of workers and management; new market strategies, innovation and diversification; and greater managerial cohesion resulting from the process of decentralization, increase of autonomy and responsibility and the social transformation of the enterprise.[43]

Changes in management style have come more slowly. That such changes are more modest is understandable, since the new heads of the nationalized and privatized firms are little different in training from their predecessors, for whom hierarchy and centralization are the stock in trade.[44] Also hindering the change are subordinates used to leaders who manage in an autocratic and paternalistic style. The new CEOs of the 1980s faced a rigidly centralized and hierarchical structure that ensured that only the highest levels of management had decision-making power and that the president alone bore responsibility for the company's activities.[45] Compared to Great Britain and Germany, France has had the strongest degree of centralization of authority, with the CEO monopolising decisions on most major issues.[46] Moreover, unlike German managers, who tend to reward individual creativity and see the organization as a co-ordinated network of rational individuals, or the British who focus on interpersonal communication and negotiation skills, and view the organization as a network of relationships among individuals who seek to influence one another, the French have looked at the organization as 'an authority network where the power to organize and control the actors stems from their positioning in the hierarchy', according to André Laurent.[47] They have traditionally emphasized the ability to manage power relationships and to work the system.

The hierarchical structure of the French firm, along with the focus on power relations, ensures that all attention is focused on the top. Add to this the fact that French firms traditionally have boards of directors and works' councils that play minor roles, and it becomes all the more understandable why, as Louis Gallois, former head of SNECMA, put it, the entire system 'leads to a solitary power at the top'. Decentralization – necessary to combat this – requires 'fighting a natural tendency'.

Such hierarchy is difficult to overcome. For Daniel Lebègue, director-general of the BNP, 'The French CEO is seen more as a monarch who makes decisions all alone, perhaps with some princes.' Still, many executives did seek to diminish the authoritarianism, decentralize operations and share some information and decision-making with managers and wage-earners. This depended on personality as much as on firm history and structure, with long-internationalized firms such as Pechiney, Rhône-Poulenc and Elf less likely to be centralised than more recently internationalized firms.

Although some firms have successfully democratized decision-making at the uppermost levels, the most progress has been made at the lower management levels. In a 1989 study of three major firms, Michel Crozier found that managers were very open to participative management, were unanimously in support of quality circles and greeted the reduction in hierarchical levels with not nearly the opposition that might have been expected, because it speeded up the decision-making process. Nonetheless, he found that many problems resulted from the fact that major decisions are still the domain of the top.[48] The progress at the lower management levels also reflects the near-revolution in personnel and labour relations, itself a byproduct of the rehabilitation of business and the end of economic ideology. Traditionally, France has had poor labour relations, with management attitudes toward workers characterized by mistrust and coldness. This translated itself into management by fiat or decree, a rejection of all worker participation or meaningful involvement of subordinates in decision-making and limited worker discretion accompanied by close supervision.

Much of this changed in the 1980s. Although the worker democracy laws were not very effective, they at least brought France up to the level of the countries that surround it.[49] In the view of the CEOs they helped facilitate better communication between management and workers, diminished the importance of unions, provided workers with better understanding of the requirements of the firm and gave management a better grasp of issues important to the workers. The 1984 Cofremca study confirms this, seeing management, on the one side, closer to the personnel, notably in the factories, and more co-operative and communicative, having abandoned its anti-union stance. On the other side, it found workers less interested in ideology, preferring negotiated solutions to battles about grand principles, and the personnel having greater trust in the enterprise and less interest in recourse to the state, which it had come to see more as temporary and dangerous.[50]

The personnel as a whole, moreover, had become more motivated. In 1986, a SOFRES study found about half of the personnel (51 per cent) ready to make extra efforts for the firm, as opposed to slightly a third (34 per cent) who did their work conscientiously but no more, and smaller percentages who saw work as a necessity (8 per cent) or who did not find it worthwhile to make the effort (5 per cent). Blue-collar workers, however, were somewhat less motivated, perhaps reflecting the still-traditional organization of some workplaces.[51] Moreover, personnel's views of management had also been transformed. By 1986, 69 per cent of the personnel had come to see top management as *sympathique*, while 78 per cent found them competent and 73 per cent felt they were worthy of trust.

Nonetheless, the graduates of élite educational institutions and members in the élite civil service corps have continued to limit upward mobility in the corporation, blocking access to the highest ranks for those making their way internally up the corporate ladder. By rewarding credentialism at the expense of achievement, this recruitment and promotion system lowers morale and fails to take full advantage of human resources within the corporation. A sense of going nowhere – of being *plafonné* – is a clear indicator of the effects of the élite recruitment system. The contrast with Germany is most striking, where the pattern of inside promotion is said to encourage employee loyalty to the firm and its objectives, leading to the development of a long-term view.[52] And because promotion to top management positions in Germany is the reward for high performance over the long haul, it also gives Germans a sense that they have something to work towards, by contrast with France, where no amount of achievement will help. Drancourt illustrates this by comparing Germany, where there are more captains and fewer generals, to France, where the generals come from elsewhere, and the captains aspire only to be colonels. This results in a profound resentment among captains, who cannot get far enough.

These internal rigidities have begun to change, albeit minimally, in large measure because of the modernization and internationalization of French firms carried out by the CEOs themselves. Now, virtually all government and business officials interviewed agree, élite recruits are entering the firm earlier, spending more years learning the business before being catapulted to the top and gaining more international experience. Moreover, the traditional management profile is beginning to diversify. University graduates are beginning to make inroads, even if not to the highest positions. Only 40 per cent of recruits to career positions in large firms now come from the *grandes écoles*, a significant change from 15 years ago.[53] Although lower-level management positions are being increasingly opened to women, higher-level positions remain male-dominated: only 4 per cent of top management positions were held by women.[54]

At the same time that more women and more university graduates are making their way up the hierarchy, however slowly, there are also larger numbers of graduates of the *grandes écoles* moving directly into business, without passing through the state first. According to Strauss-Kahn, changes are occurring because the decrease in state influence on the economy is weakening the hold of this 'closed shop': élite graduates know that state service will not necessarily net them the leadership of a major state enterprise, whereas a career in business may.

The internationalization of French business has also helped loosen the hold of the graduates of élite schools, with the MBA increasingly becoming the degree of choice among up-and-coming executives. Moreover, the internationalization of firms has also made foreign experience an increasingly important part of a manager's career profile. But this is still not true for the CEOs. In 1986, of the 144 CEOs of the top French multinationals, only 16 had foreign managerial experience, and only eight of these worked for the company they were later to lead. Of the rest, 112 lacked foreign experience.[55]

The more French firms internationalize and diversify their recruitment, and the less they value the internal market, the less likely it is that graduates of the élite schools will hold sway – unless they have the greatest international experience, the best language skills and have managed to prove themselves in the firm before they are considered for high-level positions. For the moment, the typical top management team remains remarkably like those of the past – very French, very male and very élite. But they preside over a corporation that has been transformed. Bankers and industrialists both act in a more interdependent manner and more independently of the government. And they operate in an environment in which business has been rehabilitated and economic ideologies put to rest. In consequence, at no other time in their history have French CEOs been more powerful and had fewer constraints, given the size of their empires and the relative retreat of the state.

CONCLUSION

For the moment, the French government seems willing to leave the future of French business in the hands of the CEOs. While not abandoning state interventionism altogether, it is changing its response to the pressures of European integration. From traditional *dirigisme*, where the state formulated plans and industrial policies for industry, leaving industry to implement them in consultation with the various ministries, industrial policy now appears to have taken a back seat to business plans and industrial strategies. The state has simply changed its form of interventionism.

Because the European Commission takes a dim view of direct subsidies, French governments have increasingly favoured more indirect ways of providing financing, such as through the trading of shares in nationalized industries and banks. In certain strategic areas, however, the old pattern continues, with nationalized industries receiving large infusions of investment aid with the ultimate approval of the EU. The French have also sought to institute industrial policies at the European level that are no longer possible at the national level (for example, in high-definition television and computers).

Even before state control diminished, businesses ordinarily set their own strategies, with accommodation and co-optation the key to ministry–industry relations in implementing industrial policy-making.[56] The state has strengthened the ability of French business to operate efficiently and effectively.

Finally, although governments may become uneasy about how much freedom they have given business, they still have indirect ways of exerting control. They continue to influence business not only through more supply-side macroeconomic policies and microeconomic incentives but also through personalities. The state's colonization of business, by way of state-trained, former civil servants at the head of major French banks and industries means that there remains a single interpenetrating élite setting the course of the French economy. As a result, the retreat of the state has not brought the end of state influence over business, only a different kind that matches the modernization and internationalization of French business itself.

Notes

1. Portions of this chapter were published in 'An End to French Economic Exceptionalism? The Transformation of Business Under Mitterrand', *California Management Review* 36, no. 1 (Fall 1993) pp. 75–98; and 'A Profile of the French CEO', *International Executive* 35, no. 5 (September/October 1993) pp. 413–30.
2. On the deindustrialization, see Jean-Louis Levet, *Une France sans usines?*, 2nd ed. (Paris: Economica, 1989); Elie Cohen, *L'Etat brancardier: Politiques du déclin*

industriel (1974–1984)* (Paris: Calmann-Lévy, 1989); Pierre Dacier, Levet and Jean-Claude Tourret, *Les Dossiers noirs de l'industrie française: Echecs, handicaps, espoirs* (Paris: Fayard, 1985).

3. For a fuller explanation, see Schmidt, 'An End to French Economic Exceptionalism'.

4. The more than 40 interviews with top government and business officials from February to July 1991 included Ministry of Industry officials, including two ministers; top managers of major public, private, privatized and nationalized firms in heavy and light industry, the energy sector, electronics and high technology, retail, and banking and insurance; and management consultants and heads of business associations.

5. For example, André Lévey-Lang, head of Paribas (interview with author, 26 April 1991) and Daniel Lebègue, No. 2 at the BNP and former director of the Treasury (interview 26 April 1991).

6. For example, Jean Gandois of Pechiney (Interview with author, 2 July 1991).

7. For example, Louis Gallois, current head of Aérospatiale, former head of SNECMA and former director-general of Industry, 1982–6 (interview, 3 May 1991); Roger Fauroux, Minister of Industry under Michel Rocard and former CEO of Saint-Gobain; José Bidegain, Fauroux's right-hand man at the ministry and a former top director at Saint-Gobain (interview, 7 March 1991).

8. For a full discussion of the nationalizations, see André Delion and Michel Durupty, *Les Nationalisations* (Paris: Economica, 1982). See also Lionel Zinsou, *Le Fer de lance* (Paris: Olivier Orban, 1985) pp. 68–71.

9. Interview, 16 May 1991.

10. Schmidt, 'Industrial Management Under the Socialists in France: Decentralised *Dirigisme* at the National and Local Levels', *Comparative Politics* 21, no. 1 (October 1988).

11. Durupty, *Les Privatisations en France* (Paris: Documentation Française, 1988).

12. *International Herald Tribune*, 17 November 1986.

13. *Le Point*, no. 757, 23 March 1987. For a general discussion of the pre-1981 situation of French banking and industry, see Bertrand Bellon, *Le Pouvoir financier et l'industrie en France* (Paris: Seuil, 1980).

14. Michel Bauer and Bénédicte Mourot, *Les 200: Comment devient-on un grand patron?* (Paris: Seuil, 1987) p. 107, fn. 7; and François Morin, *La structure financière du capitalisme français* (Paris: Calmann-Lévy, 1974).

15. 'Stratégie du capital et de l'actionnariat', working document, Institut de l'Entreprise (January 1991).

16. 'L'Etat et les chefs d'entreprises', *L'Observatoire de la Cofremca*, no. 5 (1981).

17. *Le Monde*, 28–29 September 1986.

18. SOFRES, *L'Etat de l'opinion 1987* (Paris: Le Seuil, 1987) pp. 141, 143.

19. 'Le Nouveau réalisme', *L'Observatoire de la Cofremca*, no. 11 (1983).

20. SOFRES, *L'Etat de l'opinion 1988* (Paris: Le Seuil, 1988) p. 31.

21. *Ibid.* p. 30.

22. *Le Monde*, 10 May 1991.

23. See Schmidt, 'Industrial Management'.

24. *The Economist*, 24 May 1986.

25. For a discussion of this élite, see Pierre Birnbaum, Charles Barucq, Michel Bellaiche and Alain Marie, *La Classse dirigeante* (Paris: Presses Universitaires Française, 1978); and Birnbaum, *The Heights of Power* (Chicago, IL: University of Chicago Press, 1982). For the Socialist recruitment pattern, see Elie Cohen, 'L'Etat socialiste en industrie: Volontarisme politique et changement socio-économique', in Birnbaum, ed., *Les Elites socialistes au pouvoir (1981–1985)* (Paris: Presses Universitaires de France, 1985); and Bauer and Mourot.

26. In more than forty interviews with the author between February and July 1991, all noted these exceptions to the rule.

27. Bauer and Mourot, p. 187.
28. For a more extensive comparison, see Schmidt, 'Profile'.
29. These statistics and those in the following five paragraphs are from Bauer and Mourot.
30. *The British Entrepreneur 1988*, cited in Christel Lane, *Management and Labour in Europe: The Industrial Enterprise in Germany, Britain and France* (London: Edward Elgar, 1989) pp. 91.
31. Bauer and Mourot, pp. 247–8.
32. See Pierre Bourdieu, *La Noblesse de l'état: Grands écoles et ésprit de corps* (Paris: Editions de Minuit, 1989) p. 518; and Bauer and Mourot, pp. 127–32.
33. Bauer and Mourot, p. 183.
34. Bourdieu, p. 354.
35. Jacques Julliard, 'Mitterrand: Between Socialism and the Republic', *Telos*, no. 55 (Spring 1983).
36. François de Closets, *Le Pari de la responsabilité* (Paris: Payot, 1989).
37. *Le Monde*, 11 May 1991.
38. Interview with author, Paris, 17 April 1991.
39. Quotes in this paragraph are from 'Patrons '78–91', a documentary film by Gérard Mordillat and Nicolas Philibert, produced first in 1978 but censored at the time because several CEOs objected to the editing. The film was only aired recently, with an update and commentary by a few of the 'new generation' of CEOs.
40. *Financial Times*, 25 January 1986.
41. *Le Monde*, 11 May 1991.
42. See, for example, Renaud Sainsaulieu, ed., *L'Entreprise, Une Affaire de société* (Paris: Presses de la Fondation Nationale des Sciences Politiques, 1990); G. Archier and H. Sérieyx, *L'Entreprise du 3e type* (Paris: Seuil, 1984); and Antoine Riboud, *Modernisation, mode d'emploi* (Paris: Union Générale d'Editions, 1987).
43. 'Meilleur Pilotage dans les Entreprises', *L'Observatoire de la Cofremca*, no. 12 (1984).
44. See, for example, Pierre Dupont Gabriel, *L'Etat patron c'est moi* (Paris: Flammarion, 1985).
45. For empirical pieces on French management before the eighties, see Roger Priouret, *La France et le management* (Paris: Denoël, 1977); André Harris and Alain de Sédouy, *Les patrons* (Paris: Seuil, 1977); Dominique Xardel, *Les Managers* (Paris: Grasset, 1978) and Philippe Vasseur, *Patrons de gauche* (Paris: Lattès, 1979).
46. Lane, p. 105; J. Horovitz, *Top Management Control in Europe* (New York: St. Martin's Press, 1980) p. 67; and G. P. Dyas and H. Thanheiser, *The Emerging European Enterprise: Strategy and Structure in French and German Industry* (London: Macmillan, 1976) p. 246.
47. Laurent, 'The Cross-Cultural Puzzle of International Human Resource Management', *Human Resource Management* 25, no. 1 (Spring 1986) p. 96. For the implications of this for internal management in France, by comparison with the United States and the Netherlands, see Philippe d'Iribarne, *La Logique de l'honneur: Gestion des entreprises et traditions nationales* (Paris: Seuil, 1989).
48. Michel Crozier, *L'Entreprise à l'écoute* (Paris: Interéditions, 1989).
49. For information on the Auroux Laws, see Michèle Millot and Jean-Pol Roulleau, *L'Entreprise face aux lois Auroux* (Paris: Les Editions d'Organisation, 1984); Richard Holton, 'Industrial Politics in France: Nationalisation under Mitterrand', *West European Politics* 9, no. 1 (January 1986) pp. 77–8. For their limited effectiveness, see W. Rand Smith, 'Towards *Autogestion* in Socialist France? The Impact of Industrial Relations Reform', *West European Politics* 10, no. 1 (January 1987).
50. 'Meilleur Pilotage', *Cofremca*.
51. SOFRES, *Opinion 1987*, pp. 145, 148.

52.   J. M. Bessant and M. Grunt, *Management and Manufacturing Innovation in the United Kingdom and West Germany* (Aldershot: Gower, 1985).
53.   *Le Monde*, 14 May 1991.
54.   NEDO, *Making of Managers*, cited in Lane, p. 89.
55.   Bauer and Mourot, p. 255.
56.   See Schmidt, 'Patterns of State Intervention: The Case of Industrial Policy-Making', paper prepared for presentation at the American Political Science Association, Chicago, IL, 2–6 September 1992.

7 French Socialism and the Transformation of Industrial Relations since 1981[1]

Chris Howell

This chapter describes and explains the transformation that has taken place in French industrial relations during the Mitterrand era, and discusses some of the consequences for workers and trade unions in France. It will be argued that the nature of French industrial relations, or what I term labour regulation,[2] characterized for the bulk of the post-war period by a heavy emphasis upon legislation, weak trade unions inside the firm, and very poorly-developed firm-level collective bargaining, has given way in the 1980s and 1990s to a more firm-centred system of industrial relations. There is a growing disjunction between highly politicized but weak national trade union federations on one hand, and more quiescent and autonomous enterprise unions, representing workers inside the firm but not beyond its boundaries, on the other. However, while labour is weak in the sense of having limited collective resources outside the firm, it is organized *within* the firm. The emerging form of labour regulation can be termed microcorporatism, because, in Wolfgang Streeck's memorable phrase, it encourages 'wildcat co-operation', in the form of a firm-level bargain, akin to corporatism, in which wage and work flexibility is traded for job security.[3] Labour regulation in France was particularly vulnerable to this mutation, and the Auroux reforms of the first Socialist government, allied to the economic conditions of the 1980s, and the transition from a Fordist to a post-Fordist economy (see Chapter 8) encouraged this shift.

POSTWAR LABOUR REGULATION IN FRANCE

Labour Exclusion: 1945–68

The weakness of France's post-war labour movement is well-known. After World War II and the subsequent breakup of the tripartite coalition that governed France from the Liberation until 1947, what George Ross has termed a 'labor-exclusionary post-war settlement' emerged.[4] France did not develop a historical compromise between capital and labour either in the 1930s or 1940s, as did West Germany, Austria, Britain and the Scandinavian countries. In contrast, France lacked an institutionalized collective bargaining system, its trade unions were weak and legally insecure, wage determination occurred primarily through the labour market, and Left parties played little or no role in the political life of the country. In short, both unions and the Left were essentially excluded from the political and economic structures that emerged from World War II, a situation that did not begin to change until 1968.

The French trade union movement fragmented after the war largely for political reasons. The public sector federations of the dominant union, the *Confédération Générale du Travail* (CGT), split to form the *Force Ouvrière* (FO), and the large education federation formed an independent union, the *Fédération de l'Education Nationale* (FEN), in protest against Communist domination of the CGT. In 1964 the growing ideological division within the *Confédération Française des Travailleurs Chrétiens* (CFTC) concerning deconfessionalization became an organizational division, and the *Confédération Française Démocratique du Travail* (CFDT) was formed.[5]

Historically, French trade unions have faced tremendous disadvantages. The predominance of small firms has meant an environment deeply hostile to trade unions, and indeed to any form of workers' organization. In 1967 half of those firms that, by law, should have created works councils (*comités d'entreprises*) had not, and since such councils were mandatory only in firms employing 50 or more employees, the overwhelming majority of firms had no works council.[6] Unions had no legally secure place in the firm until 1968, and even after 1968 firms employing fewer than 50 were not obligated to allow union sections. The intimidation of union activists in the firm was widespread.

In addition, French unions have had very limited funds and tiny organizational apparatuses. There are neither dues check-offs nor closed shops, except in a few unusual cases. The result was a low and strongly fluctuating level of unionization. The average union density for the post-war period was close to 25 per cent, which compared unfavourably with most West European countries.[7] Furthermore, sudden gains in membership due to particular political and economic conditions – the Popular Front, for instance – were lost completely once the conditions passed.

The big exception to low and inconsistent union density was the public sector, where greater job security and less repression have been more conducive to unionization. The public sector was overrepresented in all the unions. In 1975 the public sector accounted for 27.3 per cent of all employees but made up 42.6 per cent of CGT membership, more than 50 per cent of FO membership and in 1972, 32 per cent of CFDT membership.[8]

Because of this deep-seated union weakness and the absence of a friendly Left party in power in the 1950s and 1960s, labour regulation was highly conflictual and poorly institutionalized. In the 11 February 1950 law on collective bargaining, which though amended remains the basis for French industrial relations, the state was accorded a wider role and significant legislative restrictions were placed on the bargaining process.[9] The legislation privileged branch- (or industry-) level collective agreements, with the intention that firm-level accords *follow* and *modify* agreements reached at a higher level. In addition, agreements could be extended by the government so that they applied more widely than the signatories intended. Thus a partial agreement might be extended to an entire industry, or a whole region.

In the context of bitter shop-floor relations between unions, workers and employers, collective bargaining grew only fitfully after the war period, with wild swings corresponding closely to the state of the economy, government economic policy and the strike level. Collective bargaining increased rather than decreased as the strike level rose, particularly after 1954.[10] Thus bargaining was not an *alternative* to industrial conflict so much as a *response* to it. This underscores the fragility of collective bargaining and its lack of an existence independent of the business cycle.

French industrial relations were a constant conflict in which neither side recognized gains as legitimate or durable. Negotiations occurred when unions were strong enough to impose them on management (often following industrial action) or when management needed workers' co-operation. In the first 20 years after World War II neither of these conditions occurred with any regularity, with the result that collective bargaining was unable to develop a regular and stable existence independent of economic conditions and cyclical waves of industrial militancy.[11] Thus, in contrast to much of Western Europe, and particularly the social democratic model of industrial relations (where regular collective bargaining took place between trade unions and management, each of whom recognized the other as legitimate), France saw a form of perpetual guerrilla warfare in the workplace, where unions had a tenuous existence at best, and collective bargaining occurred only at those rare moments when workers could force their employers to negotiate.

Thus labour regulation in 1950s and 1960s France was a hybrid of mechanisms with three main components. First there was the slow development after 1955 of firm-level decentralized collective bargaining in a small number of leading sectors of the economy, such as automobiles and chemicals. Here stronger labour combined with firms' need for steady, predictable wage increases and industrial peace to make collective bargaining both possible and necessary. But these sectors were limited until the rapid modernization of the French economy that began in the 1960s. For the most part, collective bargaining took place at the branch level, and involved the setting of minimum wages. Real wages were determined at the firm level, where unions were weak or absent.

The second component of labour regulation involved state intervention. The state was involved in labour regulation, though to a lesser degree than it would be in the 1970s. The minimum wage was scarcely used as an economic or social tool; rather, it provided a safety net for sectors completely uncovered by collective agreements, and hence without branch-negotiated wage minima. The process of extension of collective agreements had some impact, particularly for the diffusion of social benefits, such as the three-week paid vacation.

The third and most important component of labour regulation was provided by the labour market. France had a very weakly institutionalized labour market, in that supply and demand were very important in wage determination. The needs of reconstruction ensured that the French economy could absorb most of the available labour. But while unemployment remained low, many new workers entered the labour force as result of either rural migration or immigration (particularly following decolonization). By 1970 there were 2 million immigrants in France, 10 per cent of the employed labour force.[12] These workers were, at least initially, less open to organization and militancy. Furthermore, the French labour market closely resembled a 'restricted, compartmentalized market' with low labour mobility.[13] Thus small increases in unemployment could have an effect on wage demands.

For the 15 to 20 years following World War II, the labour market worked to diffuse strong working-class pressure on wages. Rarely were real wages negotiated collectively; they were either set unilaterally by the employer or followed closely the branch minima. In this period, employers were largely content for the state to remain aloof from labour regulation so that wages could be set at the firm level, where workers were weak, unions non-existent and the overall balance of power favourable to employers. Wage rises tended to be the result of cyclical explosions of militancy, largely unmediated and underinstitutionalized.

In addition, state economic policies regulated the level of wages and responded to strike waves using labour market tools. For instance, the wage explosion of 1955–7 was dealt with by a stabilization plan involving deflation to generate unemployment and sap the militancy of workers. When the state did choose to intervene in wage determination, it did so through the labour market rather than through statutory controls or encouragement of a voluntary incomes policy. Above all, this was a mode of labour regulation in which workers were not integrated – into unions, works councils or regular collective bargaining – at the firm level. This helps to explain the high strike levels of the first two post-war decades and the scale of the events of May 1968.

The New Society and its Aftermath: 1968–81

This form of labour regulation collapsed in the general strike of May and June 1968. The combination of unemployment and deteriorating working conditions, resulting from Charles de Gaulle's economic modernization programme and the absence of established unions and collective bargaining practices inside the firm, led discontent to boil over into mass industrial unrest and a politicization of the dispute that threatened the regime. It is interesting that in the official response to May 1968, the industrial relations system was identified as a major culprit. The driving force behind the reforms that came to be known as the 'New Society' was the notion that economic modernization required a modern set of social relations and social structures, and hence that the continued archaic nature of industrial relations was a brake on France's greatness. As Jacques Delors put it when he was social adviser to Prime Minister Jacques Chaban-Delmas: 'The point of departure is clear. An industrial society can only function well if its industrial relations are strong and properly adapted to the diverse issues which face them.'[14]

Chaban-Delmas was chosen by Georges Pompidou as prime minister after de Gaulle resigned following the defeat of his referendum proposals in 1969. Chaban-Delmas launched an ambitious package of reforms that sought to strengthen trade unions and stimulate regular collective bargaining, particularly at the firm level. It was hoped this would reduce conflict and allow decentralized negotiation to become the dominant form of labour regulation. In the public sector Chaban-Delmas experimented with multi-year *contrats de progrès*, which provided for the indexation of wages to prices *and* to the success of the particular industry or service, plus no-strike pledges. In the private sector the strategy sought to build upon one of the major gains from May 1968, the provision of legal protection for union sections. Thus, a 1971 law amended the original 1950 legislation on collective bargaining to make it easier to sign firm-level agreements.

This strategy had some success. Collective bargaining took hold in the public sector, where the government had the most influence, and there was an increase in bargaining at the industry (or branch) level in the Fordist sector of the private economy. But the end result was far from the hopes of the architects of the New Society. In the large traditional sector of the economy, and particularly at the firm level, unions remained largely excluded and collective bargaining was very limited.

The reforms were predicated upon strong unions because only strong unions could entice employers to the bargaining table. But convincing employers that they could deliver industrial peace was too heavy a burden for French trade unions. Trade unionism remained structurally weak in 1968 and 1969; it depended on the threat of strike action to maintain organizational control. Thus both trade unions and collective bargaining remained very weakly implanted at the firm level.

However, there was no return to the *status quo ante*. While the rhetoric of the New Society was rich with calls for the withdrawal of the state from its regulatory role in society, the paradoxical, and largely unintended, consequence of this period was a greatly enlarged role for the French state in labour regulation. The state was active in setting the terms for wage bargaining in the public sector and used the minimum wage to influence the lower end of the income scale in the private sector. At the same time the state took the initiative in the area of social modernization, using legislation or exhortation to create the basic social infrastructure appropriate for a modern economy.

In 1970 the minimum wage legislation was amended so that the minimum wage was indexed not just to prices but to the average hourly wage, with an additional annual increase left to the government's discretion. Also, the extension of collective agreements was made easier. And, finally, in 1974 and 1975 a series of laws and national/confederal agreements introduced the requirement of administrative authorization for layoffs and provided high unemployment benefits. The effect was to curb the disciplinary impact of the labour market by partially insulating workers from the risk of unemployment and substantial income loss.

The major change during this period was in the attitude and role of the state, rather than the class capacity of labour. In some sense, in light of the disappointing results of the New Society programme, the French state came to *substitute* for the weakness of trade unions and collective bargaining. The state provided many of the benefits that unions in other countries did, through the minimum wage, the extension procedure and the curbing of the labour market. It proved much more difficult to strengthen trade unions than to substitute for them using the resources of the state. Thus, by 1974 France could be said to have a dualistic form of labour regulation: collective bargaining was becoming implanted in the modern, Fordist parts of the private sector and in the public sector, and the traditional sector became ever more subject to state intervention and regulation. Even collective bargaining in the public sector rested upon the continued willingness of government to buy peace and legitimacy with high real wage increases. Workers remained largely unorganized and unintegrated at the firm level.

With the continued weakness of labour, the shift in the mode of labour regulation in France remained contingent upon the favour of employers and the state, and upon a strong economy. After 1974, both these conditions collapsed. The oil shock soon revealed the weakness of Fordism in all advanced capitalist economies. In the face of a profits squeeze, ballooning budget deficit and economic uncertainty, the pillars of the New Society began to erode. Lucrative public-sector wage contracts were no longer affordable, extensive state intervention now appeared to obstruct the ability of firms to adapt to economic uncertainty, and even large firms, which had spearheaded the drive for collective bargaining after 1968, began to question its utility.

Collective bargaining did not disappear after 1976, but it did change its form. Now, bargaining happened when employers wanted, on their terrain, and trade unions were chosen for their ideological affinity with management. Bargaining was more about legitimacy than about negotiation between opposing class forces. The tenor of collective bargaining in the public sector was captured well by Delors: 'There remains all that is left of a mass celebrated at the eleventh hour without faith: a liturgy empty of sense. . . . [They] maintain it as a rite, so as to save face. But the heart is not in it.'[15]

As for the second pillar of labour regulation, France remained a nation in which state regulation of labour was important, but from 1978 onward that role was reduced, and the function of state regulation changed. Until the mid-1970s state regulation had taken the place of labour regulation based on collective bargaining and strong trade unions. In order to extend Fordism into the traditional sector, state regulation needed to be more reactive, designed to 'manage' unemployment and protect those who slipped through the cracks of collective bargaining.

In this context Valéry Giscard d'Estaing and his prime ministers, Jacques Chirac and Raymond Barre, attempted a series of industrial relations reforms, including a reform of the firm in 1975–6 and an effort to reinvigorate collective bargaining after 1978. But these efforts largely failed, because trade unions were still too strong, and workers too important in political terms, to be ignored, and yet the material base for collective bargaining had collapsed. The result was, to paraphrase Antonio Gramsci, a crisis in which the old mode of labour regulation was dying but no alternative had yet been born.

SOCIALIST INDUSTRIAL RELATIONS REFORM

The 1981 landslide majority in the National Assembly of a Socialist government signalled a new departure in French industrial relations. The Socialists proclaimed a radical agenda of modernizing and humanizing the workplace, and promised to strengthen trade unions in their conflict with employers. However, a certain degree of mutual suspicion has always marked the relationship between the Socialist Party (PS) and organized labour. In part this derives from the lock the Communist Party (PCF) has historically had on the largest of the union confederations. Strengthening organized labour, then, looked a lot like strengthening the PS's enemy on the Left.

But the position of the PS on labour issues is more complicated than this. The PS entirely lacks the sort of institutional ties between Left party and union movement that colour policy in Britain or Sweden. Its members are so broadly dispersed among different trade union confederations that an alliance with any one would be deeply divisive. Further, its social base is not overwhelmingly working-class, even if workers constitute the largest single electoral bloc. Rather, the new middle classes (especially teachers) are overrepresented in the PS electorate, in the party's few workplace sections and, most strikingly, in the party itself.[16] The PS proved able in the 1970s to win the battle for the new middle classes, and this constituency heavily influenced the PS project.

There is much disagreement among scholars on the precise nature of Socialist Party ideology. It is widely argued that while *autogestion*, or self-management, exercised an important influence on the party in the 1970s, it was primarily rhetorical excess, and *autogestion* dropped off the map as soon as the PS took power in 1981. This would be to miss the *function* an *autogestionnaire* ideology played for the PS. There was an intelligible correspondence between the Socialist Party's ideology and its social base. It would have been remarkable if the PS *had* adopted a social democratic ideology in a society in which the type of labour movement necessary for the social democratic project did not exist. Rather, the *autogestionnaire* ideology was a logical response to a decentralized and fragmented labour movement, whose strength lay in firm level mobilization and action, and the interests of the rapidly expanding and electorally crucial new middle classes.

Too often the *autogestionnaire* aspects of the Socialist government's reforms are dismissed. Certainly, workers' control was not introduced in France, and Yugoslavia was not the model for the Auroux Laws, which, in fact, explicitly reaffirmed the legitimate right of owners to manage. The radical version of *autogestion* was immediately dropped once the PS took office, and indeed was probably never taken seriously by party leaders. But this ignores the essential plasticity of ideology, the multiple directions in which a given ideology can lead and the influence that *autogestion* exercised over policy well after its radical version died.

Autogestion tended to focus on the firm and on power relations within the firm. Its subject was workers rather than unions; it emphasized self-transformation through daily struggle in the workplace. One concomitant feature was a certain wariness, not so much of trade unions *per se* but rather of the social democratic model of centralized, highly disciplined and bureaucratic trade unions.[17] The PS was genuinely critical of corporatist-style arrangements because corporatism implied deals made above the heads of workers, who were passive participants. In addition, such arrangements usually concerned quantitative wage issues and left authority relations essentially untouched. Above all, social democracy mediated workers' interests and actions through trade unions rather than allowing direct expression of workers' demands.

This ambiguous relationship between the governing Socialists and the labour movement formed the backdrop for the Auroux reforms of 1982–3. The initial reform proposals were made in the Auroux Report in September 1981, and five pieces of legislation followed between August 1982 and July 1983. The proposals prompted a good deal of debate – within the PS, between the PS and the trade unions, and between the Left and the Right in the National Assembly – and the legislation that finally emerged was clearly a compromise. Of the unions, the CFDT was most successful in getting its goals incorporated in the legislation and found itself the reforms' main defender outside the government. The CGT wanted the reforms to go further in giving concrete powers to prevent layoffs, while FO was deeply suspicious, seeing the reforms as ultimately weakening unions.[18]

These reforms contained two distinct and coherent, but incompatible, logics. One logic led toward a model of decentralized collective bargaining between employers and trade unions, in which bargaining was articulated between branch and firm levels, and in which the relationship between the various forms of worker representation in the firm was one of mutual reinforcement. In this model, trade unions would have the critical role of privileged representatives of the working class, and workers inside the firm were connected, via national union organizations and articulated bargaining, to workers in other firms and sectors.

The second logic led toward a model of microcorporatist bargaining between employers and firm-specific organizations of workers, in which labour regulation centred on the firm. Trade unions were either banished from the firm or assigned a peripheral role in bargaining, as firm-specific forms of worker representation bargained with management. In this model workers would be cut off from a wider collectivity of workers, and firm-level bargaining would be independent of bargaining at higher levels.

The central question for the fate of the Socialist reform project was whether the Auroux Laws would become beachheads for union activity in the firm, or rather create potential *alternatives* to union organization. In the early and mid-1980s – not a good time to construct a model of labour regulation based on trade unions – the latter prevailed. The trade union crisis deepened. Membership loss was only briefly halted by the arrival of the Left in power before the slide began again. The French *patronat*'s response to the Auroux reforms was initially negative, and it maintained both its deep hostility to trade unions and its search for alternative forms of mediation that did not rely upon trade unions as the privileged interlocutors of the working class.

There is no doubt that the primary goal of the legislation was to encourage the first model of decentralized collective bargaining. The Auroux reforms deepened and extended the innovations of Delors' New Society: where the New Society provided legal safeguards for trade union sections in firms employing 50 or more people, the Auroux Laws extended that protection to all firms regardless of size; the New Society encouraged firm-level collective bargaining, while the Auroux Laws made it obligatory.

However, the Auroux Laws contained two kinds of dangers. The first was that such a project depended upon the strengthening of trade unions, and, surprisingly, the Auroux Laws did practically nothing in this direction. In particular, unions received formal legal protection in smaller firms, but none of the benefits – paid leave, facilities – afforded unions in larger firms. This lack of protection in part was due to fear of the costs to smaller employers, and in part to the hope that unions would benefit *indirectly* through a strengthening of the works councils. This proved to be a fatal gamble.

The second danger was that in a number of ways the reforms strengthened the microcorporatist features of the French industrial relations system. By expanding works councils' powers, the legislation blurred the difference between unions and works councils. As Raymond Vatinet has pointed out, there is a fine line between consultation and negotiation,[19] and the Auroux reforms encouraged the small but growing trend of agreements '*de fait*' between management and works councils. These were technically illegal (as only union sections had the legal right to conclude agreements) but operated nonetheless. In 1985, of all the firms that did not bargain with their union delegates despite legal obligations, half signed illegal agreements with their works councils.[20]

In a similar way, the requirement in the Auroux reforms that larger firms create a 'right of expression' for workers inside the firm became – in the context of weak unions and a resurgent managerial emphasis upon firm-level labour regulation – a form of obligatory quality circle, dominated by the existing management hierarchy, and hence acting to increase productivity and integrate workers into the firm.[21] Because it so feared this eventuality, the FO opposed the Auroux Laws. It argued: 'Under cover of democratization, the object [of the reform] remains the elimination of unionism, a process which will take place by an atomization of workers and by an integration of the worker.'[22] Thus both the increased powers for the works councils and the new worker expression groups encouraged alternative *firm-level* and *firm-specific* forms of worker representation to trade unions.

A third microcorporatist innovation was the right of firm-level agreements to 'derogate', or exempt themselves from the non-wage elements of a branch-level agreement or even legislation, so long as no veto was exercised by 'majority' unions. Clearly this eroded the traditional hierarchical relationship between legislation and the various levels of collective bargaining embodied in the 1950 law.

This erosion was dramatically accelerated by the Auroux Laws' obligation to bargain at the firm level. In practice, given the weakness of unions in the firm, employers now shifted their bargaining from the branch level to the firm level. The annual codicils to branch-level collective agreements (the best measure of the vitality of bargaining at this level) dropped by half, from 1385 in 1982 to 695 in 1986, before stabilizing at 840 in 1989.[23] Meanwhile, the number of firm-level agreements rose steadily in the 1980s, almost tripling from 1955 in 1983 to 5793 in 1989.[24]

The impact of the Auroux reforms has been a kind of decoupling of the system of industrial relations in France. The Auroux legislation did encourage collective bargaining. The coverage of collective bargaining increased at the branch as well as firm level, which helped to legitimize a partial withdrawal of state protection from the large block of workers previously not covered by collective agreements.[25] While in 1981, 2 million workers (about 25 per cent of the labour force) had no coverage, that had been reduced to 1.3 million by 1985.[26] A 1987 Ministry of Labour study estimated that by that date only about half a million workers remained without coverage.[27]

However, the traditional hierarchy – in which legislation and high-level bargains formed a floor under collective agreements at lower levels – broke down and began to invert under pressure from derogation and the obligation to bargain at the firm level. Thus the abilities of the state to substitute for trade unions was weakened, as was the ability of trade unions to use their strength at the branch level to benefit workers even in the absence of strong firm-level unions.

Moreover, the fundamental prerequisite for the Auroux Laws to encourage regularized collective bargaining was a strong trade union movement. But in the 1980s the decline of French unions accelerated, by several measures (see Chapter 9). Union density is now estimated to be between 5 per cent and 10 per cent of the workforce (and that is concentrated in the public sector), and non-union candidates dominate works council elections.[28]

This suggests a marginalization of unions, or an integration of the union section into the firm and a loosening of the ties among various union delegates. Raymond-Pierre Bodin's detailed study of the application of the Auroux Laws in small firms led him to suggest that the 'position of the trade union confederations play little part in negotiation. . . . [I]t is rather a case of firm bargaining in the strict sense of the term'.[29] Thus there is a kind of cutting off at the knees of France's trade unions because of the isolation of firm-level union delegates from the regional or sectoral unions, let alone the confederation as a whole. The Auroux reforms also opened the way for new, firm-specific forms of labour organization to grow out of the enhanced powers for works councils and worker expression groups.

The *Projet Socialiste* had argued in 1980 that the public sector would be 'the primary terrain for advances in self-management' and a model for the private sector,[30] and the Auroux Report in 1981 promised that 'public and nationalized firms must play an exemplary role'.[31] But the July 1983 law grandly titled 'Democratization of the Public Sector' barely went beyond private-sector reforms, only encouraging a negotiated decentralization of works councils to smaller work units.

Faced with economic crisis, the Socialist government chose to use the public sector as the centrepiece of its wage restraint programme. From 1982 on, the government set targets for nominal wage growth that were strictly adhered to in the public sector, even if it meant not signing an annual wage agreement. In addition, Delors, as Minister of Finance and the Economy, successfully broke the rigid wage-price indexation that had operated in the public sector since the New Society.

The result was a success in terms of the government's anti-inflation policy, as public-sector workers bore the brunt of wage restraint and saw their purchasing power actually fall after 1982.[32] However, the subordination of industrial relation reforms to the austerity programme not only ensured that the public sector could not be used as a model for worker democratization, but also weakened collective bargaining in the one area it had been strongly implanted. Trade union strength has remained sufficiently high to resist much of the disorganization of unions that occurred in the private sector (where unions have, to all intents and purposes, disappeared), and to launch successive waves of strike action (while strikes have become very rare in the private sector). Nevertheless, while the microcorporatist logic of the Auroux Laws was much weaker in the public sector, the quasi-corporatism of French public-sector labour regulation inherited from the 1970s collapsed as a result of Socialist economic policy.

CONSEQUENCES

There has been much discussion both in and out of the academy of the 'normalizing' or 'modernizing' role of President François Mitterrand.[33] This volume provides evidence that Mitterrand has engineered a thaw in the deep ideological divide between Left and Right, which has existed since at least the founding of the French Communist Party, and perhaps since the French Revolution. The experience of government has moderated the French Socialist Party, while the Communist Party is getting smaller every day. It is in economic and education policy, and above all in ideological discourse, that most discussions of normalization take place, and the Socialists' 'end of illusions' noted.[34]

At least as important, however, is the realm of industrial relations. As Pierre Rosanvallon has pointed out, the Auroux Laws paradoxically marked the end of a century of debate over, and movement towards, greater democratization of the firm.[35] The French Socialist Party's most important contribution to the 'modernization' of France has been the creation of a system of industrial relations with a structural bias toward co-operation rather than conflict. Any discussion of future transformation of the firm now concerns greater management-labour co-operation and worker participation, not the elimination of private ownership and worker control. Socialist governments after 1988 translated the austerity policies of the early 1980s, which were designed as short-term responses to economic crisis, into a permanent policy bias toward wage restraint, fiscal conservatism and reduced corporation tax.[36] As Elie Cohen has said: 'The arrival of the Left in the context of crisis was necessary to prove to the unions that in an open economy there existed incontrovertible rules of the game.'[37] Thus at both the level of discourse and the level of Left political projects, there has been important change.

At the same time Socialists and trade unionists have scaled back their expectations, employers have demanded further marginalization of both trade unions and legislation. The growth of managerial interest in 'human resource management' and initiatives to bypass trade unions in the firm has had consequences for the legislative agenda of French employers. In 1985, *Entreprise et progrès*, representing the progressive wing of the French *patronat*, proposed a *contrat collectif d'entreprise*. In place of the bargaining monopoly of the trade unions, workers in a given firm would elect representatives to negotiate and sign contracts with management. These contracts would be for a fixed duration (one to three years), and contain an indivisible package of wages, work conditions, flexibility measures and so on. The right to derogate from existing legislation and collective agreements reached at higher levels would also be greatly expanded because, as the report said, 'legislation is no longer capable of comprehending the reality of our complex and changing society'.[38] Thus this proposal simultaneously attacked the role of trade unions and the role of the state inside the firm.

A proposal from the *Centre des jeunes dirigeants d'entreprise* in June 1986 was only slightly less radical. It too called for the end of union monopoly on bargaining, to be replaced by a *conseil d'entreprise*, which would take the place of all other representative institutions in the firm and then negotiate with management.[39] Such proposals – which would accelerate a transformation of labour regulation that is already much advanced – would not have been considered serious before the Left arrived in power. But as the unionized segment of the labour force has shrunk, providing unions with a monopoly on bargaining seems increasingly anachronistic and adds plausibility to new managerial initiatives.

The defining feature of the newly emerging microcorporatist mode of labour regulation is that the firm becomes the dominant locus of labour regulation, and its boundaries become evermore impermeable to outside influence, be it that of the state expressed through legislation and the Labour Code, or of a wider collectivity of workers represented by trade unions. The point is that the new organizational forms tend to create or reinforce 'micro-collectivities' of work, and have a 'de-unifying [*désolidarisant*] effect not only at the level of the union organization, but on the workers' movement itself'.[40] Jean-François Amadieu has put forward the reasonable hypothesis that what is taking place now in France is the creation of an *enterprise unionism*, whether it be genuine, in the sense of firm-specific unions, or *de facto*, when local unions *act* as enterprise unions.[41]

This leaves the national union organizations as 'semi-public' service organizations,[42] who lobby governments, legitimize government initiatives in social and economic policy[43] and support spontaneous strikes. As Daniel Furjot and Catherine Noël note in their study of strikes in France, in the future unions will appear more 'as experts, putting their experience, their infrastructure and their technical competence at the disposition of strikers who would maintain control [of the strike]'.[44] There is thus a widening gap between trade unions at the national and industry level and trade unions at the firm level.

There are two wider consequences of this transformation. First, the emerging form of microcorporatist labour regulation has been much more conducive to deregulation of the labour market and the implementation of flexibility in the firm.[45] In the mid-seventies, the demands for greater flexibility – in hiring, firing, work contracts, wages, work time and so on – began to multiply in France, as elsewhere. The extensive role of the state and high-level collective bargaining in labour regulation was, in fact, particularly obstructive to flexibility. But repeated efforts to introduce greater deregulation and flexibility by the conservative government of Raymond Barre and the Socialist government of Laurent Fabius (after what Daniel Singer terms the 'conversion' of the PS to neoliberal economic policies[46]) failed.

However, the Socialist industrial relations reforms encouraged flexibility in several ways. They permitted derogation from legislation and high-level collective agreements, which was precisely what flexibility meant for employers, and most agreements involving derogations appear to have concerned issues of flexibility.[47] They encouraged bargaining at the firm level, where flexibility made most sense. The number of firm-level agreements on flexibility of work time almost doubled between 1984 and 1987, while similar branch-level agreements practically disappeared.[48] Finally, the reforms created and encouraged firm-level organizations of workers that tend to be less able to resist employer demands for flexibility agreements. Five years after the Auroux Laws went into effect, the CGT believed that there had been such a fundamental shift in the balance of power against trade unions that: 'It is not a case of collective bargaining, that is to say, the negotiation of workers' demands, but the negotiation of employer demands [and] the ratification of employer decisions.'[49]

So the reforms unblocked French labour regulation's resistance to flexibility. It should also be noted that in the absence of strong unions, the flexibility was fairly brutal, reflecting the interests of employers rather than workers. Firm-level agreements on work time overwhelmingly concerned flexibility (usually an employers' demand) rather than work time reduction (generally a union or workers' demand).[50] In addition, statistical as well as anecdotal studies have argued that labour-market dualism is being exacerbated.[51]

The second wider consequence of the transformation has to do with worker militancy. The number of days lost to industrial action declined from 3.67 million in 1977 to 0.9 million in 1989,[52] and strikes have become less frequent, shorter and involve fewer workers.[53] To some extent the dramatic reduction in the strike level is due to adverse labour market conditions and might be expected to revert if unemployment is reduced. For instance, the persistence of public-sector strikes could indicate that worker combativeness has returned as economic conditions improve.[54] Yet these strikes have occurred in only heavily protected and highly unionized parts of the public sector – rail, metro, airlines, the postal system and so on, industries with long traditions of militancy. These are precisely the sectors where microcorporatist labour regulation has made the least inroads and where trade unions remain relatively strong.

However, more important than the number of strikes (which have, after all, declined in almost all advanced capitalist societies) is their form. Conflicts tend increasingly to be very brief, spontaneous stoppages rather than extended strikes. These conflicts make a great deal of sense in the context of microcorporatist labour regulation, because they originate in the firm, require limited organization and resources and are intended more to make a point than to threaten the financial viability of the firm. But these conflicts prevent wider industrial action and limit the *experience* of collective action. Furjot and Noël write that 'without memory, they are also usually without a tomorrow.'[55]

CONCLUSION

French industrial relations have undergone a transformation in the course of the Mitterrand era. In the 1960s and 1970s, France was distinguished by a rigid, hierarchical mode of labour regulation and a very weak trade union movement. But, paradoxically, the role of the state in labour regulation gave unions an influence beyond their numbers. So long as unions were able to present themselves as the single most legitimate representatives of labour, the state, in effect, extended the weak real influence of trade unions to the wider economy, to create a kind of ersatz trade unionism – unionism without the unions, as it were. And workers benefited from wages, work contracts, job security, work time regulations and so on, which they would have been unable to win on their own.

The emerging microcorporatist form of labour regulation, by contrast, is characterized by the insulation of the firm and firm-level worker organizations from the wider influence of trade unions, high-level bargains and state legislation. Thus, the main feature of microcorporatist labour regulation is the focus upon the firm, where both collective bargaining and any form of worker organization had been largely absent. Workers have not simply been *demobilized* by unemployment, they have been *remobilized* and reorganized in ways that place structural limits upon collective action and imply a new, stronger identification with the firm. Thus we are not observing only quantitative change – a decline in union membership and strike levels – but also qualitative change, in which the labour movement is restructured and conflicts between labour and capital change in form. A new form of worker representation is emerging in France, one that is antithetical to traditional social democratic trade unionism and instead centred on, and limited to, the firm.

Microcorporatism has a structural bias toward co-operation rather than conflict, because workers in a given firm, isolated from the protection of a wider collectivity of workers or legislation, begin 'to identify their interests with those of the firm'.[56] Clearly this is an enforced co-operation and does not necessarily imply any change in the attitudes of workers.[57] Indeed there is plenty of evidence of the frailty of the recent experiments with quality circles and worker expression groups.[58] Rather, the point is that if the main resource of labour is its capacity for collective action, microcorporatist labour regulation implies a diminished capacity for French unions.

French industrial relations had always been vulnerable to this shift because of the persistent weakness of labour organization. Trade unions never cultivated deep roots in the working class. The influence of unions had derived not from the strength and unity of workers but from the framework of labour law, which privileged the branch-level and peculiar statist form of labour regulation. Two changes after 1981 facilitated a shift toward a microcorporatist mode of labour regulation. First, the state began a withdrawal from its previously dominant role in labour regulation, at first in response to economic crisis but later to encourage flexibility in the firm under new industrial relations legislation. Second, French workers, who had previously been largely unintegrated (into the firm or trade unions), were now more likely to be organized into firm-specific organizations.

One result of the weakness of labour organization in France has been that the generalized phenomenon of post-Fordism came to France in a peculiarly distorted form.[59] In contrast to Michael Piore and Charles Sabel's notion of a 'flexible specialization', which enhances the job security and skills of workers,[60] French post-Fordism has emphasized flexibility in the sense of the precariousness of employment, labour market deregulation and exacerbated wage competition.

The paradox of the Auroux reform project is that the reforms have indeed had profound consequences for French industrial relations, as this chapter has suggested, but those consequences have not been what the French Socialists intended. The Auroux Laws have not simply been a failure; on the contrary, they have had a lasting impact upon labour regulation and have brought about fundamental changes in the role, locus and nature of collective bargaining in France and in the organizational resources of labour. Though economic crisis, employer pressure and labour weakness all conspired to ensure that the result of the reform was not what initially had been intended, the reforms were not irrelevant.

I have argued that there was always a fatal ambivalence in the relationship between the PS and organized labour. The *autogestionnaire* project of the 1970s was less deeply buried after 1981 than one might believe. The problem for the French Socialists and the trade union movement was not that the Auroux Laws had a series of unfortunate and unexpected by-products, but rather that they contained within them two entirely different logics and two very different models of labour regulation. Clearly, the extent to which legislation can have results in the face of an adverse economic situation and a hostile business class is questionable. But it would be to trivialize the Auroux Laws to argue that they were simply a failure, mis-timed and essentially irrelevant. The double logic contained within the legislative package encouraged the shift toward a microcorporatist form of labour regulation, and made the transition toward such a model easier.

Meanwhile, French trade unions were poorly placed to resist the shift. Their limited resources were concentrated at the national level. The Auroux reforms, in decentralizing labour regulation to the firm, bypassed the unions. Thus once the national political debate over the scope of the reforms had died down, struggle over their operation was surprisingly limited. Inside French firms change occurred on employers' terms.

Some elements of the *patronat* and its intellectuals were quick to recognize the role the Auroux Laws played in encouraging the transformation of French industrial relations, and it is important to note that the conservative government of 1986–8 did not seek to dismantle the Auroux reforms.[61] This is remarkable, considering the reaction of the *patronat* to the reforms in 1982–3. A 1984 opinion poll found that 66 per cent of employers questioned believed the Auroux Laws had been beneficial, only 6 per cent saw the legislation as reinforcing trade unions (70 per cent believed it did not), and 47 per cent believed that the reforms actually encouraged competition inside the firm with trade unions (26 per cent did not).[62] François de Closets, a best-selling author known for his opposition to the '*toujours plus*' of the unions and his support for partnership in the firm, found the Auroux Laws tremendously important in encouraging his project. As he put it: 'The French have evolved more in the last five years than the previous one hundred.'[63] The reforms generalized, by legislation, practices that a few of the most 'modernist' employers were already using. Thus, the Socialist reforms *forced* an evolution of microcorporatist practices in the firm, where before only a few employers had sought to incorporate works councils into economic management and create quality circles. In this sense the Socialists bear responsibility for the transformation of French industrial relations in the past decade.

Notes

1. An earlier draft of this chapter was presented at the conference 'Labour and the Left in France: A Decade of Mitterrand,' at Wesleyan University, 11–12 April 1992. My thanks go to Jane Jenson, George Ross, Martin Schain, Mark Kesselman, David Cameron, Rand Smith and Anthony Daley for their comments and suggestions.
2. The use of the term 'labour regulation' is an indication of my theoretical debt to the French Regulation School of political economy. I will use the term as a substitute for a system of industrial relations in this chapter. A mode of labour regulation is an institution that mediates the relationship between labour, capital and the state. Its advantage over the term industrial relations is both that it is broader – for instance, the labour market is a form of labour regulation – and narrower, in that it refers specifically to mechanisms and institutions that handle industrial conflict without necessarily constituting a system. For an elaboration of the notion of modes of labour regulation see Chapter 1 of Chris Howell, *Regulating Labor: The State and Industrial Relations Reform in Postwar France* (Princeton, NJ: Princeton University Press, 1992). The best summary of regulation theory is provided by Robert Boyer, *La Théorie de la régulation: Une analyse critique* (Paris: Éditions La Découverte, 1986).
3. Wolfgang Streeck, 'Neo-Corporatist Industrial Relations and the Economic Crisis in West Germany,' in John H. Goldthorpe, ed., *Order and Conflict in Contemporary Capitalism* (Oxford: Clarendon Press, 1984).
4. George Ross, 'Perils of Politics: French Unions and the Crisis of the 1970s', in Peter Lange, Ross and Maurizio Vannicelli, *Unions, Change and Crisis: French and Italian Union Strategy and the Political Economy, 1945–1980* (New York: Allen and Unwin, 1982) p. 21.
5. The best single account for the history, organization and activities of French trade unions is Jean-Daniel Reynaud, *Les Syndicats en France*, 3rd ed. (Paris: Seuil, 1975).
6. This figure comes from Gérard Adam, *Le Pouvoir Syndical* (Paris: Dunod, 1985) p. 66.
7. For comparative rates of unionization see John D. Stephens, *The Transition from Capitalism to Socialism* (Chicago: University of Illinois Press, 1986) p. 115–6.
8. Adam, pp. 55–60.
9. Paul Durand, 'The Evolution of Industrial Relations Law in France since the Liberation', *International Labour Review*, 74 (1956).
10. For figures on strikes and collective bargaining see René Mouriaux and Françoise Subileau, 'Données statistiques concernant le syndicalisme des salariés en France (1945–1986),' working paper (Paris: CEVIPOF, 1986).
11. There was an exception to this pattern of limited collective bargaining and focus upon branch-level rather than firm-level bargaining. In the second half of the 1950s there was a series of agreements in the metalworking, electrical and chemical industries. These 'Renault-style' agreements, modelled on the first such agreement signed at Renault in 1955 (itself very similar to the landmark 1948 General Motors-United

Auto Workers agreement), were multi-year, firm-level bargains, providing extensive benefits and cost-of-living protection plus annual real increases, and involved a commitment to avoid industrial action for the life of the contract. However, these agreements remained limited to a few core, Fordist sectors of the economy, where firms could afford this kind of deal. See 'Works Agreements of the "Renault type"', *International Labour Review*, 81 (1960).

12. See Jane Marceau, *Class and Status in France* (Oxford: Clarendon Press, 1977) p. 26.

13. Pierre Dubois, Claude Durand and Sabine Erbès-Seguin, 'The Contradictions of French Trade Unionism', in Colin Crouch and Alessandro Pizzorno, eds., *The Resurgence of Class Conflict in Western Europe since 1968*, Vol. 1 (New York: Holmes and Meier, 1978) p. 55.

14. Jacques Delors, *Changer* (Paris: Stock, 1975) p. 189.

15. Quoted in *Le Point*, 19 January 1976, p. 36.

16. David S. Bell and Byron Criddle vividly demonstrate the declining representation of workers and rising representation of the new middle class as one moves up the PS from membership to leadership positions. See *The French Socialist Party* (Oxford: Clarendon Press, 1984) p. 203.

17. This suspicion was not unrelated to the fact that the PCF had strong links to the largest trade union confederation.

18. For a useful account of the various union and employer positions on the Auroux reforms from the perspective of the CFDT, see 'Les autres et les droits nouveaux,' *Notes et documents de BRAEC* no. 22 (October–December 1982).

19. Raymond Vatinet, 'La Négociation au sein du comité d'entreprise', *Droit social*, no. 11 (November 1982).

20. *Bilan de la négociation collective, 1985* (Paris: Documentation Française, 1986).

21. See, for example, Jean-Jacques Nansot, 'Le droit d'expression des salariés dans les entreprises. Premiers constats', *Travail et emploi*, no. 24 (June 1985).

22. 'Les autres et les droits nouveaux', p. 13. Note also that FO signed the smallest proportion of the accords on the *droit d'expression*, 62 per cent. Next lowest was the CGT with 76 per cent. See Serge Volkoff, 'Expression des salariés. Bilan statistique de 3000 accords', *Travail et emploi*, no. 23 (March 85) p. 81.

23. See *Bilan de la négociation collective, 1987* (Paris: Documentation Française, 1988) p. 31; *Bilan de la négociation collective, 1988* (Paris: Documentation Française, 1989) p. 22; and for the 1989 figures see the summary of *Bilan de la négociation collective, 1989* in *Le Monde*, 16 June 1990, p. 23.

24. See *Bilan de la négociation collective, 1987*, p. 12; *Bilan de la négociation collective, 1988*, p. 11; and *Le Monde*, 16 June 1990, p. 23. The 1989 figure is approximate because it includes any agreements reached that year on setting up worker self-expression groups.

25. It is important to make a distinction between the coverage of collective bargaining, where agreements are extended to new sectors or regions and operate without expiration dates, and the amount of actual bargaining activity. The annual codicils discussed earlier measure the latter.

26. Françoise Dussert, Yves Mouton and Chantal Salmon, 'Évolution et structure du tissu conventionnel', *Dossiers statistiques du travail et emploi*, no. 27–8 (December 1986) p. 21. These figures are for firms employing ten or more workers. Estimates for those not covered by any collective agreement if firms employing fewer than ten are included were 3 million to 3.5 million in 1981, and 1.9 million to 2.75 million in 1985.

27. See *Liaisons sociales. Documents*, no. 41 (4 May 1988).

28. For figures on union membership see Mouriaux and Subileau, 'Les Effectifs syndicaux

en France', working paper (Paris: CEVIPOF, 1987). Data on the number of union sections and delegates can be found in Jean-Pierre Aujard, 'Les Délégués syndicaux en 1985', *Dossiers Statistiques du Travail et d'Emploi*, no. 27–8 (December 1986). Information on union strength in works council elections can be found in another article in that volume, Aujard, 'Les Élections aux comités d'entreprise en 1985', *Dossiers statistiques du travail et d'emploi*, nos. 27–28 and 'Les Élections aux C.E. en 1986', *Dossiers statistiques du travail et d'emploi*, no. 39 (December 1987).

29. Raymond-Pierre Bodin, *Les Lois Auroux dans les p.m.e.* (Paris: Documentation Française, 1987) p. 194.
30. *Projet Socialiste* (Paris: Club Socialiste du livre, 1980) p. 238.
31. Jean Auroux, *Les Droits des travailleurs* (Paris: Documentation Française, 1981) p. 20.
32. See the *Centre d'étude des revenus et des coûts* study, *Les Français et leurs revenus: le tournant des années 80* (Paris: Éditions la Découverte, 1989) p. 42–5. Furthermore, the weight of the public sector in France, combined with the wage restraint policy, permitted a peculiarly French version of co-ordinated wage determination in the economy as a whole. See David Soskice, 'Wage Determination: The Changing Role of Institutions in Advanced Industrialised Countries', *Oxford Review of Economic Policy* 6, no. 4 (1990).
33. See, for instance, the contributions to these conferences: 'A France of Pluralism and Consensus? Changing Balances in State and Society', New York University, 9–11 October 1987; and 'In Search of the New France', Brandeis University, 13–15 May 1988. See also Suzanne Berger, 'French Politics at a Turning Point?' *French Politics and Society*, no. 15 (November 1986).
34. See W. Rand Smith, *The End of Illusions*, manuscript in preparation.
35. Pierre Rosanvallon, *La Question Syndicale* (Paris: Calmann-Lévy, 1988) p. 139.
36. For a glowing account of the French economy's performance see *The Economist*, 19 May 1990, p. 77. See also Howell, 'The Fetishism of Small Difference,' *French Politics and Society* 9, no. 1 (Winter 1991) for an evaluation of the economic and social policy of the Rocard government.
37. Elie Cohen, 'Le "moment lois Auroux" ou la désublimation de l'économie', *Sociologie du travail*, no. 3 (1986).
38. Details of this proposal can be found in *Liaisons sociales. Documents*, no. 27 (6 March 1985).
39. Unions, however, would retain their monopoly in the first round of voting for this new body. See *Liaisons sociales. Documents*, no. 55 (18 June 1986).
40. Pierre-Eric Tixier, 'Management participatif et syndicalisme', *Sociologie du travail*, no. 3 (1986) p. 367.
41. The work of Jean-François Amadieu reaches very similar conclusions to those of this essay on the subject of emerging microcorporatism. See his 'Vers un syndicalisme d'entreprise', *Sociologie du travail*, no. 3 (1986) and 'Les tendances au syndicalisme d'entreprise en France: quelques hypothèses', *Droit social*, no. 1 (January 1986).
42. This argument is made by both Rosanvallon and Adam.
43. The issue of legitimization is important. The trade union confederations, whatever their actual degree of representation, are the single most visible representatives for labour and can influence government disproportionately to their membership. It is unclear why else governments of both the Left and Right would seek to talk to organizations whose memberships comprise less than one-tenth of the work force.
44. Daniel Furjot and Catherine Noël, 'La conflictualité en 1986: Bilan statistique et qualitatif', *Travail et Emploi*, no. 34 (December 1987) p. 67. The annual summaries and analyses of strike statistics by Furjot and collaborators are the best source of semi-digested strike data available, and the analyses are usually excellent.

45.   For this argument in a more developed form see Howell, 'The Dilemmas of Post-Fordism: Socialists, Flexibility and Labor Market Deregulation in France', *Politics and Society* 20, no. 1 (1992).
46.   Daniel Singer, *Is Socialism Doomed? The Meaning of Mitterrand* (New York: Oxford University Press, 1988).
47.   *Bilan de la négociation collective, 1985*, p. 36.
48.   For details of work-time agreements see *Bilan de la négociation collective, 1985*, *Bilan de la négociation collective, 1986* (Paris: *Ministère des Affaires Sociales et de l'Emploi*, 1987) and *Bilan de la négociation collective, 1987*.
49.   Quoted in *Négociation collective – Quels Enjeux?* (Paris: La Documentation Française, 1988) p. 221.
50.   See successive issues of the annual *Bilan de la négociation collective*.
51.   For details see *Les Français et leurs revenus*, Chapter 6, and Michel Schiray, 'La Précarisation du travail', *Problèmes politiques et sociaux*, no. 575 (8 January 1988).
52.   *Liaisons sociales. documents*, no. 64 (30 May 1990) p. 1.
53.   Information on number and duration of strikes can be found in Furjot and Noël. They also point out that smaller firms tend to have fewer strikes than large firms, and there are more and more workers employed in small firms (p. 58).
54.   For an account of the industrial conflict in the fall of 1988, and the argument that any emphasis upon consensus and the end of strikes is premature, see George Ross and Jane Jenson, '*Quel joli consensus!* Strikes and Politics in Autumn 1988', *French Politics and Society* 7, no. 1 (Winter 1989).
55.   Furjot and Noël, p. 69.
56.   Amadieu, 'Les tendances au syndicalisme d'entreprise', p. 23.
57.   For this point see Tixier. He argues that participatory management does not end alienation or domination but merely replaces bureaucratic and Taylorist domination with a 'manipulation of the subjectivity and creativity of workers', p. 360.
58.   See, for example, Frank Wilson, 'Democracy in the Workplace: The French Experience', *Politics and Society* 19, no. 4 (1991).
59.   The literature on post-Fordism is voluminous. For a good account of the breakdown of post-war Fordism throughout the Organisation for Economic Cooperation and Development see Andrew Glyn, Alan Hughes, Alain Lipietz and Ajit Singh, 'The Rise and Fall of the Golden Age', in Stephen Marglin and Juliet Schor, eds., *The Golden Age of Capitalism* (Oxford: Clarendon Press, 1990). For an argument about the diverse national forms of post-Fordism see Robert Boyer, 'Capital Labour Relations in OECD Countries: From the Fordist "Golden Age" to Contrasted National Trajectories', CEPREMAP working paper, no. 9020 (Paris: September 1990).
60.   Michael J. Piore and Charles F. Sabel, *The Second Industrial Divide* (New York: Basic Books, 1984).
61.   For a discussion of the evolution of employer attitudes to the Auroux Laws see Bernard H. Moss, 'After the Auroux Laws: Employers, Industrial Relations and the Right in France', *West European Politics* 11, no. 1 (January 1988).
62.   Cited in François de Closets, *Tous Ensemble* (Paris: Éditions du Seuil, 1985) p. 437.
63.   *Ibid.* p. 8.

8 French Labour Confronts Technological Change: Reform that Never was?[1]

Mark Kesselman

Although many accounts have documented the decline and fall of the French labour movement, most analyses focus on trends at the national level. The paucity of local-level studies is surprising, given the strong scholarly consensus that state regulation has declined in importance while firm- and plant-level regulation has become more extensive. The shift is in part a product of strategic changes by state, business and union officials. The labour movement recognized the need for greater emphasis on local initiative before the Socialist government reached power in 1981. In the late 1970s, the two largest labour confederations – *Confédération Générale du Travail* (CGT) and *Confédération Française Démocratique du Travail* (CFDT) – acknowledged responsibility for a strategic error earlier in the decade. In order to enhance the prospects of electoral victory for the Union of the Left, the two unions had restrained labour mobilization and accepted limitations on trade union autonomy. When the Left was defeated in 1978, the two unions responded by seeking to shift the focus of union efforts from the national arena to encouraging greater local initiatives.

In large measure, the change sought to make a virtue of a necessity: the new path was a response to the decline of the labour movement's capacity to engage in mobilization at the national level. Furthermore, the value of initiatives at the base was often more evident in official proclamations than concrete actions.[2] When the Socialist Party finally did achieve an electoral triumph in 1981, the labour movement confronted a crisis unprecedented for the post-war period. Trade union membership, already at low levels in the 1970s, was plummeting; union confederations were at war; and recession, economic restructuring and decades of conservative governance were wreaking havoc on a labour movement historically among the weakest of any advanced capitalist nation.[3] Despite the arsenal of important new legal rights that organized labour gained from Socialist-sponsored legislation, the movement was in an even greater crisis after more than a decade of Socialist rule. In order to understand why, studies of national trends – as in Chapters 7 and 9 – must be supplemented by attention to developments at the local level.

CONSULTATION OVER TECHNOLOGICAL CHANGE

An important and little-studied provision of the 1982 Auroux Laws created the right for works councils (*comités d'entreprise*) to be consulted regarding technological change. Modeled on similar procedures instituted in the 1970s in the social democracies of northern Europe, the reform requires company management to consult with works councils at least one month before introducing any project involving technological innovation in the workplace that will substantially affect employment levels or occupational health and safety. In 1986, the law was extended to require employers to regularly inform and periodically consult with the councils concerning the implementation of technological changes. When a proposed change promises to have a substantial impact, works councils in firms with more than 300 employees are authorized to hire independent experts at company expense to assist in their deliberations. However, the councils need management's agreement concerning whether to hire a consultant, the scope of the consultant's mandate, and choice of consultant; if management refuses, the works council can seek judicial recourse to compel assent.[4]

The consultative procedure over technological change was part of a battery of reforms contained in the Auroux Laws to strengthen unions, who usually control works councils. Better-known features include a requirement that employers bargain annually over wages, hours and working conditions, as well as increased rights and protection for union organizations. The right for works councils to be consulted over technological change is especially noteworthy in that it aims to improve the capacity of organized labour to participate in decisions regarding the firm's operations rather than merely enunciating bread-and-butter demands. The legislation could have helped the French labour movement develop a more proactive position than its traditional position in the Fordist phase of regulation, where management directs the process of production while unions seek to defend the interests of workers adversely affected by the *consequences* of economic decisions.

One might have expected the organization of consultation over technological change to have far-reaching consequences, as Jean-Daniel Reynaud, a respected specialist of French industrial relations, predicted.[5] Moreover, to the extent that the labour movement gained a significant (albeit advisory) voice in organizing production, this might compensate for its declining capacity to organize strikes. The result would thus be quite different from the strategic impasse that Guy Groux and René Mouriaux term 'unionism without members' (see Chapter 9).

In order to assess the impact of the reform, however, one cannot rely on laws or collective bargaining agreements, especially at sectoral or peak levels (as many scholars have done). Research is necessary at plant and firm levels. Yet studies of consultation organized under the aegis of the reform have found that it has had little impact and that unions have failed to increase their influence over the process of planning technological change. Indeed, the law has mostly remained a dead letter. Although its provisions apparently apply to most investments in new plant and equipment in France, relatively few cases of consultation have actually occurred. Moreover, where consultation has occurred, it has not altered the character of technological change.[6] Although, as will be suggested later, this provision of the Auroux reform has had an important indirect effect, it is worth asking why its manifest impact has been so slight.

There are two reasons for this outcome. First, management typically claims that it is not required to consult works councils, and courts have generally supported this restrictive position. Management has successfully claimed that the phrase 'new technology' requires that a given technological change must involve significant innovation in general, not merely within a particular workplace. Therefore, courts have held that most of the recent technological changes that have thoroughly transformed the French economy do not fall under the provisions of the law.

Second, management has usually succeeded in preventing works councils from hiring outside experts at company expense to evaluate the impact of technological changes. Business executives deeply resent what they regard as dangerous meddling in firm affairs by outsiders chosen by unions.[7] Because works councils find it time-consuming, costly and usually fruitless to sue employers to extract information, there have thus far been only several hundred cases of expert evaluations – a fraction of the thousands of instances in which the procedure is ostensibly mandated.[8] That few firms have even negotiated collective bargaining agreements with unions specifying the procedures for consultation at the firm or plant level (as the law stipulates) suggests how marginal the reform has been.

It may be unrealistic to expect immediate results, as reforms of this kind take years to bear fruit. Moreover, the reform has not been totally without effect. For example, the largest peak employer association, the *Conseil National du Patronat Français*, and most union confederations negotiated an agreement in 1988 to extend the provisions of the law regarding consultation over technological change. The agreement mandated bipartite negotiations between sectoral business associations and unions to develop sweeping guidelines and regulations concerning the design of new technology and its social impact – for example, by regulating safety, pay equity, working conditions and retraining for displaced workers. Worker participation, the agreement proclaims, constitutes a key element in improving the quality of technological change: 'Informing workers and providing possibilities for them to express themselves, as well as linking this process to consultations with the appropriate representative mechanisms, provides the best means for identifying how to satisfy workers' expectations as well as serve the interests of the firm.' By the early 1990s, about 22 sectoral agreements were concluded, some of which had been negotiated before the 1988 national-level agreement, in the banking, metalworking, food processing, printing, chemical and textile industries.[9]

The legally mandated obligation for employers and unions to consult must be placed in a broader context. Although most scholars are correct to claim there has been little direct impact of consultation on technological change according to the legally mandated procedures, the reform has had a considerable *indirect* impact, albeit one difficult to measure. This claim is based on studying the consultative process in the chemical and banking industries, two of France's most dynamic, technologically advanced and internationally competitive sectors.[10] In both industries, there has been substantial reorganization of the labour process linked to the introduction of information-based technology. Although the two sectors are of course very different, they exhibit strikingly similar tendencies regarding the character of change in organization and content of production. In both, traditional repetitive tasks – such as regulating valves or typing – have been replaced by operations on computer terminals that often require considerable skill and judgment.

In virtually every case studied, when consultation occurred, it did not influence management's plans. Most of the time, management evaded the need to engage in the formal process of consultation and was quite unresponsive when works councils did make proposals. Works council members, for their part, are not qualified to analyse management proposals, and management successfully resisted councils' attempts to hire external consultants.

When consultation does occur, it is usually quite limited in scope. Lacking the capacity to evaluate issues of technological design, works councils contest the consequences of technological change – above all, the layoffs that typically accompany rationalization. Not surprisingly, in most cases management and labour seek divergent results from technological change. Workers' representatives accord highest priority to the impact of technological change on employment levels; next in importance are issues of occupational health and safety, skill levels, wage scales and the kind and amount of vocational training management plans to provide workers who will operate the new equipment. Works councils often contest management's projected employment targets. However, since management's aim in investing in technological change is to raise productivity – which perforce usually involves downsizing – technological change nearly invariably puts management and labour on a collision course. Works council representatives also assert that workers should receive better training to operate the new technology and should be compensated by higher skill classifications and wages. And they charge that management underestimates the risks to occupational health and safety involved in technological changes.

Given these obstacles to exercising their right to be consulted over technological change, works councils rarely invoke the law. Consultation does occur, however, and in several cases works council proposals were partially accepted. For example, the works council in one plant persuaded management that engineers had underestimated the difficulties of installing and operating new equipment, so that additional jobs would be needed. Yet even when consultation is described as effective, the outcome is often more ambiguous.

Modernizing ATOCHEM-Grande Paroisse

After investments in new plant and equipment had languished for a decade, the management of ATOCHEM-Grande Paroisse, France's largest fertilizer producer, decided to invest 200 million francs to introduce computer-controlled production at one of the plant's facilities near Rouen. Prior to doing so, plant managers requested that the National Agency for the Improvement of Working Conditions (ANACT), a tripartite parapublic agency, organize consultations between management and workers.[11] Management decided to consult because when it had modernized facilities at another plant several years earlier, a bitter strike ensued, which management attributed to its failure to consult.

In order to organize consultation, an ANACT expert assembled study groups of managers and workers to review specific features of the project. Labour unions were quite enthusiastic about the proposed investment because it symbolized management's commitment to keep the plant in operation. Given the fact that it used outmoded equipment and was a heavy polluter close to Rouen, its future had been highly uncertain.

Labour representatives differed with management in two respects: they opposed projected job reductions, and they proposed that workers chosen to operate the new equipment receive greater training and higher skill classifications than management was prepared to provide. The unions' demand that re-skilled workers be promoted to the rank of technician, despite their lack of educational qualifications, was unprecedented at this plant (and unusual elsewhere in France). Management initially rejected both demands but eventually agreed after a brief strike erupted.

Following the consultation, ANACT portrayed the process in glowing terms. Indeed, the ANACT expert who directed the consultation proved so successful in gaining the respect of both sides that ATOCHEM later hired him as assistant personnel director at the Rouen plant. Several years later, however, both management and union officials agreed that the results had been considerably less positive. Consultation had served primarily to minimize possible disruptions resulting from technological innovation, not to broaden participation in the process of planning the change. Moreover, whatever success had been achieved had little impact on labour-management relations elsewhere in the plant. Indeed, when management planned another investment at the plant in 1992, it did not initiate a similar process of consultation. This case, and others I studied, corroborate Groux's claim that conflicts over technological change have not involved 'technological innovation in itself but rather the effects of innovation on working conditions, job classifications, and skill requirements, all in all a rather traditional set of labour issues'.[12]

TOWARD AN EXPLANATION

Three factors explain why the French labour movement has failed to confront management in such a vital sphere. First, as mentioned above, two provisions of the law mandating consultation limit the scope of the regulation. And when consultation does occur, works councils lack adequate time to deliberate. The law specifies that the works council must issue its report evaluating a project within one month after it receives the proposal. The results can hardly fail to be superficial.

A second hindrance to union attempts to intervene in the domain of technological change is the tenacity of traditional understandings of the appropriate terrain of union activity, often shared by business executives, union leaders and rank-and-file workers alike. In the tacit division of labour, management is deemed exclusively responsible for organizing production (including the design of technology), while unions are responsible for challenging what are misleadingly characterized as the social consequences of economic and technological decisions. Thus, organized labour is inclined to contest the social costs of rationalization – for example, layoffs that result from technological choices – but in an essentially defensive manner. As noted above, the CGT and CFDT have revised their official doctrine in this respect. But although the CGT proclaims the need for organized labour to intervene in the economic and technological sphere, its dwindling resources preclude achieving its ambitious goals. The CFDT is often inclined to swallow the bitter pill of layoffs in exchange for gaining a favoured position in negotiations over the terms of layoffs. But it takes two to tango – or even, given France's plural unionism, more than two. And French management is generally reluctant to accept CFDT overtures since, for reasons of ideology and organizational self-interest, other unions would respond by trying to sabotage the effort.[13] In brief, management is not persuaded that benefits would accrue from making unions a privileged interlocutor in consultation.

When business executives were asked for an explanation of why the consultative process had failed to produce significant results, they replied that shop stewards and works council members had little to offer. 'How can works council representatives, with at most one week of economic training, make a valuable contribution?' asked the human resources director at a petroleum company plant. An executive responsible for organizational development for a green-field facility of a giant chemical firm described an elaborate set of procedures for recruiting new workers and associating them in the decision-making process.[14] When questioned about the unions' role in the new plant, he replied, 'We want to do things our way, and unions are rigid and unresponsive. They are far removed from the preoccupations of people. Unions will eventually become organized here – but hopefully not too soon.'

A third reason unions have been limited derives from the changing balance of labour relations and class forces more generally. To illustrate, an official of the chemical industry trade association suggested in an interview that a 1990 branch-level agreement over technological change was linked to other agreements recently negotiated in the chemical industry involving procedures for regulating layoffs and scheduling work. 'When our social partners accepted the value of greater flexibility in using equipment and restructuring employment', he said, 'we drew the consequences and signed the agreement on technology.' Given the general weakness of organized labour, however, management has little incentive to make substantial concessions to gain its co-operation. Collective bargaining in France, as in other comparable countries, has shifted from exchanging benefits to union concessions.

In this connection, business executives regard France's industrial relations framework, including the Auroux reforms that mandated expanding requirements for bargaining and consultation, as archaic and unhelpful. They rail against what they consider the top-heavy, formal character of the labour code, which imposes a plethora of requirements restricting their freedom of action. One human resource director said, 'Laws are gadgets. We need to comply with the law, but that's all.' Legal requirements are seen as hindering flexibility.

LAWS AND ACTIONS

If one confined attention to the consultative procedures regulating technological change mandated by the Auroux Laws, the conclusion would be – as it has been for many studies of the process – that it represents a case of a reform that never was. But confining attention to the manifest impact of the reform obscures its indirect contribution to an extraordinarily significant process of change that is revolutionizing the system of labour regulation in France. At the same time business executives evade a host of legal requirements to negotiate and consult, corporate initiatives proliferate to involve workers and their representatives more fully in the firm's operations. French managers, often assisted by US management consulting firms, devote great effort to developing participative management, semi-autonomous work teams, 'flat' hierarchy and task enrichment. The labour movement is left far behind as management sponsors crash programmes to promote workers' flexibility, initiative and attention to product quality, as well as training programs geared to future employment projections (*gestion prévisionnelle de l'emploi*).

Until the 1980s, collective bargaining and consultation at firm and plant levels were practically non-existent. The Auroux Laws powerfully contributed to altering this situation by strengthening legal protection for union locals and mandating annual bargaining over wages, hours and working conditions. Despite the sharp decline in union membership in the past decade, the number of union *locals* has sharply increased – producing Groux and Mouriaux's unionism without members. The Auroux Laws also enlarged the space for consultation by expanding the jurisdiction of the works councils to require employers to consult with councils about the firm's economic situation. At the same time, in large firms, firm-level works councils were created, which meet periodically at firm headquarters. The Auroux laws further strained union resources by ordering firms to organize shop-floor assemblies in which workers were given the right to discuss working conditions. Unions sought to play a leading role in these meetings, which meant an

additional burden for militants. Finally, management created a host of consultative devices of its own, such as quality circles.

The cumulative effect of the new initiatives is staggering. Union leaders (as
well as works council representatives, who are usually union militants) spend
inordinate time in meetings – on the shop floor, at plant offices and company
headquarters in Paris or elsewhere. One study of 20 union locals in the chemical
industry reports that more than half of union delegates' legally mandated released
time was devoted to meetings of various representative mechanisms.[15] The new
tasks have been added to the traditional job of representation and mobilization at
the very moment union membership has plunged and there are fewer militants to
help. As a result, the gulf has widened between many overworked militants and
rank-and-file workers. Paradoxically, the rapid expansion of consultation has
deepened a crisis of representation in the French labour movement.[16] Far from
constituting a reform that never was, then, the Auroux reform mandating consultation over technological change indirectly contributed to a powerful movement
that has fundamentally transformed labour regulation in France. It provided further impetus for French business to seize the initiative in order to transform
confrontation to integration in the workplace and office.

CHANGING PERSPECTIVES

Although it is impossible to determine exactly how the existence of a Left government in the 1980s and early 1990s affects the outcome of this story, Socialist
policies appear to have directly and indirectly strengthened a process already
underway. First, the Auroux reforms contributed significantly to modernizing
French industrial relations. Here, as in other areas, despite some chaos and contradictions, the Socialist government sponsored enlightened conservative reforms
that were far more effective than policies of the stagnant governing coalition of
the 1970s. Second, it is noteworthy that this was a *Left* government: it was far
better equipped than its conservative predecessors to discredit the 'ideological
illusion' (in the words of a Socialist Party leader) that political activity could
achieve substantial social progress. Recall that the Auroux reforms – quite pallid
stuff when viewed from the perspective of northern Europe – were legislated
during the initial reformist phase of Socialist rule.

In the area of technological change, the Socialist-sponsored reform at least
indirectly served to integrate the labour movement far more closely into the
process of capitalist rationalization. In the 1990s, it is activists outside the ranks
of union leadership who are organizing wildcat strikes and protests to challenge
management.

There is a close link between the Socialist government's orientation and the
revolution – or counter-revolution – in shop-floor and office relations that occurred
when the Socialists were in office. The integration of workers on management's

terms has further eroded the memory of collective worker protest that for generations was a key feature of French working-class struggles. What emerges from this analysis is that, as in many other areas of its social life, the long era of French exceptionalism is apparently declining.[17] This is not to claim that the contours of 'normalcy' are either static or transparent. But it does suggest that the cycle of change in the sphere of labour regulation is only partially linked to the cycle of partisan change. If the date that separates the close of the Mitterrand era from its successor may have little significance for the system of labour regulation, the advent of the Mitterrand era coincided with the transformation of the traditional system of labour regulation in France into the (brave?) new world beginning in the 1980s.

Notes

1. Earlier drafts of this paper were presented at the Ninth International Conference of Europeanists, Chicago, 31 March–2 April 1994, and at the annual meeting of the American Political Science Association, Chicago, 3–6 September 1992. I am grateful for suggestions from Anthony Daley, Jane Jenson and Lowell Turner. Field research on which the paper is based was supported by a Fulbright Senior Research Fellowship in 1991–2.
2. See Mark Kesselman, with the assistance of Guy Groux, ed., *The French Workers' Movement: Economic Crisis and Political Change* (London: Allen & Unwin, 1984). Among the few studies of local union activity, and virtually the only one in English, is W. Rand Smith, *Crisis in the French Labour Movement: A Grassroots Perspective* (London: Macmillan, 1987).
3. For some general analyses, see Guy Groux and René Mouriaux, *La C.F.D.T.* (Paris: Economica, 1989); Groux and Mouriaux, *La C.G.T., Crises et alternatives* (Paris: Economica, 1992); Dominique Labbé and Maurice Croisat, *La fin des syndicats?* (Paris: L'Harmattan, 1992); Pierre Rosanvallon, *La Question syndicale* (Paris: Calmann-Lévy, 1988); and Pierre Eric Tixier, *Mutation ou déclin du syndicalisme? Le cas de la CFDT* (Paris: Presses Universitaires de France, 1992).
4. For analyses of the reform, see ANACT's 'Changements technologiques et négociations', *La Lettre d'information* (September 1988) pp. 3–7; *Introduction des nouvelles technologies: Concertation et négociation* (Paris: ANACT, 1989); *Organisation du travail et participation des salariés* (Paris: Editions ANACT, 1990); Stéphane Beaud, 'L'Introuvable négociation des nouvelles technologies: Un point de vue sociologique', *La Note de l'IRES*, 20 (2nd semester 1989) pp. 11–24; Institut Entreprise et Politique Industrielle, 'Technologies nouvelles, efficacité sociale et économique: Intervention des travailleurs dans la gestion' (unpublished transcript of conference held at Nanterre, 9–10 March 1988); Gérard Martinez and Ahmed Silem, 'Nouvelles technologies dans les entreprises: Les opinions des salariés sur l'information et la consultation', *Humanisme & Entreprise*, no. 302 (1988) pp. 57–69; Véronique Sandoval, 'La "négociation" de l'introduction des nouvelles technologies dans l'entreprise', *La Note de l'IRES*, 20 (2nd semester 1989); and Michèle Tallard, 'La négociation des nouvelles technologies: Eléments pour

une comparaison de la France et de la RFA', *Droit Social*, no. 2 (1987) pp. 124–30.

5. See Jean-Daniel Reynaud's assessment of negotiations in the steel industry, 'La négociation des nouvelles technologies: une transformation des règles du jeu?' *Revue française de science politique* 38, no. 1 (February 1988).

6. François Eyraud, Alain d'Iribarne and Marc Maurice, 'Des entreprises face aux technologies flexibles: Une analyse de la dynamique du changement', *Sociologie du travail* (January 1988) pp. 55–76; and V. Genestet and J.-Y. Potel, *L'Introduction des nouvelles technologies et sa négociation en entreprise* (Paris: ANACT, 1988). One illustration of how insignificant the reform has been: in their extensive analysis of the CGT's efforts to influence decisions within the economic and technological domains, Groux and Mouriaux did not even mention the existence of the legal requirement for employers to consult with works councils (*La C.G.T.*, ch. 4).

7. Union confederations and federations have organized agencies of professional consultants, including accountants, economists, lawyers, ergonomists and engineers, to assist their organizations. Business executives especially opposed consultation in cases where the CGT controlled the works council, on the grounds that the union would use consultation to damage the firm's interests.

8. Approximately 5000 firms are subject to the provision. See Martine Blanc, Elsie Charron and Michel Freyssenet, *Le Développement des systèmes-experts en entreprise*, Cahier no. 35 (Paris: GIP-MI, 1989); Pierre Cam, 'Le Droit à la lumière ou les ambivalences du savoir,' *Travail et emploi*, no. 43 (January 1990) pp. 9–28; Cam and Patrick Chaumette, *L'expertise d'entreprise*, report prepared for the Commissariat Général du Plan (Paris: Commissariat Général du Plan, 1988) and 'L'expertise technologique du comité d'entreprise', *Droit Social*, no. 3 (March 1989) pp. 220–8; Dominique Carré and Auslag Johansen, *L'expertise en nouvelles technologies: Une nouvelle dynamique de la concertation sociale en entreprise* (Paris: ARETE, Commissariat Général du Plan, 1987); GIP-MI, *Points de vue sur l'expertise non patronale en entreprise*, Cahier no. 18 (Paris: GIP-MI, 1988); Johansen, 'L'expertise technologique pour le comité d'entreprise: Un démarrage difficile', *Travail et emploi*, no. 34 (December 1987) pp. 71–9; and Didier Lochouarn, 'L'Expertise nouvelles technologies et prévention des risques graves', *Travail et emploi*, no. 43 (January 1990) pp. 22–8.

9. For an analysis of sectoral-level bargaining, see Francis Ginsbourger and J.-Y. Potel, *Les Pratiques de la négociation de branche* (Paris: Service des Etudes et de la Statistique, Ministry of Labour, 1987). Reynaud provides a detailed analysis of negotiations in the steel industry.

10. I studied the process of consultation over technological change and related issues in several banks and chemical, petrochemical and pharmaceutical companies. I participated in meetings at the firm and plant levels, and interviewed officials from trade associations, companies, unions and works councils.

11. The consultations were not conducted under the provisions of the Auroux Laws, however. Given the magnitude of the project, the legally mandated procedures for works council consultation should have been followed. Instead, ANACT proposed its own procedure, to which the works council and management agreed.

12. Groux, 'Trade Unionism and Technology', in Kesselman and Groux, p. 139. To bring Groux's observation up to date, one should add job protection to the list of traditional labour issues.

13. The structural tendency has been well analysed by Martin A. Schain, 'Relations between the CGT and the CFDT: Politics and Mass Mobilisation', in Kesselman and Groux, pp. 257–76.

14. The battery of tests and interviews used to select new employees at this plant was

quite formidable. One can understand why: the plant cost between 250 and 400 million dollars but operates with a total work force of 250 employees.

15. Pascal David, *Vers un syndicalisme sans adhérents*, unpublished Master's essay (Grenoble: Institut d'Etudes Politiques, 1989), cited in Labbé and Croisat, p. 109.

16. I analyse this dilemma in 'The New Shape of French Labour and Industrial Relations: Ce n'est plus la même chose', in Paul Godt, ed., *Policy-making in France: From de Gaulle to Mitterrand* (London: Pinter Publishers, 1989) pp. 165–75.

17. I have analysed other aspects of the change in 'La Nouvelle Cuisine en Politique: La fin de l'exceptionnalité française', in Yves Mény, ed., *Idéologies, Partis Politiques, et Groupes Sociaux, Pour Georges Lavau* (Paris: Presses de la Fondation Nationale des Sciences Politiques, 1989) pp. 159–74.

9 The Dilemma of Unions without Members

Guy Groux and René Mouriaux

The economic recession of the 1970s had several effects on union action in most of the industrialized countries. The constraints to greater or lesser degrees have affected union practices: unions have had to explore new strategies within the context of new modes of regulation and class compromise.[1] The consequences on memberships have varied widely among nations. National traditions have been historically constructed; they have depended on previous union presence, recruitment practices (the closed shop in Britain, for instance) and the shapes assumed by national union offices. In northern Europe, unionization remains traditionally strong, reaching and even surpassing a density of 80 per cent of the work force in Sweden, Denmark and Finland. Elsewhere, real declines in membership have not precluded continued union influence: in the United Kingdom and Italy union density has dropped to between 35 per cent and 40 per cent, but unions continue to wield authority.

Within this context, French unionism and the profound crisis that affects it seem marked by a particularity so strong that few informed observers in France hesitate to envision a unionism *without* members. Historically several peculiarities have characterized French unionism. It was founded on a representative institutionalization that prioritized a mass unionism and has always relied on a militant structure. It conceived of membership as an act of conviction rather than as a simple commitment linked to immediate interests. In general, it remained devoid of genuine service functions aimed at members.[2] Most of all, however, the establishment of French unions held little importance for the labour movement.[3] French unionism never brought together more than 20 per cent to 25 per cent of the workforce, and was always strongest in the public sector, nationalized companies and certain large industrial groups in the private sector. With the crisis, the traditional weakness of the union presence has been even further highlighted, in breathtaking proportions. France's unionization rate, between 8 per cent and 10 per cent, is by far the lowest in the European Union and in the states belonging to the Organization for Economic Co-operation and Development.[4] Paradoxically, the development of negotiation – and notably direct bargaining – expanded but hardly led to a reinforcement of union influence. This disengagement now touches the public was well as the private sector.

THE PARADOX: CONTRACTUAL INSTITUTIONALIZATION AND UNION DISENGAGEMENT

The largest number of France's collective bargaining agreements were signed in the 1980s. At the national, cross-sectoral (*interprofessionnel*) level, the productivity of contractualization from 1986 to 1991 rivalled that of the early 1970s, previously the principle benchmark for collective bargaining.[5] The recent expansion of direct bargaining, however, can be distinguished from previous periods by the emergence of the *firm* as the space for bargaining. By the end of the 1970s, firm-level agreements in France were more the exception than the rule, unlike the practice in so many other Western countries.[6] Under the dual pressure of the Auroux Laws and the new workplace practices of French employers – initiated not simply on the emergence of new techniques of social management but also on the implementation of a new social compromise – the firm-level accord has reached an unprecedented level. In 1950 there were 17 such accords. In 1970 there were 658, but many of these constituted attempts to resolve immediate conflict. In 1990, almost ten times as many accords (6496) were signed, despite the lower level of industrial conflict.

Traditionally, the majority of accords touched on immediately tangible advancements linked to the workplace, including salaries, working conditions and skilling levels. Today, however, the content of accords increasingly touches different domains – for example, the introduction of new technologies, personnel management, the adjustment of working time and profit-sharing. These accords transcend both the individual worker and the employment collectivity to focus on the specific reproduction of production mechanisms.

The over-institutionalization of negotiation that has taken place can be described by three attributes. First, the primacy of the local-level and firm-level accord occurred within a traditionally centralized industrial relations system where the state assumed a major role.[7] Second, new contractual themes emerged that target the economic as much as the social realm. Third, these numerous accords have been negotiated independent of industrial conflict or collective worker mobilization. A system based on 'cold negotiations' has been institutionalized, whereas in the past social regulation frequently rested on a dialectical relationship between conflict and negotiation (or on a balance of power more than on compromise).

It has been overwhelmingly clear that the heightened institutionalization of direct negotiation has brought no corresponding increase in union activity, nor has it brought a greater organizational legitimacy to the workforce. The union disengagement has continued and even accelerated in spite of the increase in accords, whether or not union organizations have taken part in this institutionalization.

The number of days lost to strike activity in the French private sector has decreased from 5 010 700 in 1976 to 665 500 in 1991.[8] In the public sector, statistics have only been kept since 1984, so any long-term comparison is impossible.[9] Still, the effervescence of the 1986 to 1989 period has clearly slackened.[10] The retreat from strike activity requires a careful examination that is agnostic to intellectual fashion. Not to explore this labour quiescence within the context of mass unemployment would be to recall the thin analyses found in a number of popular works.[11] Economic factors, however, do not play a mechanical role, as the behaviour of workers can be marked by a phenomenon of hystasis or inspired by anticipation. The heavy tendency since the onslaught of the economic crisis has had different phases and different conditions that must be taken into account.

Private sector protest was significant in 1979, 1982, 1986 and 1988. In the context of a tranquil social landscape, the rail strikes of December 1986 and January 1987 marked the appearance of a new juncture, one in which the advancement of wage demands did not exclude other more qualitative claims. These included a willingness to pursue actions in a more direct fashion toward the rank-and-file and the maintenance of clearly segmented approaches. The singularity of the Peugeot conflict in 1989 was part of this movement.[12] A sense of injustice resulted from the manner in which remunerations were handled. The strike was conducted in a democratic manner, but its practices were not diffused into the automobile sector.

To interpret correctly the weakening of industrial conflict in France, it is necessary to understand the political context. From 1981 to 1986, the labour movement spared the Socialists in power. Cohabitation of a Right government with a Socialist president, in contrast, favoured a resumption of contestation that continued in the public sector during the early phase of the Socialist minority government led by Michel Rocard. The crisis in the Persian Gulf froze the labour movement from August 1990 to March 1992. To a lesser degree, the beginning of the social calendar (*rentrée sociale*) in 1992 was overshadowed by the 20 September referendum on the Maastricht Treaty.[13]

The marginalization of the *Confédération Général du Travail* (CGT) – from the rupture of its alliance with the *Confédération Française Démocratique du Travail* (CFDT) to its proposition for greater concertation in 1992 – has also played a considerable role in the overall weakening of French labour. Cold negotiations precluded successful mobilization. In October 1985, the Secretary General of the CFDT, Edmond Maire, declared he was against the 'mythology reducing union activity to the strike'.[14] The CFDT called for a return among the railworkers in 1986–7. Jean-Paul Jacquier, a confederal secretary at the time, disavowed his own Finances Federation in October 1989 by claiming that a reasonable compromise had already been reached. In contrast, the workforce in the Ministry of Finances claimed that their conflict – of a size and intensity never before seen in this sector – had not produced results in proportion to the effort expended.[15] Beyond the case of the Finance Ministry, the cautiousness of workers must be placed within the context of national authorities and the employers who have sought to substantiate the idea that workplace struggles simply do not pay off.

Along with work stoppages, demonstrations have also diminished. May Day has wilted. September meetings (for the *rentrée*) have become thinner.[16] It was the Right that hit the streets in 1982 and 1984. It was students who were attracted to solidarity around Malik Oussekine after his death at the hands of the Parisian police in 1986.[17] Since the CGT managed an impressive demonstration on 22 March 1987 in support of Social Security, union crowds have been thin. Collective action has not fallen into disuse – look at the 8 July 1989 cry of 'Enough already' against the desecration of the Jewish cematary in Carpentras, the 12 January 1991 rally for peace in the Persian Gulf and the 25 January 1992 demonstration against racism. The union movement, however, no longer has the capacity to intervene decisively in favour of social demands.

Diminishing participation in social and professional elections provide further evidence for the diminishing attractiveness of French unions. The abstention rate for works council elections has climbed five percentage points from the 1976–7 to 1989–90 annual cycles. For the bipartite administrative committees in the public sector, abstention increased from 18.1 per cent in 1978–80 to 24.1 per cent in 1989–91. Reestablished in 1983, the elections for Social Security boards attracted only 47.3 per cent of eligible voters; the next vote has been delayed ever since. Meanwhile, for elections to the conciliation boards, abstention rates have steadily risen from 36.8 per cent in 1979 to 58 per cent in 1992. By showing the declining overall union vote, these data suggest that the argument that a 'unionism of electors' has been substituted for a 'unionism of members' obscures as much as it clarifies.[18]

The last indicator of union crisis is furnished by the rate of membership. In France, working out the precise ratio of union members to those who can be organized is particularly difficult. The available information comes from the unions, who either embellish or hide reality. And dues are generally payable on a monthly basis, but union organizations rarely sell 12 stamps to each member. More importantly, if affiliation constitutes a gradual relationship, then any statistical series must be viewed with a critical eye regardless of how carefully constructed it might be.

Overall, the French labour movement has lost roughly two-thirds of its membership since 1976 (see Table 9.1). While union density hovered around 25 per cent in 1974, it dwindled to 8 per cent in 1992. Table 9.2 provides an initial inventory of internal and external factors that explain this haemorrhage.

The manifest retreat of French workers from the union movement has translated into scepticism, disappointment and demobilization. Does it also indicate a relative satisfaction, or even a morose realism? The available studies seem to indicate the existence of an abundant 'protest terrain' that for production workers applies first to employment and wages but also concerns career trajectories and interest in work itself.[19] Management personnel prioritize their concerns as career, followed by working conditions, retirement, employment and then salary.[20] The explosion of diverse work conditions and worker expectations has made the

Table 9.1   Estimates of Union Membership, by Observer

	Pierre Rosanvallon 1988	Michel Noblecourt 1989	Pierre Cours-Salies 1990
CGT	600 000	600 000	515 000
CFDT	400 000	470 000	335 000
FO	400 000	450 000	270 000
CFTC	–	100 000	–
CGC	–	100 000	–
FEN	200 000	300 000	300 000

Notes: FO = *Force Ouvrière*; CFTC = *Confédération française des travailleurs chrétiens*; CGC = *Confédération générale des cadres*; FEN = *Fédération de l'Education Nationale*.

Sources: Rosanvallon, *La question syndicale* (Paris: Calmann-Levy, 1989) p. 15; Noblecourt, *Les syndicats en questions* (Paris: Editions Ouvrières, 1990) p. 34; Pierre Cours-Salies, 'Syndicats, état des lieux', *L'Homme et la société*, no. 4 (1990) p. 43.[21]

aggregation of interests around which unions need to focus extraordinarily arduous. The appearance of 'co-ordinations' demonstrates a refusal of union divisiveness among railworkers, a concern for direct control among social workers and nurses and a desire for management to use creative means to save employment. It indicates a distancing between the base and the union apparatusthat de-unionization has aggravated.

FRENCH EXCEPTIONALISM: FROM THE PRIMACY OF THE STATE TO THE 'PRIVATE CONTRACT'

The paradox of the institutionalization of direct negotiation during union decline reveals that the current crisis and the forms of collective withdrawal that accompany it are more serious than any problems that have previously confronted French labour. One cannot simply refer back to previous crises of unionism from the *Belle Epoque* to the scission of the immediate post-war period that have so shaken the 'crisis cycle' history of the workers' movement.[22]

In France, as in other nations, unionism has suffered the effects of exogenous traits tied in various degrees to the character of the world market, unemployment, the increasing precarity of employment, the different reconfigurations of the workplace and managerial policies to mobilize the workforce.[23] And, as elsewhere, endogenous factors – including organizational centralism and ideological division among the unions – continue to play a critical role. One critical structural element that can help explain union decline, however, is unique to France.

The crisis of French unionism is first of all a crisis in its relationship to the

Table 9.2 Factors Contributing to the Union Crisis[24]

Political	Economic	Social	Organizational
Crisis of French communism and socialism	Unemployment	Development of service industries	Institutionalization
CGT electoral support for the PCF	Destruction of worker collectivity	Feminization of Work	Bureaucratization
Factional struggles in PCF	Decrease in purchasing power / draw on union dues	Expansion and diversification of immigration	Absence of internal debate
Refusal to unify in action	Precarious contracts / runaway shops	Individualization of salaries Individualism	Cumulative losses (members, electors, militants, permanent officials)
Withdrawal and reorganization of the state	Subcontracting	Firm-level bargaining	
End of the primacy of labour law	Efficiency losses	Direct expression	Lack of realism; infighting
Repression	Insertion into European Community and world markets	Cycle of social retreat	Abandonment of labour claims and worker struggles
Government support		Firm-level decentralization	
Crisis of Secularism		Generational shift	

state and its legal institutionalization, a relationship that could not take the place of new forms of association based on direct negotiation, firm-level negotiation and private contracts.[25] The current French system of industrial relations developed after World War II with all its peculiarities, stemming directly from the various themes within the programme of the *Conseil National de la Résistance*. Through its control of new nationalized companies in key sectors of the economy, the state became not only the largest employer in France, it also appointed itself the modernizer of social relations in the name of economic interventionism. Through a series of regulations, the state exercised until the mid–1980s an increasingly extended influence on various aspects of social life – salaries (through minimum wage-setting), employee representation in the firm, profit-sharing, the role of bipartite commissions (for working conditions and training), the definition of industrial citizenship, the codification of social insurance, the legislation of contractual safeguards. Thus, state initiative frequently determined the content of collective bargaining when it did not completely replace direct negotiations between economic and social actors.

Over the long term, the primacy of law on negotiations explained union behaviour and strategy, both of which tended to be defined along political lines. 'National days of action', a very French-specific form of mobilization, also played a role, especially in the private sector, where unions remained weak and poorly developed. They were intended to exert a direct pressure on the state – legislators, the executive and the judiciary.[26] Other strategic tapestries were woven simultaneously at the legislative level, and these tended to politicize most of the 'representative' unions.[27] In exchange for electoral influence over the workforce, the unions became political lobbies and promoted the legal implementation of organizational demands.

The relationship between unions and the state was increasingly affected by changes in legislative discretion and by the crisis suffered by those parties closest to the union organizations. The progressive decrease in power of the National Assembly throughout the Fifth Republic and the crisis of Left values in the 1980s – affecting both Communism and social democracy – also played a considerable role. The weakening of the union-party relationship – and therefore of state modes of union institutionalization – derived first and foremost from state action, starting in 1984.

The paradox here is not its initiation, for the relaxation of state intervention is not necessarily linked to the abdication of political will. Rather, it was inspired by an increasingly hegemonic theory of the economy and mode of individual decision-making.[28] From the mid-1980s on, a new political discourse confronted not simply a Left newly inspired by the business community but it also confronted an existing set of economic factors. Keynesian policies to revive the economy through an increase in consumption and employment were afterwards torpedoed. In their place, governments of Left and Right prioritized the revival of investment, which, in turn, brought wage restraint and a new element: a rehabilitation of both the firm and the market that *ipso facto* implied a relaxation of regulatory constraint. Consequently, the relationship between law and (negotiated) contract was redefined. In the first period (1984–6), compromise was managed by state initiative, and ministries imposed increasingly fewer new rules. In fact, the application of law became increasingly dependent on direct negotiation between the concerned parties at both the sectoral level and the base. Then, after 1986, in the process of deepening this new form of social regulation, negotiation and agreements increasingly dictated the content of legislation (and other forms of state decision-making). This can be seen in such critical domains as employment (redundancies, precarious work, flexibility of working time), technological change, the various industrial conversion measures and vocational training.

As a result, we have witnessed a powerful new institutionalization of social relations, in the midst of which direct negotiations have taken priority over law in industrial relations. The autonomy of industrial relations, the legal retreat and the gradual elimination of the state as a critical prop for the unions, however, have all taken place during a period in which the weakening of union demands is far advanced and the intervention of union organizations has become increasingly empty within these forms of regulation. The declining representativeness and influence of unions have played key roles, as have the external economic constraints that have pressured unions to grant concessions. Unions remain divided in the face of these concessions, especially in that they have problems mastering the technical elements of collective bargaining that they are in the process of conceding.[29] Thus, the former system of industrial relations, with the state as kingpin, has been superseded. The new system, influenced by liberal tenet, has a credibility seldom challenged because of the diminished union legitimacy, the new balance of forces that dominate the economy and the compromises now being signed. In other words, alongside union divisions and the historically weak union presence in the workplace has been the challenge to the legitimacy of the former system of regulation, which was founded on public regulation and has yet to be fully supplanted. It is therefore not surprising that the responses of worker organizations have been delicate. Any organization faced with the exhaustion of practices in place for so long could only respond tentatively.

THE SEARCH FOR SOLUTIONS

In the face of de-unionization, the reduction in mobilizational capacities and the decline in influence of collective bargaining, the unions have not remained lethargic. They have explored the reasons for their weakening and have searched for ways to reverse it. A study of union congresses remains indispensable not only to ascertain the meaning the actors themselves derive from their own behaviour, as Max Weber suggested. It also enables us to catch a glimpse of the stakes involved in any form of confederation 'normalization', the struggle between various strategies and the dynamic between union leaders and members.

The succession of André Bergeron, secretary general of the *Force Ouvrière* (FO) after 1963, gave rise to a sharp confrontation before and during the 16th Confederal Congress held in January and February 1989. There was a consensus on the current problems – and on the untimeliness of publicly displaying the real situation of unionization.[30] Instead, a debate developed over the appropriate strategies to initiate. Much of the tension began with the negotiations over employment flexibility in 1984. The secretary general, who was at the peak of his power within the confederation, decided to sign the agreement, but the national confederal committee refused to give him a majority vote. According to Bergeron,

We were at the end of our prospects. It infringed on the Labour Code. Our militants don't want anything to do with that. It is a religious maxim. I cannot go over the heads of our militants. We remain a democratic organization.[31]

The different opinions on what was to be done in the context of a long economic crisis structured the leadership transition and election of a new secretary general. In the beginning of 1986, Marc Blondel, from the office workers' federation, placed himself in competition at the same time Trotskyites were accused of infiltrating the organization.[32] Undoubtedly encouraged by Bergeron, Claude Pitous, from the postal workers' federation, announced his candidacy shortly thereafter. The contest came to revolve around two different strategies.

A year before the congress that was to settle the leadership transition, Pitous published a cautious manifesto, *Principles and Perspectives of Reformist Unionism*.[33] In it he denounced 'sterile incantations' and made a plea for greater realism in union action. His adversaries shadowed him with several tactics – a refusal of all dogmatism, praise for organizational adaptation and proposals of an 'intermediary corps'. They painted him as a partisan of service unionism – in effect, fellow-travelling with French managers – indicated by the very character of his supporters in the Metalworkers' Federation (Michel Huc) and the Paris departmental union (Jacques Mairé). In contrast, Blondel declared himself comfortable with a protest unionism, all the while paying attention to societal evolution and declaring himself pragmatic. His oral report and his response to interventions during the 17th Congress in 1992 reflected a majority position in the confederation: 'Revolutionary in its aspiration but reformist in its practice, our unionism will be the motor of history.'[34] The contractual way, he continued, remained privileged, although not every text merited a signature. The best defense of worker interests was independent unionism. Blondel justified the strike of 24 October 1991 as necessary vis-à-vis an austerity imposed upon the workforce, the dismantlement of public services and the pretence of public-sector wage settlement. While unionism was passing through difficult times – a loss of membership, and diminishing capacities – it would not extricate itself by denying its vocation or by erasing conflict 'in the name of I don't know what modernism'. For Blondel, FO had to rejuvenate and reinforce its organization. It needed to improve its position and counter-attack. 'It has not changed direction.'

The CFDT has seen itself in different terms. Evolving over a 20-year period from the CFTC and Catholic unionism, the organization conceived of itself within a larger movement, developing its structures, ideology and strategy. After the alliance with the CGT signed on 10 January 1966 and having participated in the events of May 1968, it declared itself in favour of self-managing socialism (*socialisme autogestionnaire*) in 1970. Having frequently appeared alongside the CGT in demonstrations and in a variety of local workplace disputes, the CFDT began to diverge from its positions in the 1977–8 period. The 'recentreing' (*recentrage*) consecrated by the Brest Congress had four different meanings:

contractualism would take precedence over legislative avenues, cold negotiations were endorsed, unity of action would take place at several speeds, and economic constraints would be recognized in the name of larger solidarities. This orientation expanded in the following years. In 1988, the 39th Congress confirmed a second *recentrage*. Preceded by the elimination of Pierre Héritier from the Executive Commission and followed by the exclusion of militants who later created autonomous unions in the postal services and hospitals, the congress designated Jean Kaspar (against the outgoing secretary general's heir apparent, Nicole Notat) to succeed Edmond Maire.[35] It also approved three supplementary emphases for a 'resolutely reformist' unionism – the abandonment of all references to socialism, the development of service unionism and the participation in a union 'recomposition' (in other words, alliance with other 'reformist' unions). At its 1992 congress, the CFDT admitted the logic of the market and recommended France's full participation in Economic and Monetary Union (the Maastricht Treaty). But Kaspar's goals did not receive universal acclaim, and a new set of opposition forces developed. An amendment against the abolition of departmental unions received over 60 per cent of the vote, an unforeseen resistance to confederal leadership.[36]

In October 1992, a palace revolution took place. Kaspar was forced to resign his position, and Notat was elected secretary general by the National Bureau.[37] How should we interpret this sudden shift in fortunes? 'Management crisis' was the official explanation.[38] Kaspar's fall can be partially explained by his casual style of leadership and lack of authority within the confederation. A more political explanation for this 'triumph of might', however, can be found in the gap between the current orientation of the confederation and its tradition of protest.[39] The most reformist wing feared a new majority was developing that would revert to earlier practices of local struggle.

The CGT too has changed course several times. From 1972 to 1977, it combined unity in action with support for the Common Programme. The 40th Congress in Grenoble brought to the fore a clash between a desire for autonomy vis-à-vis the PCF and participation in the rupture of Left unity. Support for the Communists dominated the period from 1978 to 1984. Still, Secretary General Henri Krasucki tried to distance the union from the PCF's departure from the Left government. His successor, Louis Viannet, has expressed the concern of traditional militants about the possibility of a drift in the organization's orientation. A meeting of the National Confederal Committee in June 1991 seriously examined union independence, and the Congress of January 1992 promoted it as a means to overcome de-unionization and demobilization. Revitalization of the union was made all the more difficult by a struggle between Communist factions – those supporting Georges Marchais (secretary general of the PCF) were fighting those defining themselves as 'reconstructors', 'refounders' and 'confrontationalists'. Such infighting was attenuated but not eliminated after Marchais' departure from his leadership position, and it continued to prevent the development of dynamism

Unions without Members

within the union and to discourage members conscious of the need for clarity and efficiency.

The three union 'strategies' must be situated in relationship to each other. The FO's commitment to maintaining a reformist unionism (in its classic version) has accompanied an incessant critique of the CFDT and the CGT. By lambasting the CFDT's modernism, the FO runs the risk of avoiding new questions, even though some of Blondel's policy positions – a reduction of working time to 30 hours a week by the year 2000, for instance – are quite daring.[40] Its anti-communism derives from the Cold War, a time already passed. Union unity is an imperative the FO will have to face squarely. The recomposition of French unions in a reformist pole has failed. Certainly, the CFDT can point to a slight increase in membership in the early 1990s. While its following has stabilized, however, many of its local militants diverge from the confederal leadership in both actions and vocabulary. And the defeat of Jean Kaspar translated into a general malaise within the organization.

Another failure in the recomposition of French unions was the rupture of the teachers' union – the *Fédération de l'Éducation Nationale* (FEN). The expulsion of two affiliated unions (covering secondary school and physical education teachers) cost the FEN 111 000 members – almost one-third of the organization. The leadership of Guy Le Néouannic has been largely discredited because of the way the union used bureaucratic procedures to achieve organizational conformity. In general, the recomposition of a reformist pole has resulted in a crumbling of organizations and in de-unionization.

The renovation sketched out by the CGT has not yet taken shape. Calls for unity fall on deaf ears because they are not followed by any substantial gestures.[41] In summary, the dominant impressions for workers at the base are the routinization of interorganizational rivalry, the splintering of initiatives, the impotence of union attempts to respond to unemployment, the reduction in purchasing power and the autocratic management of French firms.

CONCLUSION

Except in rare moments (1918, 1936, 1944), the French workers' movement has always been a weak presence. The CGT in the early 1900s only organized roughly 5 per cent of the workforce. There have been exceptions in individual sectors – for instance, among printers and teachers. Still, the rule has been skeletal organizations and minimal resources. On several occasions, doubt has surfaced as to whether unions would survive at all.[42] And this question has returned quite strongly in the 1990s as the unions' strength spirals downward. The decrease in dues leads to a reduction in the number of permanent officials and an overload of work for volunteers. The shrinkage of militancy echoes throughout the union movement.

Union actors have been called into question by the crisis of the Fordist compromise – a game involving the state, employers and unions in a context of economic growth and productivity gains linked to the extension of Taylorism – because they were used to continual economic expansion. Unions in most advanced industrial countries have been affected by economic upheaval, a change in the role of the state and a transformation of the labour force. In France, however, the shock was much harsher, because state interventionism had been so important and because union divisions made each component of the workers' movement all the more vulnerable. At this low point in the history of French unionism, organizational pluralism has proven itself to be unrealistic.

translated by Anthony Daley

Notes

1. Geneviève Bibes and René Mouriaux, eds., *Les syndicats européens à l'épreuve* (Paris: Presses de la Fondation Nationale des Sciences Politiques, 1990).
2. The *Bourses du Travail*, the originators of modern French unionism, delivered such services in the latter part of the 19th century. See Peter Schöttler, *Naissance des bourses du travail: Un appareil idéologique d'Etat à la fin du XIXe siècle* (Paris: PUF, 1985); and Jacques Julliard, *Autonomie ouvrière: Etudes sur le syndicalisme d'action directe* (Paris: Gallimard/Seuil, 1988).
3. The exceptions have been only brief historical periods – 1920, 1936 and the Liberation. On the Liberation period, see Denis Peschanski and Jean-Louis Robert, eds., *Ouvriers français pendant la seconde guerre mondial* (Paris: Publications de l'Institut d'histoire du temps présent, 1992). See, in particular, Chapter 4.
4. Among diverse sources, see the synthetic treatment by Jelle Visser, 'Tendances de la syndicalisation', in *Perspectives de l'emploi* (Paris: OECD, 1991) pp. 101–37.
5. See Pierre Morville, *Les nouvelles politiques sociales du patronat* (Paris: La Découverte, 1985).
6. Jean-Daniel Reynaud, *Les syndicats, les patrons et l'Etat: Tendances de la négociation collective en France* (Paris: Editions Ouvrières, 1978).
7. Thus, for example, the adjustment and flexibility of working time was the object of many local agreements before being ratified by a national accord concluded in spring 1989 between the employers' confederation (CNPF) and several unions, including the CFDT.
8. See *Cahiers du CEVIPOF*, no. 3 (1988) and no. 7 (1992). See also 'Les conflits du travail en 1991', *Premières Informations*, no. 302 (5 October 1992).
9. Jeanne Siwek-Poudesseau, *Les syndicats de fonctionnaires depuis 1948* (Paris: PUF, 1989) p. 247.
10. Data on the public sector are published in annual reports.
11. This includes the writings of François Simiand, Robert Goetz-Girey, Edouard Andéani and Victor Scardigli. See the bibliography in Guy Groux and René Mouriaux, *La CGT, Crises et alternatives* (Paris: Economica, 1992). See also Anthony Daley, 'The Steel Crisis and Labour Politics in France and the United States', in Miriam Golden and Jonas Pontusson, eds., *Bargaining for Change: Union Politics in North America and Europe* (Ithaca, NY: Cornell University Press, 1992) pp. 146–89.

12. See *Cahiers de CEVIPOF*, no. 7 (1992). This conflict, however, did not exemplify industrial conflict in France.
13. The notion of *rentrée sociale* is debatable. Still, in a certain sense, wage outlooks in the private sector begin to take shape in August and September for the following year. In the public sector, the preparation of budgetary debates plays an even greater role.
14. Minella Verdie, ed., *L'État de la France et de ses habitants* (Paris: La Découverte, 1987).
15. A survey carried out from September to November 1992 showed the unease with which civil servants viewed the state's offers in 1989. See Cégolène Frisque and Catherine Villanueva, '39 entretiens semi-directifs sur le syndicalisme auprès de fonctionnaires des impôts' (Paris: CEVIPOF, 1992). It should be added that on 20 November 1992, Nicole Notat, only a month into her leadership of the CFDT, came out against the striking Paris metro unions for 'sabotaging' the social dialogue.
16. The CFDT eliminated its Parisian meeting in 1981.
17. Pierre Favre, ed., *La Manifestation* (Paris: Presses de la Fondation Nationale des Sciences Politiques, 1990); and Nonna Mayer and Pascal Perrineau, *Les comportements politiques* (Paris: Colin, 1992) pp. 140–2.
18. Mouriaux, 'Remarques sur la question syndicale', *Cahiers du GIP Mutations industielles*, no. 27 (April 1989) p. 75; and Antoine Bevort and Dominique Labbé, *La CFDT: Organisation et audience depuis 1945* (Paris: Documentation Française, 1992).
19. See also Bernard Vivier, 'Les organisations syndicales', *Liaisons sociales*, special issue, no. 113 (1992).
20. This enumeration of causal factors draws from Groux and Mouriaux, p. 259. We have modified the schema to take into account all French unions.
21. Jacques Capdevielle, Hélène Y. Meynaud and Mouriaux, *Petits boulots et grand marché européen: Le travail démobilisé* (Presses de la Fondation Nationale des Sciences Politiques, 1990) p. 205.
22. This comes from a variety of SOFRES polls. See Michelle Commergnat *et al*, *Les cadres et le syndicalisme* (Paris: CGT-CCEES, 1992) p. 21. It is interesting to note that polling institutes now seldom survey worker demands. For civil servant claims, see the study by the CFDT-UFFA in *Syndicalisme*, no. 2402 (30 April 1992).
23. For an elaboration of the argument of 'historical cyles of French union crisis', see Groux and Mouriaux, pp. 49–65.
24. In 1988, 9 million work contracts were signed, of which 5.5 million were for temporary work, 2.5 million for limited-term, and only 1 million resulted in a permanent recruitment. Thus, the labour market is characterized by a radical rotation of precarious functions gearing down the number of long-term contract and developing a cycle of 'hire-and-fire' that both affects an increasing number of employees and freezes any sort of union proselytism.
25. In France any agreement, even one signed by unions enjoying only a minority of support within the workforce, is granted the status of general rule. By private contract, we refer here to a contract signed directly between non-state representatives – employers and unions.
26. On the role played by 'national days of action' in the 1960s and 1970s, see George Ross, 'The CGT, Economic Crisis and Political Change', in Mark Kesselman, ed., *The French Workers' Movement: Economic Crisis and Political Change* (London: George Allen & Unwin, 1984) pp. 51–74.
27. This was true of the CGT and the PCF. However, historically and more recently, linkages developed between other union and party organizations, even when the former denounced the 'politicization of certain unions'. This was the case with the

CFTC and the MRP, of the FO and the SFIO, more recently between the CFDT and the PS, and even the CGC and certain parts of the Gaullist movement.

28. References to the market were certainly critical to this developing orthodoxy, but the market itself – even when hyper-liberal orthodoxies prevail – has never been purely an economic institution. Deregulation even implies a higher level of political action. In this regard, the 'Single European Market' is a revealing case.

29. A number of concessionary agreements (Bull, Péchiney) have been applied only with great difficulty. Likewise, industrial conflict (as at Renault and Peugeot) has broken out after the signature of such agreements. The FO and the CGT remain opposed to a logic of 'give and take' – trading concessions for certain advances. At the level of firm agreements, this logic frequently results in a circumvention of labour law. See Marie-Armelle Rotchild-Souriac, 'Les accords collectifs au niveau de l'entreprise', doctoral dissertation (University of Paris I-Sorbonne, 1986).

30. A promise was made but not kept to publish congressional votes according to individual unions. This would have revealed a breakdown of mandates and permitted a real evaluation of membership. See Force Ouvrière, *Compte-rendu du XVIe Congrès confédéral* (Paris: FO, 1989) pp. 330–1.

31. *Année politique 1984* (Paris: Ed. Moniteur, 1985) p. 359.

32. Claude Levy, *Les trois guerres de succession* (Paris: Alain Moreau, 1987) p. 90.

33. Claude Pitous, *Principes et perspectives du syndicalisme réformiste* (Fontenay-sous-Bois: SEI, 1988).

34. The quotations in this paragraph come from Force Ouvrière, *Compte-rendu du XVIIe Congrès* (Paris: FO, 1992).

35. In the postal service, local CFDT unions sought to ally with the co-ordination in November 1988 and were expelled for having defied the federation directives. Those sanctioned created a new organization, *Solidaires-Unitaires-Démocratique*. Likewise, in the hospitals, CFDT nurses disagreed with their federation's recommendation to end conflict and sign an agreement. They were expelled over the relationship with the co-ordinations in 1988. They created *Coordonner, Rassembler, Construire*, which later became the *Fédération Nationale des Syndicats Santé-Sociaux*.

36. *Syndicalisme*, 30 April 1992, supplement to no. 2402, p. 53.

37. This leadership change was especially ironic since Kaspar had been re-elected to the National Bureau with 91.2 per cent of the vote while Notat received only 67.27 per cent at the congress that spring.

38. Michel Noblecourt, 'Une crise de management', *Le Monde*, 21 October 1992.

39. Jean-Marie Pernot, 'Le passage en force', *Témoignage chrétien*, 24 October 1992.

40. *Force Ouvrière Hebdo*, no. 2127, 11 June 1992.

41. Louis Viannet, 'Pour une dynamique de renouveau du syndicalisme', *Le Monde*, 19 June 1992.

42. The question was asked by serious observers in 1909, 1921 and in the 1950s. See Groux and Mouriaux, 'La crise de 1909: textes et commentaires', *Analyses et Documents Économiques*, no. 47–8 (December 1991) pp. 31–5.

Part III
Political Mobilization and Left Politics

10 The Shifting Advantages of Organizational Formats: Factionalism and the French Socialist Party

Serenella Sferza

What sort of party is the French Socialist Party? How does it fit into the partisan families of Left politics and the developmental typologies identified by political scientists? From the days of the First International, political scientists and participants alike have debated these questions without coming to any agreement beyond the basic fact that the Socialist Party (PS), like its predecessor, lacks the links to organized labour characteristic of social democracy.

The French Socialist Party, in fact, never followed dominant patterns nor corresponded to a single party type. In the years of party formation, the salience of regime stabilization and the primacy of political over social issues led French Socialists to adopt organizational and ideological traits that were less class-specific than those of most of their European counterparts. While committed to working-class interests, the *Section Française de l'Internationale Ouvrière* (SFIO) framed its representation within a larger republican project. The party never developed an integrated labour-movement format based on close links with unions, and it came to resemble more a citizens' than a class-mass party.[1] Moreover, its operations varied so widely that separate federations were often compared to a variety of regional models – for example, the Belgian, Neapolitan and Radical.[2]

French Socialism, an outlier in the golden age of class-mass parties, was also an outlier in the new age of catch-all ones. In the 1970s, just as political analysts were predicting the advent of catch-allism, the PS underwent a spectacular ideological revitalization and electoral expansion that flew in the face of such expectations. Although the party expanded its support beyond the traditional boundaries of the Left, it did not abandon Left ideology and programmes. Socialist supporters retained a strong left-wing identity, and the party won votes on the basis of a very radical project and alliance strategy.[3] When the United Left won power in 1981, the PS was widely regarded as the most successful *and* radical European Left party. At the same time, however, the PS continued to differ from social democracy in its organization and relation to the labour movement. Moreover, the party's remarkable renaissance was short-lived: in the 1993 legislative and 1994 European elections, the PS won less than 30 per cent and 15 per cent of the vote, respectively.

At a time in which the typologies French Socialism never fit into are losing their usefulness, it is important to focus instead on those distinctive features that do seem to explain the dynamics of the PS's evolution and provide insights about its prospects. Prevailing approaches to party development, however, are ill-equipped for this task. By portraying the party development as the byproduct of environmental factors, they largely ignore party-specific institutional resources and, in particular, organizational ones. Yet the differential capacities of parties to respond to external challenges and opportunities are largely a result of these internal factors. In the case of the PS, both its successes of the 1970s and early 1980s and its subsequent crisis were for the most part caused by the match, and then the mismatch, between the party's organizational format and the challenges posed by the socio-political context. Factionalism, in particular, was a crucial link between the environment and party strategy and a key shaper of party performance.[4]

EXPLAINING THE PARTY'S TRAJECTORY

Most accounts of the PS's renaissance in the 1970s adopt an 'externalist' approach: they analyse, whether through sociological or institutional explanations, how environmental variables influenced party strategy and performance. The party's trajectory is therefore presented as the inevitable product of its environment. Thus, the rapid modernization of French society since the late 1950s, as manifested in the dramatic increase in educated, white-collar and urban sectors of the population, is said to have created a 'natural' constituency for the PS. Moreover, the PS is presented as the major beneficiary of the Fifth Republic's electoral and party systems, which, it is argued, created a 'positional rent' for a party located to the Centre–Left of the political spectrum.[5] Seen against the background of these environmental conditions, the Socialists' success is portrayed as unproblematic: the standard text on the French Socialist Party calls it 'a party whose time had come'.[6]

Closer scrutiny, however, reveals major logical and empirical flaws in these explanations. Consider first the rapid modernization of French society – the factor most often used to explain the explosion of support for French socialism in the 1970s. Developments associated with this modernization can hardly be said to have dictated party strategy, or to have guaranteed its success once chosen. It is far from clear, for example, why the increased size of the middle class or cultural modernization alone should have enhanced the appeal of socialism rather than that of Valéry Giscard d'Estaing's liberal reformism. Indeed, it is precisely these sorts of social changes that are routinely invoked to account for the triumph, in other comparably developed societies, of catch-allism – a form of party organization and strategy that stands in marked contrast to the radicalism and increased activism of the PS throughout the 1970s.[7] Since similar structural changes can produce such opposing political outcomes, sociological indicators appear to be a poor predictor of party strategy and performance.

Moreover, while the mobilization of new actors and 'new politics' themes in the wake of the events of 1968 created a great pool of potential recruits for socialism as well as a catalyst for its ideological revitalization, the PS's prospects for tapping these sources were anything but certain. The mobilization that followed May 1968 was intensely anti-political, at least in its initial stages, reflecting a profound disillusionment with the prospect of change through political means and an even deeper distrust for traditional political formations.[8]

Similarly, the systemic logic of the Fifth Republic also had ambiguous implications for party strategies. Conventional wisdom has it that the polarizing and centripetal forces generated by the party system confer a key advantage to the moderate components of each bloc – hence the widely shared assumption that the optimal strategy for the PS was to occupy the Centre–Left. This analysis, however, takes for granted the existence of a political space that was actually created through party craft. In order to benefit from the centripetal drive, French Socialists had to displace the Communist Party (PCF) as the dominant formation within the Left. But the PS could only achieve this by presenting itself as a credible replacement for the Communists, a challenge that entailed radicalizing its programme and exacerbating the system's polarizing drive. Moving in such a direction, however, did not bode well for its capacity to win the support of groups that were opposed to the PCF and its statist and Jacobin Left tradition. Had the PS's initial status as the weaker partner in the Union of the Left not been reversed, the centripetal force that ultimately favoured the Socialists might have been suppressed within the Left. This would have resulted in an altogether different scenario, one in which the Communist Party might have benefited from the polarizing effect of the electoral system at the expense of the Left as a whole.

In the early 1970s, therefore, the societal and institutional contexts of the Fifth Republic pulled the PS in opposite directions, either of which alone would have been insufficient for the party to succeed and which, taken together, appeared to be a recipe for incoherence and paralysis. The rapid expansion of an urban, highly-educated, white-collar sector and the centripetal drive of presidential elections seemed to call for a catch-all strategy. But the polarization of the party system, the conditions of intra-Left competition and the extraordinarily high level of mobilization called for a more militant approach associated with class-mass parties. Faced with these contradictory demands, French Socialists shunned the catch-all approach and went backward in a sense. They moved not to the class-mass stage but to elements of their legacy, by reviving a form of party organization – factionalism – that was part of their traditional repertoire. This organizational format allowed the PS to combine features associated with class-mass, catch-all and even framework parties.

THE COMPARATIVE ADVANTAGES OF ORGANIZATIONAL FORMATS

Party organization is critical to party performance in two major ways: It structures and influences internal debates over how to interpret and respond to environmental conditions, and it affects the resources – ideological, institutional and human – that parties can deploy to implement their strategies. The major organizational reform the new PS introduced was a shift from a territorial organizational format – in which geographically defined units (federations) were the main loci of political debate, coalition formation and party governance – to a primarily factional one – in which ideologically defined units (factions) took that role.[9] This shift, which was spurred by the need to keep together the heterogenous coalition headed by François Mitterrand that took control of the party at the Epinay Congress of 1971, deeply affected the PS's political culture and internal operations, as well as its growth potential.[10]

During periods of high social mobilization, factionalism has several advantages over territorialism as an instrument of growth.[11] Territorial models of party organization are patterned to reflect local, electoral and administrative concerns; they are likely to favour issues and forms of recruitment and mobilization that 'fit' with existing electoral alliances and power structures. Hence they appear better suited to conserve resources and ensure party reproduction at times of low mobilization. The factional model, which prevailed in the PS by contrast rested on vertically integrated units that competed on ideological grounds. The factions served as a conductor for the energies unleashed by high mobilization. As factions eclipsed departmental federations as the main loci of activism, socialization, political debate and party governance, they became a major factor of symbiosis between the party and its environment.

The existence within the party of distinct political projects and organizational networks that targeted specific audiences enabled the PS to pursue simultaneously strategies usually associated with different types of parties. Factionalism allowed the PS to differentiate its political 'offer' without renouncing its programmatic content and promoted an ideological and institutional dynamic that helped the party gain proximity to new political actors and renew its relations with labour. As a result, the PS became both more catch-all and more militant. Most important, Socialists managed to combine horizontal growth – the widening of their following beyond traditional partisan and sociological borders to include newly mobilized sectors and previously hostile groups – and vertical growth – the deepening of support among the Left's core electorate.[12] These two types of growth allowed the PS to dislodge the PCF as the dominant component of the Left and capture a sizeable share of the centre.

The relative advantages of specific models of party organization, however, are not constant across institutional and political contexts. By the mid-1980s, these contexts had changed dramatically. The political agenda and the terms of political competition were modified by the conquest of power in 1981 and the breakup of the Union of the Left in 1984, the exhaustion of the ideological and militant reservoirs created by the mobilizations of the late 1960s and early 1970s, the inability of Left governments to bring about economic growth and their subsequent abandonment of more radical policies, and the emergence of new issues that cut across pre-existing alignments. At the same time, the emergence of Mitterrand's followers as the clearly dominant faction altered the logic of interfactional competition. These developments eroded the advantages of factionalism. In this later period, the PS's performance was negatively affected by a growing mismatch between its organizational format and its environment.

ORGANIZATIONAL MATCH: FACTIONALISM IN THE 1970S

In the early 1970s, factionalism was primarily an ideological phenomenon.[13] Some factions, most notably the one associated with Michel Rocard, adhered to a society-centred view of political and economic transformation that would simultaneously empower workers and citizens and introduce change through the practice of *autogestion*.[14] Hence, the Rocard supporters aimed at building a framework party informally linking a wide array of groups and associations, and sought to emancipate the Left from the ideological and organizational hegemony of the PCF, which they saw as inherently authoritarian and even conservative. Others, including the faction identified with Mitterrand, combined more conformist views rooted in the republican tradition of the French Left with its emphasis on statism and laicism with a unitary Left strategy, one in which the alliance with the PCF was both instrumental to the Socialists' electoral expansion and justified by a shared historical past. Still others, notably the *Centre des Etudes, Recherche et d'Education Socialiste* (CERES), presented an original synthesis of old and new demands combining statism and mass participation, openness to modernist technocratic themes and attachment to republican values. Extremely critical of the transformative potential of the Left as long as it remained divided, CERES sought to transform the PS into a class-mass party with solid working-class support and to promote its fusion with a reformed Communist party.

Competition between these alternative strategies of party-building and societal transformation was a crucial factor in the PS's ideological and militant renewal.[15] The mechanisms of internal representation, which made participation in the party's leading bodies dependent on the support mustered by congressional motions, encouraged factions to engage in ideological debate and develop permanent organizational networks. They also turned congresses into major occasions for programmatic confrontations and political and leadership choices. The raised stakes and vitality of intraparty politics, in turn, gave Socialist sympathizers incentives to join the party. At the same time, since none of the factions gained total hegemony over the party until 1981, each had powerful motives to seek out new members and ideas in order to strengthen its relative position.[16] As factions engaged in a competitive drive to gain proximity to collective actors and to impart political coherence to the demands of a wide variety of groups, from regionalist and women's groups to Catholic unionists and secular associations, they wove multiple ties between the party and mobilized sectors of society. In addition to encouraging the opening of the PS, factionalism also expanded its reach. By allowing the PS to differentiate its offer – and hence achieve the electoral effectiveness usually attributed to catch-allism – while at the same time eschewing the ideological and militant demobilization associated with this type of party, factionalism acted as a widener *and* deepener of the Socialists' appeal.[17]

On one hand, the coexistence of different discourses and projects allowed the PS to stretch across the political spectrum. With each faction targeting a distinct audience, the party as a whole succeeded in giving expression to a variety of currents that had developed outside of mainstream party politics and whose appeal extended well beyond the Left, while at the same time renewing longstanding commitments to the traditional goals and audiences of the French Left. Some factions, like the Mitterrandists, Pierre Mauroy's followers and, in part, the CERES, emphasized ideas and policies long part of the Left's repertoire (for example, laicism and nationalizations). The factions were especially effective as instruments of vertical growth by competing with the PCF for the support of those occupational and cultural groups – such as civil servants, public school teachers, secular 'red' peasants and sectors of the working class that comprised the Left's core support base.[18] Other factions, namely the Rocardians but also the early CERES, incorporated into the Socialists' symbolic discourse and programmes a wide array of demands, ranging from *autogestion* and decentralization to gender issues, that had become extremely popular after May 1968.[19] Hence, they were especially effective as instruments of horizontal growth: they attracted newly mobilized groups that had no prior ties to the Left, such as peasants in western France, progressive Catholics, regionalists and mid- and upper-level cadres; promoted the rapprochement between the *Confédération Française Démocratique du Travail* (CFDT) and what was still a largely anti-clerical party with weak links to organized labour; and presided over the party's expansion into France's most conservative regions.[20]

On the other hand, compartmentalizing audiences allowed the PS to reconcile its ideological and electoral eclecticism with a militant and programmatic stance. Throughout the 1970s, factions created separate microcosms with distinct paths of recruitment, activism and political career. By publishing their own bulletins, organizing conferences and summer schools, promoting political tourism, housing their members in separate hotels at party congresses and discouraging cross-factional fraternization, factions created very high levels of factional identification and insulation among party members. This compartmentalization re-created within factions the political coherence that their coexistence may have obscured at the global party level. As a result, factionalism served as an antidote to the ideological blandness and decline of militancy that usually accompany the diversification of a party's ideological and sociological appeal.[21]

The impact of factionalism as a deepener, not just a widener, of party appeal was essential in the highly mobilized and polarized context of the 1970s, when the PS needed access to ideological and militant resources to displace the PCF as the dominant component of the Left.[22] Newly mobilized groups and collective actors, such as the CFDT, that controlled these resources were not likely to respond favourably to the individualistic appeal and weak message associated with a catch-all strategy. The groups were steeped in the anti-politics ethos of 1968 and deeply committed to forms of collective action that had grown outside of traditional political channels. They put a high premium on ideological consistency and direct political participation and distrusted parties as inherently bureaucratic and opportunistic.

Factions helped bridge the ideological and institutional gap between these groups and the PS in a variety of ways. First, factionalism offered potential recruits an extensive menu of choice and a strategy of 'qualified entry'. By joining a faction, activists could embrace those elements of party ideology and programme that they shared, while neglecting – or even outwardly opposing – those with which they disagreed. For example, as a former CFDT official put it: 'One joined the CERES, not the PS.'[23] This made party membership congruent with a variety of prior beliefs and militant practices. Second, factionalism seemed to be an antidote against the stifling of debate and participation associated with large organizations. By channelling participation into small, ideologically defined sub-units, factions multiplied the symbolic and, in part, the selective incentives that sustain activism, thus replicating within the PS the energizing dynamic that tends to develop in small and cohesive groups.[24] Third, factionalism was seen as a guarantee of internal pluralism: newcomers believed they could easily reconcile their pre-existing ideological affinities and solidarities with party membership.[25]

In addition to facilitating the absorption of the new, factions also eased the shedding of the old. The PS had inherited a rather decentralized organization, in which party notables were free to pursue a variety of alliance strategies tailored to their local needs. This power structure was bound to produce strong pockets of resistance to the innovations endorsed by the PS in 1971 and, in particular, to its nationwide alliance with the PCF. By creating direct links between the national and local level that cut across geographic locales, factionalism recast lines of solidarity and provided national leaders with a chain of command that bypassed territorial structures. Since in most federations factional loyalties were stronger than geographic-based ones, this system of internal governance was quite effective in overcoming parochialism.

Moreover, factionalism promoted a style of party politics that accelerated the renovation of party leadership, a feature critical to the PS's credibility. As ideological and political-programmatic considerations informed by factional solidarities and inter-factional rivalries took precedence over territorial loyalties, the criteria for access to leadership shifted from technical expertise, personal notoriety and seniority to more explicitly political criteria.[26] At the same time, the existence of competing factional networks encouraged the spreading of political vocations and increased the supply of new leaders, thereby making the selection process more competitive.[27] Many territorial-based party leaders and power brokers who remained outside the symbolic discourse set by the factional axes of conflict were disarmed. In their place, new types of leaders came to the fore: ideologues bred by the factional system and militants whose activist background entitled them to speak on behalf of mobilized societal actors. Hence, renewal at the rank-and-file level quickly extended to the party's intermediate level. This, in turn, enhanced the PS's presence in social struggles and lent credibility to its rhetoric.

Finally, factionalism contributed to party governance by buffering the strains caused by increased differentiation. By organizing recruits on the basis of explicit political projects, factions softened the confrontation between sociological and religious identities at a time in which the inflow of both Catholics and Marxists in the party made such conflict inevitable. Most notably, the fact that the two most politically opposed factions, the CERES and the Rocardians, recruited heavily among Left Catholics lessened the relevance of the religious-laic cleavage as a raw source of intra-party conflict. In addition, by effectively compartmentalizing their followers within distinct micro-parties, factions played a role similar to that of vertically integrated 'pillars' in consociational societies.[28] In this way, factions contributed not only to the PS's capacity to host multiple political projects and audiences, but also to contain the conflicts engendered by its diversity.

For all these reasons, throughout the 1970s factional pluralism and interfactional competition were a major factor of party extroversion and a powerful instrument of party building. They gave credibility to the Socialists' claim of representing both traditional left-wing demands, from nationalizations to a more labour-inclusive system, and new ones, such as *autogestion* and gender issues. And they largely explain the PS's ability to satisfy apparently incompatible requirements through a hybrid strategy that combined elements associated with different party types.

ORGANIZATIONAL MISMATCH: FACTIONALISM IN THE 1980S

As political circumstances changed, however, factions degenerated from instruments of flexibility into ones of conservatism and paralysis. To be sure, many of the difficulties encountered by the PS are unrelated to the party's organizational format. Access to power in an international system highly unfavourable to the Left's expansionary economic programme and a variety of policy failures and political errors contributed to the disarray of, and disillusionment with, French Socialists (see Chapter 3). Yet as the favourable circumstances of the 1970s are not sufficient to explain the PS's success, so the difficult context of the 1980s cannot fully account for the party's inability to consolidate its earlier gains. It is significant, for example, that party membership began to stagnate before the PS's access to power and that in 1990 Socialist activists were happier about the Socialist government than about their party.[29] The inability to consolidate gains, anticipated by the membership stagnation, was largely caused by a growing mismatch between the party's organizational format and its environment.[30]

Three developments related to changes in the party's external environment and in the logic of factionalism itself were especially important to this outcome. First, beginning in the late 1970s, mobilization declined sharply. This depleted the reservoir of ideas and activists that had nurtured the PS's renewal. It also devalued many of the societal linkages on which factions had been built. Second, the reduction of the Socialist–Communist alliance to a purely electoral one and the retreat of the Socialist-led government in 1983 from many of its more controversial and radical policy commitments undermined the factions' programmatic *raisons d'être*.[31] At the same time, the Socialists were confronted with a new agenda – one that dealt with economic stagnation and such issues as immigration, the environment and European integration. Third, the PS's 1981 victory consolidated the Mitterrandists' hegemony over the party and gave them extensive access to governmental resources. All these factors transformed the logic of inter-factional rivalry from a competitive, extroverted one into a collusive, introverted one.

Factionalism made it impossible for the PS to adapt to the new challenges of the 1980s. As party leaders sought to maintain their bases of support, factions reproduced within the party a freezing of alignments similar to that which parties strive to maintain in the political system at large.[32] This tendency was strengthened by the centrality of factional criteria in the distribution of governmental and party posts.[33] Throughout the 1980s, factions clung to ideological frames which the narrowing of policy options and the decline of mobilization had rendered obsolete. That seemed especially misplaced given the transformation of factions into instruments of power acquisition and maintenance. As new initiatives were blocked or delayed by factional preoccupations, the politics of the PS appeared increasingly detached from the concerns and issues facing the Left and labour. After having lent the PS ideological and programmaic credibility, factions became associated in the public mind with the most Byzantine, opaque aspects of intraparty politics. The need for factional affiliation deterred even Socialist sympathizers from joining the party.[34]

As it became clear that no faction or coalition of factions could challenge the hegemony of the Mitterrandists, moreover, party leaders came to value the preservation of the complex constellation of local and national factional deals more than the uncertainty of growth. In many federations and sections where power equilibria were vulnerable to marginal shifts in membership, party officials, irrespective of their factional affiliation, saw the entry of new members of uncertain factional allegiance as a source of destabilization and a risk not worth taking.[35] Indeed, the PS even called this negative attitude toward recruitment 'Malthusianism'. Needless to say, this did little to stop the fall in membership. Losses were especially pronounced in federations where intense factional rivalries had corroded territorial-based forms of partisan conviviality and participation and among those groups that best symbolized the horizontal growth of the 1970s and whose members were particularly disgusted by the discovery that factional politics meant power politics as usual.

At the same time, factions became less effective as instruments of party governance. As personal ambitions and loyalties displaced ideological convictions, national leaders lost the ability to enforce the inter-factional deals through which the party was governed. The breakdown at the local level of national agreements which apportioned among factions the expected loss of parliamentarians at the 1986 legislative elections, is a typical example of the factions' reduced capacity to act as vertical chains of command.[36] Since factions also bequeathed to the party a surplus of leaders armed with distinct networks of support, their diminished capacities to command loyalty led to bitter local infighting and even to the appearance of rival Socialist slates at national and local elections.

The implosion of factions was particularly destabilizing since the PS, having always relied on factional mechanisms for conflict resolution, lacked routine procedures for handling party problems. Hence, conflict tended to spread from issues to procedures, endangering the legitimacy of decision-making. In the 1988 election of Pierre Mauroy to succeed Lionel Jospin, for example, there was controversy over not only who would be the party's new first secretary, but also which body was entitled to elect him. Similar procedural issues surrounded the election of Michel Rocard in 1993. Moreover, as conflict became more personalized, it also proved more difficult to mediate – as in 1991, when the factions failed to agree on a common platform at the party congress. This unprecedented outcome – which was ironic, given that the draft versions presented by the factions were virtually identical – was a major blow to the PS's image and morale.

In summary, the recent evolution of the PS shows that factionalism is a mode of party organization whose advantages are highly contextual and that tends not to age well. Once the conditions in place when factions are formed subside, this format is likely to degenerate into a vehicle for intra-party rivalries and party inflexibility. If not severely curtailed or counterbalanced by territorialism in the longer run, factionalism is likely to turn into an instrument of party introversion and sclerosis. In the case of the PS, factionalism proved unsuited to consolidating the growth it had made possible and directly contributed to the squandering of the party's resources. It is significant, in this regard, that federations where factionalism had been kept at bay by strong departmental leadership, or where local factional leaders achieved a consensual understanding, the drop in membership, and to a lesser extent votes, that characterized the PS from the mid-1980s on was less pronounced.[37]

THE RESILIENCE OF FACTIONALISM

If the analysis presented above is correct, the PS might have responded to stagnation and decline by reverting to a territorial format or by recasting old factions. In fact, both organizational responses had vocal advocates, yet neither proved viable. For the PS, factionalism was 'sticky' – that is, the party did not depart from that format after it had clearly lost its advantage over territorialism. To be sure, factionalism is sticky partly because it provides private benefits to powerful groups in the party (would-be presidential candidates and entrenched factional leaders being the most obvious examples), but it also has normative roots. Contrary to territorialism, factionalism is a politically motivated format, based on the notion that internal party democracy should satisfy the same criteria of competition and pluralism that obtain in the broader political system. As a result, it cannot be easily defeated on efficiency grounds.

In the case of the PS, a variety of factors made factionalism especially resilient. A first set of factors has to do with party-specific legacies. Factionalism has almost always been part of the organizational repertoire of French Socialism. The SFIO, formed in 1905 out of the merger of competing socialist parties, was from the outset a coalition of factions. The factional structure, thus, was woven into the party's constitution and identity. A tradition of ideologically charged politics, the existence of a pluralist Left and weak links to mass organizations ensured the reproduction of factionalism, and it has always resurfaced at times of major ideological and political mobilization. Moreover, decades of intra-Left competition, during which Socialists consistently used intra-party pluralism as an indicator of their commitment to democratic tolerance and as an ideological weapon against the PCF, lent factionalism additional legitimacy.[38] In 1971, like in 1905, the recognition of factions was the price of reuniting all socialists in the same party. Factions sought legitimacy by claiming a close affiliation with the founders of the SFIO.[39]

Once factionalism becomes part of a party's political culture, it is very difficult to dislodge. This was even truer with the PS, whose renaissance has been marked by the reintroduction of factions. During the party's most intense years of rebuilding, territorialism became identified with electoral and organizational stagnation. The few federations that managed to thrive without converting to a factional format were too isolated or too much identified with the old SFIO to serve as the bearers of an alternative model of party organization. Moreover, territorialism itself had been transformed and co-opted by two decades of factional dominance. As factions lost their ideological ethos, territorial leaders acquired a vested interest in preserving a system they had learned to manipulate. Factional affiliation became a bargaining chip that local leaders, encouraged by factions' willingness to outbid each other for support, used to improve their own proximity to the national leadership and the resources it commanded.[40] In extreme cases, factions actually became the creatures of local leaders who went so far as to create phoney branches of rival factions in order to preserve their own power.[41] The combination of a rigid factional format and a static territorial one resulted in a system with a low potential for reform.

A second set of factors that made factionalism sticky has to do with institutional arrangements, both at the systemic and at the party level. With ideologically based factions in particular, the smaller the distance between party and government, the stronger the pressures against factionalism are likely to be.[42] This is because factionalism requires a broad ideological space, whereas party-based government encourages intra-party uniformity and consensus. Because the role of majority parties in French policy making is relatively marginal, the capacity of political power to reduce factions in parties such as the PS has been rather limited.[43] To the extent it has been present, it is largely countered by the centrality of factions as informal channels of presidential influence and launching pads for would-be presidential candidates.[44] Moreover, these system-wide influences were strengthened by the party's institutional makeup, in which powerful departmental structures, the federations, provide factions with stable bases on which to build.[45]

Yet the embeddedness of factionalism does not explain why individual factions did not recast themselves, or why new ones did not emerge to represent new issues and actors. To be sure, the 1980s witnessed several attempts to transcend old factional cleavages – the formation of so-called '*transcourants*' and other mini-factions, the flourishing of less formal political clubs loosely linked to the PS, and the efforts of some factions to ingratiate themselves with social movements such as the *Beurs*, the students and the ecologists. Unlike in the 1970s, however, these attempts ended up undermining and splitting the movements they targeted, as in the case of *SOS-Racisme*, or causing Socialist activists to defect to outside groups, as in the case of the ecologists (see Chapters 12 and 14).[46] This was largely because the movements that emerged in the 1980s lacked the mobilizational strength to break the hegemonic hold of pre-existing factions. Under these conditions, factional infighting tended to spill over from the party to collective actors. Hence, whatever realignment that did take place occurred through the implosion of old factions rather than through the creation of new ones. In summary, factionalism was too embedded in the ideological and power structures of the PS to be easily displaced from inside the party, and external pressures were too weak to cause a major realignment among factions.

CONCLUSION

Though underlying sociological and institutional factors had a lot to do with both the PS's renaissance in the early 1970s and its current crisis, such factors take us only so far. Conventional treatments underestimate the uncertainties and risks that confronted the PS at the time of its foundation, and they take its subsequent decline too much for granted. The analysis presented here is premised on the notion that organizational resources play a central role in mediating the impact of environmental conditions on party performance: it was the initial match, and then the mismatch, between the PS's factional format and its environment that best explains both ends of the Socialists' trajectory.

This approach lends itself to a rather open-ended view of the PS's future and, in light of the party's currently dismal situation, to a relatively optimistic assessment of its prospects. A great deal of the pessimism currently surrounding the future of Left parties derives from the widespread belief in the structural decline of traditional parties and from the well-recognized difficulties of replacing old parties with new ones. As mentioned, the past development of the French Socialist Party does not easily fit dominant evolutionary schemes. Cycles of renewal and decline in the history of French Socialism, together with the role of organizational resources in causing these patterns, put the party's current difficulties in perspective. Factionalism in particular provides an effective – and underexplored – instrument for renewal from within. In this sense, the advantage of the factional format is that it offers parties an opportunity to update their programme and expand their audience without the wholesale sacrifice of their existing patrimony. It is interesting, then, to examine to what extent the preconditions for such renewal are present in the French case.

Recent developments are mixed, at best. Some of the factors that contributed to the stickiness of factions in the past – their control over political spoils and their contribution to party governance – no longer exist. Moreover, the hiatus between the issues that served as the ideological basis of factional politics and current issues has grown so wide that no faction has survived unscathed, and even some of the surviving factional leaders have supported a change in the party's organizational format. Old factions have imploded but they have not yet opened up, nor have they been re-absorbed within territorial structures. In this context, attempts to overhaul the party's factional format inevitably read, and are inevitably opposed, as the triumph of one old faction over its rivals. This is exemplified by the failure of efforts at party reorganization in the aftermath of the legislative defeat of May 1993, which began with Rocard's promise of a 'big bang' and ended with the uninspiring and fully faction-controlled slate the PS presented at the 1994 European elections. Moreover, the institutional incentives for reproduction of factions are still present and are likely to disappear only if the PS falls so low as to become a handicap for presidential candidates.

What about social mobilization? As we have seen, this has been a key condition in the revitalization of the PS, yet it is also the most unpredictable element in the equation. Here as well, the current situation is ambiguous. On one hand, the demobilization of traditional collective actors has left the PS with a dearth of likely sources of recruitment and even shrunk the bases of its vertical reproduction. On the other hand, the difficulties encountered by French green parties in consolidating their presence, despite the apparent existence of a large audience for new politics in France, suggests that there may still be a reservoir for the PS to tap. Thus far numerous Socialist leaders have payed only lip service to Green concerns, and it would be wise to remain sceptical about the convergence between Socialism and new politics. Nevertheless, in light of the Socialists' past comebacks and the advantages of their factional heritage, such a possibility cannot be ruled out.

Notes

1. For a definition of class-mass parties, see Otto Kirchheimer, 'The Transformation of the Western European Party Systems,' in Joseph La Palombara and Myron Weiner, eds., *Political Parties and Political Development* (Princeton, NJ: Princeton University Press, 1966).
2. See Alain Bergounioux and Gérard Grunberg, *Le long remords du pouvoir* (Paris: Fayard, 1992); Hugues Portelli, *Le Socialisme français tel qu'il est* (Paris: PUF, 1980); and Serenella Sferza, *The Building and Rebuilding of the French Socialist Party*, book manuscript.
3. See S. Lewis and Sferza, 'French Socialists between State and Society: From Party Building to Power', in George Ross, Stanley Hoffmann and Sylvia Malzacher, eds., *The Mitterrand Experiment* (New York: Oxford University Press, 1987); and Jacques Capdevielle *et al, France de gauche, vote à droite* (Paris: Presses de la Fondation Nationale des Sciences Politiques, 1985).
4. While this analysis acknowledges the importance of strategic choices on the part of party leaders, it focuses on the nature, sources and limitations of the organizational resources that conditioned the success or failure of these strategies. In this sense it differs from most other internalist approaches to the PS, which have emphasized the strategic role of François Mitterrand.
5. The PS, like some firms, enjoyed an extremely high rate of return, given its occupation of a protected market space.
6. David S. Bell and Byron Criddle, *The French Socialist Party: Resurgence and Victory* (Oxford: Clarendon University Press, 1984).
7. See Kirchheimer. For a recent criticism of catch-allism in comparative terms and with respect to the French PS, see Wolfgang Merkel, 'Between Class and Catch-all: Is There an Electoral Dilemma for Social Democratic Parties in Western Europe', and Gérard Grunberg, 'Le Parti Socialiste Francais. Parti de Classe, Parti Populaire, Catch-all Party?' in *Socialist Parties of Europe II: of Class, Populars, Catch-all?* (Barcelona: Institut de Ciencias Politicas y Sociales, 1992).
8. See Suzanne Berger, 'Politics and Anti-Politics in Western Europe in the Seventies', *Daedalus* 108, no. 2 (1979).
9. The Congress introduced proportional representation of ideological currents on the party's governing bodies at the federation and national levels. While the PS continues to forbid the existence of factions, the distinction between currents and factions is extremely slippery.
10. While there is an abundant literature on factional dynamics within specific parties, there has been little attempt to analyse systematically the consequences of factional formats. See, however, Giovanni Sartori, *Parties and Party Systems: A Framework for Analysis* (Cambridge: Cambridge University Press, 1976); Angelo Panebianco,

Political Parties: Organization and Power (Cambridge: Cambridge University Press, 1988); David Hanley, *Keeping Left? Ceres and the French Socialist Party* (Manchester: Manchester University Press, 1986); Bergounioux and Grunberg; and David Hine, 'Factionalism in West European Parties: A Framework for Analysis', *West European Politics*, no. 1 (1982).

11. This dichotomy does not cover the full range of party configurations. Since almost all parties contain a certain amount of factionalism, and, as long as parties contest elections, factions never fully replace territorial units, it downplays similarities across types and ignores critical differences within formats, such as those between ideology- and patronage-centred factionalism and between centralized and decentralized territorial formats.

12. For a more extended discussion of these types of growth, see Sferza, *The Building and Rebuilding*. Horizontal growth, in the sense meant here, is not synonymous with catch-allism. During periods marked by the emergence of new collective actors and demands associated with heightened levels of social mobilization in particular, potential supporters may have strong ideological preferences and collective identities that make them impervious to a catch-all appeal. In this case, horizontal growth hinges upon a party's capacity to develop strong programmatic affinities with these groups as well as innovative ways of integrating them into pre-existing partisan structures, thereby leading to what I call 'thick' horizontal growth. This was precisely the case with the PS. On the evolution of the Socialist electorate in France, see Bell and Criddle. For a discussion of cultural liberalism as a component of the Socialist vote, see Capdevielle *et al*; Elisabeth Dupoirier and Gérard Grunberg, *La drôle de défaite de la gauche* (Paris: PUF, 1986); and Daniel Boy and Nonna Mayer, *L'electeur Français en questions* (Paris: Presses de la Fondation Nationale des Sciences Politiques, 1990).

13. Attempts to analyse various factions by locating them on a Right–Left continuum or by looking at the social characteristics of their supporters have led to rather unsatisfactory results. In the 1970s, what was at stake was precisely the definition of the Left and hence of the various criteria traditionally used to identify it. On the Socialist factions, see Bergounioux and Grunberg, Hanley, and Henri Rey and Françoise Subileau, *Les militants socialistes a l'épreuve du pouvoir* (Paris: Presses de la Fondation Nationale des Sciences Politiques, 1991).

14. *Autogestion* primarily referred to the demand for participation in a wide range of contexts, from municipalities to factories.

15. *Autogestion*, the most popular and decisive ideological innovation adopted by the PS, was almost singlehandedly imported into the party by the CERES. It would later become the axis of major Left debates.

16. On the relationship between internal coalitions and growth, see Panebianco.

17. On the concept of 'political offer', see Daniel Gaxie, ed., *Explication du vote* (Paris: Presses de la Fondation Nationale des Sciences Politiques, 1985).

18. The point is not that these groups are inherently socialist, but that they had been captured within the Left's sphere of influence during a phase of previous horizontal growth.

19. On the factions' differential appeal, see Françoise Subileau, 'Les systèmes de valeurs des militants socialistes français', paper presented at the European Consortium for Political Research, Amsterdam, 1987.

20. The CERES and the Rocardians, for example, played a central role in organizing the 1974 *Assises du socialisme*, which marked the PS's opening to Catholics and the deepening of its links to the CFDT. On the regional presence of factions, see Hanley.

21. See Alessandro Pizzorno, 'Introduzione allo studio della partecipazione politica', *Quaderni di Sociologia*, nos. 3–4 (1966).

22. The underlying assumption here is that the composition and the size of a party's membership are an important component of party performance: they anticipate electoral growth and, more importantly, are crucial to the renewal of the party in programmatic, ideological and personnel terms. See Herbert Kitschelt, 'The Internal Politics of Parties: The Law of Curvilinear Disparity Revisited', *Political Studies* 37 (1989).

23. Etienne Chauvet, quoted in Steven C. Lewis, *The New Politics in the Old Politics: Institutions and Social Forces in the Remaking of the French Left*, book manuscript.

24. See Mancur Olson, *The Logic of Collective Action* (Cambridge, MA: Harvard University Press, 1965).

25. This was the case with the CFDT union confederation, for example, whose most politicized unions affiliated informally to the PS in this period by identifying closely with particular factions. See Lewis.

26. By casting competition among leaders in ideological terms, factionalism also ensured that such conflicts for the most part took on a political aspect, thereby reducing the negative effects of purely personal rivalries.

27. During the years of party rebuilding, semi-official leadership positions within the factional networks were valued as much as, if not more than, official territorial office.

28. On consociationalism see Arend Lijphart, *Democracy in Plural Societies: A Comparative Explanation* (New Haven, CT: Yale University Press, 1977). On the consociational aspects of factions, see Hanley.

29. *Libération*, 14 March 1990.

30. Party membership increased from about 70 000 in 1970 to 180 000 in 1978, peaked briefly to 213 000 in 1982 and subsequently declined to about 170 000 by the end of the 1980s. See Annie Philippe and Daniel Hubscher, *Enquête a l'intérieur du Parti Socialiste* (Paris: A. Michel, 1991).

31. On the irrelevance of factional alignments in light of the economic dilemmas of the early 1980s, see Chapter 3.

32. See Seymour M. Lipset and Stein Rokkan, *Party Systems and Voter Alignments* (New York: Free Press, 1967), and Sartori.

33. The founding leaders of the main factions enjoyed a monopoly on power positions in the party and the government. Thus, by the mid-1980s, they were commonly known as the 'elephants'.

34. By the late 1980s, relations among factions had so deteriorated that in many urban centres with multiple sections factional criteria had displaced geographical ones in determining the members' affiliation to a section. See Philippe and Hubscher. On conviviality as a reason for membership, see Subileau, 'The Strategy of Reconstruction of the French Socialist Party', paper presented at the European Consortium on Political Research workshop 'Party Strategies and Party-Voter Linkages', Rimini, 1988.

35. See the case of Ille-et-Vilaine discussed in Sferza, *The Building and Rebuilding;* and D. Deleris, *La section socialiste d'Epinay-sur-Seine de 1947 à 1981*, unpublished Master's essay in Contemporary History (University of Paris XII, 1983).

36. See F. Sawicki, *Application de la sociologie des organizations a l'étude du PS*, unpublished Master's thesis in Sociology (University of Paris V, 1986).

37. This was notably the case in the Pas-de-Calais and Loire Atlantique.

38. At the Congress of Tours, Léon Blum's indictment of the PCF rested primarily on the latter's adoption of non-democratic principles of organization. It was in these organizational principles, rather than in doctrinary divisions, that Blum saw the divide between Socialists and Communists. From then on, French Socialists have taken pride in the democratic functioning of their party, often using it as a paragon to expose the Communists' disregard for democracy.

39. See factional journals such as *Répères* and *Synthèse Flash*; and Yves Roucaute, *Le parti socialiste* (Paris: Huisman, 1983).

40. This was the case, for example, during the intense bargaining between national currents and local groups in Marseilles in the aftermath of Gaston Defferre's death.

41. This was the case in Ille-et-Vilaine, where a fake neo-Rocardian faction was sponsored by the Mitterrandists and CERES in order to prevent the Rocardians from controlling the federation.

42. This does not apply to patronage-based factions. While the motivations for factionalism may shift from ideology to patronage, the state structure in France is not conducive to this transformation. See Martin Shefter, 'Party and Patronage', *Politics and Society*, no. 4 (1977).

43. The obvious comparison is with Britain, where the constraints of 'party government' are such that even when a party is in the opposition it has to adopt an internal format that closely mimics the one it would assume when in government. This, together with close ties to trade unions, has been a major obstacle to the viability of factionalism in the Labour Party. See David Kogan and Maurice Kogan, *The Battle for the Labour Party* (London: Kogan Page, 1982).

44. Throughout the 1980s, for example, weekly meetings with the Mitterrandist faction allowed Mitterrand to control the PS while professing the aloofness from party matters required by his institutional position.

45. See Panebianco.

46. See Rémy Leveau, 'Les partis et l'integration des "beurs"', Yves Mény, ed., *Ideologies, partis politiques et groupes sociaux: Essais pour Georges Lavau* (Paris: Presses de la Fondation Nationale des Sciences Politiques, 1989).

11 French Communism: Party Construction and Party Decline

Martin A. Schain

A considerable literature has explored the rise of the French Communist Party (PCF), and a growing literature is examining its decline. In this chapter, I argue that the two are linked, that the party was constructed in different ways in different places, and that its decline is related to the bases on which it was originally built. Within this general exploration, I examine the role of immigrants and immigration in the rise and decline of the party.

The electoral fate of the PCF has changed with more general patterns of electoral realignments during each of two periods, the first after the Second World War and the second after 1978. There have been two bases for partisan realignment. The first, which has always been given the most attention, is *conversion*, the movement of voters from one party to another; the second, to which little attention has been paid, is the *mobilization* of new voters, either through generational turnover or through immigration and naturalization.[1] During the period of its expansion, the Communist party constructed three different types of constituencies, each of which depended on different balances of conversion and mobilization and was related to a different style of mobilization and a different basis of legitimacy. One important ingredient of this balance was the political mobilization of immigrant labour. The electoral decline of the party can be explained in terms of the deterioration of these three constituencies and the inability of the PCF to develop new bases of mobilization of support.

Although the implications of this exploration are national, the focus will be local and departmental, particularly on those areas in which the roots of French Communism were sunk most deeply – the so-called 'bastions'. Like the post-World War I breakthrough of the United States Democratic Party in V.O. Key's analysis,[2] the PCF's organizational and electoral breakthrough seems to have taken place gradually, first in rural areas with a Left tradition, then in urban areas where industry was being established or expanded. The electoral following of the party then grew, and, after some time, it dominated many of these areas until the late 1970s. The expansion of the party was due in part to conversion of voters who had previously supported other parties (particularly those of the Left), but the PCF was also able to achieve local electoral dominance by mobilizing a *new* electorate and integrating it into French political life.

The implied comparison of the PCF with the US Democratic Party is limited, of course. The Communists never saw themselves as a coalition of sometimes conflicting political forces at the national level as the Democrats did (although they can be seen that way), nor were they ever a majoritarian party that dominated French political institutions. For a period of time, however, they were the largest party in France and were dominant in specific areas of the country. Moreover at the local and departmental levels, the revolutionary vocation of the party was often muted and distant.

THE CONSTRUCTION OF THE PCF ELECTORATE: THREE MODELS

French voting studies have offered various explanations for the electoral emergence of the French Communist Party in the 1920s. The first solid areas of Communist implantation were in the rural areas of south-central France. The emergence of rural Communism has usually been explained in terms of *sinistrisme*, or the movement of successive generations of French voters in specific areas as far to the Left as possible through conversion of established voters. According to this explanation, the republican tradition that emerged with the French Revolution was expressed by support first for the Democrat–Socialists in 1849, later the Radicals, the Socialists during the pre-World War I Third Republic, and then increasingly for the Communists after 1920.[3]

The explanation of how Communism emerged in industrial areas is less clear-cut. Georges Lavau has argued that the PCF solidified its working-class bond from 1935 to 1937, a period in which new party members and voters were first initiated into the mass industrial unions of the *Confédération Générale du Travail* (CGT). While at the leadership level the party was created in 1920 by a split in the Socialist ranks, by the time of the Popular Front it was creating something new at the mass level. The leadership conflict within the Socialist Party (SFIO) was not necessarily reproduced at the level of members and voters. 'In reality,' Lavau writes, 'during this decisive period, the PCF conquered in the working-class milieu a place that had been largely *vacant*' among the blue-collar workers and unemployed, who became the core constituency of the party.[4] Where the party was forced to take on the Socialists directly, they were far less successful. The establishment of urban, working-class Communism in France was therefore something new, rather than a continuation of a left-wing voting tradition as it was in rural areas.[5] Jacques Fauvet summarizes the two different electorates as:

> one of a worker and social character in the Paris industrial region and a bit of the Nord, the other peasant and political [in character] that crosses the rural departments of the Centre. One expresses a renewed revolutionary tradition, the other an old republican tradition.[6]

In fact, there were two somewhat different working-class constituencies that the PCF constructed from scratch. In the new industrial suburbs of Paris (and a few other areas), Communist strength was built among workers who had migrated from other, mostly rural parts of France. In 1931, well over half of the population of Bobigny, a Paris suburb in which the party became established before World War II, was born somewhere else. Eight per cent were immigrants from other countries – mostly Poland, Italy and Spain. Bobigny's population grew 475 per cent between 1911 and 1931, and PCF strength was built among these migrants.[7] This pattern was reproduced in other Paris suburbs, as well as in the industrial suburbs of Lyons and Marseilles.[8]

Where the PCF was established in areas of high foreign immigration, the pattern was somewhat different. Here, too, the Communist Party was building anew, but through a process of political incorporation that involved several generations of the same immigrant community. In this century, four overlapping waves of immigrants were recruited into France from neighboring countries. The early part of the century was dominated by Italian and Belgian immigration, followed by a period of Polish immigration (and significant 'internal migration' from Algeria), and then after World War II there was a wave of immigration from Portugal. Since the mid–1960s, many immigrants have been arriving from the former French colonies of North Africa.

Each wave of immigration has been directed in various ways into specific industries in specific areas of the country, and within a generation of their arrival, each wave has formed a potential constituency (and problem) for the French Communist Party. With a stagnant native population, the number of resident immigrants increased from just over 1 million at the turn of the century to 2.7 million in 1931. About 60 per cent of this population was active in the labour force in 1931 (about the same percentage as in 1901), and 63 per cent of immigrants in the labour force worked in industry and transport (also about the same as in 1901).

A great deal has been written recently of the high concentrations of immigrant labour in specific industries and at specific skill levels in the 1980s.[9] However, the pattern of the 1980s was not substantially different from the one that developed after World War I. In 1901, only 6 per cent of workers in industry and transport were immigrants, compared with 17 per cent of a larger industrial work force in 1931. By the 1930s, a political party claiming to represent workers could not avoid dealing with immigrants in some way, particularly given the higher concentrations of immigrants in industries of particular interest to the emerging PCF (see Table 11.1). In specific geographic areas, such concentrations were even greater. In the coal mines of the Nord, 62 per cent of the workers (and 75 per cent of underground workers) were immigrants in 1931, as were 70 per cent of the iron miners and 90 per cent of the workers in certain factories in Lorraine.[10]

These concentrations have been attributed largely to a pattern of state intervention that had begun before World War I. The loss of manpower during the war accentuated the need for immigrant labour, and both public and private means were set into place to recruit workers and direct them into specific areas. In 1919 and 1920, the French government concluded bilateral agreements with a number

Table 11.1 Percentage of Foreigners in Specific Industries

OCCUPATION	1906 %	1931 %	% CHANGE
Mining	6.2	40.1	548
Steel Mills	17.8	34.8	96
Quarrying	8.7	26.1	200
Construction	10.2	24.1	132
Rubber/Paper	3.6	10.7	197
Chemicals	10	14.7	47
Metalwork	4.5	10.5	133

Source: *Résultats statistiques de recensement général de la population*, I, no. 5 (1936) p. 51, as reprinted in Gary S. Cross, *Immigrant Workers in Industrial France* (Philadelphia: Temple University Press, 1983) p. 160.

of countries (most notably, Poland, Italy and Czechoslovakia) for labour recruitment, and in the years that followed, commercial agencies organized by employers were authorized to recruit immigrants directly for particular work sites. Polish workers from the same regions of Poland, for example, were sent to the same areas of France. This way of organizing immigration assured that there would be high concentrations of immigrants with similar backgrounds installed in places where labour was in short supply, and in occupations that native French workers were less willing to fill. Of course, the dynamics of the process also modified the occupational and geographic structure of the French working class.[11]

Indeed, each wave of immigration has altered the structure of the working class, and each has reacted politically in a somewhat different way.[12] Emmanuel Todd has argued that the different cultural inclinations of immigrant groups had different effects on the PCF:

[I]mmigration, by pure ethnological accident, reinforced the Communist Party during the years 1930–50, and weakened it, within the working-class world, during the sixties and seventies. . . . Each of these groups influenced . . . the global ideological evolution of the French working class – no immigration is purely passive.[13]

The existence of three different kinds of electorates – rural, urban and immigrant – implies three styles of party mobilization and organization, and three somewhat different bases of loyalty. New evidence indicates that in agricultural areas (particularly in Limousin and the Dordogne), the PCF mobilized a diverse rural electorate, 'a balanced mix of small-holding peasants, tenant farmers, agricultural workers, temporary workers, artisans and shopkeepers' before World War II. These voters' fortunes were closely tied to the fluctuations of the agricultural economy. In spite of pressures from the centre to build proletarian coalitions,

Communist organizers focused their propaganda on the peasant economy.[14] The majority of the new PCF voters in the 1924 elections, the first after the split, were converts from the Socialist party, but a substantial proportion were mobilized from among former abstainers and new voters. In subsequent elections, however, there were few conversions in rural areas, and the PCF vote remained stable.[15]

In new industrial areas, party mobilization was related to the fluctuations of trade union mobilization and was largely based on class solidarity. Where the immigrant population was highly concentrated, party mobilization had many of the same characteristics it did in other industrial areas, with the added ingredients of ethnic bonds. If in native French industrial areas the PCF served to integrate large numbers of workers into French political life, in immigrant areas the party established institutions based on ethnic working-class identity. Like the Irish 'takeover' of US urban centres from the white, Anglo-Saxon establishment through the Democratic Party, the Communist victories in these communities (for the most part after World War II) represented a kind of ethnic vengeance of a newly enfranchised electorate that endured in part because the party and the community had been interpenetrated.[16] Both the PCF and the Unified General Confederation of Labour (CGTU, the Communist-dominated confederation that resulted from the split in the trade union movement in 1922) tried to mobilize and *encadrer* immigrant workers. After a series of confusing policies, the CGTU in 1926 developed a position highly supportive of immigrant interests. In his report to the 1925 Congress of the CGTU, the national secretary declared, 'If you do not support the foreign workers, they will be formed in the hands of the capitalists as a mass of labour that can be used to beat you in all the demands which you make.'[17] By 1926, 16 per cent of the confederation's budget was devoted to propaganda directed toward immigrants, mostly publication of foreign-language newspapers. Both the CGTU and the party organized separate divisions by language, and at the departmental and national levels, the party organized immigrant manpower commissions. Finally, the party supported ethnic organizations and demonstrations among immigrant groups.[18]

In principle, the PCF's mobilization of ethnic differences was not inconsistent with Patrick Ireland's characterization of the party as an 'assimilationist machine' (see Chapter 14). The process recognized, rewarded and reinforced collective identities in the public realm in ways similar to those used by the US Democratic Party during the same period. How successful were these efforts? In one sense, the numbers are not impressive. By 1930, the confederation had recruited about 17 000 members born outside of France, 5 per cent of its total claimed membership. This represented less than 2 per cent of immigrants working in industry. But during this period, the total CGTU membership in industry comprised no more than 4.3 per cent of industrial workers.[19] The construction of an organizational structure dependent on immigrants was more impressive. The effectiveness of this structure only became evident when the party and its electorate began to expand after 1936: 'Italians and Poles, above all, often furnished the only party organizations [in some areas], sometimes in liaison with the party through the MOE [*main-d'oeuvre étrangère*] organizations.'[20]

In the iron and steel areas of Lorraine (Meurthe-et-Moselle), a large proportion of militants and elected officials of the PCF, even in the 1960s, were second- and third-generation Italians. Trade unionism gained influence in the area when the first generation arrived before World War I, and the PCF gained strength when the immigrants became naturalized citizens. The second generation of anti-fascist militants provided additional recruits for the party – and after 1946, when they too were naturalized, additional votes. In 1936, less than 7 per cent of the population of two Italian immigrant mining areas in northeastern France were registered to vote; this increased to 24 per cent in 1946 (when women were granted the right to vote), and 38 per cent in 1954, an increase that can be attributed to naturalization. During this same period, the vote for the PCF rose from less than 1 per cent to 42 per cent.[21] '[I]n those communes where the proportion of Italians is highest,' Gérard Noiriel writes, 'where naturalized citizens are most numerous . . . the PCF has gained most rapidly.'[22]

Similarly, the influx of Polish workers into towns in the Nord and Pas-de-Calais became the basis for the establishment and expansion of the PCF during the post-war period. Until 1936, the tight organization of company towns, combined with the activities of the anti-union and anti-Communist Polish Workers' Association, made union activity difficult to organize. However, the region's sit-in strikes of 1936 marked a sharp turn. By the end of the strike wave, it was estimated that 80 per cent of the Polish miners were members of the CGT (now reintegrated with the CGTU). In the long run, the PCF benefited from this massive influx of workers who could not yet vote, but many of whose children would become party militants after the war.[23]

In addition to the success of the PCF in establishing regional bastions among Poles and Italians, there are numerous instances of the establishment throughout the country of more isolated, but nevertheless important, bases. Near Toulon on the Mediterranean Sea, a concentration of Italian immigrants in La Seyne-sur-Mer formed the basis for PCF control of the municipality in 1947. In the Nord, Flemish immigrants did the same in Halluin, a town so controlled by Communists that it was called 'Halluin the Red'. The PCF also developed a formidable bastion among Spanish immigrants in the 16th *arrondissement* of Marseilles. The Communists were not the only party to benefit from the wave of immigration before World War II – second-generation Italian immigrants became the core of the dominant Socialist electorate in Marseilles in the 1930s – but because they were a rising party, they were in a particularly good position to exploit the opportunities offered by immigration.[24]

Thus, the emergence of the PCF can be seen in terms of stages. The earliest breakthrough was in the predominantly rural departments in west-central France (Lot-et-Garonne, Dordogne, Corrèze, Allier, Cher and Haute Vienne). The second, overlapping breakthrough was in the industrial areas in the Paris and Marseilles regions and, to a lesser extent, in the coal basin of the Nord and the Pas de Calais. Finally, after World War II the party gained support in the industrial area around Lyons and, less so, in the Catholic areas of eastern France. The first breakthrough has been attributed to the conversion of Socialist and some Radical voters (as well as the mobilization of new voters). The breakthrough among industrial workers has been linked to the massive population changes in the new industrial areas in the suburbs of large cities. As we have seen, however, at least part of the expansion of the Communist electorate during the post-war period is related to the influx of Polish, Italian and some Spanish immigrants in northern and eastern France.

This is paralleled by the development of the PCF organization. It has been estimated that PCF membership in 1944 was about 60 000 cards placed, but by 1946 it had increased to more than 800 000.[25] The distribution of this membership growth, however, was uneven. The density of membership increased most in the old rural bastions, where, by the end of 1946, it was as great as in the industrial areas (and greater than in semi-industrial regions). Even within industrial areas, such as the Paris region, the party gained members far more rapidly than it did in the industrial suburbs.

In the Nord and Lorraine (particularly Meurthe-et-Moselle), membership grew only modestly at the departmental level but from all accounts grew rapidly in mining areas with high Polish and Italian immigration. Pierre Belleville explains the difference between Communist implantation in Meurthe-et-Moselle and Moselle after the war by the preponderance of Italian PCF militants in the *cités minières*.

> The PCF benefited when, after 1945, a second period of naturalization began. It gained in one single blow active militants, members and an audience. . . . The consequences are still being felt. As a general rule, the dynamism of the militants of Italian origin is considerable. After having largely contributed to the orientation of the CGT, to the elimination of the SFIO in the working class community, they continue to make their mark on the CGT and the PCF.[26]

There is no way to isolate the proportion of PCF membership made up of cells dominated by members of immigrant origin, but available analyses indicate that in the Nord and Meurthe-et-Moselle, areas in which overall membership expanded only modestly after the war, these cells were dynamic and rapidly expanding. They also indicate that these were not areas of Communist conversion, but new territory. Membership expansion there did not represent increased recruitment into *established* cells, but rather new areas of strength. Thus, immigrant communities contributed to the establishment and expansion of the PCF in industrial areas where its strength was either relatively stagnant or even diminishing after the war.

DEMOBILIZATION AND DECLINE OF THE PCF: VOTING AND ORGANIZATION

In the late 1980s, electoral support for the PCF reached a level comparable to what it was between 1924 and 1932.[27] After recovering from the setback of the 1958 legislative election, the PCF attracted a steady 20 per cent to 22 per cent of the vote in all of the subsequent national elections during the Fifth Republic, until 1981. Then, in the presidential elections of April 1981, Georges Marchais lost 25 per cent of the 'normal' Communist vote (with 15.3 per cent of the vote), and the legislative elections in June confirmed the falloff.

From 1981–6, during the period of Socialist government, the Communist vote was reduced by another 40 per cent, to 9.7 per cent. The shakiness of this remaining vote was revealed by the elections of 1988. The pull of the PCF was brought into question in the presidential election, when the Communist candidate won just 6.8 per cent of the vote. A month later the locally popular mayors were largely responsible for almost doubling that score in the legislative elections, to 11.3 per cent. A year later, in the European elections of June 1989, the party list won only 7.7 per cent of the vote. In regional elections in 1992 and legislative elections in 1993, Communist support increased somewhat, to just over 9 per cent of the vote.

Thus, from 1978 to 1993, the PCF vote declined by 60 per cent, from 5.9 million to 2.4 million votes. Moreover, by 1993 the party no longer had a 'normal' vote and no longer seemed capable of stabilizing its electoral following: its legislative candidates could attract as many as 2.8 million votes, but the national party seemed incapable of attracting more than half that vote in presidential or European elections.

Since 1973, the PCF has been gradually losing electoral support in its strongest areas.[28] Until 1981, these losses were masked largely by gains in areas where the party was helped by its alliance with the Socialists, and by the level of national support, which remained more or less constant. The steady state of its national electoral following also masked a complex pattern of increases and declines in various localities. For example, in the 1973 National Assembly elections, when the PCF generally regained its 1967 level of electoral support, the party reported that 58 per cent of the towns governed by Communists (with populations of more than 10 000) lost votes from 1967. Among the 42 per cent that gained votes, the gains were greatest in the *newer*, less established municipalities.

Similarly, in 1978 the PCF vote remained stable nationally. There were gains from 1973 in 44 departments, but in its traditional Paris bastions in the Seine-St. Denis and the Val-de-Marne, the party generally declined. Once again, losses in established areas were compensated by gains in newer areas of strength.[29] This changing balance of geographic support is summarized by François Platone, who demonstrates that since 1967, the maintenance and growth of electoral support for the PCF has been entirely in provincial France, and the gap between Paris and the provinces has been growing.[30]

Table 11.2 Relative Strength of the PS and PCF in the Constituencies

	1967	1973	1978	1981
No. of constituencies with PS ahead	212	276	321	429
No. of constituencies with PCF ahead	258	197	153	45

Source: Gérard LeGall, 'Le Nouvel ordre électoral', in *Revue Politique et Parlementaire* (July/August 1981) p. 17.

What was most characteristic of the newer areas of strength was the dependency of the PCF on the support of broader class coalitions, as well as political coalitions with the Socialists. We can see this in two ways: by the kinds of localities in which the party was building its electoral strength, and by the kind of coalition-building typical in these areas in the 1970s. The success of PCF electoral efforts in the 1970s was greatest in areas outside of the Paris region with low working-class populations: at the local level, three-quarters of the towns governed by Communist mayors were in the Paris region in 1968, compared with less than 60 per cent ten years later.

Thus, the stability of Communist electoral support during the 1970s masked a transformation of historic importance. The party had become increasing provincial, and the bases of its support had become increasingly diverse. It had also become increasing dependent on its relationship with the Socialists, a situation from which the Socialists were gaining. Looking at the relative weight of the Communist and Socialist votes in constituencies between 1967 and 1981 shows a shift from PCF dominance to Socialist dominance (see Table 11.2). During the entire period covered by Table 11.2, the PCF vote remained nationally stable, but its structure was changing in important ways.

The problem in the bastions became more evident in 1981, when, for the first time since 1958, the Communists suffered a sharp reduction in overall electoral support. PCF candidates lost 25 per cent of their 1978 vote nationally, but 31 per cent of their electoral support in these zones of strength; for the first time since World War II, the PCF did not receive a majority of the vote in its towns in the Paris region.

Since 1981, the three core electoral constituencies of the party have declined at different rates. The greatest decline has occurred in the industrial bastions of Paris, Lyons and Marseilles, which had been constructed around the working class of mostly native French labour. There has been a slower decline in its electoral bases in Lorraine, Nord and Pas de Calais, which had been built in the constituencies dominated by naturalized immigrant labour, while the decline has been slowest in the rural bastions of centre-western France.

In Lorraine towns of Italian settlement that had been dominated by the Communists, the 1981 losses were significant (including 11 per cent in Longwy), but not as overwhelming as in the Paris region. In Polish areas of the Pas de Calais, the losses were larger (22 per cent in Bethune). By 1988, however, when the Paris bastions at least temporarily stabilized and in many cases increased their electoral strength, those in Lorraine and Pas de Calais continued to drop in support.[31]

Nevertheless, like the industrial suburbs of Paris, Lyons and Marseilles, the old immigrant bastions generally have continued to attract electoral support at twice the national average of 9 per cent to 10 per cent, and in this sense they are more important for the party now than they were in the 1970s, when the electorate was expanding into new areas. Then the core was better able to absorb even greater losses than the periphery, but now only the core remains to play out the endgame.

The durability of the core is also conditioned by the changing structure of the PCF organization. Historically, there has been a considerable correspondence between concentrations of electoral strength of the PCF and areas where the party had its greatest concentrations of organizational strength. The organizational capacity of the PCF has depended upon its ability to recruit members and to support its organization with the political and economic resources of a network of local and national officeholders.

PCF membership, which had reached its peak in 1946 with about 800 000 members, dropped precipitously (more than 60 per cent) through the 1950s, to a low of an estimated 300 000 in 1960–61. The Fifth Republic, provided a more favourable environment for the expansion of membership, which began to rise again after 1961, and especially after 1968, when the party began to build its strength on the Union of the Left. Membership peaked again at about 520 000 in 1978–9, and then began to drop sharply, to about 330 000 in 1987.[32] Thus, during the post-war period, there were two important cycles of membership rise and decline, and there is every indication that the present decline is not yet at an end.

These two cycles have been quite different in their structural implications. During the post-war period of growth, concentrations of party membership expanded beyond the Paris region, the historic rural areas of the centre, the eastern area of the Mediterranean coast, the Rhone valley and the immigrant areas of the Nord/Pas-de-Calais. The Cold War contraction left most of these concentrations intact, but with reduced membership levels. The most significant membership losses were outside of the PCF areas of strength. Although membership increased by 60 per cent between 1962 and 1978, its distribution was concentrated in smaller areas within the post-war areas of strength. No new important concentrations were established, despite the expansion of electoral strength, and the concentrations in the Paris region and the Rhone valley (mostly in the Lyons region) were reduced, according to Philippe Buton.[33] During the early period of downturn, after 1946, the party was able to maintain its electoral following in its core membership areas, and membership losses did not prevent the PCF from surpassing its 1946 voter level in 1956 (5.5 million votes). Even when the PCF lost 1.5 million votes in 1958, it maintained its electoral strength in roughly those areas where it was organizationally strong.

When the party increased its vote after 1962 in areas where it was organizationally weak, though, and the structure of its electorate changed, it was unable to translate electoral success into organizational expansion. In the 1970s, the party was actually losing votes where its membership implantation was strongest and was gaining votes where its implantation was weak. Its electoral gain can be understood as a result of Union of the Left co-operation, rather than the *encadrement* capability of its organization.[34] The increasing inability of the PCF to maintain stable electoral support in its areas of organizational strength and build organizational strength in its areas of electoral expansion was most obvious in the case of the city of Paris, where the PCF has disappeared electorally, but is also evident in the Lyons and Bordeaux regions, as well as the bastions in the Paris suburbs, the rural centre and the north and east of the country. Now, once again, with the electoral decline of the past decade, the reduced core of organizational strength seems to correspond with the reduced core of electoral strength, but it is unclear if the organization can stabilize electoral strength, or even slow down the decline.

Moreover, if only the core remains, the party cannot survive. This is the lesson of the expansion of the 1970s. Each of the three areas of core implantation have been declining for somewhat different reasons, but in each case, the reason for the decline is an ineluctable process that is destroying the very heart of the bases for party organization and loyalty. The rural bastions are all in departments where the population on which the party has built its traditional coalition – small landholders, tenant farmers, agricultural workers, artisans and shopkeepers – is ageing and disappearing. As the French peasant population fell rapidly in the 1970s, the proportion of peasants among the Communist electorate also fell (from 9 per cent to 2 per cent). These departments look impressive on a map of France as strong regional centres for the party, but they represent less than 10 per cent of the total PCF vote.[35]

The urban industrial departments have been drawing on a narrowing base of support for some time. In 1968 one-third of the PCF-governed towns still had a majority working-class population, compared with 13 per cent ten years later. Even among the Communist bastions – those towns in the Paris region governed by the PCF since 1947 – less than 10 per cent had majority working-class populations by 1978. In addition, a significant percentage of the remaining working-class population in these bastions was composed of immigrant workers, most of whom could not vote, thus diluting the working-class electoral strength even more. In the Communist bastion of the Seine-St. Denis, where a majority of the active population was working-class in the early 1960s, only a little more than one-third were workers by the 1980s, and more than 17 per cent were immigrants (see Table 11.3).[36] Finally, many of the factories in which communist working

Table 11.3 Workers and Immigrants in the Paris Region

	Paris	Inner core	Outer core	France	Seine-St. Denis
1968: % of workers in active population	26.1	39.9	36.6	37.7	46.3
1982: % of workers in active population	19.7	29.9	28.4	28.3	36.1
1968: % of immigrants in total population	10	8.9	7.4	5.3	10.4
1982: % of immigrants in total population	16.8	14.7	10.1	6.8	17.4

Source: Henri Rey and Jacques Roy, 'Quelques réflexions sur l'évolution électorale d'un département de la banlieue parisienne: la Seine-St. Denis', in *Hérodote*, no. 43 (1986) pp. 13–4.

class culture has been nurtured over the years have closed, or are in the process of closing.

In the Communist areas long dominated by workers of immigrant origin, the changes have been more complicated. The steel industry in Lorraine has been in crisis for 30 years. Since the 1960s, jobs have been diminishing rapidly, and the old communities have been in decline. The grandchildren of Polish and Italian immigrants have been leaving the region, and are being replaced (in smaller numbers) by immigrant workers from North Africa. Even among those who remain, the ties to the PCF have become progressively weaker, tied to a period of history that is no longer meaningful. In addition, Gérard Noiriel argues that, although the Italian and Polish workers were mobilized and organized on the basis of their origin and immigrant status, party and local PCF officials have progressively de-emphasized the immigrant basis of these communities. 'But, by acting in this way,' he writes, 'the party tends to eliminate the reasons on which the confidence of the group in itself are based.'[37] During the 1970s, the party was able to maintain its base of electoral support in the same way that it did in other parts of France, through its political alliance with the Socialist Party and by broadening its social base. In the process, it diluted its local ethnic working-class base among elected officials and among voters. It was unable to regain much of this support during the period of decline in the 1980s.

MAINTAINING AND CONSTRUCTING: STRATEGIC CONSIDERATIONS

Could the electoral decline of the French Communist Party have been abated despite the changes in the traditional bases of party support? Could new bases have been constructed that would compensate for the inevitable change? Perhaps, but this would have necessitated important changes in the strategic thinking of party leaders about electoral expansion and coalition-building, thinking constrained by the party's decision-making process.[38]

As noted above, the elections of the 1970s presented the PCF leadership with both good news and bad news. The good news was that Left unity was succeeding: the national electoral following of the party was being maintained, and the number of Communist-governed municipalities was expanding. The bad news was that this success depended on an alliance with the Socialists that, after 1973, increasingly worked to the benefit of the Socialists. The good news, and the alliance strategy built around the union, brought large numbers of new recruits into the party, and, as George Ross notes, 'Entire federations – Paris in particular – took on a Eurocommunist colouring', upsetting a delicate balance of forces within the leadership.[39] The bad news, however, lent credibility the claims of the militant autonomists within the party leadership that the PCF was simply being used to advance the ambitions of the dynamic Socialists. By autumn 1977, the balance of power had shifted within the leadership, and the party broke with the Common Programme alliance with the Socialists, a costly decision that, in retrospect, marked a turning point in the fortunes of the PCF.

In the years that followed, the leadership attempted to reassert symbols and themes (*ouvrièriste* pro-Soviet and anti-Socialist rhetoric) that had been bypassed by the very bases on which the party had expanded in the 1970s. Thus, in an attempt to reassert its old identity, the PCF leadership attacked the core of its new identity. Ross writes:

> For this to succeed, the bulk of the party had to be brought along. More than two decades of frontism had made a substantial number of Communists into believers, however. Perhaps more important, the years of *Union de la Gauche* had attracted hundreds of thousands of new Communists, particularly from the intelligentsia and urban middle strata, who believed themselves part of a massive project to rebuild French Communism and the French Left, which the new line clearly rejected. The reassertion of pro-Sovietism, which occurred in the middle of a tremendous anti-Soviet conversion experience on the part of the French Left intelligentsia, did further damage.[40]

That tens of thousands of Eurocommunist members and voters rejected the party after the breakup of the alliance and the débâcle of the 1978 legislative elections effectively left it in the hands of the more traditional militant autonomists. The electoral victory of President François Mitterrand in 1981 left the PCF with the choice that the leadership had hoped to avoid: either to support the ascendant Socialists (who had an absolute majority in the National Assembly after the June legislative elections), or remain in ineffectual opposition. The participation of four Communist ministers in the Socialist governments from 1981–4 did little to change the balance within the leadership, and the shift by the

Socialists toward industrial modernization after 1983 further strengthened the position of the militant autonomists.

One of the most striking aspects of the major strategic decisions of the PCF leadership during the 1980s has been their divergence from the opinions and commitments of the party electorate. A majority of the party voters opposed the anti-Socialist campaign during the presidential campaign in 1980 and 1981, as well as the PCF support of the Soviet war in Afghanistan; 65 per cent were sympathetic to the expelled *rénovateur* ('renewal') current, and 56 per cent supported the replacement of Georges Marchais as general secretary. Two-thirds of the party voters supported Charles Fiterman as the party's candidate for the presidential elections in 1988. (The party ran André Lajoinie, who was supported by only 16 per cent).[41]

Thus, George Ross's argument that the PCF leadership, driven by its own organizational constraints and dynamics, made a series of decisions that amounted to 'deciding to decline' has meant that the party was unable to learn the lessons of the good news of the 1970s and instead concentrated on the bad. This argument is supported by the way the party dealt with the potential opportunity of mobilization among new immigrant groups. Although the voting population of Communist-dominated areas is shrinking, the immigrant population is increasing, particularly among potential working-class voters. For the moment, few of the new immigrants can or do vote, but the numbers are growing and are concentrated in key areas – the Marseilles region, the Paris region and the Nord.[42] All of the evidence, however, indicates that this is another opportunity the PCF has not been capable of exploiting.

The ability of the PCF to integrate Italian, Polish, Spanish and Jewish workers into the French political system and to strengthen its own position from this process was related to the acceptance by the party of these immigrants as a potential clientele. From the earliest years – even before World War II – North African immigrants were seen as temporary workers, who would – and indeed, should – return to their countries of origin.[43] The party represented the interests of these workers with its legal staff and elected officials but never co-opted North African militants into the CGT and party hierarchy, and never attempted to mobilize the increasing number of voters of North African extraction (*beurs*) in the same way it mobilized other immigrant groups. Instead, in a pattern parallel to the French state, the party preferred to maintain direct relations with North African governmental authorities in developing local programmes for the increasingly large immigrant populations in the municipalities the PCF governed.

None of this seemed to matter very much in the 1970s, when the party was growing and the North African immigrant populations remained relatively small. By 1977, however, 55 per cent of the larger municipalities governed by PCF mayors had populations with more than 10 per cent immigrants, and by 1982 the dominant immigrant groups were generally North African.[44] The problem was compounded by the increased presence of non-white French migrants from the overseas departments and territories, who were treated in much the same way as immigrants.[45] Thus, by the 1980s, the Communists had not developed any concerted process for the mobilization and the *encadrement* of what amounted to the growth sector of the working class. For the Communists, part of the problem was that the interests of these new immigrants were, or were seen to be, in conflict with the established interests of the working class (both of French and immigrant extraction). This conflict among working-class generations has always existed to some degree[46], but during the earlier period the mobilization of immigrant communities was most effective where it represented a new Communist implantation. Now, this mobilization meant an effective challenge to the established structure of PCF power already in place.[47]

Nevertheless, because of the weighty presence of North African workers in key sectors of industry, the Communists have not been able to ignore them. During the 1970s, in response to what they perceived as attempts by the government and management to use Muslim workers to weaken the bargaining strength of the unions, the CGT attempted to mobilize and integrate them by supporting demands for religious practice in the workplace.[48] However, the union has been wary of such an approach, and in 1983 complained to the government (in the midst of a strike wave dominated by immigrant workers) of the dangers of Iranian influence in the workplace and in social conflicts. In fact, the CGT generally sees the organization of workers around Islam as a direct challenge to union organization, rather than as a means of union mobilization of Islamic workers.[49] Since the 1960s, the number of immigrants among the delegates at the national congresses of the CGT has increased somewhat, but in 1985 they still only represented just over 6 per cent of those present.[50]

In Communist-governed towns, there has been a flowering of associations among North African immigrants. Here, too, the PCF has been unable to co-opt the leadership of these groups, which are becoming the key to the mobilization of the growing number of North African voters, and the party has generally seen them as competitors (see Chapter 14).[51] The Socialists, on the other hand, made considerable efforts to establish links to the two most important national organizations that spoke for immigrant youth: *SOS Racisme* and *France Plus*. These efforts have met with mixed success, but the PS, at least until now, has been a more 'natural' home and target for the political aspirations for voters of new immigrant origin than the PCF has been.[52]

Surveys during the election cycle in 1988–9 demonstrated the inability of the PCF to access these new voters. Of 102 *beurs* surveyed in 1988, only eleven of the 73 who identified with a party of the Left considered themselves 'close' to the PCF. (Only four felt close to a party of the Centre–Right.)[53] It is worth noting, however, that only five respondents *strongly* identified with any political party. The loss of the capacity to mobilize and integrate new immigrants is an important break in the historical pattern of the French Communist Party – although of course only one of numerous factors that help explain its decline.

CONCLUSION

The PCF emerged during a period of expansion, both of French industrial labour and of the flow of immigrant workers into the industrial work force. The initial breakthroughs came in rural areas, where the new party was able to attract from other parties a coalition of peasants, artisans and shopkeepers all dependent on the fluctuations of the rural economy. But within a few years, party influence spread to the rapidly growing centres of new industry, where the Communists mobilized large numbers of new voters who had either migrated into these areas or who had immigrated from abroad. After World War II, the PCF finally harvested the crop of membership and support that had grown from the seeds it had planted among immigrant communities before the war. Thus the post-war PCF emerged from change, but also from growth, in the French electorate.

During the period when growth had abated, the Communists were able to maintain support through a network of systems of local hegemony that at one time appeared to be impregnable. When the bases for this system began to give way in the 1970s, the party was able to maintain its influence by gaining support in new areas through an alliance with the Socialist Party.

By the 1980s the geographic bases for Communist political power were in a period of what has been called 'a complex process of deconstruction of a hegemonic local system, in the course of which the eclipse of a formerly dominant party generates a diffuse modification of political behavior, the effects of which go beyond its own electorate'.[54] The complexity was due in part to the fact that Communism was constructed somewhat differently in rural areas, in the areas of new industry and in areas of immigrant conversion. In each of these sectors the decline was related to changes particular to that sub-system.

For any political party, the reconstruction of its political base would be a formidable task, but for the French Communist Party strategies that appeared to be leading toward qualified success were hampered by an organizational framework that magnified the resistance to the lessons of that success. The alliance strategy threatened the very identity of the party and what George Ross has called its 'core stock of symbolic resources'. Confronted with a choice between maintaining identity and averting decline, the organization chose maintaining identity and thus inevitable decline. The ultimate dilemma of the Communist Party was its inability to dominate or profit from the emerging changes in the French working class that are linked to immigration. North African workers have been mobilized around an Islamic identity that clashes with the established identity of the party, and North African political organization in former bastions has posed a challenge rather than an opportunity for the declining party.

Perhaps the real lesson of this analysis, however, is the contrast between the strategic flexibility of the PCF when it was ascending and the strategic rigidity of the party in decline. In the early years, the Communists adapted well to the variety of constituencies in which they constructed the core of their party. In the declining years they rejected adaptation in the name of symbols that no longer had any mobilizing capacity outside of the party organization.

Notes

1. These bases of partisan realignment are explored by Kristi Anderson in *The Creation of a Democratic Majority* (Chicago, IL: University of Chicago Press, 1979) Chapter 1.
2. V. O. Key, 'A Theory of Critical Elections', *Journal of Politics*, 17 (February 1955). Also see the follow-up article 'Secular Realignment and the Party System', *Journal of Politics*, 21 (May 1959).
3. See François Goguel, *Géographie des élections français sous la troisième et la quatrième Républiques* (Paris: 1970) p. 78; and Daniel Halévy, *Visites aux paysans du centre (1907–1934)* (Paris: 1978) p. 182.
4. Georges Lavau, *A quoi sert le parti communiste français?* (Paris: Fayard, 1981) p. 72.
5. Jacques Girault, 'L'implantation du parti communiste dans la région parisienne', in Girault, *Sur l'implantation du parti communiste français dans l'entre-deux-guerres* (Paris: Edition Sociales, 1977) pp. 115–7.
6. Jacques Fauvet, *Histoire du parti communiste français 1920–1976* (Paris: Fayard, 1977) p. 69.
7. See Tyler Stovall, *The Rise of the Paris Red Belt* (Berkeley: University of California Press, 1990) pp. 67–70.
8. Raymond Pronier, *Les municipalités communistes* (Paris: Ballard, 1983) pp. 261–2.
9. The best estimates of immigrant employment in the 1980s can be found in Jeanne Singer-Kérel, *La Population active étrangère au recensement de 1982* (Paris: Presses de la Fondation Nationale des Sciences Politiques, Service d'étude de l'activité économique, 1985).
10. Catherine Wihtol de Wenden, *Les Immigrés et la politique* (Paris: Presses de la Fondation Nationale des Sciences Politiques, 1988) p. 54.
11. The organization of immigration in the 1920s is described by Gérard Noiriel in *Le Creuset Français: Histoire de l'immigration XIX–XX siècles* (Paris: Seuil, 1988) pp. 306–12; and Gary S. Cross, *Immigrant Workers in Industrial France* (Philadelphia: Temple University Press, 1983) pp. 52–63.
12. See Noiriel, Chapter 6.
13. Emmanuel Todd, *La Nouvelle France* (Paris: Seuil, 1988) p. 232.
14. Laird Boswell's work contradicts most of the literature on peasant communism in France, by demonstrating the importance of artisans and shopkeepers in the Communist vote in these rural areas. See Boswell, 'The French Rural Communist Electorate', *Journal of Interdisciplinary History* 23, no. 4 (Spring 1993) pp. 746–7.
15. Boswell, pp. 738–40, and Danielle Tartakowsky, *Les Premiers communistes français* (Paris: 1980).
16. Noiriel, 'Communisme et immigration, éléments pour une recherche', *Communisme*, no. 15–6 (1987) p. 95.
17. Cited in Cross, pp. 147–8.
18. De Wenden, p. 50.

19. The number of immigrants in the CGTU is reported by de Wenden, p. 52. The best comprehensive source for union membership for this period is Antoine Prost, *La C.G.T. à l'époque du front populaire* (Paris: Armand Colin, 1964) Annex I, pp. 177–94.
20. See Jacques Girault, 'L'Implantation du parti communiste français dans l'entre-deux-guerres: Quelques jalons,' in Girault, *Sur l'implantation*, p. 51.
21. See Pierre Belleville, *Une Nouvelle classe ouvrière* (Paris: Julliard, 1963) pp. 91–2, and Noiriel, *Longwy: Immigrés et prolétaires 1880–1980* (Paris: PUF, 1984) pp. 355–70.
22. Noiriel, *Longwy*, p. 359.
23. See Janine Ponty, *Polonais méconnus: histoire des travailleurs immigrés en France dans l'entre-deux-guerres* (Paris: Publications de la Sorbonne, 1988) pp. 327–8.
24. Noiriel, 'Communisme et immigration: éléments pour une recherche', pp. 92–3.
25. These figures are derived from Philippe Buton, 'Les effectifs du Parti communiste français (1920–1984)', *Communisme*, no. 7 (1985) p. 8.
26. On the other hand, success was certainly not guaranteed by the integration of immigrant militants into the CGT. In Moselle, many industrial areas were dominated by PCF militants of German origin, who were, argues Belleville, 'isolated and sectarian' and far less successful in mobilizing both members and voters. Belleville, *Une Nouvelle classe ouvrière*, pp. 91–2.
27. Four articles have probably best summarized the evolution of the PCF: Jean Ranger, 'Le Declin du PCF', *Revue française de science politique* 36, no. 1 (February 1986); François Platone and Jean Ranger, 'L'Échec électoral du parti communiste', in Lancelot, *1981: Les Élections de l'alternance* (Paris: Presses de la Fondation Nationale des Sciences Politiques, 1986); François Platone, 'Parti communiste: Sombre dimanche, triste époque', in Elisabeth Dupoirier and Gérard Grunberg, eds., *Mars 1986: La drôle de défaite de la gauche* (Paris: PUF, 1986); George Ross, 'Party Decline and Changing Party Systems: France and the French Communist Party', *Comparative Politics* 25, no. 1 (October 1992).
28. Schain, *French Communism and Local Power* (New York: St. Martin's Press, 1985) p. 48. This trend was first reported in the PCF's own analysis of the 1973 legislative elections. See *Bulletin de l'élu communiste*, no. 45–6 (1973) pp. 2–3.
29. *Bulletin de L'élu Communiste*, nos. 45–6 (1973), pp. 2–3; and *Le Monde, Les Elections législatives de mars, 1978* (Supplément aux dossiers et documents du monde, March 1978) p. 76.
30. Platone, 'Parti communiste', p. 196
31. See Platone, 'Parti communiste,' pp. 195–9; and Stéphane Courtois, 'Parti communiste: Les dernières cartouches?' in Philippe Habert and Colette Ysmal, eds., *Elections legislatives 1988* (Paris: Le Figaro/Etudes politiques, 1988) p. 27.
32. See Buton.
33. Buton, p. 21.
34. See Platone, 'Les Adhérants de l'apogée: la composition du PCF en 1979', *Communisme*, no. 7 (1985) pp. 36–8.
35. Platone, 'Parti communiste', p. 197.
36. For an excellent analysis of demographic changes in the Paris region, see Harold V. Savitch, *Post-Industrial Cities: Politics and Planning in New York, Paris and London* (Princeton, NJ: Princeton University Press, 1988) Chapter 4.
37. Noiriel, *Longwy*, p. 387. See pp. 371–91 for some challenging ideas on the decline of Communism in the region.
38. See Ross, 'Party Decline', pp. 43–61.
39. *Ibid.* p. 49.
40. *Ibid.* p. 51.

224 French Communism

41. See surveys in *L'Express*, 11 April 1981 and *Le Matin*, 14 March 1981, as well as *Libération*, 9 July 1986.
42. There are perhaps 500 000 so-called 'immigrant' voters, most of whom are young and were born in France. See Fatiha Dazi and Rémy Leveau, 'L'Integration par la politique: le vote des "beurs"', *Etudes* (September 1988) p. 182.
43. See Leveau, 'Les partis et l'intégration des "beurs"', in Yves Mény, ed., *Ideologies, partis politiques et groupes sociaux, études reunies pour Georges Lavau* (Paris: Presses de la Fondation Nationale des Sciences Politiques, 1989).
44. The largest single immigrant group until the late 1980s was Portuguese. However, these immigrants from Northern Portugal generally voted for the Centre and Right when they became citizens, and were never an important potential constituency for the Left or the Communists.
45. See Martin A. Schain, 'Immigration and Changes in the French Party System', *European Journal of Political Research*, 16 (1988).
46. The PCF excluded a group of Italians in the Lyons region in 1927. See Jacques Girault, 'L'Implantation du parti communiste français', pp. 51–2.
47. See Raymond Pronier, *Les Municipalités communistes*, Chapter 4 and pp. 396–7.
48. The link between organization and religion did not begin with Muslims. See Ralph Schor, 'Le Facteur religieux et l'intégration des étrangers en France 1919–1939', *Vingtième siècle*, no. 7 (July–September 1985) pp. 103–15.
49. See René Mouriaux and de Wenden, 'Syndicalisme français et Islam,' and Stéphane Courtois and Gilles Képel, 'Musselmans et prolétaires,' in Rémy Leveau and Gilles Képel, eds., *Les Muselmans dans la société française* (Paris: Presses de la Fondation Nationale des Sciences Politiques, 1988).
50. Mouriaux and de Wenden, p. 44.
51. Leveau, 'Les partis et l'intégration des "beurs"', pp. 253–7.
52. See the analysis of Marie Poinsot, in 'La Concurrence des associations nationales dans l'espace politique locale: SOS Racisme, France Plus et Memoire Fertile', presented to the European Consortium on Political Research Joint Sessions of Workshops, Leiden University, The Netherlands 2–8 April, 1993.
53. Fatiha Daze and Leveau, 'L'intégration par le politique', p. 184.
54. Henri Rey and Jacques Roy, 'L'Evolution électorale d'un département de la banlieue parisienne', *Hérodite*, no. 43 (1986) p. 38.

12 Green Politics and Political Mobilization: Contradictions of Direct Democracy[1]

Tad Shull

The ecology movement has entered into politics with a new model of party mobilization. Nurtured in small grass-roots activist groups, greens who have formed parties have continued to practise their radically democratic mode of organization. They have held steadfastly to their ethic of civic activism and individual autonomy in politics even while competing with the mainstream parties. Remarkably, the experiment yielded positive political benefits for France's first significant ecological party, *Les Verts*. But mobilization with the direct democratic model of organization has been difficult to sustain.[2]

The irony of the direct democratic experiment is that features that can help mobilize support for the party have consequences that ultimately undermine that support.[3] In direct democratic parties such as the *Verts*, there are few formal hierarchical structures. Party rules allow members and local-level branches an active role in selecting its leadership and programme.[4] Open participation gives activists an incentive to support the party and helps establish its identity as a democratic tribune within the party system.[5] Yet the party has an unhealthy tendency to turn inward. Required to secure internal support for any given strategy, the *Verts* are weighed down by debates over strategy. These debates degenerate into personal crusades and endless infighting and lead to contradictory or rogue initiatives. The resulting stagnation or chaos runs counter to the principle of responsible representation – and in the process the party's core activists and electors become alienated. A newer green party, *Génération Écologie* (GE), which portrays itself as more efficient and responsible, has been troubled by some of the same problems.

After a promising start, anarchy and anti-democratic drift in France's two ecology parties became painfully evident in the two most recent national elections (the 1993 legislatives and 1994 European elections). Conflicts within and between the parties were rampant. More critically, the ecologists, who thought it was vital to have a different organizational style than the mainstream parties, may have unwittingly let down their guard against the appearance of collusion with the those parties, notably the Socialist Party (PS). (The *Verts* had promoted the idea that ecology must be 'neither Right nor Left' and were joined in this position by GE in an alliance known as the *Entente Écologiste*). While the alternative model initially helped achieve positive results for the party, it has created problems for political ecology in the long term.

FACING THE LEFT IN POWER: MOBILIZATION AND COUNTER-MOBILIZATION

For ecologists who founded the *Verts* in 1984, the mainstream parties of the French Left served as negative models.[6] The record of the French Communist Party (PCF) was at issue. Its rigid, secretive organization appeared to work against whatever desirable political or social ends the *Verts* had originally sought. Yet the PS was also a focal point.

During the early to mid-1970s, the PS headed a dynamic, broad-based left-wing political movement poised to gain power in government. Many ecologists supported that objective. Yet the immediate preparation for and exercise of power revealed the Socialists' affinity for Gaullist political institutions, and later even with free trade and monetary discipline. That, of course, imbued the alternative Left ('*deuxième gauche*'), including ecology parties, with disillusionment and anomie. The organizational features of the PS were inverted in the *Verts* model. Where the programme of the PS was marked by flexibility, the *Verts* insisted on unyielding commitment to the environmental cause. The *Verts* shunned the lust for power the PS seemed to embrace. The PS presumed the party apparatus could effectively speak for social movements; the *Verts*, in contrast, allowed a high level of activist participation and direct territorial integration of local movements within the party itself.

The ecologists were dissatisfied after having rallied in support of the PS during the seventies. François Mitterrand and the PS co-opted the environmental issue while in opposition, and tried to deflect and marginalize it while in office. Until the PS's steep decline during Mitterrand's second presidential term, the party also profited from an electoral 'vacuum-cleaner effect', to the detriment of the ecologists. Majoritarian (winner-takes-all) ballot institutions induced uncommitted left-leaning electors – some of whom might otherwise have flowed toward the greens – to cast strategic votes for the predominant Left party in order to counter a highly competitive Right. Hence the PS was able to stave off a 'new politics' challenge of the kind levelled by the German *Grünen* toward the German Social Democratic Party during this same time period.[7] Suspicions bred between French ecologists and Socialists during the early years of the Mitterrand experiment left lasting impediments to accord between the two camps. Ever since, French ecology has been marked indelibly by a struggle over the means to prevent absorption or manipulation by the politically hegemonic PS.

The electoralist format and strategy of the PS lay behind its receptiveness to progressive issues like the ones the ecologists were trying to advance. After the 1971 Epinay congress, PS strategy was to rally as broad a base of progressive forces as possible behind the one left-of-centre party with a government calling. While developing its working-class strategy with the Common Programme, the PS courted the new middle-class segment of the potential Left electorate by incorporating new politics themes that had emerged from the student rebellion of 1968. *Autogestion*, political decentralization, feminism and research on alternative forms of energy were on the programme.[8] Mitterrand's rhetorical skill, plus the party's design as a campaign machine, made possible this image of a 'modern' Socialist Party. Mobilizing the potential new Left electorate meant tapping the energies of militants from the *deuxième gauche* within the party factions. The PS also sought the support of other organizations with ties to the new social movements such as the *Confédération Française Démocratique du Travail* (CFDT) or Left Catholic organizations, and satellite parties such as the Unified Socialist Party (PSU).[9]

Events later would reveal élitist tendencies in the party. As Serenella Sferza points out in Chapter 10, PS leadership factions became more rigid after the demise of the United Front around 1978. That meant that mobilization of new Left militants within the PS was seen as destabilizing, and new entries were discouraged. Further, as the Communist Party would discover, supporting or allying with the Socialists meant being controlled or politically outflanked. Independent left-of-centre organizations or candidates (including ecologists) were expected to rally behind the PS, and there was little they could do to ensure their own political relevance afterwards. In return for perennial electoral alliances supporting the Socialists, France's first New Left party, the PSU, received only a secretary post.[10] That hardened the *Verts'* resolve to reject political alliances that would not bring them any clear policy concessions.

In the dawn of the Mitterrand era, few of the PS's proposed environmental measures came to fruition. Mitterrand's promises for a moratorium and referendum on nuclear power were dropped. (The government did cancel a proposed extension to a military base at Larzac, however, as well as a nuclear power plant at Plogoff, Brittany.) In addition, Mitterrand's assumption of control of the Gaullist-designed defence structure sealed a consensus between Right and Left on France's nuclear programme and independent nuclear capability.[11] With the nuclear question a closed book, French ecology had lost a potent issue that helped launch the green movement in German party politics.

THE VERTS: ADVANCING THE ECOLOGICAL MODEL OF PARTY MOBILIZATION

A cadre of environmental veterans within the *Verts* led the party out of its chronic political isolation. After 1986, when they rose to command a majority within the party, activist mobilization and voter support surged. These fundamentalists, labeled 'pure ecologists', or '*ni droite, ni gauche*', rejected alliances with other parties.[12] They felt the green movement – with its emphasis on direct action to save the environment and its demand for transparency in public policy – had the power, like no other contemporary ideology, to speak to the concerns and aspirations of ordinary citizens. Even if this appeal was ultimately limited, the idea did convey the promise of political rejuvenation to the party's faithful, and to a youthful electorate hungry for change.

Most pure ecologists had had little background in or sympathy for socialist politics or the working class movement. Like Antoine Waechter, the individual most fully associated with this current and with the party later, many were environmentalists by profession as well as conviction. Almost all had had their formative political experiences in politically non-aligned environmental or citizens' activist groups. Hence they wanted to steer French ecology away from the themes and alliance practices of the Left that the party's previous majority had endorsed. The dispiriting course of the Socialist experiment outside the party would strengthen these 'militant autonomists' within it (see Chapter 11).

The eco-socialist, or Left-ecological, current that led the *Verts* prior to the arrival of the pure ecologists could not reverse the tiny new party's political fortunes. The Left-ecologists headed the party from its founding until the ascendancy of the militant autonomist 'Waechterians' in 1986. By that point, they had not arrived at a clear or viable political strategy, and they faced a crisis in their ability to mobilize activists.

Left-ecologists, such as Yves Cochet and Didier Anger, had come to ecology from politics, not the reverse. Their inclination was to prove that ecology had a social conscience, and that it was responsive to a broadly based left-of-centre political constituency. Their strategy was to enter into alliances with other progressive forces and thus multiply the electoral effects buoying a united New Left political front. While the PS moved more toward the Right, the Left-ecological *Verts* made several attempts to form a front of all progressive forces to its left. Before the 1986 legislative elections, for example, the ecologists negotiated a tentative alliance with the *Fédération Gauche Alternative*, remnants of the PSU, the Trotskyist *Ligue Communiste Revolutionnaire* and other leftist splinter groups. (Later, they proposed alliances with the Socialists themselves.)

This strategy opened the Left-ecologists to charges from within their own ranks that they were weakly committed to the movement (despite the solid background these individuals had in environmental or anti-nuclear activism). In the eyes of some militants, their proposals for instrumental alliances with the Left skirted dangerously close to Socialist politics-as-usual, or risked infiltration through Leninist-style tactics. Another problem was that the Left-ecological current's hybrid programme of social redistribution with environmentalist themes was advanced at a politically inopportune moment. At a point when the PS's radical macroeconomic program had been tried and ignominiously withdrawn, the burden was on any challenger to specify what it could accomplish that was truly different. What the *Verts* had offered instead were simply vague calls for solidarity with the extra-parliamentary Left, leaving the party dismally marginal.[13]

In contrast, the pure ecologist Waechterians were more effective than the Left-ecologists at rallying the party rank and file. Waechter's winning programmatic motion was aptly titled '*Affirmer l'identité de l'écologie*'. Drawing sharp moral and political boundaries between the environmentalist 'we' and the technocratic 'they', Waechter raised the weakness and isolation of the movement to the status of a virtue and a strength. His unyielding faith in ecology struck a chord with activists and members devoted since the movement's low years and demoralized at this ebb in the party's fortunes.[14] Pure ecologists such as Waechter were also more effective than the Left-ecologists at communicating what was truly different about political ecology. They defined the party around its direct democratic themes and its distance from the political class. Reforms proposed under the pure ecological strategy opposed the statist or centralist forms then associated with French Socialism. Along these lines, the *Verts* demanded specific institutional reforms, such as opening the party system to proportional representation, guaranteeing minority rights and further decentralizing France's administrative structure.[15]

Any loyalty the pure ecological motion and its fundamentalist rhetoric helped secure was instrumental for later successes in the electoral arena. As Waechter had argued, the *Verts'* ties to the grassroots environmental movement proved to be their main source of strength (though they were aided by a favourable coincidence of institutional factors).[16] After a rash of local environmental problems broke out by the mid-1980's, veteran private organizations had gained credibility and recognition in their communities. By stressing the links between the party and these local movement organizations, the *Verts'* in turn benefited from the latter's campaign activities and sponsorship of candidates.

The municipal elections in March and the European elections in June 1989 put ecology on the French political map. With all the preparation in previous local mobilizations behind them, the ecologists were well placed to campaign in the regional elections of 1992, the period of their highest aggregate electoral scores for ecology. (*Verts* and *GE* scored 6.8 per cent and 7.1 per cent respectively.) These elections were favourable for the small parties, such as the greens, because they had proportional representation or a variant and did not affect any office at the national level. Further, the programme of decentralization initiated under the first Socialist government in 1981 may have made politics at the regional level appear more significant to voters.

Throughout their electoral takeoff, the *Verts* had their highest scores in regions with a long history of mobilization around environmental issues or populations inclined to activism (such as university students): Bretagne, Rhone-Alpes and the Nord and Paris regions. Alsace until recently has had some of the highest scores (for example, 20.48 per cent for Bas-Rhin and Haut-Rhin combined in 1989). Alsace is paradigmatic of the social roots of environmental activism. Like the regions directly across the Rhine, Alsace has a tradition of citizen activism, including an environmental movement that reached back to the last century, not to mention palpable levels of environmental degradation and strong population pressure.[17] Those features set Alsace apart from the rural areas of *la France profonde*, where environmentalism has not made similar political advances.

Génération Écologie made inroads into these territories and others (notably Aquitaine). The arrival of GE, which had a more conventional mode of party organization, was an early symptom of the underlying political fragility in the *Verts'* radical democratic mode of organization. To GE's founder, former Minister of the Environment Brice Lalonde, the environmental cause was hindered, not helped, by the sectarianism of the radical social movements that Waechter represented. What he thought was needed was acceptance of partnership in government and competent, pragmatic leaders in high offices.

Accordingly, GE would not rely on mobilizing activists engaged *sur le terrain* to support the party as the *Verts* had done. The party apparatus was designed to make it an efficient campaign machine. GE's organization was held under the firm control of Lalonde, its extremely popular and charismatic leader. It was staffed by paid employees, and most of its politically active members were not environmental militants but electable candidates with independent local stature (although, Lalonde's excessive concern for his own electability strained their allegiance to his cause).

ELECTORAL MOBILIZATION: IDENTITY AND ISSUES

Ever since French ecologists entered national elections in 1978, the structure of the ecological vote has been remarkably stable.[18] One category of green voters is former *'peuple de gauche'*, mostly middle-class, in search of new mobilizing ideas. A second group is young or previously non-aligned voters. A growing portion of both groups seemed to support the Waechterian principle of political autonomy: they either vote green or abstain. (In some recent elections, though, many have abstained even when green candidates were on the ballot.) In addition, both groups respond favourably to the *Verts'* radically democratic themes.

By attracting this progressive-minded, new middle-class electorate, the ecologists clearly posed an electoral challenge to the mainstream parties of the Left, especially the Socialists. From election to election, the *Verts'* (and later GE's) numbers have consistently included many new defectors from the PS. For example, 44 per cent of those who voted for Antoine Waechter in the 1988 presidential elections had voted for the Socialists in the parliamentary elections of March 1986. Of those who voted for the Waechter list in the European elections of June 1989, 39 per cent had voted for Mitterrand in the first round of the 1988 presidentials. In the second round, 54 per cent of Waechter's voters had gone to Mitterrand. Between 1986 and 1989, there was an increase first by 5 per cent and then 12 per cent in the number of Socialists who voted green in consecutive elections. In the legislatives of 1993, 45 per cent of those who had voted ecologist in the first round supported a PS candidate in the second. Other transfers to the *Verts* came from alternative Left parties and the Communists. In the 1989 Europeans, the Waechter list gained the support of 22 per cent of those who had voted for alternative Left candidates in the 1988 presidentials, and 8 per cent who chose the Communist candidate. Some of these voters may maintain their leftist affiliations: about 29 per cent of the voters for either the *Verts* or GE in the 1992 regional elections chose a leftist candidate – PS, PCF, extreme Left or 'diverse Left' – in the 1993 legislatives.[19]

Although some ecological voters did not necessarily support the parties of the Right or Left, when pressed, a majority tended to come down clearly in favour of themes associated with the Left. On an ideological scale from Left to Right, 12 per cent of green voters placed themselves on the Left or extreme Left, and 43 per cent on the Centre–Left.[20] Voters for the first green lists in France in the late 1970s had been more moderate. Many ecologists also supported programmatic themes traditionally associated with European socialism – the right to employment, the right to strike, workplace democracy and nationalization of enterprises.[21]

Twenty-eight per cent of *Vert* voters place themselves at the Centre, with 14 per cent on the Right or Centre–Right combined. Some have voted for the Right in two-way races: for example, 16 per cent of first-round *Vert* voters chose Jacques Chirac in the 1988 presidentials in the second round.[22] The right-wing voters may not have supported the more radical features of the *Verts'* programme, and cast their vote for greens more out of concern for specifically environmental issues.

A significant portion of the *Verts* electorate refused to place themselves on a Left–Right scale of preferences, reject strategic support for other parties besides the greens and abstain if a green candidate is not present.[23] Agnes Roche interprets this trend as an indication that the *Verts* gradually built up a loyal following who are socialized to the idea that ecology is 'neither Right nor Left'.[24] Their refusal to identify themselves as 'Left' or 'Right' does not necessarily imply support for centrist politics, nor alienation from politics altogether. Instead, it reflects protest against what they saw as an illusory choice offered by the available set of party alternatives.[25]

Some of these non-aligned voters may have been young people who had never voted for any other group, or who never professed any other major political affiliation. Others may have been former leftists who simply no longer identified themselves as such. Still others may have been veterans of various new politics movements not directly represented by any other major party organization besides the *Verts*: feminists, regionalists or *'tiers-mondistes'*.[26]

The sociological background and political preferences of *Verts* voters suggest a strong inclination to support the radical participatory themes the party advanced. They belong to the 'new middle class', who are noted for the value they place on these radically democratic or libertarian themes.[27] Salaried professionals in intellectual or service occupations are the largest socio-economic group within the ecologists' ranks. In 1984, 33.5 per cent of ecologists were employed in service-sector or middle-management positions; that number was 29 per cent in 1989 and 26 per cent in 1993.[28] In 1989, 40 per cent had household income above 10 000 francs per month.[29] The proportion of working-class voters was 9.5 per cent in 1978, and 8 per cent to 9 per cent in 1993.[30] The ecologists are also relatively youthful: in 1989 15 per cent were between ages 18 and 25, and 31 per cent were between 25 and 34.[31] Finally, the *Verts* voters had a high level of education. In 1989, 34 per cent had degrees beyond high school, a higher figure than for France as a whole.[32]

The *Verts'* new middle-class supporters' political preferences tend toward what Gérard Grunberg and Etienne Schweisguth have called 'cultural liberalism': the right to choose one's own identity and mode of living.[33] Such values include strong support for individual civil rights and opposition to coercion or moral or cultural authority. Fifty-three per cent of the *Verts'* voters reject the death penalty. (Among the total population, 61 per cent support it.)[34] Only 50 per cent say they are 'proud to be French', versus 69 per cent of the population. Sixty-six per cent feel it is 'normal' for Muslims to practise their religion, versus 51 per cent of the population. Cultural liberals tend to support women's rights, approve of extramarital cohabition, tolerate homosexuality and support the rights of socially or culturally marginal groups, such as immigrants or the unemployed. In these preferences, green voters surpass those of the extreme Left parties, otherwise generally considered to be the most flexible or open-minded.

Supporters of the *Verts* place high value on political participation. The green voter is also very likely to have taken part in some militant association, whether Left, alternative or environmental. *Vert* voters also register strong dissatisfaction with established parties. As just noted, many *Vert* voters refuse to identify with an established political party. Seventy-six per cent feel that the distinction between the parties of the Right and Left has little meaning, versus 67 per cent of the French public.[35] Forty-seven per cent claim to have no confidence in their elected deputies, and 42 per cent do (a proportion paralleled only by National Front voters). Well-educated, but not at *grands écoles*, *Vert* voters may be less sympathetic to mainstream parties perpetually fronted by *énarques*.

Analysis of *Génération Écologie*'s electorate suggests that its support resembles that of the *Verts*. In its promising first electoral contest, the March 1992 regionals, GE won 7.1 per cent, the *Verts'* 6.8 per cent. According to some exit polls, GE picked about 25 per cent of former *Verts* supporters.[36] GE, whose voters tend to be more politically moderate, picked up first-time defections from the Socialist and Centrist parties.[37]

Analysing the ecological parties' electorates may provide some clues for recent signs of apathy or alienation from political ecology. A portion of the ecological voters may have been 'soft supporters', since many made their voting decisions at the last minute. Further, if green voters tend toward abstention, that can hurt the ecologists as much as other parties. Protest against the system can just as well be expressed by staying away from the ballot box as by casting a vote for protest parties. Further, the more the ecologists become established in the party system, the more they may be perceived as being made of essentially the same stuff as the established parties. In some ways, the actions of the ecology parties in political competition might have actually contributed to this perception.

SUSTAINING MOBILIZATION: AN UNCERTAIN FUTURE?

The fate of a radically democratic party competing in a less-than-democratic system might appear to be sealed in advance.[38] There is ample evidence, however, to suggest that purely endogenous factors can create problems as well. Herbert Kitschelt has noted that radically democratic party organizations are likely to encounter 'perverse effects', as the aggregate of individual actions and decisions lead to unforeseen and unwanted outcomes.[39] The *Verts'* experience confirms some of Kitschelt's scepticism.

One perverse effect is personalization: the control of the party's identity and programme by certain exceptional individuals. Where formal power is denied to leaders, personal power takes up the slack. Power flows to the strongest personalities, to the most intensely motivated, perhaps simply to the ones with the most free time. With no clear chain of command within the party, no career premiums for toeing a party or factional line and few controls on the initiatives of elected officials, these ambitions can hardly be slowed.

A second perverse effect in direct democratic organizations is that deliberately weak structures of internal authority create a void in discipline. Even if individuals with exceptional personal qualities or motivation exercise influence over the party's direction, others may not believe they are acting in the party's best interests, and they may have the power to block initiatives. The disputes that erupt can only be resolved through raw interpersonal struggle.

In turn, the conflicts of direct democratic parties undermine their ability to mobilize support. *Verts* members have been alienated by the party's hardball politics, the endless preoccupation with political strategy and an absence of fresh ideas. Membership has declined, from a high of about 5700 in 1993 to only 4000 by 1994. There are no sanctions on exiting the organization for rank-and-file members – precisely those on whom the party depends to perform its daily activities and mobilize local troops. Finally, if the divisions *within* ecology parties create an appearance to the voting public that life inside them is nothing but a clash of personalities and unchecked ambitions, the divisions *between* the two parties simply exacerbates that negative image.

The power struggles that have racked ecology parties turn on ideas as much as on raw personal ambition. Lively debates may be healthy in a new movement, and most of the opinions that get aired do offer valid perspectives. Still, ideas – especially ones that have the potential to frame the direction of the party and the movement – become entangled with personal crusades and vendettas. The perception of personal affronts and demonization of those with opposing viewpoints often overtakes real debate.

The most striking example of the drift from original intentions to personalization and paranoia is the rise of Waechterianism – or, more precisely, of Waechter himself – within the *Verts*. Waechter's unexpected gains as a presidential candidate in 1988 brought a symbolic victory and much-needed publicity.[40] The more the party succeeded with Waechter as its most visible spokesman, the more the public and political class identified the party with him. Perhaps resting on their laurels, Waechter and his circle failed to expand or develop the 'pure ecological' ideology afterward.

In place of new ideas, the Waechterians transformed the principle of autonomy into something of a fetish. They exerted considerable energy on guarding the party's independence, stemming off competing ideological and political influences from within and without – most notably from influences from the political Left.[41] As a result, they seemed not to respect the democratic principles in their rhetoric. The majority's motion of 1990 that the *Verts* would reject electoral alliances even to stop a well-placed National Front candidate opened it to charges of complacency about xenophobic politics. In addition, a controversy in early 1991 surrounding the issue of party membership for Pierre Juquin (a former Communist feared because of his potential influence) did not do much more to polish the party's image in the press. The Waechterians' zeal may have been misplaced, since the Socialist and Communist Left was dropping further toward a state of intellectual and political prostration. For this reason, the Waechterian current finally succumbed to internal opposition in November 1993. The new majority was headed by Left-ecologists who advocated a 'dialogue' with progressive leftist forces such as Communist *rénovateurs* or left-wing Socialists.

If personalization around figures like Waechter has its drawbacks, the opposite tendency carries the risk of too rapid a turnover in leadership. The *Verts'* performance in the European elections of June 1994 is a case in point. The new leadership still could not agree on one of their own to head the list for the Europeans, so they nominated a relative unknown instead, European Parliament Vice President Marie Isler-Beguin. Without a recognizable figurehead, the *Verts* obtained only 2.95 per cent of the vote.[42]

The newer party, *Génération Écologie*, was fashioned to be free of the chaos and suspicions about its own leadership that have plagued the *Verts*. Yet, Lalonde's organization has not overcome the clash of personal ambitions either. An élite political club may not be any more ready to accept control by a single individual than a cohort of radical social movement activists is. Lalonde recently faced a revolt within his own party. Some key members opposed what they saw as the autocratic tendencies of its founder and his fondness for holding office for its own sake. One member, Nél Mamère, joined Bernard Tapie's surprisingly successful list for the 1994 European elections, and both he and another former GE member have formed their own new parties. In this process, the party may have squandered its main source of political capital – its image of competence and reliability. The mercurial behavior of GE's founder may also have contributed to this credibility problem. He participated in a Socialist government, then broke with them when serious troubles began in 1992, then once again entertained their proposals. When he re-entered party politics, Lalonde first opposed the *Verts*, then united with them, then was seen heading an independent list in the Europeans. (In fairness, the *Verts* themselves had denied him second place.) The conflicts and contradictory messages appear to have critically damaged GE's prospects. It has had only one promising electoral result in three major contests – 7.1 per cent in the 1992 regional elections. (GE sank to 2.01 per cent in the 1994 Europeans.) GE, then, is an electoralist party without electors – a familiar refrain to observers of the contemporary PS.

In the end, the disorder within the political ecology movement has undermined its ability to shape its external environment. Voters misunderstand what the parties' real intentions are, and other parties can manipulate ecologist leaders and their political identity. The disastrous performance of the ecological parties in the 1993 parliamentary elections is a prime example.

The failure of the united *Entente Écologiste* in the 1993 elections for the French National Assembly was the only surprise in a contest where a Socialist débâcle and the return of the Right to power seemed inevitable. The ecologists' combined score in the regional elections a year earlier had been almost 15 per cent, and their polling scores remained at this level throughout the year. As the legislative elections approached, some polls registered as high as 19 per cent.[43] Yet the ecological bloc scored only 7.8 per cent in the first round, with only two candidates remaining for the second, and won no seats. Other parties' polls were more consistent with their scores. That includes the Socialists (scoring 18 per cent on the first ballot), whose losses might once again have been the ecologists' gains.

As mentioned above, one possible explanation for the discrepancy between earlier scores and polls and the actual votes cast is that the ecological vote includes a portion of soft support, or voters inclined toward abstention. The entry of some 'new ecologists' – *ad hoc* or even spurious green parties – might also have chiselled at the *Entente*'s numbers.[44] Such *nouveaux écologistes* scored 2.56 per cent, bringing first-round ecology votes to 10.92 per cent.

Events immediately preceding the elections suggest that the ecologists had a hand in this drop of support. Emboldened by high expectations and eager to make an impact on the political debate, the ecologists may have allowed the distinction between themselves and the political class to become blurred (especially surprising for the otherwise fiercely independent *Verts*). Meetings between delegates from the *Entente* and heads of the established parties were quite conspicuous during the last two months of the campaign: Lalonde with Centrists, Waechter with neo-Gaullist Edouard Balladur. The embrace of the newcomers by a motley assortment of government parties later was widely judged – including by the ecologists themselves – to have been a poisoned kiss.

Perhaps most damaging to the ecologists' image of integrity and credibility was an episode that began with an alliance offer from the Socialists. Michel Rocard, the presumed presidential candidate of the PS, made a last-ditch proposal in February 1993, known as the 'Big Bang': a thoroughgoing political and ideological recomposition of the Left that would include the ecologists. Rocard's initiative envisioned a programme for sharing work time as a solution to France's high level of unemployment. In fact, work-sharing was an idea that the greens' own campaign had tried to promote. (Voters were evidently unconvinced by any of the rhetoric.) The *Verts*, not surprisingly, were suspicious. But Lalonde suddenly agreed to accept the outstretched hand – and then recanted. The 'Big Bang' received a massive amount of publicity, though, and the damage was done. Rocard's last-minute embrace of the ecologists' ideas, plus the idea that the exhausted Socialists could simply dissolve and regroup with the ecologists, might have sealed the latter's association with the PS in voters' minds. The association was unenviable, and at any rate did not help the PS. The PS was perceived as that undemocratic 'other' against which French ecology had come to know itself.

CONCLUSION

Ecological parties, such as the *Verts*, have viewed radical democracy as a valued goal in itself, and have tried to live up to their commitment. The significance of their experiment reaches beyond the values and agendas of the post-1968 generation or the environmental movement, and should not be discounted out of hand. The ecologists' emphasis on individual autonomy and initiative in politics reflects a growing interest in the resurgence and dynamism of civil society in the last generation.[45] The ecology party model also epitomizes a classic problem for democratic institutions – the dilemma of effective representation within the context of social fragmentation or 'difference'. Opening itself to heterogenous demands and initiatives, ecology has embraced and even celebrated difference without truly confronting or resolving the contradictions it creates.

The more ecology chooses to place priority on a radical democratic format as an end in itself, the more that move contradicts other goals the party may seek. Ecology parties, in France as elsewhere, may have to become more efficient to survive in politics and advance the aims of the environmental movement. The ecologists need to focus their energies on getting out their message of respect for the environment and self-development in politics more clearly and effectively.

To advance their ideas, it might nevertheless be possible for movement-based parties like the *Verts* to retain their local-level forms of mobilization (media personalities like Lalonde come and go, and thus have not been a promising alternative). Yet they would also have to accept a fairly élitist premise – for example, that the party organization itself should actively encourage mobilization at grass-roots level, and not depend on the self-motivation of intensely interested individuals. Perhaps they may discover some means of *encadrement* that could engage people in various activities in and out of the party, even in the workplace.

To send a clearer message, ecology will also need to restrain the conflicts among its various leaders – though change will depend on these leaders themselves. Alternatively, there might be some strategic accord between Left-leaning ecologists and more progressive elements from the socialist movement. The current vacuum in effective opposition to the neoliberal Right could open the door to such an accord. Even in this case, though, the two camps face the formidable task of defining their agenda. An ideological gulf lies beneath the political one dividing the Left and the greens – between the social and the ecological, between collective empowerment and individual autonomy. The new current animating the *Verts*, has recognized this divide and made tentative moves toward closing it. They have placed debate and dialogue with the progressive Left before strategic alliances. In that, they recognize that socialist politics, as much as green politics, need to be rethought before the twain can ever meet.

Notes

1. I would like to thank Kent Worcester and Sigrun Kaland for their perceptive and meticulous readings of several drafts of this chapter.
2. 'Radical participatory democracy' is the most precise term for the concept behind the ecological party model, though 'direct democracy' or 'radical democracy' are used for the sake of brevity. See David Held, *Models of Democracy* (Stanford, CA: Stanford University Press, 1987); and Carol Pateman, *Participation and Democratic Theory* (Cambridge: Cambridge University Press, 1970).
3. The analysis here and throughout has been enriched by the work of Herbert Kitschelt, especially his *Logics of Party Formation* (Ithaca, NY: Cornell University Press, 1989).
4. Regional branches elect three-quarters of the party's internal parliament, the *Conseil Nation Interrégional* (CNIR). Individual members – all with equal voting rights – elect the other quarter at an annual *Assemblée Générale*. This body also debates and votes on the party's programmatic material and strategic orientations. The CNIR selects a *Collège exécutif*, which oversees the party's regular affairs, and includes four public spokespersons. Other direct democratic institutions include an internal referendum that can be initiated with signatures from only 10 per cent of the party's members, or the requirement that elected officials cede their positions halfway through their terms. See Guillaume Sainteny, *Les Verts* (Paris: Presses Universitaires de

France, 'Que sais-je?' 1991); and Raymond Pronier and Vincent Jacques le Seigneur, *Génération Verte: Les écologistes en politique* (Paris: Presses de la Renaissance, 1992).

5.   The idea of a modern party as a 'tribune of the people' was applied to the French Communist Party by Georges Lavau, in Donald L. M. Blackmer and Sidney Tarrow, eds., *Communism in Italy and France* (Princeton, NJ: Princeton University Press, 1975).

6.   This motive for the direct democratic experiment was repeatedly expressed in interviews, conducted in March and April 1992, with *Verts* spokespersons or veterans who came from both Left–ecological and pure environmentalist currents. On similar patterns in German political ecology, see Andrei Markovits and Phillip Gorski, *The German Left: Red, Green and Beyond* (New York: Oxford University Press, 1993).

7.   Herbert Kitschelt, 'La gauche libertaire et les ecologistes français', *Revue français de science politique* 40, no. 3 (June 1990) pp. 339–65; Brendan Prendiville, 'France: Les Verts', in Ferdinand Muller-Rommel, ed., *New Politics in Western Europe* (Boulder, CO: Westview Press, 1989); Robert Ladrech, 'Social Movements and Party Systems: The French Socialist Party and New Social Movements', *West European Politics* 12, no. 3 (July 1989) pp. 262–79; and Frank Wilson, 'When Parties Refuse to Fail: The Case of France', in Kay Lawson, ed., *When Parties Fail* (Princeton, NJ: Princeton University Press, 1988).

8.   On the similarities between the programmes of early ecological groupings and the PS during the seventies, see Sainteny, *Les Verts*.

9.   Many of the *Verts'* and GE's guiding lights spent their politically formative years as activists in organizations, such as the PSU or CFDT, that had supported the PS's governmental initiatives during the seventies. Some even passed through the Socialist Party itself. Sainteny, 'Les dirigeants écologistes et le champ politique', *Revue française de science politique* 37, no. 1 (February 1987) pp. 21–32.

10. Huguette Bouchardeau, head of the PSU, became secretary of the environment in March 1993, then Minister in 1984.

11. John Grouard Mason, 'Mitterrand, the Socialists and French Nuclear Policy', unpublished doctoral dissertation (New York: CUNY Graduate Center, February 1993).

12. For more information on this current, see Jane Jenson, 'From *Baba Cool* to *Vote Utile*: The Trajectory of the French *Verts*', *French Politics and Society* 7, no. 1 (Fall 1989) pp. 1–15.

13. The score in the 1986 legislatives was only 2.74 per cent of the votes cast where an ecological candidate was present.

14. After ecology proved politically viable later, though, the party mobilized a much broader circle of activists, including many from the PSU, PCF or the extraparliamentary left. Notable among these were radical economist Alain Lipietz and Communist renegade Pierre Juquin.

15. The *Verts'* strategy for competing in elections governed by majoritarian institutions and centripetal ideological forces was to emphasize party autonomy and independence as much as possible. Specific features of this strategy were codified at the party's 1990 general assembly in Strasbourg. For example, it stipulates that the party will refuse to withdraw its candidate in favour of that of another party or, if scoring less than 10 per cent, will refuse to advise voters for the second turn. Entry into government is not closed off, but predicated on a contract stipulating some 'non-negotiable' objectives, such as moratoria on nuclear testing or the construction of new highways.

16. Sainteny, 'Chez les écologistes la désunion fait la force', *Revue politique et parliamentaire*, 958 (March–April 1992) pp. 28–34; and Jane Jenson, 'From Party Formation to Paradigm Shift: The Experience of the French Greens', unpublished

paper of the annual meeting of the American Political Science Association (San Fransisco: August 1990).

17. Roger Cans, 'La France écolo', *Le Monde*, 10 June 1992.

18. Daniel Boy's work on the ecologists over the last decade has uncovered these patterns. See three of his articles: 'Ecologistes, les frères ennemis', in Philippe Habert, Pascal Perrineau and Colette Ysmal, eds., *Le vote éclaté: Les elections régionales et cantonales des 22 et 29 mars 1992* (Paris: Presses de la Fondation Nationale des Sciences Politiques, 1992); *L'écologisme en France: Evolutions et structures* (Paris: Cahiers de CEVIPOF, 1990); and 'Le vote écologiste en 1978', *Revue française de science politique* 31, no. 2 (April 1981) pp. 394–416.

19. These figures are from CSA, SSU exit poll, April 1988; cited in Sainteny, *Les Verts*; Jean-Luc Bennhamias and Agnes Roche, *Des verts de toutes les couleurs: Histoire et sociologie du mouvement écolo* (Paris: Albin Michel, 1992); and BVA-Liberation, March 1993.

20. 'Enquête SOFRES sur les lecteurs écologistes', September 1989; cited in Bennhamias and Roche.

21. Boy found that in 1978 only 38 per cent of ecological voters chose a left-wing candidate on the second round, whereas 44 per cent came out for the Right. See Boy, 'Le vote écologiste en 1978'. Also see his *Evolutions et structures* on the shift toward a more left-wing orientation in the ecological electorate.

22. Bennhamias and Roche, *Des verts de toutes les couleurs*.

23. For example, abstention may account for the 30 per cent of first-round *Verts* voters in the presidential elections in 1988 who supported neither Mitterrand nor Jacques Chirac (see Bennhamias and Roche). Seventy-six per cent of Waechter's voters then remained with the *Verts* between the 1988 presidential elections and 1989 Europeans (Sainteny, *Les Verts*). Even with GE's presence, 46 per cent of the *Verts'* voters in the Europeans voted for the party again in the regionals of March 1992 (Boy, 'Frères ennemis'). Boy notes that massive abstentions even occurred between the first and second rounds in the 1992 cantonals, where *Verts* candidates were present. He also observes that a projection of cantonal scores shows that more leftists transferred to the *Verts* on the second round than vice versa.

24. Bennhamias and Roche, *Des verts de toutes les couleurs*.

25. The *Verts'* electorate has often been categorized as 'centrist', i.e., either moderate or apolitical, or both. See Kitschelt. In *Les Verts*, Sainteny presents a cogent and thorough counterargument to this claim.

26. Jenson, 'From *Baba Cool* to *Vote Utile*'.

27. See Monique Dagnaud and Dominique Mehl, 'Profil de la nouvelle gauche', *Revue française de science politique* 31, no. 2 (April 1981), for a profile of the new middle-class readers of the new politics magazine *Faire*, noting their orientation toward political activism and *autogestion*.

28. Tony Chafer, 'The Greens in France: An Emerging Social Movement', *Journal of Area Studies*, 10 (1984) pp. 36–43; Enquête SOFRES (June 1989) in Sainteny, *Les Verts*; and SOFRES, March 1993, cited in Roche, 'Mars 1993: une revelateur des faiblesses des écologistes', *Revue politique et parlementaire*, no. 964 (March–April 1993) pp. 34–41.

29. SOFRES (June–July 1989) in Bennhamias and Roche, *Des verts de toutes les couleurs*.

30. Roche, 'Mars 1993'.

31. Sainteny, *Les Verts*.

32. Thirty-four per cent of *Vert* voters have advanced education. Only the centrists' education level (36 per cent) exceeded that of the *Verts* (Bennhamias and Roche).

33. Gérard Grunberg and Etienne Schweisguth, 'Liberalisme culturel et liberalisme

240   *Green Politics*

économique', in Daniel Boy and Nonna Mayer, eds., *L'électeur français en question* (Paris: Presses de la Fondation Nationale de Science Politique, 1990).

34. Figures in this paragraph are from Bennhamias and Roche, *Des verts de toutes les couleurs*.
35. *Ibid.*
36. 'Enquête SOFRES,' March 1992, cited in Boy, 'Frères ennemis'. Boy points out, however, that the geographic breakdown of the vote makes the notion of a direct transfer of votes between the two parties problematic. In some areas where GE scored above or tied the *Verts'* 1989 results nationwide, the *Verts* had never themselves exceeded 5.5 per cent. Conversely, where GE did not present any candidate, the *Verts'* numbers were similar to the score they obtained in that area in 1989. On the basis of these observations, Boy concludes that much of the extra numbers that GE added to the ecologists' combined national score probably would not have gone to the *Verts*.
37. Of the PS list's voters in the 1989 European elections, SOFRES had GE gaining 8 per cent; BVA and IFOP, 9 per cent (exit polls in March 1992). From the Centrist list in 1989, those organizations had it gaining 7 per cent, 8 per cent or 12 per cent, respectively (Boy, 'Frères ennemis'). Boy, 'Les écologistes en France', *French Politics and Society* 10, no. 2 (Summer 1992).
38. For an analysis of the disadvantages in party competition for a radically democratic organization such as the *Verts*, see Tad Shull, 'The Ecologists in the Regional Elections: Strategies behind the Split', *French Politics and Society* 10, no. 2 (Spring 1992) pp. 13–29.
39. Kitschelt, *Logics*. The term 'perverse effects' was first used by Raymond Boudon, *Effets pervers et ordre social* (Paris: Presses Universitaires de France, 1977).
40. Jenson, 'From *Baba Cool* to *Vote Utile*'.
41. See Pronier and le Seigneur, *Génération Verte*.
42. F. Chirot, in *Le Monde*, 14 June 1994; and V. Schneider, *Libération*, 13 June 1994.
43. For example, BVA-*Libération*, January 1993.
44. The new ecologists deliberately borrowed names or designed voting bulletins that resembled those of the more familiar ecological parties (for example, '*Génération Verte*'). Their background ranged from disgruntled GE members to Moon sectarians.
45. On the significance of this shift for France, see Pierre Rosanvallon, 'Malaise dans la représentation', in François Furet, Jacques Julliard and Rosanvallon, *La République au Centre: Fin de l'exception française* (Paris: Calman-Levy, 1988).

13 The Politics of *Égalité Professionnelle*: As Symbolic Reform becomes More Symbolic

Amy G. Mazur

In the early 1980s, the Socialist government formulated and implemented a new equal employment policy for women (EEP). The 1983 *égalité professionnelle* law was intended to reduce gender-based disparities in paid employment. Like other social reforms of the Mitterrand era discussed in this volume, the 1983 law was an integral part of the Socialist Party's governing agenda. Likewise, like many social policies undertaken before the U-turn, party platform status did not necessarily translate into concrete reform. Still, in 1981, experts and advocates of equal employment policy were optimistic that the new Socialist government would formulate authoritative legislation to fill in the gaps of past equal employment laws adopted under Centre–Right governments.[1] From the very beginning of the Mitterrand era, however, it was clear that there would be constraints on the impending reform. The effect of the 1983 *égalité professionnelle* law has been limited to symbolic policy.[2]

Indeed, from the moment the Socialist policymakers agreed to sponsor the new legislation, only about a dozen advocates in trade unions, political parties, ministerial offices for women and academia were concerned with making policy that effectively improved women's inferior position in paid labour. Outside of this small and relatively powerless community, most actors in the state – ministers, heads of labour administrations and parliamentarians – and in society – representatives of employer associations and trade unions – supported EEP as long as the principles of gender-based equality in employment that the new policy encompassed were not tangibly implemented.

As the Socialist government moved toward what Anthony Daley calls 'new individualism' in policy in the late 1980s and early 1990s, the programmes generated by the 1983 law became even more symbolic. The transformation of the Left during this period, underpinned by the erosion of France's economic policy autonomy, created a political environment even less likely to concretely promote EEP. This chapter will trace the formation of the 1983 *égalité professionnelle* law through the policy process, including the stages of problem-definition, agenda-setting, formulation, implementation and evaluation.

PROBLEM DEFINITION AND AGENDA-SETTING

In the late 1970s, the EEP community had criticized the efforts of Raymond Barre's government to address gender inequities in employment through pilot retraining programmes for women sponsored by Nicole Pasquier, the Deputy Minister of Women's Employment. A 1982 study of these programmes showed retraining women and placing them in 'male' jobs did not stop job discrimination.[3] In 1981, the Women's Work Committee (*Comité du Travail Féminin*, or CTF[4]) published a disparaging report on the progress of women's rights at work, drawing particular attention to the inadequate nature of past government policy in this area.[5] In 1978, Pasquier had commissioned a report on gender-based disparities in employment.[6] The commission, headed by Jacques Baudoin, consulted labour market experts and representatives from trade unions, employer associations and women's groups to analyse the problems associated with women's employment. Reflecting critiques from the EEP community, the final Baudoin report pointed out the deficiencies of past policy and the need for new legislation. It included draft legislation that presented a firm-level approach to occupational segregation. The approach, called *égalité professionnelle*, was quite similar to the Socialist legislation that would be proposed in 1981.

The concept of *égalité professionnelle* emerged through a process in which the definition of the problem of gender discrimination as occupational segregation was being coupled to certain policy proposals. The idea of hiring quotas had been rejected by the state feminists in the CTF in a 1979 report,[7] by the tripartite Baudoin Commission and by the Constitutional Council on the grounds that the potential to discriminate against women (by setting a ceiling that could be eventually surpassed) as well as against men (by automatically excluding men from certain positions) outweighed the benefits of a quota system.[8]

Instead, policy solutions to the problem of gender-based inequalities in the work force were based on different versions of *égalité professionnelle*. In this approach, gender discrimination would be attacked at the firm-level through company-level works councils.[9] This new orientation was promoted by the Baudoin report, the 1979 CTF report, bill proposals presented by the *Parti Communiste Français* (PCF) and the PS in the late 1970s, and the positions of the left-wing trade confederations, the *Confédération Française Démocratique du Travail* (CFDT) and the *Confédération Générale du Travail* (CGT).

Supporters of EEP also agreed that trade unions and women's associations should be allowed to prosecute discrimination cases. One of the major criticisms of the 1972 equal pay law and 1975 equal treatment law was that women were left on their own to prosecute their cases. The firm-level approach of *égalité professionnelle* necessarily implied an increased role for trade union representatives in fighting gender discrimination, especially because management reports on the status of women would be presented to works councils.

Although *égalité professionnelle* had been developed by EEP activists, it appealed to mainstream policy makers because responsibility for gender-based disparities could be diffused to firms without involving additional government funds or over-burdening management, trade unions or works councils. But strong non-partisan support for *égalité professionnelle* only existed as long as provisions of the law were not made compulsory. Mainstream policy actors consistently opposed provisions that made participation in the new policy a legal requirement or precondition for any government subsidy.

In 1980, responding to the growing support for legislated *égalité professionnelle* and pressure from the Socialists given the upcoming elections, Pasquier followed the suggestions of the Baudoin Report and drafted a bill proposal that officially articulated the various strands of the notion of *égalité professionnelle*. The Council of Ministers approved the proposal two months before the presidential elections of April–May 1981. Any parliamentary discussion of the Pasquier proposal was interrupted by the elections and ensuing legislative elections, which brought in a new president and parliament.

The *égalité professionnelle* bill that Yvette Roudy, the Socialist head of Ministry for the Rights of Women (*Ministère des Droits de la Femme*, or MDF), proposed one year later reflected non-partisan appeal for weak *égalité professionnelle*.[10] The Roudy bill was formulated in a more favourable political environment than the Pasquier bill. The convergence between the definition of certain problems related to gender-based discrepancies in employment and a policy proposal appealing to a wide range of political actors coincided with the arrival of the Left to power and the appointment of an activist women's ministry in 1981. In this manner, a second policy window opened for EEP. Only this time, Yvette Roudy pushed draft legislation onto the parliamentary agenda before the window could snap shut. Even though the Socialist government was committed to acting on its agenda for social reform during the first two years of Mitterrand's term, the *égalité professionnelle* bill – proposed by the women's ministry and marginalized from the government's main policy concerns – was not a top priority.

Especially in the area of workplace reform, the Roudy bill had a lower priority than the Auroux Laws of 1982–3, which aimed to improve the rights of workers in the workplace (see Chapter 7). One such law mandated, for example, that management include a report on salaries by gender in annual reports presented to the works councils.[11] Therefore, seven days before the Roudy law would be approved by the Council of Ministers in September 1982, policy actors were asked to formulate a complex set of laws that changed the nature of industrial relations at the grass-roots level.

The Auroux Laws, which involved the same complex sectoral and ministerial consultation as the Roudy law, first monopolized the attention of unions and employers, then preoccupied the parliamentarians. When Roudy's turn came several months later, many mainstream policy makers and social partners felt that her bill replicated government efforts already in place. One official who took part in drafting the bill maintained that the government and the major trade unions were more dedicated to the Auroux Laws than to the *égalité professionnelle* law. Mainstream ministers and unions and employers resisted the stronger provisions of the original bill proposed by the MDF because of the low priority given it by the Socialist government. Because only the EEP community was interested in formulating and implementing an effective bill, the outcome of the agenda-setting process was inevitably symbolic.

FORMULATING SYMBOLIC REFORM

Immediately following the Socialists' victory in the presidential and parliamentary elections, when *égalité professionnelle* was being placed low on their decision agenda, Yvette Roudy's cabinet began to draft an EEP bill. In addition to being a top priority for the PS feminists in the MDF, justification for the bill also came from European Community policy.[12] A letter from the ministry to the French Council of Ministers outlining the draft legislation mentioned that French legislation was not up to speed with EC policy.[13] While pressure from the EC may have provided justification for moving ahead on the EEP legislation, the EC wielded little power to enforce equal employment policy for women in member countries.

Because of the wide appeal for weak *égalité professionnelle* legislation, provisions that would have given the new policy authority were eliminated by the time the bill was approved by the Council of Ministers in September 1982. One of the first casualties was the elimination of a minimum quota for women in all technically oriented national training programmes. The *Conseil National du Patronat Français*, trade unions and the ministries of Professional Training and Labour were hostile to the idea of quotas. In public, opponents to quota systems claimed that setting a minimum quota would lead to reverse discrimination.

The initial disapproval of a quota system by the major policy actors meant that models of affirmative action from the United States would not be acceptable in France. Consequently, the MDF team developed an alternative to quotas that still provided a means by which women could catch up to their male counterparts in training, salaries and promotions. This alternative, called *rattrapage*, was contained in the *plans d'égalité* first proposed in late 1981. These plans would be initiated after management made the annual report on the position of men and women in the firm to the works council. The major causes of any gender-based disparities would be identified by the works council, and a plan would be designed to remedy inequities. The plan would be turned into a contract to be signed by worker representatives and management. Together, they would outline a long term plan to reduce the inequities through preferential training, hiring and promotion.

Central to the success of these plans would be the annual report on the status of women in the firm presented by management to the works council. Guidelines for what management should include in the report were not specified in the original legislation. In the first version of the bill, firms would only receive state benefits if they filed an annual report. PS state feminists also suggested that labour inspectors fine firms that did not present the reports. However, making these reports and the subsequent equality plans obligatory rendered the legislation too strong for all but the EEP community.

For instance, in a meeting on the draft legislation the Finance Minister, Jacques Delors, expressed 'hostility to any measures that would aggravate cost to enterprises' and opposition to any state funding of equality plans.[14] The ministry eventually cut the proposed budget for the plans in half. Trade unions and employer associations resisted the added burden of another annual report. Given this non-partisan opposition to the required annual report, the final version of the bill omitted any compulsory participation in either the equality plans or the reports. As one member of the Roudy team said: 'The government cannot mandate *égalité professionnelle*.'[15]

Another key provision of the original bill was the creation of an autonomous administrative authority that would oversee the formulation of equality plans, ensure the filing of annual reports and help women with discrimination cases. Regional representatives would be the eyes and ears of the agency at the local level. These offices would also arbitrate specific discrimination cases in the same way the equal employment commissions did in the United States and Great Britain.

This provision was eliminated from the final draft legislation by the same non-partisan lineup of forces that had struck down the required annual reports. Opponents argued that the creation of such an agency outside of the system of normal policy enforcement would undermine the established pattern of labour code enforcement. The *Direction des Relations du Travail* (DRT), the national office in charge of labour code enforcement through the Labour Inspectorate, would have its authority as the 'only institution in its administrative domain to pursue work code infractions' threatened.[16] The DRT preferred instead that the implementation of the new legislation be undertaken by the existing administrative structures, suggesting that an unnecessary reorganization of the work administration would otherwise take place.[17] In light of this resistance, Roudy was urged to consider making this new agency's mandate control over trafficking of immigrant labour, a role that would give the agency little power or autonomy. The new authority would have some input into *égalité professionnelle* measures but would not supersede the authority of the established work inspectorate.

The original bill had also sought to give feminist associations the right to prosecute discrimination cases in court. However, the trade unions argued that they could be the only legitimate representatives of workers' interests in work-related litigation. Allowing women's groups to enter trade unions' domain would threaten their already limited control over the workplace. This was especially critical given the overall decline in the rate of unionization in the early 1980s.[18] Although the Women's Ministry was sympathetic to the demands of feminists who sought this legal right, it acquiesced to the trade unions, who held much more influence over the Socialist government than did the much weaker feminist groups.

The Minister of Justice found the penalties for discriminatory practices included in the original version of the bill too strict and recommended lowering the length of prison terms and the level of fines. The CGT blocked efforts to eliminate automatically all clauses in the work code that discriminated against women, such as protectionist clauses. The trade union had traditionally taken the position that the sections of the labour code that protected women should not be eliminated, but rather extended to men.

A final area of compromise that reduced the effectiveness of the 1983 law regarded the burden of proof in equal treatment and salary discrimination cases. The original bill had shifted the burden of proof to the employer. However, the ministers of Justice and Economy objected to this measure since employers would have to justify minor employment decisions. The Women's Ministry team negotiated a compromise that gave the judge authority to decide whether the defendant had to provide proof of non-discrimination.

When draft legislation was finally presented to the Council of Ministers, little opposition was expected. The Council of Ministers approved the bill on 29 September 1982 with little enthusiasm. In a letter to 'Madame le ministre et chère amie', André Labarrère, parliamentary liaison for the prime minister, communicated the government's apathy towards the bill:

> Following your note, I promise you [informal *tu*] that I will do all that is necessary so that your bill will be examined in the shortest period of time. But I do not want to hide from you, as I already indicated to you in the Council of Ministers, that the parliamentary agenda is already excessively overloaded and you would help me a great deal in my efforts to get this text adopted if, on one hand it were adopted very quickly in the Council of Ministers and on the other hand, it were limited to only the most essential provisions.[19]

With an absolute left-wing majority composed of Communist and Socialist deputies in the National Assembly, the bill was hardly altered during parliamentary discussion and was approved in a first reading in the lower house. Only 10 out of 491 deputies were present for the first debate.[20] While the press gave some coverage to the discussion and the adoption of the bill, little public debate took place. An article in *Le Monde* reported that the 1983 *égalité professionnelle* law represented 'a noiseless change'.

Feminists and employers both expressed their opposition to the bill during the parliamentary debate. Several feminist groups in Paris organized a campaign to show the lacunae of the bill; however, the campaign failed to change the content of the legislation in this final stage. In the right-wing-controlled Senate, senators with management backing tried to introduce amendments that would reduce the effects of the law. Senators from the opposition managed to prolong debate on these amendments through a series of tactics used frequently by right-wing opposition to undermine the Socialist reforms. These efforts did not succeed; after four readings in each house and a joint commission review, the *égalité professionnelle* law was adopted.[21]

Although some of the issues of concern to EEP advocates were addressed in principle, the final law did very little to change the mechanisms of the labour market that kept women in marginal employment. In individual discrimination cases the burden of proof was not entirely shifted to the employer. The plaintiff still had to provide proof of the discriminatory act. A more sophisticated definition of equal work was elaborated, including the idea of equal worth. Unions, but not feminist associations, were given the right to defend such cases.

The 1983 law eliminated from legal codes the stipulation introduced by the 1975 equal treatment law that stated employers could treat female workers differently from men if they had a 'legitimate motive'. If an employer was brought before a court for an offence, the judge could allow the employer to present specific measures that would address the causes of the discrimination instead of invoking the normal penalties (a maximum fine of 20 000 francs or two months in prison). Henceforth, collective agreements could not include any protectionist clauses for female workers only; this stipulation was not made retroactive.

Companies were supposed to present an annual report comparing the situation of women and men in the workplace to the works council.[22] From the annual report management could formulate an equality plan (*plan d'égalité*) to be negotiated and signed by union representatives and management. If approved, the government would fund half the cost of each plan.[23] The High Council for Equal Employment (*Conseil Supérieur de l'Égalité Professionnelle*, or CSEP), a tripartite advisory body connected to the ministries of Labour, Professional Training and Women's Rights would participate in the definition and the application of public policy in this area. The council's role was limited to consultation and discussion. The *Mission de l'Égalité Professionnelle* (MEP) was created to administer the council's work. Reflecting the power relationships between the policy actors in the formulation process, the overall tone of the final law was highly voluntaristic – it lacked any real authority.

IMPLEMENTING SYMBOLIC REFORM

The MDF launched a public relations campaign to promote the new policy and sent out orders containing new administrative duties to the regional and departmental directors of the work inspectorate, lower-level work inspectors and the ministry's territorial offices.[24] Firms received a detailed pamphlet on the procedures of annual reports and equality plans. To EEP advocates in the ministry it appeared that all of the necessary steps had been taken to ensure implementation of the new law; however, by 1985 it became clear that the law's weaknesses would prevent the new *plans d'égalité* and annual reports from being taken seriously by management, *comités d'entreprise* and trade unions. Only the EEP community remained actively involved with implementation of the 1983 law. As Martine Lévy, secretary general of the CTF and longtime member of the EEP community recently suggested, '*égalité professionnelle* was a policy in which no one really believed'.[25]

Studies of the annual reports and *plans d'égalité* show that although 3000 annual reports had been filed in 1985, they tended to be incomplete and poorly updated.[26] That year, of 736 reports only 17 per cent contained the seven areas of information suggested by the law to conduct a firm-level dialogue about women's status. Another analysis found the added burden of the reports on management and labour hindered compliance.[27] Without incentives or penalties, management and union representatives did not devote the time necessary to analyse the position of women in the firm. As a result, the *plans d'égalité* were severely limited.

According to a source close to the MDF, Yvette Roudy had predicted in 1985 that 300 *plans d'égalité* would have been signed by 1986. As of June 1993, only 30 plans affecting 4000 women had been completed, with half of the firms receiving a government subsidy.[28] Union activists consistently indicated in interviews that the lengthy negotiations necessary to draw up an equality plan – often taking up to two years – were not worth the time. By 1993, only half the state funds that had been set aside for equality contracts had been used by firms. One women's association, *Retravailler*, has taken an active interest in supporting the plans. Regional affiliates of the national organization helped firms draw up several equality plans.[29] While the CFDT took initiative in several of the contracts, in 1993 the national confederation's position was that the plans were not an effective means by which to address gender inequities. The CGT also has been hesitant to get involved with drafting positive action contracts.

Several businesses have used the equality contracts to retrain female employees to deal with new manufacturing technologies or to meet the demands of newly created employee structures – not to help female workers catch up to their male colleagues. The contracts seemed more likely to be used when management perceived them to be economically beneficial to the firm. In 1989, a colloquium sponsored by the Deputy Minister of Women's Rights (*Secrétaire d'Etat aux Droits des Femmes*, or SEDF) and organized by sociologist and EEP advocate Jacqueline Laufer sought to sensitize businesses to *égalité professionnelle* and to energize the stagnant policy effort. One principal thrust of the conference was to show firms how the equality plans could be used to modernize the work force.[30] But only three additional contracts have been signed since the conference.

Nor has there been much institutional enthusiasm on the part of the French state. Until 1986 the CSEP and the MEP had an extremely active agenda. With a significant budget and Roudy's support, the commission's staff organized a dizzying series of sub-commissions to further examine EEP. The MEP published a bimonthly newsletter on its work as well as annual reports on the work of the sub-commissions. It has been suggested that the large volume of work in these two years had little impact and that in fact the CSEP functioned primarily as a showcase for Roudy. Commission staff also judged that churning out study after study prevented the commission from having a more authoritative role.

From 1986 to 1988, under the cohabitation of a left-wing president and a right-wing prime minister, the work of the CSEP came to a halt. The new Delegation of Women's Status (*Déléguée à la Condition Féminine*, or DCF) replaced the MDF and was demoted to a lower rank, under the Minister of Social Affairs. Hélène Gisserot, the new delegate, did not call the CSEP into session until January 1988, and its sub-commissions were disbanded. The few staff members who remained tried to aid the ongoing equality contracts and maintain an active voice for *égalité professionnelle* within the right-wing government.

Gisserot gave the CSEP no new policy orders for an entire year and spent the first six months of her term conducting an administrative audit of the ministry. The agencies, products of PS feminism inextricably linked to the personality of Yvette Roudy (especially in the eyes of the Chirac government), did not have a favourable environment in which to work. The linkages between the implementation of the 1983 law and the electoral fortunes of the Socialist government made it difficult for a permanent administrative bureau to remain in charge of EEP.

From 1991 to 1993, Véronique Neiertz, the Deputy Minister of Women's Rights and Daily Life (*Secrétaire d'Etat aux Droits des Femmes et la Vie Quotidienne*), convened the CSEP once, following the persistent demands of the MEP staff. In 1993, the cabinet under Cohabitation II, the government of Gaullist Edouard Balladur, excluded the ministerial level office for women for the first time since 1974. The administrative services of the former SEDFVQ were left intact and were attached to the staff of the Ministry of Social Affairs, headed by centrist Simone Veil. In June 1993, Veil announced her desire to revitalize EEP through the CSEP.

Although the *Ministère des Droits des Femmes* during Yvette Roudy's tenure placed pressure on the DRT to sensitize work inspectors to gender equality, the work inspectorate has failed to oversee adequately the implementation of the law. Furthermore, any efforts to work with the inspectorate on EEP were brought to a standstill by the change in parliamentary majority in 1986. For instance, a project to make work inspectors more aware of the law was suspended under the Chirac government. After the return of the Socialists to government in 1988, no new directives were given to the labour inspectorate about the 1983 law.

There are several explanations for the failure of the work inspectorate and the DRT to implement the EEP law. The DRT has always been hostile to any added responsibilities, especially in the area of gender-related work policy. Work inspectors at all levels tend to be generally overloaded with the demands of a complex set of labour laws. Given the time limits of each inspector, he or she chooses which regulations to enforce. The additional responsibility of watching for cases of gender-based discrimination and making sure that annual reports were presented, then, was not welcomed. And many work inspectors were not even aware of the new regulations.

Labour inspectors asserted in interviews that female labour inspectors were more likely to enforce the new stipulations than male inspectors. Attempts to promote the new programmes affiliated with *égalité professionnelle* were isolated. One EEP activist in the DRT emphasized the need for more women at all levels of the inspectorate to promote the enforcement of the 1983 law. Without more female labour inspectors, she maintained, such laws fail to penetrate the culture of the work inspectorate.

Another problem with enforcement of the new law was the established approach of the work inspectorate to female workers. In the past, work inspectors had dealt with female employees through the protectionist provisions of the labour code. Reflecting the older approach to women in paid labour, after 1983 the Central Mission for the DRT continued to record infractions as violations of the protectionist clauses rather than instances where inspectors had intervened in favour of women's rights.[31]

Because Socialist governments never instructed the national school for the work inspectorate to include *égalité professionnelle* in its training programme, no new patterns of behaviour were established. The implementation of the 1983 law, then, would always be dependent on pressure emanating from the Women's Ministry. After 1986, when there was no institutionalized programme to promote EEP in the work inspectorate, enforcement of EEP programmes was increasingly subject to the discretion of each work inspector.

The regional and departmental delegates of women's rights also were supposed to monitor implementation of the law. There were delegates in all 12 regions and three-quarters of the departments. Each delegation was given a small budget and minimal staffs to oversee the administration of all policies for women. Some of the departmental delegates did not receive a salary. Regional and departmental delegates consistently complained of an overloaded work schedule and insufficient funds and staff. The programmes and policy initiatives carried out by each delegation depended greatly on the interests of the particular delegate.

Égalité professionnelle programmes were not consistently implemented by the territorial administrations. Because the national ministry gave no clear implementation orders for the 1983 law, only those delegates with expertise in industrial relations and connections with trade unions at the local level promoted the new legislation. Out of the four women's rights administrators interviewed, two of them had promoted different aspects of the 1983 law. Once the pressure from the national ministry dropped after 1986, the delegates had less impetus to oversee the EEP measures.

EVALUATING SYMBOLIC REFORM

In 1994, the policy community involved with promoting gender equity in employment agreed that government policies have fallen short of providing effective solutions to the causes of women's persistent marginalization and segregation in the labour force. A 1993 report on EEP prepared by the Deputy Ministry of Women's Rights for the International Labour Office contained four critiques. First, women's employment status in relations to men's has either stagnated or worsened in the 1980s. Second, this inferior status has been partially caused by 1980s government policies (Socialist and right-wing) to create part-time work opportunities. Third, as in the past, employment policy for women in 1993 continued to be pulled in two directions by a dual logic embedded in French labour law consisting on one hand of outdated notions of protecting women in paid labour, and on the other of promoting gender equality in employment. Fourth, in part as a result of these contradictions, EEP programmes have done little to equalize employment choices and opportunities between men and women.[32]

A more detailed examination of these arguments underlines the extent to which French observers concur that *égalité professionnelle* policy has failed to address the causes of gender-based employment disparities and, consequently, has become increasingly symbolic and less tangible in the early 1990s. First, while women continued to enter paid employment at higher rates than men in the 1980s, female workers became increasingly marginalized from higher-paying, full-time positions. In 1989, women filled 75 per cent of all low-skilled jobs in the service sector and held 28 per cent of mid-level management jobs, a 4 per cent increase since 1982. In 1992, the average gap between men's and women's hourly pay was at 30 per cent, having changed little throughout the 1980s. Women were twice as likely as men to receive the minimum wage in 1992.[33] In the late 1970s and early 1980s, significant gender-based differentials began to be identified in unemployment rates. In 1985, there were 4.5 per cent more women than men on the unemployment rolls. And young women were 8 per cent more likely than men of the same age to be unemployed.[34]

Second, in the early eighties, when the Socialist government was encouraging the creation of part-time jobs, women increasingly worked in part-time positions. From 1978 to 1985, the percentage of employed women in part-time labour increased from 15.8 per cent to 21.8 per cent. In the same time period, the percentage of men's paid labour in part-time work went from 2.2 per cent to 3.2. per cent.[35] In 1989, 83 per cent of part-time work in the service sector was held by women and one out of every four women who worked held a part-time job.[36]

Experts of women's employment patterns have argued that although policy makers assume that women seek part-time work in order to resolve family and professional conflicts, many women actually take part-time jobs because they have no other choice.[37] As critics maintain, the consensus between some unions, management and government officials around part-time work only emerged because it was viewed as an option for working mothers, not for 'real' workers who want a full-time job. Therefore, at the same time that state feminists in the MDF were developing programmes to extend equal opportunity to female workers, other policy actors were promoting a policy that helped restrict women's employment choices.[38]

Third, critics have argued since the mid-1960s that an outdated protectionist approach to female workers in French labour law has been an important obstacle to *égalité professionnelle*. EEP advocates point out that the prohibition of women from working at night in certain sectors is particularly emblematic of the lingering presence of the 19th century tradition of protecting women workers. Despite a 1986 law that partially lifted the ban on women's night work, French law still formally prevents women from working between 8 p.m. and 5 a.m. in heavy industry, public services, liberal professions and associations.[39] However, since a 1991 decision of the European Court of Justice declared that such laws violated a 1976 directive on equal treatment for men and women, this law has not been enforced. To date, government efforts to formulate legislation to formally lift the ban on night work have been stalled, however, by intense trade union opposition to the elimination of what is seen as established worker rights.[40]

Despite the new developments in European law, policy actors involved with the enforcement and implementation of employment policy tend to perpetuate this protectionist logic. More than a century before it was given the responsibility for enforcing the new equal employment laws of the 1970s and 1980s, the labour inspectorate dealt with female workers through protective regulations, and this tradition continues.[41] In interviews, labour inspectors asserted that already overloaded inspectors tend to stress the more established protective approach to women's employment over the newer, more complicated *égalité professionnelle* provisions.

Fourth, the EEP community has drawn attention to the failure of societal actors to become involved in the equal opportunity programmes first introduced by the 1983 *égalité professionnelle* law. A multitude of unofficial and official evaluations have shown that the failure of the annual reports and equality plans has contributed to the absence of effective policies to counteract the narrowing of women's employment choices and their increasing marginalization from fulltime, permanent positions.[42] Management and labour representatives have been reluctant to oversee the work necessary to fill out the annual reports on men's and women's status in the firm. While employers see the reports as an administrative constraint, union organizations, works councils and state work inspectors all could have placed pressure on management to fill them out but did not. Moreover, women's and feminist groups have taken little interest in the annual reports. As a result, only 30 per cent of all businesses submitted reports in 1992.[43]

In reaction to the indifference to EEP programmes and the relatively recent fall of women's status in the labour force, state feminists have made repeated efforts to re-energize equal employment policy for women. But these measures have done little to render EEP any more effective. In 1987, following the recommendations of the CSEP, Gisserot issued a decree that gave firms with fewer than 50 employees the opportunity to receive government funding to improve the position of individual women in the firm, usually through training opportunities. In 1992, 500 women had benefited from these grants.[44]

In 1988, the European Court of Justice condemned France for violating the

1976 European Community directive on equal treatment. France was found in violation because collective employment agreements signed by labour and management included clauses that gave working mothers dispensations – maternity leave, for example – that were not extended to working fathers. In response to the EC violation, the Socialist government passed a law in 1989 that called for a revision of the discriminatory agreements and gave labour and management representatives two years to omit the gender-biased clauses by extending parental rights to male workers. A 1991 report submitted to the *Assemblée Nationale* showed that out of 307 national collective agreements in violation, 80 still contained discriminatory wording.[45]

The 1989 law also included an article that provided the opportunity for businesses of 50 employees or more to conduct an in-depth study of women's status in the firm and eventually to sign a convention to promote women's status in the firm. According to one of the individuals who drafted the 1989 bill, this article was snuck into the bill at the last minute as the result of the pressure placed on the Socialist parliamentary group by deputy Yvette Roudy. As state feminists involved with EEP asserted, these new measures had little to do with calculated efforts to reformulate EEP. As a result, the government made no specific efforts to implement the new law and did not institute funding for the new programmes until April 1992.[46] In the summer of 1993, according to the staff of the MEP, no businesses had applied for the new funding.

In 1990, Roudy, in her new capacity as Socialist deputy, mayor and president of the women's section of the PS, presented yet another official report on *égalité professionnelle*.[47] That same year, the Socialist parliamentary group in the *Assemblée Nationale*, under Roudy's initiative, registered a bill on *égalité professionnelle entre les femmes et les hommes*, but it was never passed. Two years later, on 12 March 1992, during an official meeting of the Socialist government, the SEDF's Véronique Neiertz announced that her ministry was constituting a working group to study equal employment between men and women in the firm. This group had no connection with the CSEP. Socialist deputy and PS activist Ghislaine Toutain was put in charge of the study.[48] Toutain's report replicated the findings of previous reports: apathy of social actors in the firm and limited scope of the *plans d'égalité*.[49]

Thus, since 1984, EEP has consisted of a proliferation of reports that show the deficiencies of *égalité professionnelle* programmes and public policy statements that rehash the same failed programmes. The plethora of state feminist initiatives has had little concrete effect on employment practices toward women. Repeatedly, state feminist ministries have called upon employers, trade unions and women's associations to participate in the revitalization of EEP. Dutifully, the various groups contacted have sent representatives to CSEP meetings. At the same time, the low number of *plans d'égalité* suggests management's refusal to embrace *égalité professionnelle*, as well as the reluctance of organizations that represent working women to exert any pressure on employers. As the 1993 SEDF report observed, the two major trade union confederations have abandoned 'positive action strategies' for more 'classic' approaches to inequality, which include in large part the call for more part-time work for women, as long as the work is chosen by women and not 'forced' upon them.[50]

In 1994, the only actors actively involved with EEP are the state feminists in the *Service des Droits Des Femmes* and in the *Délégations Régionales* and *Départmentales des Droits des Femmes* and a few EEP experts in the CFDT, the PS and academia. As the members of this community argue, the bipartisan consensus on the creation of part-time jobs earmarked for female workers, and the protectionist approach of labour law, continue to limit women's employment opportunities and contradict *égalité professionnelle* policies, which aim to guarantee that women have the same labour-market opportunities as men. Moreover, because of the absence of jurisprudence to effectively sanction discriminatory employment practices, anti-discrimination laws have done little to negate the trend toward what Jane Jenson has called 'the separate but unequal treatment of women in paid labour'.[51]

The norms and practices of France's legal system have posed formidable obstacles to the pursuit of employment equity through the courts.[52] Not only have there been few discrimination cases, but only a small number of decisions have been in favour of victims.[53] Among those, none have involved class-action suits (which are virtually absent from French law) and settlements have been minimal. Although important appellate court decisions have interpreted the meaning of 'equal value' in litigation, French judicial review, in which legislation is only examined by the Constitutional Court before adoption, prevents jurisprudence from concretely affecting anti-discrimination law.[54] As a result, interest groups involved with the rights of working women have not actively used the courts to promote employment equality.

CONCLUSION

An examination of the 1983 *égalité professionnelle* law shows that the seeds for symbolic politics are sown when the political agenda is set. The low placement of *égalité professionnelle* on the Socialist agenda set the stage for the compromises of policy formulation. In all conflicts over the content of the 1983 law, the winners were the mainstream interests in labour, management and the state, and the losers were female workers who sought equality.

Outside of the very narrow circle of EEP activists, very few societal interests have contributed to the programmes initiated by the 1983 law. Not only have over-burdened trade unions increasingly lost interest in *égalité professionnelle*, but women's associations and feminist groups have done little to promote the new laws, partially due to the exclusion of those groups from taking up the defence of discrimination cases. The dearth of new discrimination cases after the passage of the law underlines the lack of institutional support for victims of direct discrimination. The failure of the state to produce a permanent administrative structure to oversee implementation of EEP programmes suggests that this policy will continue to be dependent on the presence of a strong state feminist voice within government. When governments no longer pay attention to this voice – which has been the case since 1986 – the programmes associated with the 1983 law become less tangible. While the Socialists may have introduced a more authoritative approach to dealing with gender-based inequities in paid employment than right-wing governments did, their retreat in the 1980s increasingly relegated EEP to purely symbolic reform.

Notes

1. See Amy Mazur, *Gender Bias and the State: Symbolic Reform at Work in Fifth Republic France* (Pittsburgh: University of Pittsburgh Press, 1995).
2. Symbolic reform occurs when the demands of unorganized interests for change are met in a policy settlement that 'is mostly meaningless in its effects on resource allocation'. Murray Edelman, *The Symbolic Uses of Politics* (Urbana: University of Illinois Press, 1965) p. 24.
3. Anne-Marie Grozelier, A. Labourie Racapé, M. Appert, C. Baron and G. Gontier, 'Diversification de l'emploi féminin', Centres d'Etudes de l'Emploi, Dossier de Recherches, no. 8, 1982.
4. As an advocate for women's rights at work within the government, the CTF brought together representatives from trade unions, women's groups, employers organizations and experts to discuss problems related to women in the work force. Starting as a study group, the consultative body was upgraded to a ministerial committee in 1971. The heads of this committee throughout its tenure were right-wing. For further analysis of the CTF see Martine Lévy, *Le féminisme d'état en France, 1965–1985: 20 ans de prise en charge institutionelle de l'égalité professionnelle entre hommes et femmes*, unpublished doctoral thesis (Paris: Institut d'Études Politiques, 1988).
5. CTF, *Droit et travail des femmes, Un Bilan critique*, Ministère du Travail et de la Participation (January 1981).
6. Jacques Baudoin, ed., *Le Rapport Baudoin: Les discriminations et les disparités du travail féminin* (Paris: Documentation Française, 1980).
7. CTF, *L'avis sur la question des quotas*, report for the Ministry of Labour, 1979.
8. A landmark Constitutional Council decision in November 1982 struck down a law that had stipulated 75 per cent of municipal election slates could be of the same sex.
9. Works councils give employees representation for decision-making in some job-related issues, such as working conditions, although they have traditionally been limited to more integrative activities of the company. In larger firms where workers are organized, trade unions have the potential for control. See Chapter 8.
10. The similarity between the two bills does not stop at the content. A key member of

the team of administrators that put together the Pasquier bill also contributed his expertise to the drafting of the Roudy bill. Much of his expertise had been drawn from a visit to Washington to observe the mechanics of equal opportunity policy in the United States.

11. *Syndicalisme*, 20 October 1983.
12. The women's bureau in the European Commission had initiated three major directives to enforce principles of gender equality in employment in the member nations. They were adopted in the 1970s.
13. 'Communication du Ministre au Conseil des Ministres: Rappel des Principales Dispositions du Texte', 29 September 1982.
14. 'Compte Rendu [Minutes] de la réunion tenue avec le Ministre de l'Économie et des Finances', 4 April 1982
15. Interview with François Brun, February 1989.
16. 'Note à Madame le Ministre' from Brun, 20 January 1982.
17. 'Compte Rendu de la réunion du 29 avril avec le Ministère du Travail sur le Projet de loi relatif à l'égalité professionnelle', 7 May 1982.
18. Henry W. Ehrmann and Martin Schain, *Politics in France* (New York: Harper Collins, 1992) Chapter 5.
19. Letter from André Labarrère to Yvette Roudy, 30 July 1982.
20. *Libération*, 12 June 1982.
21. For the National Assembly see *Journal Officiel* (6 December 1982) pp. 7978–8019; (13 June 1983) 2460-8; (27 June 1983) 3252–5; (30 June 1983) 2390–2. For the Senate see *JO* (11 May 1983) pp. 805–17; (21 June 1983) 1809–18; (26 June 1983) 2066–71.
22. In the first year of implementation, only those companies with 300 or more employees were requested to present the report. The following year, firms with 50 or more employees were supposed to participate.
23. Decree no. 84–136, 22 February 1984.
24. Since 1978, the government had put into place women's rights offices at the regional and departmental levels.
25. Lévy, p. 245.
26. CREDOC, *Evolution 1984–1985 des rapports sur la situation comparée des hommes et des femmes dans l'entreprise* (February 1986); CREDOC, *L'égalité professionnelle entre les hommes et les femmes – 1984 première année d'application de la loi* (December 1984); Claudine Alezra, Jacqueline Laufer, Margaret Maruani and Claire Sutter, eds., 'La mixité du travail, Une Stratégie pour l'Entreprise,' *Cahier entreprises* (3 June 1987); Laufer, 'Égalité professionnelle un atout négligé pour gérer les ressources humaines', *Revue française de gestion* (January/February 1986); Laufer, 'Egalité professionnelle et Pratiques', *Droit social*, 12 (1984).
27. Anna Arrivaben and Laurence Devillard, 'L'égalité professionnelle. Tentative d'analyse de la mise en oeuvre d'un principe à travers les premiers rapports sur l'égalite professionnelle,' *Actes juridiques* (15 September 1985).
28. GRAF, *Les Plans d'égalité professionnelle, Étude-bilan, 1983–1988* (1989) and Toutain, *L'Emploi féminin, pour une méthode de la mixité professionnelle*, Secrétariat des Droits des Femmes (Paris: Documentation Française, 1992).
29. GRAF, p. 27.
30. Laufer, 'Ressources humaines et égalité Professionnelle entre les femmes et les hommes: Stratégies et moyens d'action, Une journée d'information et d'échanges organisé par le SEDF et Jacqueline Laufer', 22 March 1989.
31. Mission Centrale d'appui et de coordination des Services extérieures du travail et de l'emploi, *L'Inspection du Travail en France. Rapport Annuel* (December 1987).
32. Annette Jobert, *Négociation Collective et Promotion de l'Egalité en France*, Rapport

pour le Bureau International du Travail, Service du Droit et des relations du Travail, Secrétariat d'État des Droits de Femmes, 1993.

33. Jobert, p. 3.
34. INSEE, *Les femmes, contours et caractères* (Paris: Documentation Française, 1991) p. 54.
35. *Ibid.* p. 49.
36. Jobert, p. 3.
37. For the most recent study see Margaret Maruani and C. Nicole-Drancourt, *La flexibilité à temps partiel* (Paris, Documentation Française, 1992). Danièle Kergoat in *Les femmes et le travail à temps partiel* (Paris, Documentation Française, 1984) presents the most cited critique of the channelling of women into part-time labour. For an excellent overview in English of the issue of part-time work see Jane Jenson, 'The Limits of "and the" Discourse: French Women as Marginal Workers', in Jenson, Elisabeth Hagen and Ceallaigh Reddy, eds., *Feminization of the Labor Force* (New York: Oxford University Press, 1988) pp. 155–72.
38. State feminists, or 'femocrats', are public officials who are appointed specifically to design, implement and evaluate women's rights policy. See Dorothy McBride Stetson and Amy Mazur, eds., *Comparative State Feminism* (Thousand Oaks, CA: Sage, forthcoming).
39. Jobert, p. 23.
40. *Ibid.*
41. Jean-Paul Antona, *Les Relations de l'Employeur avec L'Inspecteur du Travail* (Paris: Dalloz, 1991) p. 2.
42. Interviews with members of the MEP in 1988–9, 1991 and 1993.
43. Jobert, p. 27.
44. *Ibid.* p. 20.
45. Ministère du travail, de l'emploi et de formation professionnelle, 'Rapport au Parlement sur l'application de l'article 8 de la loi du 10 juillet 1989 relative a l'égalité professionnelle', *La négociation collective en 1991* (Paris: Documentation Française, 1991) pp. 372–402.
46. Yves Delamotte and Daniel Marchand, *Le Droit au travail en pratique* (Paris: Editions d'Organisation, 1993) p. 225.
47. *Le Monde*, 9 March 1990.
48. *Bulletin Quotidien*, 12 March 1992.
49. See Toutain.
50. Jobert, p. 33.
51. Jenson, p. 169.
52. For a discussion of different types of legal systems see Henry Ehrmann, *Comparative Legal Cultures* (Englewood Cliffs, NJ: Prentice-Hall, 1975) or Alan Katz, 'France', In Katz, ed., *Legal Traditions and Systems: An International Handbook* (Westport, CT: Greenwood Press, 1986) pp. 105–24.
53. Because government offices do not have to officially record such cases and non-governmental organizations do not systematically track them, it is difficult to obtain an accurate count. Unofficial sources, including the CTF archives, legal articles and the files of EEP activists who have followed these cases such that there have been approximately 50 cases tried under the equal employment laws of 1972, 1975 and 1983.
54. For a discussion of French judicial review see Alec Stone, *The Birth of Judicial Politics in France* (New York: Oxford University Press, 1992).

14 Race, Immigration and the Politics of Hate
Patrick R. Ireland

A 9 May 1991 headline in the Parisian daily *Libération* summed up a turbulent decade for France's immigrants and immigration policy since the election of François Mitterrand to the presidency of the Fifth Republic: 'From the miseries of immigration to the clashes of integration.' Indeed, the debate on immigration has undergone a major transformation since the Socialists' historic victories in 1981. It has shifted from the push-pull calculus of labour recruitment to the more contentious politics of a multi-ethnic society. Increasingly, this debate is played out in the seething housing projects of the country's deindustrializing suburbs, where, fuelled by both unemployment and racism, rioting has pitted both immigrant-origin and 'native' French youths against authorities.

Immigration has merged with the deep-rooted social problems in which it has in fact always been embedded. Integrating the sizeable foreign-origin population has become one of the most essential and formidable tasks facing France, and government officials enjoy little room for manoeuvre. A potent extremist reaction to the immigrant presence has made it politically perilous for any government to tackle the problem honestly and directly. Mitterrand and the French Socialist Party (PS) met with important political and social constraints in dealing with immigration, an issue bound to turn into a political minefield. The Socialist landslide in 1981 came at a critical historical moment. Economic forces and earlier policy choices had changed the foreign worker phenomenon into true immigration. A diverse foreign-origin population had developed into a structurally essential component of French society with a claim to rights guaranteed by the republic. In the afterglow of Mitterrand's election, he and his governments employed strategies that nourished the anti-racism movement and other forms of immigrant political mobilization. But at the same time, the Socialists' electoral tactics also helped propel France toward a new politics of hate. By the early 1990s, the sorcerer in the Élysée had lost control over his apprentices, and the Left stood divided and seemingly helpless in the face of widespread suburban unrest and racial tensions.

While the Socialists' record on immigration fuelled the explosive social conditions in France's decaying suburbs, it also contributed to the rediscovery of traditional French values of inclusion and assimilation. Thus, even the current Centre–Right government of Édouard Balladur – with its fashionably harsh stance on immigration – has only a very narrow window for policy reform.

CONTINUITY AND CHANGE IN THE IMMIGRATION PROBLÉMATIQUE BEFORE MITTERRAND

Unlike many of its European neighbors, France has long been a country of immigration. The roots of the present challenge of ethnic diversity lie in earlier developments and policies. The long process of immigrant settlement and the French institutional response to it bequeathed the Left a set of constraints and opportunities in the 1980s that differed fundamentally from those that had confronted earlier governments.

In the second half of the 19th century, the French working class underwent a rapid restructuring. The old trades were declining, and new industries, such as iron and steel, mining and chemicals, were sucking unskilled labour into Paris's suburbs, Lorraine and the Nord-Pas-de-Calais. The bulk of this new working class was formed by migrants not only from rural areas in France (Brittany, Auvergne) but also from outside the country (Italy, Poland, Belgium, Spain).

At first, the nascent French labour movement failed to welcome foreign workers. Fights broke out between French and foreign workers, especially Italians; despite their labour militancy, foreigners were seen as strike- and wage-breakers.[1] By the early 1930s, however, the French Communist Party (PCF) and the trade unions had developed a collective response to the economic crisis and organized the new working class (see Chapter 11). Wrapping their members in a web of personal and professional organizations and activities, the Communists created an encapsulated society through which immigrant workers assimilated into French society, though not without conflict. The Catholic church performed the same function for other outsiders to the political community. France's centralized school system, in the meantime, acted as the agent of political socialization for foreign workers' children.[2]

Immigrants participated alongside their French comrades in the wave of strikes and demonstrations that ushered in the Popular Front (1936–8). But the foreigners wound up serving mostly as fodder in political battles between the Right and the Left and between the Communist and non-Communist Left, causing xenophobia among the rank-and-file. By 1937, the Communists accepted the reformist position of the trade unions, adopting the slogan 'France for the French!'[3] In the end, the brief experiment in governance by the Left brought bitter disappointment and few lasting improvements for foreigners.

Their political space constricted sharply under Édouard Daladier's National Union government in 1938. Mistrust of corporations of all kinds was a legacy of the French Revolution. Not until 1884 did legislation finally legalize trade unions and recognize foreign workers' right to join them. A 1901 law eliminated the remaining restrictions on the right of individuals, immigrants included, to join and form associations. In April 1939, however, Prime Minister Daladier issued a decree that forced 'foreign' associations to obtain preliminary authorization from the interior minister.[4] The 1939 decree was born of the fear that fascist Italy and

Nazi Germany might use such associations to undermine the French government but remained in force long after France's liberation in 1944.

By the eve of World War II, the legal framework that would determine immigrants' place in the French political system until 1981 was largely in place.[5] The nature of labour immigration itself, however, would prove very different after Liberation. With a demographic gap created by more than a million wartime casualties, France needed immigrants. Officials wanted a stable, ethnically balanced inflow of workers who could be assimilated.[6] The demographic rationale for immigration and assimilation had always been as important as the demand for cheap labour in France, where worries about low population growth have gnawed since Napoleon's rule. Naturalization laws were designed 'to make Frenchmen out of foreigners'.[7]

General Charles de Gaulle sought a more consistent and co-ordinated approach to immigration after World War II. He pushed through an expansive, reformed Nationality Code in October 1945 and an *ordonnance* on 2 November 1945 that still regulates the residence and employment of foreigners in France. The creation of the National Office of Immigration (ONI) established a government monopoly over immigration. Immigration was to be a matter for technocrats.

Yet economic forces would soon override demographic concerns and change the entire immigration calculus. By the mid-1950s, the French post-war economic recovery was creating heightened demand for unskilled labour. For the first time, labour immigration into France took the form of the massive importation of an evermore diverse range of national groups: in addition to Italians (most numerous as late as 1959), waves of Iberians, Serbs, Algerians, Moroccans, Tunisians, sub-Saharan Africans and Turks followed each other in quick succession in the 1960s and early 1970s. The newcomers were increasingly unskilled workers from rural, uneducated backgrounds.

This diversification of the sources of immigrant labour was in part an intentional effort by French authorities to introduce selectivity and economic competition among the various ethnic groups and thereby depoliticize their presence. The ONI solidified the hierarchy of national groups by creating and renewing bilateral accords with homeland governments. Each nationality's situation varied with its alleged ability to melt into French society and with the political weight of the sending country, with non-European workers considered an 'unassimilable island'.[8] Industry was clamouring for more immigrant workers, though. The government lost control over the influx, and in practice French officials permitted undocumented immigration. By the end of the 1960s, 70 per cent to 80 per cent of all immigrants entered France 'spontaneously' in search of labour market opportunities.[9]

French working-class organizations were also challenged by new political and economic circumstances. In general, the 'assimilation machines' of the inter-war period, the PCF and its allied *Confédération Générale du Travail* (CGT), functioned for post-war Italian and Spanish workers. Since the government could expel any foreigner who menaced 'public order', autonomous action was risky. And in keeping with Lenin's Third International formula of 'one working class and one working-class party in every state', the PCF and CGT required foreign Communists to organize under their auspices.[10] Still, as the foreign labour force grew more ethnically diverse, it proved difficult for both the Communist and non-Communist Left to fit the newcomers into their traditional, class-based analysis.

When French organizations failed to defend new foreign workers' grievances, they adopted confrontational tactics to address the political system. They first appeared as autonomous actors during the events of May 1968. Foreign workers thereafter turned supposedly apolitical social issues into explicitly political conflicts. Racism, too, drove them to act. A law passed in July 1972 punishing racist words and deeds remained limited in its application, and physical attacks against non-European immigrants in particular were increasing in number and ferocity. Throughout the early 1970s, immigrant-led protest marches wound through the streets of French cities.

In the workplace, meanwhile, many foreign workers were struggling with the corset imposed by the French Left. In a series of wildcat strikes, the immigrants underscored that their interests did not intersect completely with those of the major French trade union organizations and left-wing political parties. The French labour movement gradually grew more sensitive to discrimination in their organizations, fearing immigrants might join rival ones.[11]

France's poorest neighbourhoods and municipalities, left-wing strongholds, bore the brunt of the costs and social tensions associated with large numbers of immigrants. Containing immigration issues in the *communes* helped national political élites defuse racial and ethnic tensions up to the early 1970s. By then, the social costs of immigration were swelling, as immigrant workers were neither returning to their homelands nor blending into French society.

The economic strain that followed the 1973 oil crisis brought the issue to a head. The immigration ban the following year quickened the stabilization of France's foreign population. The Giscard administration vowed to integrate France's immigrants into French institutions and society, a good intention doomed to fail because of lack of funding. Meanwhile, family reunification and illegal immigration continued. Immigrants' periods of residency in France were lengthening, and monetary inducements failed to encourage many non-European legal immigrants to return home.[12]

France, in effect, had *created* an ethnic minorities problem. *Ad hoc* post-war labour and housing policies, as well as the sheer magnitude of the population movements, had contributed to the formation of stable immigrant communities. The government's selective treatment of each had fostered collective, ethnic-based identities often lacking among arriving immigrants. As the French social welfare system steadily expanded, ties to the homelands weakened. Whereas French labour policies had insured that immigrants fell in the lowest levels of the working class, those from within the European Community enjoyed certain privileges, and the latest, non-European arrivals performed the most demeaning jobs. The ban on unauthorized foreigners' associations, as well as the requirement that they maintain political neutrality, remained in force. In response, immigrants continued to target social policies during the Giscard *septennat*: housing problems (the SONACOTRA rent strikes, 1975–80), discrimination and restrictive legislation and administrative procedures (the proposed Stoléru reform and Barre-Bonnet laws, 1979–80) became the object of undeniably political protests.

EARLY CHANGES IN POLICY AND DISCOURSE

François Mitterrand and the Socialist Party's platform promised better treatment and greater political rights for France's immigrants, including local-level voting rights. After Mitterrand's victory, immigrants flocked to the Place de la Bastille to celebrate, in a scene evocative of the parade of the united 'people of the Left' in 1936.

Once in power, Mitterrand and the PS moved quickly to implement several of their campaign pledges. Not surprisingly, given the immigrants' lack of political resources, many of these policies started out as symbolic reforms, such as the 1983 *égalité professionnelle* law (see Chapter 13). To be sure, their effects could sometimes be more substantial. Undeniably, they reduced the insecurity of foreigners residing in France. The Socialists significantly increased their ability to organize on the basis of class, ethnicity, race and even religion. The Left's honeymoon was relatively brief, however. Soon interfering were the forces that previous regimes engendered, as well as the new majority's own internal divisions. In a few years, the limits to governmental action, as well as the negative effects of some Socialist policies, had become clear.

Once in power, the Left reaffirmed the two main objectives of French immigration policy: stopping the influx and absorbing the immigrants already settled in France. Right away, though, the new government enacted more liberal policies toward family immigration. Also, it strengthened immigrants' protection against administrative abuses and deportation without due process and enacted a one-time 'regularization' programme for illegals.[13]

The PS recognized immigrants' right to live and work in France without abandoning their cultural and ethnic identity. Most significantly, with the October 1981 law – enacted at least in part because of immigrants' efforts – foreign associations became subject to the same conditions as 'French' associations. Immigrants likewise won the right to act as administrators of all associations and to receive public funding. This change influenced many of the immigrants' voluntary-association allies on the Left, who had received generous financial support from the French state: it appreciated their providing social services and other humanitarian assistance that would otherwise have been in its realm of responsibility and more of a political issue. Now, however, these groups had to compete with the immigrants' own associations for government largesse. The Catholic Federation of Support Associations for Immigrant Workers (FASTI), the Protestant social action committee CIMADE, the pro-Communist Movement Against Racism and for Friendship Between Peoples (MRAP) and others eventually had little choice but to respond with greater respect for the immigrants' political autonomy and a willingness to collaborate on an equal basis.[14]

The number of immigrant associations skyrocketed after the law passed, surpassing 4200 by the mid-1980s. They represented virtually all possible currents, 'from moral exhortation to calls to radical action'.[15] Many groups now broadened their actions: whereas before they primarily provided social services and organized folkloric and religious activities, now they were also demanding greater freedom of political expression and defending their cultural identity and worth. Immigrant associations learned from one another how to articulate demands and influence French politics. Inter-ethnic co-operation and organization intensified: for example, the Paris-based Council of Immigrant Associations of France (CAIF), friendly with the PCF and the CGT, united some 14 national-level, ethnic-based umbrella associations. Also, multi-ethnic women's associations quickly formed in the more tolerant political climate.

THE LIMITS OF REFORM

But during the global economic transformation that was wreaking havoc on the French labour market, the Socialists not only effected a U-turn on economic policy by 1983, they also adopted a noticeably harsher line on immigration. A series of developments provoked this shift: the increasing visibility of Islam, internal divisions within the Left, the unintended effects of earlier reforms, the rise of a politically active second immigrant generation and an organized anti-immigrant reaction.

Islam

The emergence of Islam as a locus of political mobilization severely tested the limits of the new tolerance. The vast majority of France's Muslims belong to Islam's Sunnite branch, which has no hierarchy or magistracy. Even though the Paris mosque, controlled by homeland authorities, liked to present itself as the official representative of Islam in France, in actuality there has never been a unifying structure that could speak for its Muslim population.

Spiritual demands from an increasingly sedentary population combined with the new associational possibilities to spur the construction of mosques. There were more than 600 Islamic places of worship in the country by the end of 1984, compared to 131 in 1976.[16] Alongside them, local Muslim cultural associations assisted members at social welfare offices, schools, police stations and city hall.

Islam appeared in the workplace as well. Laws in 1972 and 1975 had extended the voting and eligibility rights of foreign workers as employee committee members and trade-union delegates, though foreign candidates for election had to be able to 'express themselves' in French. The Auroux Laws of June 1982, intended to enlarge labour rights generally, removed that stipulation and made foreign workers eligible to sit on the labour relations tribunals (*conseils des prud'hommes*). Moreover, immigrants no longer risked expulsion for participating in militant trade union activity.

Such legal changes heightened opportunities for class-based action. A new wave of immigrant-led strikes hit Renault, Citroën and Talbot automobile plants in several areas of France from the summer of 1981 to early 1983. For the immigrants these conflicts were no longer just class struggles, they were calls for the official recognition of Islam within factory walls. Immigrants wanted not only work-related improvements, such as in employer-provided housing and job training, they also wanted Islamic prayer rooms in the factory. The strikers brought in religious leaders (imams) to facilitate co-operation.[17]

As before, competition within the pluralistic French labour movement worked to the immigrants' advantage. The CFDT encountered some success in organizing the less religious. The CGT, dominant among automobile workers, backed calls for factory prayer rooms and created a 'collective' of sympathetic imams at Renault's Billancourt plant to 'protect the mosque from any deviation'. Employers relented and found to their relief that practicing Muslims participated less often in trade union and strike activities. Eventually, management even adapted work on the line to the daily cycle of Islamic prayers.[18]

The movement had grown into a fight for the improved status of immigrant workers in heavy industry. Their militancy, albeit along institutional channels, rattled French authorities. Officials overreacted, fearing Islamic fundamentalism and foreign influence. The Labour Minister, Jean Auroux, asserted that 'we are a secular state, and we damned well intend to keep things that way'. The striking immigrant workers were, Prime Minister Mauroy declared, 'agitated by religious and political groups acting on agendas that have little to do with French social realities'.[19] Specifically, Mauroy was referring to attempts by Iran's ayatollahs to export their fundamentalist revolution to Europe.

Divisions within the Left and Halfway Reforms

In other respects as well, immigrants could sense that the bloom was off the rose. The promised extension of limited suffrage, for instance, never materialised. President Mitterrand declared that the country's state of values ('*l'état des moeurs*') precluded such a move, but really, political reasons were paramount. While the PS was joining the far Left in supporting local-level voting rights for immigrants by the late 1970s, the Socialists' Communist allies repeatedly opposed granting immigrants suffrage. Instead, they advocated their full social and trade-union rights in France and the fight for democratic rights in their homelands. In Communist-governed *communes*, PCF officials never failed to condemn racist sentiment and acts. However, as early as 1969, the Communist mayors of the Paris region had protested against the 'inequitable distribution' of immigrant workers and their families: working-class cities paid a disproportionate share of the costs associated with these 'victims of social discrimination'.[20] By the late 1970s, formal protests had degenerated into 'crude actions directed against both immigrants and French workers from overseas territories'. During the presidential campaign of 1981, as Martin Schain has written: 'These actions emerged as a co-ordinated campaign led by the national leaders of the Communist Party.'[21] Thus the Socialists risked the ire of their Communist partners when they moved to incorporate the immigrant population into French society outside the factory. When the PCF finally exited the government in 1984, the PS had a smaller base of political support for any immigration reform.

Further hobbling the Socialists were the consequences of their own reforms, many of which were incomplete. 'Administrative inertia' continued to 'blunt the force of progressive policies and programmes', even if some of the more flagrant bureaucratic abuses had been removed.[22] Gaston Defferre's political decentralization package in 1982, furthermore, gave free rein to local mechanisms of segregation, since immigrants did not enjoy full civil rights.

The Challenges of the 'Second Generation' and Le Pen

Although the reforms of 1981–2 were limited, the Left did dissuade foreign workers from employing confrontational political tactics by opening new participatory channels to them. The first immigrant generation was shifting to more accepted, assimilative forms of participation by the early 1980s. Protest did not disappear: more vulnerable illegal immigrants took up the unconventional tactics that more established immigrants were abandoning. Even more noteworthy in this regard was the appearance of a 'second generation' of immigrants. For the full century of large-scale immigration to France, several generations of immigrants had lived in the country. Yet it was not until the apparently 'unmeltable' sons and daughters of non-European workers after World War II cast doubts on the assimilative powers of French society that the second generation acquired collective visibility.

The governing Left did much to spur the formation of a politically active second-generation subculture, but it was the heavy volume of post-war family immigration into France that had made for the rapid growth of this age cohort and the challenges associated with it.[23] Its ethnic diversity reflected the successive waves of immigration into the country. Most second-generation immigrants were in the same undesirable occupational substratum as their parents. Unemployment rates were high (at least one-third in 1982), and those with jobs were largely in temporary positions that offered no security.

Caught between the host society and their parents' homelands, most of these young people saw themselves as being from France, the place of their birth and/ or upbringing. Most qualified for French citizenship or would automatically when they reached 18. Their expectations and demands differed from those of the first generation; their sense of identity and collective behavior had less to do with their social status or ethnic origin than with the web of local political, cultural and economic relationships in which they moved. Most refused to identify with the working class, rejecting a future as the 'second generation of street sweepers'.[24]

Such a rebuff upset the PCF, CGT and CFDT, already hard-pressed by the ongoing transformations of the French economy and work force. Like the army and the Catholic church, left-wing French political parties and trade unions were less and less able to help immigrants assimilate and socialize. Through part conscious choice and part disorientation and organizational constraints, the Communists failed to capitalize on the political potential in immigrant communities (see Chapter 11).

For the sons and daughters of immigrant workers, the task came to fall almost entirely on the schools, which tended to marginalize those unable or unwilling to adapt.[25] As a result of post-war policy choices, such people populated the *cités* and the prison-like low-income housing complexes (HLM) of France's industrial suburbs. They took in immigrants, *harkis* and *pieds-noirs*,[26] young workers from declining rural areas and older workers chased out of the central cities by urban renewal.

Not surprisingly, the first collective initiatives by second-generation immigrants emerged from the suburban housing projects in the late 1970s. The '*Beurs*' (slang for second-generation North Africans) got involved first, in particular through cultural activities. Militant theatre groups presented often farcical interpretations of daily suburban life, and *Beur* rock groups such as '*Carte de séjour*' and the '*Rockin' Babouches*' sang of the second generation's trials and tribulations.

Reacting against rising anti-immigrant sentiment, a spate of local 'Rock Against Police' (RAP) movements appeared in Paris' Red-Belt suburbs in 1980 and 1981. Like their forerunners in Britain, these loosely organized groups threw free rock concerts, which often ended in bloody confrontations with police. The RAP considered delinquency to be 'a legitimate response to the repressive actions of the state, as relayed by local authorities and especially by Communist mayors'.[27] The government moved to deport participants, instigating hunger strikes. They ended in the spring of 1981, when the new Socialist government suspended the deportations pending a legislative study.

Mitterrand's decision did not end assaults against immigrants and their children, above all North Africans. During the 'hot summer' of 1981 in the suburbs of Lyons, youths looted stores and stole automobiles, drove them wildly through the city and then burned them on street corners. These so-called *rodéos* terrified the French.[28] Quickly, the Mauroy government launched 'Operation Anti-Hot Summer', which included summer camps by the sea and training for associational leaders. Officials also designated priority educational zones (*Zones d'éducation prioritaires*) in areas of high immigrant concentration and introduced special remedial classes. French courts started to hand out harsher sentences against the murderers and harassers of immigrants and their children.

These measures defused the anger boiling over in France's suburbs and encouraged many North Africans to work within the institutions of the host society.[29] The legal changes and new programmes sparked an intensification of second-generation associational activity. Culture remained a potent – and now government-funded – form of political expression, often finding an outlet in newly legal private radio stations.

The second generation's mobilization incensed the anti-immigrant movement already building strength as France's economic crisis deepened. During the municipal elections and by-elections of 1983, local politicians of all stripes portrayed the immigrants as a problem population. Jean-Marie Le Pen and his *Front National* linked the rise of crime and insecurity to the presence of non-European immigrants. The FN did well in cities such as Dreux, Paris, Roubaix and Marseille, which had a high proportion of 'Arab' immigrants.

The far Right's electoral breakthrough rocked the political establishment. The government responded in ambivalent fashion. Children with at least one French-citizen parent and 15 years' residency in the country became eligible in 1984 for the much coveted single, renewable ten-year residency and work permit.[30] New restrictions on family reunification counterbalanced that advance, however, and the discredited *aide au retour* had returned a year earlier in revamped form as 'reinsertion aid'.

The immigration issue defied a simple Left–Right dichotomy. The PS found itself torn between proponents of a new ethnic pluralism and defenders of the traditional Jacobin model requiring immigrants' complete assimilation. The mainstream Right did not have a coherent position either. As for the PCF, by now in rupture with the PS, its strength steadily eroded, and it reaped what it had sown: 'Virtually the same rhetoric that was used so effectively by the National Front in 1983 was first used by the Communist Party and some of its representatives in 1980–81.'[31] With its 'anti-political' political discourse, the FN filled the ideological void.[32] From March 1983 to March 1985, it received close to or more than 10 per cent of the votes nationally in six elections.

Second-generation immigrants reacted immediately to Le Pen's electoral successes. The mutual respect and institutional contacts that had grown out of earlier clashes helped make the summer of 1983 'warm' instead of 'hot'. Clashes with police in the suburbs of Lyons gave rise not to riots but to the non-violent 'March Against Racism and for Equality' from Marseilles to Paris that fall. Though *Beurs* and other non-Europeans predominated, marchers of Southern European origin also participated. At first, the Socialist government and the trade unions only tacitly backed the peaceful protest. But by the time the marchers arrived at the Place de la Concorde, numbering over 100 000, Mitterrand was there to greet them.

This stunning success galvanized the second generation. Proposed initiatives called for the right to participate in the management of housing, job training and social services. One group of *Beurs* wanted to emphasize a broader, multi-ethnic perspective and organized '*Convergence '84*': five squadrons of motor scooters, each representing one of the major ethnic components of France – North Africans and Turks, Iberians, Asians, sub-Saharan Africans and the French – left from one of five French cities and converged in Paris for a multicultural celebration.[33] In the end, internal differences robbed *Convergence* of its impact, despite its motto, 'Living together with our differences' ('*Vivre ensemble avec nos différences*'), as some activists ended up denouncing the action and arguing that only a broader initiative could truly shift the focus to the fundamental problem of inequality in France. They called for a class-based, multi-ethnic movement uniting all of the politically disenfranchised.[34]

With the second-generation leadership in disarray, the Socialists moved to harness the anti-racist organizational potential. A handful of veterans of the 1983 march close to the French Socialists and militant Jewish student groups founded *SOS-Racisme* in 1984. Its charismatic leader, Harlem Désir, insisted that *SOS-Racisme* was a multi-ethnic movement of the 'buddy' ('*pote*') generation, the French and immigrant youths of the suburban housing projects.[35] From the start, *SOS-Racisme* benefited from the logistical, financial and moral support of the government, the PS and the Left-leaning press. The movement exhibited an impressive mastery of public relations techniques. Soon appearing on lapels of students, politicians, intellectuals and movie stars was a plastic pin shaped like an open palm and inscribed: 'Hands off my buddy' ('*Touche pas à mon pote*'). Thousands of immigrants and French citizens joined local branches across the country. Through cultural events, vocal defence of young immigrants' and non-immigrants' rights and media campaigns, *SOS-Racisme* advanced its eclectic, vaguely defined agenda, despite harsh attacks from the Communists and the FN. The PS maintained its support for *SOS-Racisme*, but both the divisiveness of second-generation politics and the rise of *lepénisme* shook it. It dropped its call for '*droit à la différence*' for a campaign themed 'living together' ('*vivre ensemble*'), emphasizing common ground instead of cultural differences.

In 1985, a new group, *France-Plus*, and a number of local Collectives for Civic Rights organized drives to register eligible second-generation immigrants to vote. Researchers estimated the potential electorate of foreign origin (including the children of the *harkis*) at more than one million in 1984. In the cantonal elections of that year, more than thirty *Beur* candidates and several of Southern European origin had run for office. A number of second-generation immigrants won seats on municipal councils or were appointed to municipal commissions during this period.[36] Like other manifestations of the second generation's political awakening, these developments were largely made possible by the governmental reforms of the early 1980s.

The Difficult Cohabitation

Socialists feared the approach of legislative elections in 1986. Mitterrand, hoping to divide the Right and limit his party's losses, changed the electoral system to one of proportional representation. The strategy worked to a degree, but in the process it let the *lepéniste* genie out of the bottle: the Front garnered 9.8 per cent of the vote – 38 000 more votes than the PCF – and elected 35 deputies, enough to constitute a parliamentary group. The Front seemed to be replacing the PCF as the tribune of the disaffected.

The period of cohabitation that followed the Right's narrow victory brought more repressive immigration policies. The new prime minister, Jacques Chirac, made an explicit connection between delinquency, terrorism and immigration. Identification checks and expulsions of illegal immigrants and refugees multiplied, with non-Europeans incurring much of the wrath of the new hard-line Interior Minister, Charles Pasqua. His policies, codified later that year, made it clear that the new government rejected the notion of a multicultural France. The Left remained silent, apparently terrified at the public support such measures were receiving.

An emotional and fragile movement, organized anti-racism fluctuated and evolved, partially in response to events created by its adversaries and allies. The PS had appointed *SOS-Racisme* the mouthpiece of the anti-racism youth movement. Increasingly, though, its momentum was flagging: the Palestinian issue divided its Jewish and Muslim members, and its cosy relationship with the Socialists limited its reach and effectiveness. New groups, such as the Arab Youth of Lyons and its Suburbs (*Jeunes Arabes de Lyon et sa Banlieue*) and several other *Beur* groups, sprang up and opposed the 'feel-good' anti-racism of Harlem Désir as well as the Chirac/Pasqua regime.

A turning point was reached with the student demonstrations in late 1986 and early 1987, which forced the government to withdraw planned educational reforms (the Devaquet Plan) by stressing the traditional republican values of equality and inclusion. The movement's leadership and much of its base had cut their activist teeth in the marches and rallies of *SOS-Racisme*. The students' reluctance to forge an alliance with striking railroad workers bespoke the absence of working-class consciousness that typified much of the second generation.[37]

A few months later, the government proposed a reform of the Nationality Code (the Chalandon Reform). It planned to eliminate the automatic nature of second-generation immigrants' accession to French citizenship, in order to stem the 'mass' naturalization of second-generation immigrants. When the same student groups started to take to the streets once again in opposition, Prime Minister Chirac quickly put the reform on ice. Le Pen taunted the government for 'demeaning the Republic by capitulating before the ukases of Harlem Désir and *SOS-Racisme*'.[38]

With the Right stumbling, the Left gradually rediscovered solidarity with the foreign-origin population. The Communists were realizing just how deeply the restructuring of industry and urban areas had affected the French working class. Changes in its position in society, composition and aspirations had transformed its relationship with the PCF and the trade unions.

With the upcoming presidential campaign in sight, moreover, Mitterrand retook the high ground in 1987 and 1988. Once again, he spoke of granting municipal voting rights to non-citizens,[39] rejected any tightening of naturalization laws and vowed to overturn the draconian Pasqua Law if the Left regained its governing majority in parliament. Political strategy played a role here: thanks in part to *France-Plus'* voter registration and education efforts (particularly among second-generation *harkis*), the second immigrant generation accounted for 3 per cent of the total national electorate. Most of these voters leaned toward the Socialists. In first-round balloting in the 1988 presidential election, Mitterrand won the backing of nearly half of second-generation North Africans; between 80 per cent and 84 per cent of them, stunned by Le Pen's 14.5 per cent nationally, chose Mitterrand over Chirac in the second round.[40] The President's re-election brought thousands of relieved immigrants into the streets of French cities and towns. A minority Socialist government emerged from the legislative elections that June – held once more under a two-round, majority electoral system that allowed Le Pen's party to capture only a single seat in the assembly. The political class also breathed a sigh of relief.

THE SOCIALISTS, ISLAM AND THE SUBURBAN EXPLOSION

Such complacency proved premature, as the earlier constraints on the Socialists intensified after 1988. Le Pen had shifted political discourse decisively toward an insular, right-wing populism. After Mitterrand's re-election, the immigration challenge merged inexorably with broader urban and social crises, resulting in political dynamite. And whereas the explosive potential had been building long before the Left came to power, its policy responses to immigration since 1981 helped light the fuse.

Of course, 1981 was not 1936. The Left significantly increased the foreign-origin communities' ability to protect themselves and integrate into French society. As the foreign-worker generation neared retirement age, an assertive new French-born associational leadership was emerging. Foreign workers grew bolder in exercising their expanded rights in the factory. A new wave of strikes hit France in the fall of 1989, most notably at the Peugeot plants in Sochaux and Mulhouse. Moroccan, Portuguese and Algerian immigrants spearheaded these protests and participated as other workers did, even while investing strike activity with their own demands.[41]

The second generation showed no more interest in the class struggle than before, but its political clout kept growing. By 1988, more than 600 young people of North African, Asian and Southern European stock figured on the candidate slates of all the mainstream parties. The next year, two *Beurs* won election to the European Parliament, one a Green and the other a Socialist *SOS-Racisme* activist. In the municipal elections later in 1989, more than 300 second-generation immigrants won local-level office. In addition to the candidates that French parties put forward, grass-roots 'independent' lists appeared on the municipal ballot in Lille, Saint-Étienne and Bron, where they obtained between 1 per cent and 3 per cent of the first-round vote.[42]

The second immigrant generation, then, has not rejected the French political system or republican values. The vast majority have either remained apolitical or have chosen legal and institutional means of participating in that system. Those of non-European background have nonetheless deeply rattled French society, with Islam again a major reason. Muslim fundamentalism has never won large numbers of converts in France, least of all among the younger generation of North Africans, sub-Saharan Africans and Turks. As their economic and social integration in France has stalled, however, many of these youths have mythologized the Arab world. Islam has become for them a battle cry and a negotiating tool in a painful process of integration through protest, just as the Communist Party was for French and immigrant workers from the 1920s to the early 1970s.

This transformation, and its wrenching effect on the French polity, was apparent during the so-called scarf affair in autumn 1989. Officials at a *collège* in Creil cited a 1937 decree-law against promoting religion in public schools to refuse entry to three Muslim girls who insisted on wearing the traditional scarf (*hijab*) covering the hair, ears, and neck to class. A fierce, two-month furore ensued, one that aggravated divisions within French political families and within the anti-racism movement. Members of the government opposed each other publicly, as did *France-Plus* (which like Communist and trade union officials insisted that religious symbols be banned in public schools) and *SOS-Racisme* (which demanded that the Minister of Education re-admit the students).[43]

The controversy forced the nation to debate the role of the immigrants and Islam in French society. Interior Minister Pierre Joxe doubled his efforts to encourage the selection of moderate imams and the development of a national consistory (a council of religious leaders that acts as an intermediary between a community and government), as exists for France's Jews and Protestants. Such attempts to structure a 'Gallic Islam' met with limited success, often heightening tensions within the pluralistic Muslim population.[44]

As attacks on non-European immigrants and mosques multiplied, laws passed in 1989 and 1990 strengthened legal provisions against racism. Prime Minister Michel Rocard tightened controls against illegal immigration and unveiled an

expensive program to speed up resident immigrants' integration that largely repeated measures in effect since the mid-1970s: teaching secular values in schools,
sprucing up the housing projects and developing neighbourhood parks and youth
centres. However, highly touted programmes failed to translate into discernible
changes in the neighbourhoods, where decentralization made it easier for local
political clientelism to gum up the best-intentioned national policies.

The inadequacy of the governmental response became apparent in the fall of
1990. Almost a decade after the 'hot summer' of the early 1980s, riots once again
spread across France from the tinderbox of Lyons' suburbs. In dozens of cities,
poor youth of immigrant and native French stock looted stores and set fires in
commercial districts. The disturbances often began with a clash between young
people and the French police, whom many residents accused of racism and heavy-
handedness.

In the early 1980s, the French government had answered the angry protests of
the second generation first with police repression and then with the institution of
locally based structures and subsidies that facilitated cultural and political expression. With the decline and growing irrelevance of the traditional transmission
belts linking foreign workers with French society, in fact, it was up to the social
welfare and criminal justice systems to deal with the country's marginal groups.
Through reactive institutional tinkering the system had thereby integrated the
second-generation leadership, who became the organizers of the anti-racism
movement. A '*beurgeoisie*' emerged: activists who run the local associations in
the housing projects and young suburban entrepreneurs who launch multi-ethnic
small businesses. These new élites, many of them women, have acted as brokers
between their generation and French society.[45]

But the government's tactics gradually alienated their movements, even the
privileged *SOS-Racisme*.[46] And those groups lost touch with the bulk of immigrant-
origin youths, for whom socioprofessional mobility has remained out of reach.
The industries that needed foreign workers after World War II have undergone
a drawn-out, painful period of post-Fordist restructuring and today provide fewer
and worse jobs for their children. Those who took part in 1990's 'intifada of
the suburbs' were the youngest and most marginalized, with no memory of
earlier struggles. Disaffected suburban youths have developed 'parallel survival
networks', an underground economy of petty delinquency and drugs organized
around loose youth bands, some multi-ethnic and others reinforcing ethnic and
social differences.[47]

From the onset of Mitterrand's second *septennat*, then, immigration moved to
the very centre of the French political agenda. With extremists of all ilks profiting
from the social unrest, the government tried once more to depoliticize the issue.
In March 1990, Michel Rocard instituted the High Council for Integration (*Haut
Conseil à l'Integration*), comprising nine members from the major French political 'families', to develop politically balanced, palatable solutions. In the first of
its six reports, presented to the government in February 1991, the HCI underscored the need for greater administrative coherence and 'patient, vigorous and

inventive' measures to integrate immigrants, who should 'accept the rules of French society' and adhere to a 'minimum of common values'.[48] The council, in effect, reaffirmed the traditional model of individual assimilation. As if to drive home the point, the new government under Prime Minister Édith Cresson that spring included Secretary of State for Immigration Kofi Yamgnane, a man of Togolese origin who perfectly embodies this Jacobin tradition.[49]

Unfortunately, simply reiterating the old assimilationist formula did not make it work again. Only crass, barefaced political posturing resulted. Jacques Chirac decried 'the noise and the smell' of 'the foreigners'.[50] Valéry Giscard d'Estaing referred to immigration as an 'invasion' in an interview with *Figaro Magazine* and called for naturalization based on blood ties to prevent the 'abuse' of French citizenship laws.[51] Put on the defensive, Cresson talked about chartering airplanes to deport illegal aliens. Meanwhile, French officials failed to provide a positive, inventive response to the country's very serious social problems.

They were manifest yet again in the 'suburban fever' of autumn 1991, as angry incidents between groups of youngsters and the police and commercial security forces escalated into full-scale riots. The epicentre of this wave of violence was in Mantes-la-Jolie, outside Paris, where youths primarily of North African origin looted businesses, burned cars and attacked firemen. The troubles quickly spread and preoccupied the French government, media and public.[52]

Seizing the French political class was the familiar fear that suburban housing projects were degenerating into full-blown, 'American-style' ghettoes. The third report of the HCI, in February 1992, developed further a Jacobin model of integration: equal rights and obligations for all were to generate solidarity among the different ethnic and cultural components of French society. Appearing during the highly charged period following the electoral success of the fundamentalist Islamic Salvation Front in Algeria, the report defined and defended 'French values' and rejected 'Anglo-Saxon ethnic pluralism' and the 'tribalism' it supposedly generated.[53]

Yet in practice, French authorities have always discriminated on the basis of ethnicity and nationality. The entry of immigration onto the French political stage has been the logical consequence of a long process of settlement in French society and French officials' response to it.[54] After 1981, the governing Socialists facilitated that entry, as well as that of the National Front, only to blanch when challenged by the new politics of hate and violence that they inherited and aggravated. By 1993, growing numbers of illegal immigrants and refugees were providing additional points of confrontation, more grist for the National Front's mill.

CONCLUSION: THE PASSING OF THE MITTERRAND GENERATION?

In March 1993, responsibility passed to the mainstream right, which crushed the divided and demoralized Socialists and won almost 80 per cent of seats in the

National Assembly. Once again, Charles Pasqua became Minister of the Interior. Returning with him have been more restrictive policies and more exclusionary rhetoric toward immigration.

In the first 100 days of Édouard Balladur's government, three major laws were passed that directly affected immigration. The Nationality Code, reformed in July, required second-generation immigrants born in France to make a formal request for French nationality between the ages of 16 and 21 (they used to receive it automatically at 18) and tightened the so-called *double jus soli* – the automatic right to citizenship of someone born in France to French citizens – enjoyed by the French-born children of Algerians before their country gained its independence in 1962. The police won broad powers to check the identity of 'suspicious persons' in August. And later that month, it became easier for authorities to detain and deport unwanted migrants and harder for foreigners to enter France (including under family reunification), become residents, marry a French citizen and apply for political asylum. The government also began training a special police force to suppress illegal immigration.[55]

Left-wing commentators have decried the 'Second Pasqua Law' and the 'Maginot Line mentality' breeding such 'legislation of closure'.[56] Then again, even if the current government has expressly advertised its goal of zero immigration, it too has run into political and institutional constraints that severely limit policy implementation. For example, Simone Veil, Minister of Social, Health and Urban Affairs, argued successfully against Pasqua's bill that would have prevented illegal immigrants from benefiting from emergency medical care. To his even greater consternation, local-level courts have suspended deportation orders authorized by the Interior Ministry as a 'matter of urgency' and – citing the right to family life as guaranteed under Article 8 of the European Convention on Human Rights – have ruled that even foreigners living illegally in the country have the right to marry French nationals. In August 1993, the Constitutional Council annulled eight provisions of the new package of legislation. Most were later reintroduced in acceptable form, to be sure, and after bitter debate the government even convinced Parliament to amend the Constitution and restrict the right of foreigners to ask for asylum in France. Regardless, a vigorous debate over immigration and refugee policy has ensued.

In the process it has become clear that the French Right's attacks have not seriously weakened the universalistic, egalitarian principles of the republican model.[57] The changes to the Nationality Code 'are not very drastic; they preserve the traditional *jus soli* – residence, not blood, is what matters.'[58] Likewise preserved are fundamental rights to due process, legal equality and political asylum.

Much of the political, academic and journalistic establishment shares the High Council's attachment to the values of a unitary lay republic.[59] At the same time, what is championed is a newfangled brand of Jacobinism. The HCI has admitted that 'for people who are immigrants or of immigrant origin, the process of acculturation . . . may sometimes be a painful experience. But it is not a one-way street, and the immigrants also take part in the elaboration of the national culture.'[60] The HCI has celebrated voluntary associational life as the ideal means for expressing cultural and ethnic diversity. At once innovative and contradictory, this neo-Jacobin outlook is a legacy of the Left in power. Victim and villain, the Socialists were unable to defuse the political crisis of social control; nevertheless, the intended and unintended effects of their policies and strategies have helped force France to engage in wrenching, albeit necessary, soul-searching and adaptation.

It is thus all the more surprising that François Mitterrand now stands on the sidelines of the immigration debate. After a decade during which governmental policy on immigration was strongly identified with the philosophy and strategies of the President, his current silence is deafening. Reasons for his reticence are not hard to find: the Right's massive majority, which limited parliamentary debate on the new laws; lingering bitterness within the fragmented Socialist party over his compromise on the constitutional revision on the right to asylum;[61] and perhaps most significantly, the weakening of the organized youth movement, the 'Mitterrand generation' once so powerful in blunting the Right. *SOS-Racisme* and *France-Plus*, which spearheaded the movement in the 1980s, no longer have the media resonance or the reach that they once possessed. The immigrant-origin youths who participated in the violent demonstrations in spring 1994 against the government's proposal to introduce lower 'training' wages resembled the anomic rioters of the early 1990s more than the friendly *potes* of the 1980s.

Whether or not the Right's aggressive new immigration policies will halt the inflow into France remains an open question. As France struggles to adapt to the developing Schengen system and the European Union's evolving concept of European citizenship, the issue of how to integrate the existing immigrant-origin communities will only intensify. The current government, caught between fear of European integration and fear of Muslim fundamentalism, has made the immigrants scapegoats. It might do well to consider instead the successes, disappointments and surprises of its leftist predecessors' record and work to develop a realistic policy response in line with the opportunities and constraints that it faces.

Notes

1. Algerians were present in France by the 19th century as well, yet it was primarily Europeans who were seen as the 'foreign competition'. See René Mouriaux and Catherine Wihtol de Wenden, 'Syndicalisme français et islam', *Revue française de science politique* 37, no. 6 (December 1987) pp. 794–819.
2. See Eugen Weber, *Peasants into Frenchmen* (Stanford, CA: Stanford University Press, 1976).

3.   Catherine Wihtol de Wenden, *Les immigrés et la politique* (Paris: Presses de la Fondation Nationale des Sciences Politiques, 1988) p. 68.
4.   Under the 1901 association law, Parliament authorized the President to dissolve by decree those associations that he deemed a threat to national security. Those with foreign administrators, a non-citizen membership of more than one-quarter or headquarters outside of France were deemed 'foreign' under Daladier's 1939 decree.
5.   The Vichy regime and occupation brought greater harshness toward foreigners – and disaster for French and foreign Jews – but the war did not fundamentally alter French immigration policy.
6.   Albert Bayet, *Le problème des immigrés dans la France libérée* (Paris: CADI, 1945).
7.   Georges Mauco, *Les étrangers en France* (Paris: Armand Colin, 1932) Chapter 3. Under the Jacobin model of the nation-state, which has long dominated France as a general paradigm, membership in the national community involves a voluntary commitment to the republic and its values. Religious, ethnic and regional subcultural identities have been relegated to the private sphere.
8.   Gary Freeman, *Immigrant Labor and Racial Conflict in Industrial Societies* (Princeton, NJ: Princeton University Press, 1979) p. 88.
9.   Eric-Jean Thomas, *Immigrant Workers in Europe: Their Legal Status* (Paris: UNESCO Press, 1982) p. 42.
10. Foreign Socialists also blended in largely with the PS and, by the late 1960s, the often likeminded *Confédération Française Démocratique du Travail* (CFDT). The PCF did suffer the autonomy of the offical Algerian organization, the *Amicale des Algériens en Europe*, out of respect for the party's close relations with the FLN regime in Algiers.
11. Françoise Briot and Gilles Verbunt, *Les immigrés dans la crise* (Paris: Éditions Ouvrières, 1981).
12. See André Lebon, 'L'aide au retour des travailleurs étrangers,' *Économie et statistiques* 113 (July–August 1979) pp. 37–46.
13. Some 140 000 '*sans-papiers*' took advantage of the programme, which lasted until 1983. See Claude-Marie Valentin, 'L'immigration clandestine en France', *Travail et emploi* 17 (July–September 1983) pp. 27–39.
14. Gilles Verbunt, 'Relations associations immigrées/associations de solidarité', in *Forum des associations* (Paris: CAIF, May 1985) pp. 23–5.
15. Briot and Verbunt, p. 136.
16. Gilles Kepel, *Les banlieues de l'Islam* (Paris: Seuil, 1987).
17. See Floriane Benoit, *Le printemps de la dignité* (Paris: Éditions Sociales, 1982).
18. Toma Subhi, 'Musulmans dans l'entreprise', *Esprit* 6 (June 1985) pp. 216–21.
19. For their complete comments, see *Le Monde*, 11 February 1983.
20. Personal interview with Mayor James Marson (PCF), La Courneuve.
21. Martin A. Schain, *French Communism and Local Power* (New York: St. Martin's Press, 1985) p. 81.
22. Myrto and Christian Bruschi, 'Le pouvoir des guichets,' in *L'immigration maghrébine en France: Dossier de la revue Les Temps Modernes* (Paris: Éditions Denoël, 1985) p. 296.
23. By most estimates second-generation immigrants under age 18 numbered well over 1 million by the early 1980s.
24. Cited in Jean-François Clément, 'Après la marche', *Esprit* 6 (June 1985) pp. 111–2.
25. Alain Pierrot, 'L'école française et ses étrangers', *Esprit* 6 (June 1985) pp. 143–54.
26. The *harkis* are native Algerians who served alongside the French colonial military forces and remained loyal to France, where they withdrew *en masse* after independence in 1962. The *pieds noirs* are former French colonists who fled independent Algeria at the same time.

27. 'Rock Against Police' bulletin provided by the municipal archives of La Courneuve.
28. Adil Jazouli, *L'action collective des jeunes maghrébins en France* (Paris: CIEMI/ L'Harmattan, 1986) pp. 81ff.
29. Christian Delorme, 'Le mouvement *"Beur"* a une histoire', in Association nationale de la jeunesse immigrée, *Les cahiers de la nouvelle génération* 1 (Gennevilliers: ANGI, December 1984) pp. 18–46.
30. By that date, more than 70 per cent of France's foreigners had lived there more than ten years.
31. Martin Schain, 'The National Front in France and the Construction of Political Legitimacy', *West European Politics* 10, no. 2 (April 1987) p. 239.
32. 'La perturbation Le Pen', *L'Express*, 24–30 September 1984, pp. 73–81.
33. See Nelson Rodrigues, *La ruée vers l'égalité* (Paris: Mélanges, 1985).
34. Farida Belghoul, 'Lettre ouverte aux gens convaincus', reprinted in *Presse et immigrés en France* 125 (December 1984) pp. 1–6.
35. Personal interview with *SOS-Racisme* leaders, Paris.
36. Driss El Yazami Khammar, 'Les *Beurs* civiques', in Sans Frontière, *La 'Beur' génération* (Paris: Éditions Sans Frontière, May 1985) pp. 11–4.
37. See *Libération, Le Monde* and *Le Figaro* from late December 1986 to mid-January 1987.
38. Quoted in Guy Birenbaum, 'Les stratégies du Front National', *Vingtième siècle* 16 (October–December 1987) pp. 13–4.
39. Later the Socialists would again decide that local suffrage was too inflammatory.
40. *Libération*, 28–29 May 1988.
41. Maurizio Lazzarato, 'Peugeot 89', in *L'Europe multicommunautaire*, special issue of *Plein Droit* (Paris: GISTI, 1989–90) pp. 115–9.
42. Saïd Bouamama, 'Élections municipales et immigration: essai de bilan', *Migrations-Société* 1, no. 3 (June 1989) pp. 22–45.
43. *Le Figaro*, 6 October 1989. The *Conseil d'État* eventually issued an ambiguous ruling that students may wear religious symbols in schools, provided that they do not interfere with the secular educational programme. The scarf debate rages on in local administrative courts across France.
44. Christian Lochon, 'Vers la création d'instances supérieures de l'Islam en France', *L'Afrique et l'Asie Modernes* 165 (Paris: CHEAM, Summer 1990) pp. 43–67. For more on the PS's relations with the Paris Mosque, see Kepel, Chapter 7.
45. Catherine Wihtol de Wenden, 'Naissance d'une "beurgeoisie"', *Migrations-Société* 2, no. 8 (March–April 1990) pp. 9–16.
46. Harlem Désir squabbled with the Rocard government during the scarf affair and in 1991 during the Persian Gulf War. He later broke completely with the PS. *SOS-Racisme* now has new leadership. See *Le Monde*, 14 March, 12 December and 17 December 1991; and *Libération*, 7 September 1992.
47. See the comments of Adil Jazouli in Commission nationale consultative des droits de l'homme, *La Lutte contre le racisme et la xénophobie* (Paris: Documentation Française, 1992) pp. 211–8.
48. Quoted in *Le Monde*, 19 February 1992.
49. For a defence of Jacobinism, see Patrick Weil, *La France et ses étrangers* (Paris: Éditions Calmann-Lévy, 1991).
50. *Le Figaro*, 21 June 1991.
51. *Figaro Magazine*, 21 September 1991.
52. *Le Monde*, 25 June and 30 June–1 July 1991. A few months earlier, second-generation *harkis* had occupied public buildings and clashed with French police across the South of France.
53. *La Croix*, 7 February 1992. The HCI's second report, like several later ones, concentrated on developing reliable statistics on immigration.

54. For more on the evolution of immigrant politics in France, see Patrick Ireland, *The Policy Challenge of Ethnic Diversity* (Cambridge, MA: Harvard University Press, 1994), from which much material in this article is drawn.
55. Christian Bruschi, 'Moins de droits pour les étrangers en France', *Migrations-Société* 6, no. 31 (January–February 1994) pp. 7–23.
56. Philippe Farine, 'Objectif: 'Immigration zéro', *Migrations-Société* 5, nos. 28–9 (July–October 1993) pp. 9–11, 17.
57. James F. Hollifield, 'The Migration Challenge', *Harvard International Review* 26, no. 3 (Summer 1994) p. 67.
58. Stanley Hoffmann, 'France: Keeping the Demons at Bay', *New York Review of Books* 41, no. 5 (3 March 1994) p. 14.
59. John A. McKesson, 'Concepts and Realities in a Multiethnic France', *French Politics and Society* 12, no. 1 (Winter 1994) p. 16.
60. Haut Conseil à l'Intégration, *Pour un modèle français d'intégration* (Paris: Documentation Française, 1991) pp. 33–4.
61. See the criticisms of Kofi Yamgnane in *Le Quotidien de Paris*, 10 October 1993.

Index

Agence Nationale pour l'Amélioration des Conditions de Travail (ANACT), 165
Anger, Didier, 228
ATOCHEM-Grande Paroisse, 164–5
Attali, Jacques, 63, 67, 69
attitudes toward business, 122–5
Auroux, Jean, 8, 264
Auroux Laws, 8, 13, 20, 37, 109, 130, 141, 148–50, 156, 167, 243
  small firms and, 151
  technological change provision, 162–4, 167
autogestion, 20, 25, 132, 147–8, 196, 203n
automobile industry, 103–6

Balladur, Edouard, 11, 236, 258
Banque de France, 59, 60, 64, 68, 85, 88, 89, 96n
Barre, Raymond, 57, 60, 147
Baudoin, Jacques, 242
Bébéar, Claude, 128
Beffa, Jean-Louis, 121
Bérégovoy, Pierre, 18, 20, 50, 60, 68, 75, 120
Bergeron, André, 179–80
Besse, Georges, 106
Beurs, 24, 200, 219–20, 266, 268, 269, 272
  see also immigration
Bianco, Jean-Louis, 67, 69
Blondel, Marc, 180
Blum, Léon, 84, 86–9, 90–1, 204n
BNP, 121, 131, 134
Bouygues, Francis, 129
Bundesbank, 67
  predominance of, 47
Bush, George, 83, 91

Calvet, Jacques, 105
Camdessus, Michel, 70, 78, 81n
Cartel des Gauches, 19, 83–6, 90
Cent dix propositions, 56

Centre des Etudes, Recherche et d'Education Socialiste (CERES), 36, 193, 194, 195
Centre des jeunes dirigeants d'entreprise, 152
Chaban-Delmas, Jacques, 145
Chevènement, Jean-Pierre, 49, 63, 60, 81n
Chirac, Jacques, 11, 43, 147, 269, 273
Citroën, 104–5
Cochet, Yves, 228
collective bargaining, 143, 145, 146, 150, 157–8n, 163, 167, 173
Comité du Travail Féminin (CTF), 242, 255n
comités d'entreprise, see works councils
Common Programme of Government, 7, 35, 36
Confédération Française Démocratique du Travail (CFDT), 13, 14, 101, 105, 110, 142, 161, 166, 174, 180–1, 182, 195, 227
  égalité professionnelle and, 242, 248
  legislative goals, 148
  membership in, 176
  relationship with PS, 194–5, 204n
  strikes and, 174
Confédération Française des Travailleurs Chrétiens (CFTC), 142
  membership in, 176
Confédération Générale des Cadres, membership in, 176
Confédération Générale du Travail (CGT), 13, 14, 74, 101, 105, 110, 142, 161, 166, 174, 181–2, 207, 220
  égalité professionnelle and, 242, 246, 248
  immigrants and, 260–1
  legislative goals, 148
  membership in, 176

Confédération Générale du Travail Unitaire (CGTU), 210
Conseil des Associations Immigrées en France (CAIF), 263
Conseil National du Patronat Français (CNFP), 74, 131, 163, 183n
Conseil National Interrégional (CNIR), 237n
Conseil Supérior de l'Égalité Professionnelle (CSEP), 247, 248–9, 252
Corps des Mines, 129, 130
Cresson, Edith, 50, 55n, 120, 122, 273

Daladier, Édouard, 259
Dalle, François, 132
Davignon Plan, 11
decentralisation, 9, 13, 27–8n
Defferre, Gaston, 70
Deflassieux, Jean, 61
de Gaulle, Charles, 3, 18, 34, 36, 53n, 89, 95n, 260
de la Genière, Renaud, 61, 64
Déléguée à la Condition Féminine (DCF), 249
Delors, Jacques, 37, 39, 55n, 56, 60, 64–5, 67, 71, 102, 145, 151, 245
    see also 'New Society'
de Mouy, Pierre, 84–5
Désir, Harlem, 268, 269
devaluation, 9, 59–72, 85, 88, 89, 93
de Wendel, François, 96n
Direction des Relations du Travail (DRT), 245
    and *égalité professionnelle*, 249–50
Drancourt, Michel, 131, 135

École des Hautes Etudes Commerciales (HEC), 130
École Polytechnique, 125, 126, 127–9, 130
ecology movement, 2, 17, 22, 225–6, 227–30, 232–3, 235–7
    'Big Bang' and, 236
    electoral constituencies of, 230–1
    see also party names
Economic and Monetary Union, 47–8, 181

economic policy, 3, 7–12
    l'autre politique and, 19, 68–9, 71, 74, 76, 77–8, 86
    demand stimulation, 9
    see also devaluation, exchange rate policy, '*l'autre politique*', U-turn
égalité professionnelle law, 23, 241–55, 262
    discrimination cases and, 254, 255, 257n
    emergence of, 242–3
    follow-up reports, 253–4
    formulation of bill, 244–6
    implementation of, 247–50, 252
    legislative approval of, 246–7
    opposition to, 246–7
    plans d'égalité, 247–8, 253
    protection vs. equality, 251–2
    provisions of, 247, 252
    quota system and, 244
    weakness of, 247–8, 251, 254–5
elections
    1978 legislative, 53n
    1981 legislative, 7
    1981 presidential, 1, 36
    1983 municipal, 37, 56, 69
    1986 legislative, 228
    1988 presidential, 1, 2, 11, 15, 17, 18, 22, 43, 44, 56, 83, 231
    1988 legislative, 45
    1989 municipal and European, 56, 229, 230, 232
    1992 regional, 1, 17, 22, 229
    1993 legislative, 1, 17, 50, 56, 189, 201, 225, 231, 235, 274
    1994 European, 1, 25–6, 56, 189, 201, 225, 234, 235
    1995 presidential, 51, 56
    lack of party loyalty within, 25–6
Emmanuelli, Henri, 94
Entente Écologiste, 226
    electoral results for, 235
Entreprise et progrès, 152
Equal Employment Policy (EEP), see *égalité professionnelle* law
European Community (EC)/European Union (EU), 11, 39–41, 48, 54n

European Community (EC)/European
Union (EU) (*continued*)
Commission, 39, 40, 137; White
Paper, *Growth, Competitiveness,
and Employment*, 48
EEP and, 244, 252–3
French support of, 40
Thatcher government and, 39
European Monetary System (EMS), 10,
48, 65, 66, 67, 68, 77, 79n, 87–8,
98
devaluation and, 58, 60, 62–4
proposed withdrawal from, 69–71,
78
Exchange Rate Mechanism (ERM), 50,
57, 58, 59, 68, 71, 73, 82n
exchange rate policy, 58–60, 72–3
export industry and, 74–5
financial sector and, 75
franc fort policy, 47, 75
labour and, 73
see also devaluation, EMS, ERM

Fabius, Laurent, 10, 14, 42, 46, 50, 64,
102
Fédération de l'Education Nationale
(FEN), 14, 142, 182
membership in, 176, 182
*Fédération des Associations de Soutien
aux Travailleurs Immigrés*
(FASTI), 263
Fédération Gauche Alternative, 228
Fifth Republic
constitution of, 33
electoral system of, 5
presidents and parties in, 33–4, 41,
44, 53n, 191
PS and, 191
Force Ouvriére (FO), 13, 142, 148,
150, 179–80, 182
membership in, 176
France-Plus, 220, 268–70, 271, 275
Front National (FN), 15, 43, 54n, 273
as alternative to PS and PCF, 51

Gaullism, 5
see also RPR
Génération Ecologie, 17, 22, 225,
229–30

electoral results for, 232, 235, 240n
influence of Lalonde, 234–5
Giscard d'Estaing, Valéry, 3, 7, 36, 38,
60–1, 147, 190, 261, 273
Guigou, Elisabeth, 69, 75
Gisserot, Hélène, 249, 252
Gomez, Alain, 132
grandes écoles, 118, 119, 125–31
grands corps, 126, 127–30
Guillaume, Henri, 65
Gulf War, 10

Haberer, Jean-Yves, 61, 63, 64, 121
Hanon, Bernard, 106
Haut Conseil à l'Intégration (HCI),
272–3, 274–5
Héritier, Pierre, 181
Herriot, Edouard, 83–5, 88–9, 92–3

immigration, 23–4, 144, 208–10, 217,
258–75
Auroux Laws and, 264
Balladur policy toward, 274–5
Chalandon Reform, 269
demonstrations, 267–8, 269, 272,
273
FN stance toward, 267, 273
harkis, 276n
HCI and, 272–3, 274–5
immigrant associations, 263
Islamic immigrants, 263–4, 271
Mitterrand era policies, 262, 264–5,
270
Nationality Code, 274
pre-Mitterrand history, 259–62
PCF and, 207–11
PS policy toward, 262–3, 266
'second generation', 265–8, 269–70,
271–2, 276n
'U-turn', 263
industrial relations, 147–71, 173,
176–9, 185n
microcorporatism in, 141, 148–51,
153, 155–6
Socialist reforms, 147–54, 156–7
see also Auroux Laws, Labour, 'New
Society', trade unions
industrial policy, 8, 19, 97–9, 117,
119–21, 177

industrial policy (*continued*)
　noyau dur, 120–2
　restructuring, 100–6, 109–10
　see also automobile industry, steel
　　industry
inflation, 37, 58–9, 80n, 119
Inglehart, Ronald, 6
Isler-Beguin, Marie, 234

Jacquier, Jean-Paul, 174
Jeunes Arabes de Lyon et sa Banlieue,
　269
Jospin, Lionel, 46
Joxe, Pierre, 271
Juquin, Pierre, 234, 234–5, 237

Kaspar, Jean, 14, 181
Kirchheimer, Otto, 6
Kohl, Helmut, 69
Krasucki, Henri, 181

labour
　attitudes toward business, 123
　exchange rate policy and, 73
　gender bias within, 253
　immigrants and, 259, 261, 264, 270–1
　mobilization of, 155
　movement, 2, 12–13, 169
　reforms, 8–9, 152–4, 177–8
　regulation of, 143–4, 153–4, 157n, 178
　relations with management, 123–4,
　　134–5, 167–8
　relations with PS, 147, 189
　role in industrial policy, 110, 148
　strikes, 16, 144, 154, 160n, 162,
　　173–4, 264, 270–1; by
　　immigrants, 270
　technological change and, 162–4
　weakness of, 74, 110, 124, 146,
　　174–5
　see also trade unions, *individual
　　union names*
Lahnstein, Manfred, 66
Lajoinie, André, 219
Lalonde, Brice, 230, 237
Laufer, Jacqueline, 248
l'autre politique, 19, 76–7, 86
Laval, Pierre, 86
Lebégue, Daniel, 61

Le Néouannic, Guy, 182
Le Pen, Jean-Marie, 267, 269–70
Lévy, Raymond, 106
Ligue Communiste Revolutionnaire, 228

Maastricht Treaty, 11, 25, 48–9, 54n,
　174, 181
　referendum, 50
Maire, Edmond, 181
Mamére, Nél, 235
management
　background of managers, 127–8, 136
　recruitment, 125–9, 136
　reforms in, 133–4
　relations with labour, 134–5, 152,
　　162–4, 165, 167–8, 170n
Marchais, Georges, 15, 24, 181
Mauroy, Pierre, 7, 46, 65–7, 69, 87, 102
minimum wage, 143, 145, 146
Ministère des Droits de la Femme
　(MDF), 243–4, 249
Ministry of Finance, 37, 61, 67, 75–6,
　126
　Trésor, 61, 64, 69, 70, 73, 75–6
Ministry of Industry, 102, 119, 120
Ministry of Labour, 11
　labour inspectors in, 245, 247, 249,
　　250, 252
　see also DRT
Mission de l'Égalité Professionnelle
　(MEP), 247, 248
Mitterrand, François, 18, 193
　110 Propositions of, 56, 60, 78n
　cohabitation and, 42, 50
　decline of PS and, 50–2
　devaluation and, 61–2, 63, 66, 70–1,
　　73, 78
　economic policy of, 78, 87–8, 90–1,
　　93
　election of, 1, 7, 15, 56
　first presidential term and, 36–43
　French Right and, 42–3
　German unification and, 55n
　immigration policy of, 275
　industrial policy and, 102, 109
　Maastricht treaty and, 48–9
　PCF and, 36, 53–4n, 151–2
　policy changes by, 26
　political skills of, 18, 45, 53n, 227

Mitterrand, François (*continued*)
  PS and, 34–6, 38
  re-election strategy of, 43–4
  relations with EC members, 40
  relations with Michel Rocard, 28n
  strategy of, 38–9, 40–2
  succession battle over, 14
  U-turn and, 37
  monetary policy, 57–8, 76, 84–94, 95n
  history of, 84–7
*Mouvement contre le Racisme et
  l'Anti-Sémetisme et pour l'Amitié
  entre les Peuples* (MRAP), 263
Mouvement Générale des Fonds, 85, 93
Mouvement Républicain Populaire
  (MRP), 4

nationalization policy, 8, 100–1, 119–22
  '*ni-ni*', 117
  public opinion of, 124
  see also privatization policy
National School of Administration
  (ENA), 125, 126, 127, 130
Neiertz, Véronique, 249, 253
'New Society', 144–7, 149
Notat, Nicole, 181, 184n
nouveaux ecologistes, 235

Office National d'Immigration (ONI),
  260

Parti Communiste Français (PCF),
  1–2, 7, 14, 221–2, 226
  CGT and, 181
  constituencies within, 22, 147,
    207–10, 213–14
  decline of, 15, 17, 54n, 82n, 152,
    213, 220, 221
  dissent within, 24–5, 38
  economic policy and, 73–4
  égalité professionnelle and, 242
  electoral results for, 1–2, 206,
    212–17
  emergence of, 207–12, 221
  immigrants and, 208–11, 217,
    219–20, 221, 224n, 259, 260–1,
    265
  in urban areas, 207, 216
  leadership of, 219

  limitations of, 5, 74
  membership of, 212, 215
  peasantry and, 207, 216
  PS and, 218, 221
  strategy of, 219–22
Parti Socialiste (PS), 1, 3, 7, 14–16,
  34–6, 189–90, 201–2
  1971 creation of, 35
  and Mitterrand, 44, 205n
  as alternative to PCF, 191, 194, 195,
    199, 220
  business policy of, 117, 127, 129–30
  CFDT and, 13–14, 194–5, 204n
  courants, 15, 21, 25
  dissatisfaction within, 25, 77
  ecology movement and, 225–6, 227,
    236
  electoral results for, 1, 79n, 189
  Epinay Congress of, 34, 192, 227
  erosion of support for, 54n, 56–7,
    197
  factional organization of, 192–8,
    201, 202n; failure of factionalism,
    197–8, 204n; resilience of
    factionalism, 199–200
  growth of, 194, 204n
  immigrants and, 262, 265, 266, 275
  industrial policy and, 98–9, 107,
    109, 123, 168–9
  leadership of, 15, 21, 45–6, 51–2
  monetary policy and, 87, 94
  presidency and, 34–5, 45
  relations with labour, 147, 153, 156,
    189
  relations with management, 124,
    131–2, 137
  relations with social forces, 201, 225,
    226
  Rennes Congress of, 46
  revitalisation of, 21, 83, 193
  selection of 1995 presidential
    candidate, 50–1
  success of, 190
  transcourants, 200
Parti Socialiste Unifié (PSU), 227
party system, 4
Pasqua, Charles, 269, 274
Pasquier, Nicole, 242, 243
Péchiney, 100, 106, 122

Pélat, Roger-Patrice, 50
Peugeot Société Anonyme (PSA),
 103–5
Peyrelavade, Jean, 61, 65, 126
Pitous, Claude, 180
Plescoff, Georges, 66
Poincaré, Raymond, 84, 85, 92, 93
political exchange in France, 12–18
Pompidou, Georges, 3
Popular Front, 19, 90–1
presidency of France
 central role of, 3, 14–5, 18–9, 33–4,
  51–2
 direct election to, 34
 PS and, 34–6
 see also Fifth Republic
Prigent, Loïk Le Floch, 126
privatization policy, 10, 120, 122, 124,
 133
 public opinion of, 125
Projet socialiste, 36, 66
Przeworski, Adam, 6

Ralite, Jack, 105
Rassemblement pour la République
 (RPR), 43
Reagan, Ronald, 40
recession of 1991–2
 effect on European unity, 48
Renault, 103–4, 105–6, 264
Rhône-Poulenc, 100, 121, 122
Riboud, Jean, 63, 66
Rocard, Michel, 2, 10, 14, 36, 37,
 45–6, 47, 193
 1994 European elections and, 51
 appointment of, 45
 auto industry and, 105
 'Big Bang' and, 2, 201, 236
 immigration policy of, 271–2
 industrial policy of, 121
 Mitterrand and, 28–9n, 45, 54n
 resignation of, 43
 'virtual candidacy' of, 29n
Roudy, Yvette, 243–5, 248–9, 253
Rueff, Jacques, 90

Sacilor, 100, 101–3
Saint Gobain, 100, 120, 121, 122
Sautter, Christian, 67

Schwietzer, Louis, 106
*Secrétaire d'Etat aux Droits des
 Femmes* (SEDF), 248, 253–4
*Secrétaire d'Etat aux Droits des
 Femmes et la Vie Quotidienne*
 (SEDFVQ), 249
*Section Française de l'Internationale
 Ouvriére* (SFIO), 4, 5, 189, 199,
 207
Servan-Schreiber, Jean-Jacques, 66,
 70
Service des Droits Des Femmes, 254
Single European Market, 8, 11, 18, 40,
 47
Socialisme et République, 46
Société Générale, 120
SOS Racisme, 25, 200, 220, 268, 271,
 275
Stasse, François-Xavier, 67
steel industry, 99–103, 111n
Stoltenberg, Gerhard, 71
Strauss-Kahn, Dominique, 120

Talbot, 104–5, 264
Tapie, Bernard, 25, 26, 29n, 51, 235
TF1, 120, 129
Thatcher, Margaret, 39, 83
Toutain, Ghislaine, 253
trade unions, 12–14, 16, 20, 153–4,
 159n, 165–6
 Auroux Laws and, 149–50, 167–8
 composition of, 142
 history of, 141–5, 259
 immigrants and, 267–8
 legislation affecting, 142–3, 145
 membership in, 2, 29n, 142, 149,
  150, 161, 172, 175–6
 weakness/decline of, 21, 33,
  150–1, 156, 174–5, 176–7, 179,
  182–3
 see also labour, *individual union
 names*
Trésor, 61, 64, 69, 70, 73, 75–6

Union de la Gauche, 35, 218
Usinor, 100, 101–3
U-turn, 3, 9–10, 14, 16, 18–19, 25,
 37–8
 Delors Plan and, 102

Veil, Simone, 274
Verts, 17, 22, 225, 229–34, 237, 238n
  electoral results for, 229–31, 234,
    239n
  ideological composition of, 231–2,
    239n
  influence of Waechter, 234
  membership in, 233
  organizational structure of, 225, 226
  weakness of, 225, 228–9, 233
Viannet, Louis, 181

Waechter, Antoine, 228, 229, 230–1,
  234

women
  as electoral constituency, 22–3
  gender-based employment disparities,
    251
  rights for, 23, 250–1
  see also égalité professionnelle law
works councils, 142, 144, 149–50, 151,
  156, 162–4, 166, 167, 168, 170n,
  244, 255n
  elections to, 150, 175
  égalité professionnelle and, 247–8
  see also Auroux Laws, labour

Yamgnane, Kofi, 273